Business in Kenya

Business in Kenya
Institutions and Interactions

Edited by

Dorothy McCormick • Patrick O. Alila • Mary Omosa

University of Nairobi Press

First published 2007 by

University of Nairobi Press
Jomo Kenyatta Memorial Library, University of Nairobi
P.O. Box 30197 – 00100 Nairobi
E-mail: nup@uonbi.ac.ke
http://www.uonbi.ac.ke/press/

The University of Nairobi Press supports and promotes University of Nairobi's objectives of discovery, dissemination and preservation of knowledge, and stimulation of intellectual and cultural life by publishing works of highest quality in association with partners in different parts of the world. In doing so, it adheres to the University's tradition of excellence, innovation and scholarship.

University of Nairobi Library CIP Data

HF 5341 B9	Business in Kenya: Institutions and Interactions/ed. by D. McCormick, P.O. Alila and M. Omosa. – Nairobi: University of Nairobi Press, 2007.
	360p.
	Business I. McCormick, Dorothy. II. Alila, Patrick O. III. Omosa, Mary.

ISBN 9966-846-95-6

Printed by:

Starbright Services Ltd.
P.O. Box 66949-00200
Nairobi

Table of Contents

Part III: Conclusions

List of Tables

List of Figures

List of Boxes

List of Contributors

Patrick O. Alila is a Research Professor, Institute for Development Studies, University of Nairobi. He graduated from the University of East Africa and Indiana University, Bloomington, USA. He was IDS Director from 1993 to 2001. His major areas of research include: public policy, rural change and institutions of local development. His publications are mainly on credit, micro and small enterprises and participation in development. He recently co-edited a book on *Negotiating Social Space: East African Micro Enterprises.*

Rosemary Atieno is a Senior Research Fellow at the Institute for Development Studies, University of Nairobi. She holds a PhD from the University of Giessen (Germany). Her research and teaching focus on development economics. She has publications in the areas of labour market participation issues, finance and enterprise development as well as poverty and socio-economic development.

Paul Kamau is a Research Fellow at the Institute for Development Studies, University of Nairobi. He holds a BA in Economics (University of Nairobi) and MSc in Economics (University of Zimbabwe). He is also a PhD student at the University of Nairobi. His research focuses on trade and development issues.

Karuti Kanyinga is a Senior Research Fellow at the Institute for Development Studies (IDS), University of Nairobi. He holds a PhD in Social Sciences from Roskilde University, Denmark. He has carried out many research projects on development and published extensively on the local politics of development in Kenya. Some of his recent articles include 'Ethnic Inequalities and Governance of the Public Sector in Kenya 2006' and 'The Civil Society and Democratization Process in Kenya' (2004).

Meleckidzedeck Khayesi is a Transport Geographer currently working as Technical Officer in the Department of Injuries and Violence Prevention at the World Health Organisation, Geneva, Switzerland. He holds a PhD degree in Transport Geography. His current research is on development of successful practices in urban transport, long-term consequences of road traffic crashes, political economy of road safety and the role of informal public transport in the economy of Kenya. He is a member of the International Editorial Board for the *Journal of Transport Geography*.

Mary Njeri Kinyanjui is a Senior Research Fellow at the Institute for Development Studies, University of Nairobi. She holds a PhD degree from the University of Cambridge. She is an economic Geographer with a focus on industrial development, micro and small enterprises and gender. She has published extensively and has received several research awards.

Peter Kimuyu is a Professor of Applied Microeconomics and the founder director of the recently established School of Economics in the University of Nairobi. He is the current chairman of the Export Promotion Council in the Government of Kenya and a director with one of the large commercial banks in Kenya. Peter Kimuyu is also a research associate with the Kenya Institute of Public Policy Research and

Analysis and a former Executive Director of the Institute of Policy Analysis and Research. He is a member of the New York Academy of Sciences and has co-authored several books and authored/co-authored many journal articles. His current research interests include the economics of inheritance enterprise development, corruption and moral issues pertaining to economics.

Dorothy McCormick is Associate Research Professor and Director of the Institute for Development Studies, University of Nairobi (2001-2007). She holds a PhD from the Johns Hopkins University, USA. Her research and teaching focus on the study of small enterprise development and broader issues of industrialisation.

Winnie V. Mitullah is an Associate Research Professor at the Institute for Development Studies (IDS), University of Nairobi. She holds a PhD in Political Science and Public Administration majoring in Urban Development. She has researched, consulted and published in the areas of provision and management of urban services, policies, institutions and governance, including participatory development. She belongs to a number of local and international networks including: the UN-HABITAT Advisory Board of the Global Research Network on Human Settlements (HS-Net); and Women in Informal Employment: Globalising and Organising [WIEGO]. She is Chair of the Kenya National Commission for UNESCO Social and Human Science Programme Committee and Project Director of 'Facilitation of Street and Informal Traders Associations in Kenya'.

Walter Odhiambo is a Research Fellow at the Institute for Development Studies, University of Nairobi. He holds PhD and Masters degrees in Economics. His current research areas are trade and development, business systems and regional and international trade.

Benjamin Okech was, until his death, Associate Research Professor in the Institute for Development Studies, University of Nairobi. An economist, he specialised in energy issues and also had interests in industrial development.

Mary Omosa is an Associate Research Professor at the Institute for Development Studies, University of Nairobi. She holds a PhD in Development Sociology from Wageningen Agricultural University, The Netherlands. She is engaged in teaching and research with a focus on food security, rural poverty, information communication technology, and popular participation and engagement. Currently, she is the UNESCO/UNITWIN Chair at the University of Nairobi.

Joseph Onjala is a Research Fellow at the Institute for Development Studies (IDS). He holds a PhD in Environmental Economics from Roskilde University (Denmark). He teaches Environment and Natural Resources Management and Environmental Economics. His research focuses on natural resource and environmental issues, with particular attention to the analysis of water policies.

Poul Ove Pedersen is a senior researcher (now retired) at Danish Institute of International Studies in Copenhagen. He has written widely on small towns and small enterprise development in Africa and on the development of freight transport and logistics in Africa.

Preface

Business in Kenya: Institutions and Interactions is based on research that was carried out between 2000 and 2003 by a research team from the Institute for Development Studies (IDS), University of Nairobi. The overall aim of the research was to describe and analyse Kenya's business system in order to characterise it and assess its prospects for further development. The research also aimed at proposing strategies for improving the quality of life of Kenyans through industrialisation. It is based on the premise that business is carried out in different ways in different parts of the world. As such, the team began research expecting to find features that make Kenyan business recognisable as a business system.

The focus of this work is on processes internal to Kenya but we realise that Kenya exists within an increasingly globalised world. Actions taken locally are shaped by global events and have the potential to shape institutions and actors located elsewhere. Our task in this volume is to explore these ideas using the lenses of specific productive sectors in Kenya. From the analysis, we draw conclusions and examine their practical and theoretical implications.

The major focus of the research was on the system as a whole but we recognised that viewing the system from the perspective of particular sectors would give depth to the study and allow for useful comparisons. A number of considerations influenced the choice of sectors to include in the research. We first resolved to include production and services since both are necessary parts of the business system and we believed that they would reveal different patterns of institutional interaction. On the production side, we chose two manufacturing sub-sectors and two in the area of agro-processing. In choosing the textile and metal sectors to represent manufacturing, we considered various sub-sectors' importance to the Kenyan economy, the expected institutional variation, and the presence in the sector of micro and small enterprises as well as larger firms. We also considered our own individual and institutional experience with these two sectors. The choice of the coffee and tea sub-sectors to represent agro-processing was based on their longstanding importance as export earners and on the recent changes in each of them. Trade and transport, were chosen because of their direct contribution to the economy and the fact that they feature in nearly every other economic activity.

The authors of the sectoral chapters in *Part Two* of the book carried out the project fieldwork. Primary data were gathered using combinations of structured questionnaires, semi-structured interview guides, and checklists. The main unit of analysis was the firm, though in the case of micro and small enterprises, considerable information on the entrepreneurs was also gathered. Key informant interviews, focus group interviews, and case studies were also used to provide in-depth information. More detailed descriptions of methodology are available in the sectoral chapters but the overall analysis can best be described as synthetic. We have used primary data from field research carried out as part of the IDS/Centre for Development Research (CDR) Business Systems Project; primary data from related research; secondary data from a variety of published and unpublished sources; and feedback from a series of stakeholder workshops. Data were analysed both quantitatively and qualitatively. Working and conference papers were developed and presented. These form the backbone and main resource for the sectoral chapters.

The volume is in three parts, but in writing the book, we have attempted to create a structure and linkages that weave into a coherent whole. Thus, *Part One* of the book establishes the theoretical and practical context for business in Kenya. It has seven chapters. Chapter One gives an overview of business systems and serves as an introduction to part one. Chapter Two explores the theoretical underpinnings of the business systems approach. The detailed discussion of economic, political and social institutions and their potential impact on business provides the foundation for the analysis of business in Kenya

Chapter Three takes up the crucial issue of government policies and regulations, examining in detail four groups of policies – macro-economic, incentive, institutional, and infrastructure – together with a number of related sets of regulations. It is noted that, although many of these have been supportive of business development, some have actually impeded development of the private sector in Kenya. The negative outcomes are attributed to poor quality of government institutions, corruption, and poor implementation of policies and programmes. Chapter Four examines the current state of Kenya's power, water, and sanitation infrastructure. A number of key questions are raised concerning the adequacy of these services, which are very important to business activity. The chapter then goes on to look at the need and prospects for their improvement.

Chapter Five describes Kenya as a multi-ethnic country with a diversity of cultural practices and beliefs. The areas examined comprise Kenya's growth performance, demographic trends, rural-urban linkages, and the distribution and magnitude of poverty, human capital, physical infrastructure, and natural resources. Chapter Six reviews trade and production systems in Kenya since independence. It focuses on institutions believed to facilitate trade and production such as cooperatives, parastatals, labour markets, technology, and foreign aid. Chapter Seven argues that a well functioning financial sector is necessary for development. The areas examined include the establishment and evolution of the financial system, the financial sector reform effort, and the blossoming of micro-finance institutions. It concludes with the implications of these institutions for the growth of the business system.

Part Two takes a sectoral perspective and has five chapters. Chapter Eight focuses on linkages and competition in the metal products sub-sector. The nature of competition, the size of the market, pervasive mistrust and rivalry, as well as a weak technological system working against firm linkage, are highlighted. It is noted that lack of appreciation of what business associations can or should do means that firms fail to benefit from collective action. Chapter Nine identifies three separate tiers of firms in the textile industry. The first tier consists of thousands of micro and small enterprises, most of which are making clothing. The second tier contains about 150 small to large firms spanning the full range of textile activities from fibre to final products. Most of these have existed since the import substitution era and have struggled to survive in the era of market liberalisation. The third tier is the relatively small number of global exporters that are benefiting from greatly increased trade in textile products. The detailed analysis of each of these tiers clearly demonstrates the book's hypothesis that both sector and firm size are important for understanding the impact of various institutions.

Chapter Ten provides an overview of the tea industry in Kenya, and then goes on to discuss the relationship of the new free trade (*Soko Huru*) on small producers. The detailed description of market changes and the interactions between formal and informal actors highlight the importance of information and suggests a need to improve the quality of information available to small producers. Chapter Eleven examines the impact of liberalisation on coffee production and marketing. It describes the retreat of the state and the emergence of new actors and institutions.

Chapter Twelve returns to the theme of business linkages. The chapter analyses the scope, pattern, and trends of the interrelated process of trade and transport in Kenya, taking a network perspective. The conclusions highlight the importance of historical factors dating back as far as the pre-colonial period in shaping current patterns of trade and transport. The ways in which government has used legislation on trade to achieve social as well as economic objectives are noted; and the importance of structural adjustment, especially import liberalisation, in changing the economics of trade in the country, are underscored. Changes in ownership and new actors, networks, and relationships as important factors in the transformation of trade are pointed out. It is predicted that trade is likely to transform even further with the advent of the Internet.

Finally, *Part Three* reflects on what the findings have to say about doing business in Kenya. It focuses on the analysis of interactions as revealed by the sectoral studies: interactions between business and government, business and society, and businesses with each other. This leads to an examination of the incentive structure and investment patterns within the business system, which suggest the elements of a strategy for building a more competitive business system.

We are grateful to many people for making this work possible. The Danish Government, through its programme for Enhancing Research Capacity (ENRECA), provided financial support for the research programme. The Centre for Development Research (now Danish Institute for International Studies (CDR) in Copenhagen was our link institution and provided many of us with opportunities to visit, analyse data, and write. Poul Ove Pedersen, senior researcher at CDR, was a constant source of insight and encouragement. The authors responded most graciously to our queries and requests for revisions. We thank them, along with those who provided secretarial and editorial assistance, especially Josephine Mong'are and Linet Misati. The production of the book has benefited immensely from the support of the University of Nairobi Press.

Dorothy McCormick
Patrick O. Alila
Mary Omosa
July 2007

Part 1

Kenya Business Context

Chapter 1

Business Systems: An Overview

Mary Omosa, Dorothy McCormick and Patrick O. Alila

INTRODUCTION

This chapter gives an overview of business systems. It serves as an introduction to the book's first part, which deals with the business context. Government policy is a critical component of that context everywhere in the world, especially in the countries of Africa, which gained their independence at a time when many believed that the state must drive development. Understanding the policy process is, therefore, essential to understanding how business has evolved in Kenya. Not only does business in Kenya differ from that in other continents and countries, but also earlier investigations suggest that business systems in Africa tend to be internally fragmented (Pedersen and McCormick, 1999). Both internal and cross-country differences are rooted in the interactions of the economic, political, and social institutions that make up the context for business activity.

The chapter has four sections. The first touches briefly on the business context, which is dealt in greater details later in the book; the second looks at the way various actors participate in the business process; the third one examines the boundaries between the public and private sectors; while the last section outlines some of the milestone policy developments.

BUSINESS CONTEXT

The business context basically consists of those forces, present conditions, and institutions that have the power to affect the establishment, growth, and development of business. Although our emphasis in this book is on the national level, we nevertheless, recognise that the national interacts with both the local and the wider regional and global contexts.

The business context is important because, like other living organisms, businesses tend to adapt to their environment. They learn, for example, to compensate for weak demand, take advantage of a strong legal system, substitute for missing infrastructure, or self-finance when banks are unfriendly.

Globalisation is a major force affecting business in the world today. By affecting businesses' present conditions and influencing the way institutions change, globalisation shapes the future of business in most parts of the world. The broad theme of globalisation runs through the book because it affects aspects of the business context ranging from the changing tastes of urban consumers to improved communications in remote rural areas. The power of globalisation is felt differently in different sectors, as the case of textiles in this volume clearly shows.

Present conditions form the ground on which business rests and from which it grows or withers. Present conditions are economic, social, political, technological, and cultural. Perhaps, one of the most important 'present conditions' affecting the business system is a country's level of wealth and income. It makes a difference whether a country is rich or poor, well endowed with resources or struggling to find the means to develop. Although Kenya is the third largest economy in Sub-Saharan Africa, it is a poor country by most standard measures. Gross Domestic Product (GDP) per capita income was US$395 in 2003 (Kenya, 2004). More than 50% of the population was absolutely poor and over one-third suffered from the low incomes, illiteracy, and poor living conditions associated with human poverty (UNDP, 2004). Under such circumstances, it is not surprising that businesses struggle to find markets, or that they operate with poor infrastructure and fail to invest.

The final element of the business context is the one we believe to be critical for business development: the institutions that shape the interaction of individuals and organisations. Institutions are rarely created in a day. More often, they grow and develop over time; and for this reason, in the concise words of an eminent economist, "History matters" (North, 1990: vii). In Kenya's case, the most relevant parts of history include the migrations that brought the country's current inhabitants to this part of East Africa, the period of British colonisation, and the post-independence era that began in 1963. This history is important, not only for its positive and negative lessons, but also because these times and events gave birth to the norms, values, rules, regulations and informal ways of doing things that form the present institutional context for business in Kenya.

The institutions that shape business are, therefore, many and complex. They range from the economic institutions of markets, firms and relational contracting, to political and social institutions, such as the state, family, gender, and ethnicity. In form, they include formal rules, such as constitutions, policies, laws, and regulations, as well as the less formal norms, customs, and codes of conduct. These come together and are in constant interaction in the notion of the business system, which is central to our analysis (Whitley, 1992; Whitley and Kristensen, 1996).

ROLES AND MODES OF PARTICIPATION IN BUSINESS

A number of factors define the ways in which various actors participate in business. These include who owns business, how policy is formulated and related regulations developed, how business and labour participate in the process, the socio-cultural status of business owners, and the operations of businesses within and beyond national boundaries.

Actors in the Policy Process

Policy process is a key factor that defines formal roles through involvement by various actors in policy formulation relevant to business. This is broadly in terms of contributions to policy inputs, mostly demands, or having responsibility for policy outputs by way of implementation and/or just being recipients of policy enacted already. The formal roles of actors in policy formulation and modes of participation in business can be described as follows:

Government

The government is the major actor in policy formulation and generally has a dominant presence throughout the process. In most cases, policy initiatives/prescriptions originate from the public bureaucracy or parliament in the form of Acts of Parliament, Sessional Papers, and Legal Notices governing actual participation in business. There are several policies covering life of a business right from registration to the time of winding up or closure. A policy environment conducive to participation in business will result in business growth, hence the persistent calls in the ongoing policy reforms debate that the government provides an enabling policy environment for the growth of businesses, especially small and medium enterprises. This is in relation to both policy prescriptions and more so implementation, since it is through policy implementation that government has frequent and pervasive interactions with business.

Stakeholders

The stakeholders are generally people affected by a particular policy comprising key actors that are involved and actively participate in the policy formulation process and the general public mostly indirectly involved. It is therefore useful in identifying key players in policies affecting businesses to bear in mind the policy target(s) and coverage. This is in terms, for instance, of different sizes of business such as small or large, smallholder farmers or estate; commodity type such as cash crop or metal products; geographical locations, whether in the urban or rural sector, and economic sector such as agriculture, industry, transport services etc. The main actors participating in formulation of policies affecting business include business entities, business associations and lobby groups, government departments, Provincial Administration, professional groups and associations, non-governmental organisations (NGOs) and Community Based Organisations (CBOs), parliament, labour unions, media houses, and the Judiciary.

Ownership

It is ownership or proprietary rights that determine the stakes one has in an enterprise and therefore participation in business. Proprietary rights originate from owning or controlling business resources, notably through investment financing by way of start-up or working capital. At the broadest level, ownership of enterprises can be private, public, or some combination of public and private. Private businesses may be owned by an individual as a sole proprietor, or by more than one person in partnership or various forms of limited liability companies. Public enterprises are those in which the state is full or partial owner. In 1998, the Kenya government fully owned 155 out of 325 public enterprises, and held a controlling interest in another 53 (Ikiara, 2000). The formal status of an enterprise sometimes fails to reveal the full reality of its ownership. For example, formally, two enterprises may be entirely separate sole proprietorships, but are owned by two members of the same family who work closely in certain aspects of their businesses. Larger enterprises may be linked through overlapping directorships, and apparently, local firms may be subsidiaries of multinationals. The problem of controlling stakes in business has been the source of ownership crisis in many enterprises, especially state ventures being privatised.

Although not owners as such, financiers, landlords, and even agents may wield considerable power in certain circumstances. A case in point comes from the transport sector where the financier has drastically altered a bus company's operations by re-possessing vehicles for failure to meet scheduled debt payments. Decisions of landlords or agents can have comparable impact on an enterprise's ability to operate profitably.

Business Regulators

The government exercises both power and authority over businesses and is the key dominant actor in the regulation of business. The starting point is policy setting and rules enactment by central government and local authorities followed by policy implementation, enforcement of rules and arbitration over regulations for business. The regulations also impact on businesses differently depending on size and level of operations, commodity type, geographical and sectoral location. The regulatory framework is commonly perceived as punitive and extractive, mainly due to taxation and control measures by government. This view, however, often overlooks the positive dimensions of the framework, notably ensuring quality, security measures, information and the maintenance of institutions for regulation purposes.

There has been likewise controversy regarding policies deemed to be foreign inspired. For instance, a number of aspects of privatisation policy have been criticised and faulted for being imposed by development partners. This position, however, needs to be balanced with the positive role of the development partners in institution capacity building for business regulation. A persistent major problem in these institutions and state enterprises and/or those where government is commanding majority shares is patronage that continues to undermine efficiency and productivity. In any case, the government formally has governance instruments for enforcement of rules/contracts, regulation and control of businesses and monitoring and evaluation of policies, which if properly used, should result in desirable business practices and development.

Business and Labour Representatives

Those owning businesses have several interests, which in short, can be stated as making profit or high returns to capital invested and remaining in business. As for labour, the critical issue around which interests revolve is fair remuneration for work done. These interests are served by organisations charged with formal role of representation of business and labour. The organisations comprise Business Associations, Chambers of Commerce, Cooperatives, Professional Associations, Labour Unions, NGOs, Religion and Faith Organisations, and Political parties.

Social Cultural Status

It is often the case that social cultural norms assign individuals and/or group status that formally determine their participation in business. In many societies, social ties and social status also affect access to state resources, including public services. The key relevant aspects of social ties are kinship, subsuming family, household and clan, gender, and ethnicity, subsuming tribe and race. These social ties have been instrumental in starting businesses in the provision of start-up capital for individual businesses and joint ventures/partnerships. Relatives form the bulk of business employees/labour in the case of micro and small enterprises and smallholder farms. Kinship and other social ties constitute a significant basis of business connections and networks. Ethnic connections have proved useful in establishing business and even accessing credit, notably, in the case of Asian families and also certain tribal groups.

In contrast, gender remains a negative factor, specifically, for women thereby constraining their participation in business. There is conclusive evidence of little or no access to credit from formal financial institutions by women and overall limited business opportunities to be exploited by women. Women compared to men tend to engage in fewer and only certain types of enterprises.

In line with the practice of patron-client politics at the national and local levels, patronage has been a significant factor in gaining access to business opportunities and subsequently, participation in business. Relatives, tribesmen and/or friends have helped in clinching business deals in many different ways at various levels of power hierarchy. In some cases, such deals have turned out to be the breakthrough to participation in big business. In the same vein, joint ventures between family members and even with foreign firms have been literally put together to clinch deals.

Transnational Business Operators

Business operations that take place beyond national boundaries have significant implications for business in terms of participation in the different national business systems. In the first place, nationality may confer certain privileges and at the same time impose restrictions on participation. For instance, a multinational firm may have relatively easy access to investment capital but its operations remain restricted to certain products and particular geographical locations. In contrast, indigenous businessmen may have serious constraints of access to capital but not face restrictions in terms of product type or location. All in all the nationality status of business operators whether indigenous, immigrant or foreign is of crucial importance for participation.

Secondly, the firms which export or import products operate in two or more different national business systems having varied market structures, rules and conditions. These firms have to tailor their participation accordingly to conform to the rules and procedures of a particular business system.

Thirdly, firms in export and import have greater government presence in their business, for example, being involved with the foreign office and state backed international bodies especially for trade. The terms and conditions to be fulfilled, including capital outlay and business connections abroad, restrict entry into export-import business and participation is limited to a relatively small number of firms.

PUBLIC SECTOR AND BUSINESS STRUCTURAL BOUNDARIES IN KENYA

Government is an entity whose analytical boundaries can be identified with relative ease through delineation of its institutional components. Government exercises constitutional sovereignty arising from internationally recognised nation-state status, geographical location and historically demarcated political boundaries. The key components include central government, comprising public bureaucracy, subsuming the civil service, parastatals and commissions; and local government, subsuming local authorities and district administration. The foregoing components largely fall within the executive branch that works in tandem with parliament and the judiciary, second and third branches respectively. There is an underlying fundamental principle of separation of power between the three branches, mainly for purposes of checks and balances and basically, for the proper functioning of government.

In contrast, business has generally no geopolitical boundaries and takes place between firms and individuals within and across national boundaries and even between governments. Thus, there is a wide variety of business types, widespread location of firms globally, and variations of links between business and governments/political regimes, all of which pose difficulties for demarcating boundaries for institutional components of business.

In any case, for purposes of examining interactions with government, the core of business consists of private firms operating with the aim of making a profit. These engage in manufacturing, trade, services, or some combination of these activities. In terms of origin and location, the firms can be national/indigenous and operating nationally or multinationally. A second group of organisations also "does business" with government. These are private, not-for-profit organisations such as churches, foundations, NGOs and CBOs. Notable among them for our analysis are the NGOs and CBOs. NGOs are both local and international, while CBOs are by definition rooted in the local community. The activities of both are mainly in the realm of services, but in their operations they engage both government and commercial business firms in buying and selling goods and services. The transactions result in two- and/or three-way interactions between them and government. The lynchpin of NGOs' interaction with government, CBOs and even amongst themselves, are the large amounts of resources such organisations marshal for public projects. The resources are deployed mostly through purchase/orders of material inputs in the foreign and local markets and it is mainly the commercial firms that are the suppliers.

GOVERNMENT INTERACTION WITH BUSINESS: MILESTONE POLICY DEVELOPMENTS

In Kenya, there are key developments, mostly policy and economic management decisions that have been instrumental in giving form and content to government interactions with business. First and foremost is the Kenyan historical experience of nearly half a century of a colony status. The carving out of a Kenyan state on a racial and foreign, white settlement basis gave rise to African nationalism which spearheaded the successful fight for political independence bringing high hopes and excitement to realise equality of citizens. This has never come to pass and the legacy of racial/ethnic inequality, particularly in the economic/business sphere, is left instead, and is in fact growing. The colonial economy principle of primary commodity production for export remains entrenched. The description of such an economy as one where "people produce what they do not consume and consume what they do not produce" essentially remains true of independent Kenya's economy which is dominated by tea, tourism, horticulture and coffee. The colonial legacy of establishment of government machinery has meant an operational administrative structure, law and order. However, a strong dominant public bureaucracy has thus far meant dwarfing of the private business sector that remains relatively weak. Also, the Asian community's dominance in business is a colonial relic, having origins in the colonial administration policy of making commerce and trade in towns and trading centres outside Nairobi, a preserve for Asians. While white settlers grew cash crops, the major economic/business assignment for the Africans was provision of labour.

Secondly, the independence pronouncement of equality of Kenyan citizens was a landmark development and a turning point for government business interaction, especially for the Africans' business initiatives. A related policy step was the African Socialism and its Application to Kenya, Sessional Paper No.10 of 1965 which provided ideological backing for private property ownership and protection as a fundamental and constitutional right. In the same spirit, barely two years later, the sessional paper was followed by the Trade Licensing Act of 1967, mainly geared towards more favourable location of African businesses in the central business district in the main Kenyan towns, Nairobi, Mombasa, Kisumu and Nakuru. The rationale for the two pieces of legislation was to redress the disadvantaged position of Africans under the colonial regime by according Africans the necessary recognition and opening up business opportunities for them through government effort and policy support.

Thirdly, the informal sector, and specifically the micro small enterprise sector gained recognition and subsequent government support due to three key policy decisions. The first was adoption of the 1972 International Labour Organisation (ILO) report on the informal economy that meant official recognition of the sector. The next step was a declaration of commitment to develop the sector through the launch of Sessional Paper No.1 of 1986 on Economic Development and Renewed

Growth which underscored the important role of the sector in national socio-economic development. The Sessional Paper No.2 of 1992 on Small Enterprises and the *Jua Kali* Development in Kenya was the third step. It was, however, the first instance the government came up with a policy framework for promoting small-scale enterprises through policy interventions thus creating an enabling environment for this type of business, channelling of credit to them and addressing gender related issues peculiar to the sector.

It is in the same vein of enhanced involvement of Africans in business, and also to strengthen the private sector being transferred into the hands of the indigenous population, that a landmark policy decision was taken. The Kenya government to this end adopted the Ndegwa Commission Report of 1972, well known specifically for allowing civil servants, still in public service, to engage in private business. The broad issue that arose is the intertwined relationship between government and business which impacts negatively on free operation of the market and good governance. The reality is that civil servants in business have to take time out to run their businesses which means divided loyalty, less devotion and questionable commitment to public service that translates into a weak, inefficient, corrupt and ineffective civil service. A critical concern here is, however, conflict of interest for public servants engaged in private business, who are suppliers and at the same time virtually customers for goods and services purchased by government, or those using their position to influence purchase decisions.

Finally, developments influencing government interaction with business have been the result of landmark macro economic policies that directed economic development attention, specifically first towards agriculture and then later focused on industrialisation. The latter in turn has also subsequently seen policy change in the recent past. In the last two decades or so, there has been a major shift to policy reforms, comprehensively addressing the whole economy, that are still ongoing.

The historical policy decision regarding agriculture that led to a transformation of the sector was taken in the 1950s, shortly before independence. It was under the Swynnerton Plan for agriculture that a new policy was introduced then, allowing African smallholders to grow cash crops, specifically coffee, tea and pyrethrum, which hitherto they were barred from growing. The coming into existence of the African smallholder was a phenomenal structural change in agriculture ending sole reliance on estate farms during the colonial period. The new development also meant greater African participation in agricultural business and playing a major role in the overall economy.

The quest for industrialisation on attaining independence led the government to embark on an import substitution strategy for industrial development or Import Substitution Industrialisation (ISI). The strategy was inward looking, seeking to produce locally what was previously imported by local producers protected from foreign competition. The policy step led to rapid development of some industries, notably plastics, pharmaceuticals, paper, textiles and garment manufacturing, and food processing. The strategy was however biased against the agricultural sector, directing resources disproportionately to the manufacturing sector with no tangible evidence of the objective of rapid industrialisation being ever realised. In any case, weaknesses of immediate concern were failures regarding saving foreign exchange, increased domestic control of the economy and generation of employment.

The more comprehensive economic policy reforms the government embarked on were initiated in the 1980s under the World Bank/IMF sponsored Structural Adjustment Programmes (SAPs). These policy reforms were in essence, outward-looking and specifically in the case of trade, involved phasing out import substitution and pursuing export promotion. The policies embraced were the free market principle, notably, advocating for privatisation with the aim of moving away from the historically established practice of government dominant civil bureaucracy control and protection. Likewise, the key cost-sharing idea in the reforms meant that service provision costs should not be government responsibility in entirety but should be instead shared, for instance, by way of resources being marshalled from non-government/private sector to meeting part of at least the service cost requirements for education, health, water, etc.

In relation to geography/regions, the policy perspective that viewed the economy as dichotomous with two separate components, namely, an urban and a rural sector, was found wanting. For instance, due attention was not being accorded to the wide ranging inter-linkages between the two sectors in terms of rural labour supply to the urban enterprises, rural production of both food and raw materials for urban workers and manufacturing firms in towns/trading centres respectively and the larger rural market for mostly urban businesses goods and services. The new policy direction puts emphasis on rural-urban linkages starting with Sessional Paper No.1 of 1986. Consequently, poverty afflicting the majority of rural dwellers remains at the top of economic but more so, social development agenda.

CONCLUSION

All in all, both the internal and cross-country variations between systems, traced to forces determining the business context, notably, institutions, different socio-economic, political and technological conditions, and also globalisation, are remarkable. Businesses themselves are shaped by institutions which are wide ranging in type and complex in form, such as markets, the state, family, ethnicity etc. The institutions and the relevant actors involved, interacting with each other mostly over policy making for business and implementations, make up the core of a business system. The government is the major actor in the policy process and plays a pivotal role universally in virtually all business systems. The Kenyan experience with policy and economic decisions discussed in this chapter briefly indicates that the government plays a relatively more pronounced role in a business system in an African context.

REFERENCES

Ikiara, G.K. 2000. "The Public Sector in Kenya since Independence." In Nyong'o, P. Anyang'; Ikiara, G.K.; Mwale, S.M.; Ngugi, R.W. and Aseto, Oyugi. *The Context of Privatisation in Kenya*. Nairobi: African Academy of Sciences.

Kenya, Republic of. 2004. *Economic Survey 2004*. Nairobi: Government Printer.

North, Douglass C. 1990. *Institutions, Institutional Change and Economic Performance*. Cambridge: Cambridge University Press.

Pedersen, Poul Ove and McCormick, Dorothy. 1999. "African Business Systems in a Globalising World." *Journal of Modern African Studies* 37(1): 109-135.

UNDP. 2004. *Human Development Report 2004*. New York: United Nations Development Programme.

Whitley, Richard. 1992. *Business Systems in East Asia: Firms, Markets and Societies*. London: Sage.

Whitley, Richard and Kristensen, Peer Hull (eds.). 1996. *The Changing European Firm: Limits to Convergence*. London: Routledge.

Chapter 2

Business Systems Theory: An African Perspective

Dorothy McCormick and Peter Kimuyu

INTRODUCTION: INSTITUTIONS AND BUSINESS

The institutions that shape business are many and complex. They range from the economic institutions of markets, firms and contracting, to political and social institutions such as the state, family, gender, and ethnicity. In form, they include formal rules, such as constitutions, policies, laws, and regulations, as well as the less formal norms, customs, and codes of conduct. These come together in the notion of a business system, which is key and forms the major part of this book's analytical framework.

Few would deny that a society's institutions affect the way its businesses are organised and operate (Williamson, 1985; Nabli and Nugent, 1989; North, 1990; Evans, 1995; Hollingsworth and Boyer, 1997). We use North's (1990) now classic definition of institutions as 'humanly devised constraints to human interaction'. Some constraints are formal, in the sense that the rules are written down, while others are informal norms or codes of conduct. Institutions operate in different spheres of a society's life, with some being mainly social, others political, still others economic. It is important to recognise, however, that what may on one level be viewed as purely social institutions, may have significant economic consequences. For example, in many places, the social institution of marriage carries with it the expectation that the wife will carry certain domestic duties and responsibilities. This has a clear effect on the amount of time she can spend in business activities (McCormick, 2001a).

In everyday language, the terms 'institutions' and 'organisations' are often used interchangeably. The two are not, however, identical in meaning. To use North's (1990) sports analogy, institutions are the 'rules of the game' while organisations are its players.[1] As already pointed out, institutions include such rules as a country's constitution and a community's social norms. Organisations are the embodiment of the institutions. They are bodies formed to carry out the rules. They are, quite simply, the players. Thus, if the state has a constitution, it requires various governmental organisations to implement its provisions. At a much more micro level, the rules of contribution and distribution that characterise the rotating savings and credit organisations are embodied and acted out in specific ROSCA groups.

This chapter lays the theorêtical and conceptual foundations for the book. Our point of departure is the observation that there are significant differences in business organisation and conduct in different countries and, to some extent, in different regions of the same country. Over the last several decades there has been growing consensus that the state and market alone cannot fully explain differences in business organisation and operations.

Institutions Shaping the Business System

The literature on business systems attempts to examine the forces that direct and influence the way individual businesses operate and, ultimately, the organisation of business activity in general (Pedersen and McCormick, 1999). It does this by looking at various groupings of institutions, both separately and in their interactions with one another. At least twelve such groupings can be identified: the state, goods markets, firms, business associations, laws and contracts, trust and related institutions, financial institutions, labour markets, education and innovation systems, family and community, ethnicity, and gender. Although the importance of any group or individual institution can vary from one setting to another, all are sufficiently important to be worth considering in this overview.

State and Government

The state is a critical actor in the economic activity of most nations. Yet, not all states participate in the economy in the same way or to the same degree. Although state and government are intertwined, we tend to view the state as the overarching political reality of a particular country, and the government as its organisational structure or ruling authority. In this section, we look first at the nature and basic orientation of the state, and then at the systems of support for industrial development that are usually provided by government.

Nature and basic orientation of the state

States differ in their basic orientations. Politically, some are autocratic while others adopt varying forms of liberal democracy. Their relationship to the economy can, in theory at least, range from pure laissez faire to centrally planned. Even within

---

1   This is not the only possible distinction between institutions and organisations. In the organisational development literature, organisations are technical instruments designed as means to definite goals. Institutions, whether conceived as groups or practices, are products of interaction and adaptation that hold ideals and values. In this view, organisations may *become* institutions if they take on value beyond the technical requirements of the task at hand (Selznick, 1966).

liberal democracies there is considerable variation in the type and degree of intervention that is considered appropriate.

As we will see in Chapter 3, most sub-Saharan African states adopted a developmental approach at independence. The Structural Adjustment Programmes of the 1980s and 1990s changed the approach somewhat, but many, including Kenya, continue to be broadly developmental both in their ideological underpinnings and in their attempts to direct administrative and political resources to achieve development objectives (Mkandawire and Soludo, 1998). This is not to say that all, or even many, of these states have been successful in achieving their development objectives. Many fail because they lack the internal cohesion or the financial or human resources necessary to carry out their policies (Evans, 1995; Weiss, 1998; Chibber, 2002), but even these remain 'developmental' in their orientation.

Defining a state as 'developmental' has implications for the likely configuration of state institutions affecting industry and industrial development. Drawing on secondary sources and his own research in Asia and Europe, Whitley (2003) argues that the key characteristics of the developmental state are its high level involvement in economic development, its limited encouragement of business associations, and its low tolerance of labour organisations. Limited studies in Africa of business associations and labour movements suggest that these observations are likely to hold true (McCormick et al., 2001; Sachikonye, 1993).

The issue of cohesion is also critical. Evans (1995) argues that, "To deliver collective goods, states must act as coherent entities". Yet, many African states lack coherence. Planning documents gather dust on shelves, but are never followed by regulations and specific programmes. Not only are policies not implemented, but they may even be contradicted by action on the ground.

Systems of support for production and distribution

Support institutions can help firms meet the information, skills, finance and other needs that are difficult to satisfy in the open market. The key support mechanisms are policies, regulations, infrastructure, and programmes, practice, and informal ways of operating.

Government policy is a major support mechanism. Policy sets the broad framework within which production and distribution take place. Policy is in that sense an institution or 'rule of the game' at a given point in time. As will be discussed in Chapter 4, both macro-economic policies and incentive policies can either support or constrain industrialisation. The need for appropriate macro-economic policy can hardly be disputed, though it is not always easy to achieve. The case for incentive policies is less clear. The classic 'developmental states' of Japan, Taiwan, and Korea are credited with succeeding at industrialisation by using selective interventions. At least one analysis, however, suggests that the contribution of such interventions to these countries' growth was only marginal, and that their success was due instead to their macro policies and their export bias (Noland and Pack, 2003).

All states formulate and enforce rules, but the thrust of regulation varies. Some act as stimuli or incentives. Others prevent or restrict certain activities seen as inappropriate or even dangerous. New policies usually require new or revised rules to make them operational. Over-regulation acts as a disincentive to business activity, but under-regulation can also be problematic if it means that key policies are not implemented for lack of specific guidelines.

Production and distribution require certain supporting facilities that are ordinarily provided by government or public corporations. Services such as telecommunications, power, transportation, water, and sanitation – often called "physical" or "hard" infrastructure – are vital for productive performance and economic growth. Support institutions constitute the "soft" infrastructure. These include economic institutions such as the monetary system, the system of property rights and contracting, and various formal and informal financial arrangements.

Governments also affect business activity through programmes, practice, and informal ways of doing things. Government programmes are actually an extension of rules and regulations, acting as positive incentives for the target group. Programmes shape industry by offering information, financial or other benefits to certain categories of businesses, for example, those of a certain size, in a particular sector, or located in a target area. For instance, South Africa's Black Economic Empowerment (BEE) programme is attempting to compensate for the uneven economic playing field created during the apartheid era by offering special concessions to businesses run by Black South Africans.

Markets

Broadly speaking, a market is any context in which the sale or purchase of goods or services takes place. Taking an institutional perspective, we define a market as a set of rules for the exchange of goods and/or services.

Markets can be viewed and categorised in different ways. One of these is the purpose to which the good or service is to be put. Thus, firms speak of their supply or input markets and their product markets. Economists categorise markets according to the degree of competition or, conversely, their domination by one or more actors. In this conceptualisation, markets range from perfectly competitive to monopolistic, with various shades in between. Businesses categorise markets according to what customers they are trying to reach. Some aim at high-income consumers, others at institutional buyers, still others at the youth. Each of these groups defines a particular market. One of the fundamental choices that a business has to make is whether it will try to appeal to a mass market or position itself in a particular niche.

Business and industry often find it useful to describe markets by their geographic reach, speaking of the local or domestic market, regional markets, and the global market. This designation is important because the characteristics of customers in different places shape the nature, quality, and price of the products being offered, the logistics of getting those products to market, and the strategies that have to be employed to compete successfully.

Firms

Firms are the basic building blocks of the system of business. They occupy a key position between the market and the state, and their nature and functioning are determined by the activities of both. Volumes have been written defining the concept of the firm and theorizing about its role in the economy (see, for example, Coase, 1937; Penrose, 1959; Nelson and Winter, 1982; Williamson, 1985; North, 1990; Hart, 1995). A full discussion of this literature is outside the scope of this book, but we will briefly make the case for an understanding of the firm that goes beyond the traditional neo-classical 'black box' approach.

The neo-classical firm makes a single product and is defined by that product's production function. Inside the firm, inputs are turned into outputs steadily and smoothly, so that all variations in internal organisation can safely be ignored. Here our focus on the variations that occur across business systems requires a different definition. Drawing on Coase (1937), North (1990) and others, we define a firm as an institution that buys or hires resources and organises them to produce goods and/or services. Such a definition allows firms to vary, not only with the product being made, but also according to the characteristics of the owner and the firm's institutional environment. Real-world firms, therefore, are not black boxes, but differ in size, form of ownership, internal organisation, and external linkages.

Businesses vary in size, ownership, and legal status. Size differences come about, not only because of available economies of scale, but also because of differences in the owners' resources, their preferences for production strategies, and the institutional environment that may favour larger or smaller firms.

Firms also vary in the type of ownership. By far, the most prevalent, especially in developing economies, is the single owner firm. Also common are partnerships where two or more persons go into business by each contributing to the firm's capital and its operations. Finally, there are various forms of limited liability companies. These operate under the laws of a particular jurisdiction, which limits the liability of the company's members or shareholders for debts or other liabilities incurred by the company. A variant of the limited liability company, often found in African countries, is the parastatal. These limited liability companies are wholly or partly owned and fully controlled by the state. Also common in African economies are producer cooperatives: societies jointly owned and run by members to produce and distribute goods and services.

The legal status of private firms is often summed up in the shorthand terms 'formal' and 'informal' sector; public firms can be added by naming a 'parastatal' sector (Pedersen and McCormick, 1999). The notion of 'formal sector' is generally used to describe the group of larger, well-capitalised, legally established firms. These are recognised by the authorities of the place(s) in which they operate, usually because they have registered or obtained a business licence. The term 'informal sector' is used to encompass the mass of self-employed individuals and micro- and small enterprises common in developing countries. Typically, these are not registered or licensed, have little capital and few employees. Although the two terms offer a useful typology at the extremes, there is a considerable grey area consisting of registered micro-firms and unregistered or non-compliant medium-scale enterprises that makes it difficult to apply analytically. We will, therefore, use these designations sparingly.

Firms also differ in what they do and how they do it. Firms are typically classified by sector and within sectors, by industry. Thus, some firms belong to the manufacturing sector, while others are traders or service providers. Manufacturing firms make different products, service firms offer services ranging from barbering to computer software design. Traders can be categorised as wholesalers or retailers, general merchandisers, or specialists in a particular product line. Many firms engage in multiple activities.

Even within a single sector, firms differ considerably in the way they organise their business. The term "firm-level institutions" is sometimes used to capture these differences. As the name suggests, these are rules, norms, and practices that govern what happens within firms (Whitley, 1992; McCormick 2001b).

Some differences have to do with size, others with the available technology or the skills of the workers, and still others are functions of history or the preferences of the owners. In small-scale manufacturing, for example, it is common to add machines gradually as capital becomes available (Sverrisson, 1993). This means that at any given moment, firms in the same sector may differ considerably in their production technology. It also means that businesses often link with others to borrow or buy the services of the missing machines. Finally, manufacturing firms differ in the way they organise their production. The largest usually use some variant of mass production, with division of labour and one or more production lines. Some small firms also use a modified mass production approach (see Ongile and McCormick, 1996), but others prefer craft or 'make through' models.

Business Associations

Although the firm is the basic unit of business activity, firms often find it advantageous to join together in networks, linkages, and subcontracting relationships. Such external relationships often enable firms to do things that would not be feasible to do alone. We focus here on one form of linkage, the business association, because it cuts across sectors and has the potential to offer widespread benefits to the business community.

Associations are formed for the joint benefit of the members. Observers have identified two main reasons why people join associations: to benefit from collective influence, and to benefit from particular services. What has been called the logic of influence focuses on the role of an association in acting collectively on behalf of its members' interests (Olson, 1971; Streeck and Schmitte, 1991; Bennett, 1998). Thus, a business association will lobby government for policies and programmes believed to be beneficial to its members. The logic of services leads associations to respond to members' individual and specific need for services (Bennett, 1998). Service-oriented associations provide training, market information, directory services, industry research, technical advice, and a host of other services to their members and sometimes to outsiders.

Business associations vary in size. For example, the national chambers of commerce, associations of manufacturers, and the like, are usually large and draw membership from across several sectors. Businesses often organise into smaller groups, such as sub-sectoral associations, location-based associations, credit groups, and other special interest groupings. Theoretical and empirical studies suggest not only that smaller groups are more cohesive, but also that larger groups are unlikely to act or even to form themselves into an association without the inducement of services or other selective incentives (Olson, 1971; McCormick et al., 2001).

Laws and Contracts

Firms are constantly entering into formal and informal contracts (Coase, 1937; Ricketts, 1994; Langlois and Robertson, 1995). The ability to enforce those contracts depends on laws and access to legal and extra-legal enforcement mechanisms. We first discuss the legal side of contracting.

Exchange requires actual property rights and the ability to enforce these rights. Laws provide mechanisms for both. They spell out who has the right to own or use property, under what conditions, and for how long. They also specify how rights can be transferred and what mechanisms are available for enforcing property rights. The vitality of markets draws from the sharpness with which rights over property are defined, protected and enforced by law. When the law is either absent or weak, exchange contracts are undermined since such contracts are difficult to enforce.

When contracting must proceed despite unclear property rights or poor enforcement, the parties must fall back on legal substitutes for enforcement and protection. Legal substitutes may include arbitration, reputation, norms, altruisms and trust. Enforcement may also rely on family alliances, threat of violence or actual violence, and other self-protection mechanisms. Such substitutes are inherently inefficient and incapable of supporting generalised exchange. Legal substitutes embody hidden costs that restrict the extent of exchange by favouring simple, simultaneous cash exchanges not prone to opportunistic behaviour. The rule of law is therefore important for efficient enforcement of exchange-related property rights and promotion of commerce.

Laws are easier to enforce and most supportive of markets when they are aligned with social norms. Laws that are out of step with social norms are either disobeyed or obeyed out of fear. When the law and social norms are aligned, morality becomes a guide to legality. This reduces the costs of legal counsel and enforcement. When citizens perceive the law as just, they have reason for obeying it out of respect.

Norms, Trust and Social Capital

Although enforcement of contracts often depends on the law and state action, businesses frequently use other avenues such as norms, trust and institutions of social capital either because the legal system is deficient or because non-state relationships seem more appropriate or more effective.

Exchange thrives in cooperation that grows as different persons share a common ethos. In this case, cooperation is made possible by forces that reside in moral norms. A norm is an institution that specifies what action a set of people regards as proper or correct, improper or incorrect. Norms are created and reinforced by socialisation. Acceptable patterns of behaviour are only sustainable when there are widely understood and firmly enforced by sanctions. Norms, then, can be viewed as standards of individual conduct that people follow in order to avoid sanctioning (Kimuyu, 2000).

Sanction is more effective and less necessary when people are able to privately monitor and require compliance from each other. This is more likely in smaller groups that interact closely and continuously. When exchange has a wide outreach and is between anonymous groups, or when the exchanges are separated by time such as in credit and insurance markets, moral norms become inadequate for enforcement. Information asymmetries – the fact that one party to a transaction has better information about the good or service being exchanged – also allow one party to take unfair advantage of the other. Protection from such opportunistic behaviour may require laws or other additional institutions.

Trust is an expectation that others will not exploit one's vulnerability. Trust allows people to take risks. Trust is demonstrated when economic agents take risky actions in an environment of either uncertainty or informational incompleteness. It permits exchanges in these circumstances but conditions such exchanges in specific ways (see Zucker, 1986; Platteau, 1994; Fafchamps, 1996; Schmitz, 1999 among others). This in turn shapes the business system.

For business to continue, a high level of trust must be maintained, and when trust is abused, there must be mechanisms for recourse. When such mechanisms are absent or are too cumbersome to use, firms tend to work in ways that do not require trust, especially by inspecting all supplies before buying, requiring large upfront deposits, and eliminating credit transactions. Such approaches add to costs and reduce the number of potential customers.

Norms and trust allow the formation of social capital. Social capital is often viewed as an asset analogous to financial or physical capital. Unlike these, however, it inheres not in objects, but in relationships (Coleman, 1990). It can be broadly defined as encompassing such things as 'institutions, relationships, attitudes, and values that govern interactions among people and often contribute to economic and social development' (Grootaert and Bastelaer, 2002). Some argue that it can be measured according to the number and size of networks of connections that someone has access to (Fine, 2001). Two broad elements are embodied in this general definition; one that has been referred to as structural social capital, which is assumed to include such elements as institutions, associations and networks as well as the procedures and rules that they embody. The other element is referred to as the cognitive social capital, and includes subjective and less tangible elements such as behavioural attitudes and norms, shared values, trust and reciprocity.

Researchers distinguish different elements of social capital based on its scope.[2] At the micro level, social capital manifests itself as horizontal networks of households and individuals, with the associated values and norms that underlie such networks. There is also the meso-level of social capital that embodies both horizontal and vertical relationships among groups. In other words, a further scope of social capital is the level between individuals and society as a whole, illustrated by regional groupings of local associations. Social capital is also observable at the macro level where it is embodied in the broader institutional and political environment.

Looking at social capital, this broadly gives room for the analysis of and substitution between the different levels. Complementarity can for example obtain when national institutions make the environment for local associations such as business associations more enabling. Micro and meso level social capital can in turn either improve or weaken the state. Local associations can, for example, sustain national and regional institutions, enhancing their legitimacy and stability. On the other hand, excessive ethnic identification in local associations can undermine the development of successful policies. Social capital unites members of a community while excluding others. It is, therefore, not necessarily unifying. The structure of social capital can be the basis of evolution of business sub-systems.

Substitutions are also present among different levels of social capital. Many communities in the developing world use social pressure and reputation to enforce agreements between different parties that may be either individuals and groups. As modern forms of government develop, forms of governance that have clear structures and systems of rules and laws replace the community as the guardian of business, social and personal contracts.

Finance Institutions

The term 'financial institution' is used in two ways. According to Whitley (1992), these are first, sets of rules and regulations governing who gets access to capital and whether and how that capital is returned to its original owner; and second, rules indicating how and to whom a firm's management is accountable.

Access to capital

All businesses need capital. Where and how firms obtain their capital and what form it takes determines how businesses start, their growth, their ability to withstand shocks, and ultimately, their survival. Capital generally takes the form of equity, or ownership capital, and debt. Many firms have some combination of the two, though it is not uncommon, especially for very small firms, to be entirely self-financed through equity.

---

2 Other categorisations of social capital include the communitarian perspective that focuses on local groups and organisations, the network view that describes horizontal and vertical linkages, and the institutional perspective that views social capital through the lens of its legal, institutional, and political contexts (Grootaert and Bastelaer 2002).

A country's financial system consists of at least four main elements: Capital markets, banks, insurance, and other formal institutions; supplier credit; small-enterprise credit programmes; and informal sources. Formal financial organisations are registered with the state or another governmental body and are usually highly regulated. Capital markets are those in which capital in monetary form is lent and borrowed on varying terms and for varying periods. Treasury bills, commercial paper, bonds, and equities are the most common instruments traded. Banks provide both deposit and lending facilities and are, therefore, key to satisfying the financial needs of business. Similarly, banks, including commercial banks, development banks, and merchant banks, usually have minimum capital requirements as well as regulations on deposit insurance, loan-to-deposit ratios, and other operating matters designed to prevent bank failure and protect depositors from loss. Insurance companies, savings and credit organisations, building societies, and other formal institutions ordinarily have their own sets of laws and regulations for the same purpose.

Supplier credit is an institution that may be formal or informal. Formal supplier credit is expressed in written terms specifying the length of available credit, its cost, and any penalties to be levied for failure to pay on time. Where such formal credit exists, it is usually spelled out on the invoice in terms such as 'net 30 days', followed by an interest rate to take effect on the expiration of the 30-day grace period. In many places, formal supplier credit is rare, but good customers can make informal credit arrangements with their suppliers. For such informal supplier credit, reputation substitutes for formalisation of the credit contract.

Small-enterprise credit programmes come in basically two forms: government or government-guaranteed loan programmes and NGO credit. Many governments, including those in industrialised countries continue to support small business through special loan programmes. The business loan programmes of the US Government's Small Business Administration are just one example. The past twenty years or so have witnessed the rise of a new form of credit, available to the smallest businesses in many developing countries. Non-Governmental Organisations (NGOs), often with an aim of alleviating poverty or promoting economic development in poor areas, have established programmes that offer credit to micro- and small enterprises. The amounts are usually small, but increase as the borrower successfully repays the first loan. The loans carry interest at either market rates or at subsidised rate slightly below market. Sometimes the credit facility is accompanied by training in business management or technical skills.

Informal sources of finance include those that are supported by clear institutions, such as rotating savings and credit associations, and those that are purely informal, such as occasional borrowing from a relative. Who has access to what types of finance is a major feature of the financial system that determines its role in the overall business system. In most industrialised countries, for example, nearly all citizens have access to some banking facilities, generally including current and/or savings accounts, credit cards, home mortgage, consumer loans, and if their credit rating is satisfactory, other loans as well. In many developing countries, banks are the preserve of government, larger formal firms, and well-off individuals. If ordinary people have access at all, it is only to the deposit facilities (usually savings accounts) and not the lending.

Financial accountability

Generally speaking, the nature of financial accountability depends on the sources of finance, and the wider the sources, the greater will be the burden of accounting. At one extreme, the micro-enterprise financed solely through the owner's savings may have no external accountability requirement beyond that of reporting income to the tax authority. At the other, the publicly held company whose liabilities include bank loans and corporate bonds is accountable to shareholders, bondholders, banks, the tax authority, and in many countries, to government regulatory bodies.

Whitley (1992) argues that the prevalence of capital market-based financial systems in some countries elevates the financial function within firms and creates systems that tend to use financial means of control as a management tool. This observation leads one to expect that when the main source of capital is self or family, rather than the market, strict financial controls may be less important.

Labour Market Organisation

Labour market organisation is a major institution that structures and enables different business systems to develop and become established. Whitley (1992:16) includes under this heading, not only those factors directly affecting the supply and demand for labour, but also more general and diffuse attitudes and beliefs about work, material values, and authority relations. Under the first category, we consider matters such as trade union structures and power, job search and placement practices, and job quality. We then raise what appear to be the most pertinent attitudinal issues.

When their strength is high, labour organisations can have an important influence not only on rates of pay, but also on work organisation and control. Unions' power to bargain over wages and benefits is a check on the price mechanism of the labour market. When unions are weak, as they often are in labour abundant economies, workers must settle for what the market dictates. Strong unions also have an impact on work organisation and control. This is especially true; when the unions are craft-based or when prior negotiations have resulted in strict work rules.

Job search and placement practices are a practical manifestation of the labour market's organisation and functioning. For example, open and transparent search and hiring are the result of labour markets where information about available positions flows freely and where institutions protect the interests of both workers and employers. Where broad information sharing is lacking, markets are likely to be fragmented and job seekers will tend to rely on family or ethnic networks to gain access to jobs.

The term 'job quality' refers to a range of inter-connected employment concerns that are rooted in the fundamental human rights of workers (Standing, 2002). Job quality encompasses, among others, the level and form of remuneration, working conditions, and employment security issues. How such matters are handled can have an impact on costs and on employers' latitude in reorganising work to attain greater flexibility.

Although many sets of attitudes undoubtedly help to shape labour markets, we choose to focus on two. The first of these is the place of business in the country's value system. Is business considered to be a worthy occupation, or is employment in a business firm, whether large or small, a second-best career choice? The second is the general work ethos. How do people view work? Hofstede (1997) speaks of those who 'live to work' and those who 'work to live.' In his country and regional studies, he found that East Africans occupy a middle ground between the two extremes of strong inner drive to work and strong preference for leisure.

Education, Technology, and Innovation Systems

Innovation involves use of existing knowledge and acquisition, generation and sharing of new knowledge. Learning and research are therefore important for innovation. The innovation process itself involves shifts from existing knowledge and learning patterns to new ones through discovery and invention. The literature refers to this process as heuristic, as a strategy or procedure for solving a problem or moving towards solving a problem.

An innovation system is interwoven with a knowledge system. The latter is a less well-defined but broader system that includes both an underlying knowledge and learning framework and specific innovation processes. Since innovation is application of knowledge, knowledge can be viewed as repository from which items are picked up in inventing things and in creating new ways of doing things. For this reason, a knowledge system is a nebulous and vague collection of elements, some of which are useful but forgotten and others that are redundant, ignored, irrelevant or even wrong. The knowledge system together with the innovation system provides what literature refers to as the technology infrastructure. When combined with institutional frameworks, the technology infrastructure provides the basis for technical innovation.

Education and the process of learning are central to a knowledge system. Learning provides the cement for binding innovation and production together. Learning therefore plays a central role in development and refinement of educational and innovation systems. Learning occurs at micro/individual and macro/organisational levels. It is also inter-firm, inter-organisational and cross-institutional. Although the context of learning involves clear collective and interactive dimensions, a collection of firms, organisations, and institutions is unlikely to have single and clear knowledge-associated processes. Although knowledge systems can be associated with learning frameworks and parts of the system involved in collective learning, the literature posits that knowledge itself resides in individuals.

A knowledge system therefore consists of two sub-systems. One relates to individually centred knowledge, referred to in the literature as a knowledge sub-system in which knowledge circulates between and within individuals through social interactions. For this sub-system, knowledge is created and shared in organisational and social contexts, so that the more important institutions for this sub-system are socio-cultural. Although this knowledge sub-system tends to be location specific, such sub-systems may operate at different spatial scales. Examples given in the literature include Research and Development (R&D) workers in multinational firms participating in geographically dispersed teams through e-mail and video conferencing complemented by repeated travels that permits face to face contacts. These possibilities make the scope of the knowledge sub-system international. The second sub-system, referred as the quasi-knowledge system, involves the sharing of codified knowledge, and draws from a host of institutions including economic, political and socio-cultural.[3] These two sub-systems are interdependent.

Institutions shape the growth of knowledge. In different fields of application of knowledge, individuals' thoughts and actions are influenced by the existing institutional structures. Information is never passed on raw, but is perceived, selected and arranged by institutions. For this reason, literature argues that information is culturally processed. Because institutions are 'informational devices' that shape perceptions, they are at the core of the learning process (Lundvall, 1992). In a complex society, social interactions help social agents to develop a basis through which to understand, learn, and act accordingly.

Customs, rules, traditions, norms and habits transfer knowledge from across generations. Some of such knowledge may later retard future development by preserving unproductive habits, while the other may be conducive to future development and accumulation of knowledge. Without these institutions, it would be difficult to remember what has been learnt.

There are different reasons for learning, but its real motivation is a mixture of idle curiosity, the instinct of workmanship, prestige such as the one accorded to successful researchers, and pecuniary attraction including the fear of loss. Different societies have different motivations for learning. There are also different types of learning, the most productive of which is described as the 'systematic and organised searching for knowledge' (Lundvall, 1992:30) and observed in the modern industrial society with its different types of research institutes, universities and R&D departments[4]. This extreme form of learning involves complex, intense interactions within the research community as well as between researchers and other individuals and communities.

Family and Community

Since Hofstede's (1980; 1997) landmark study of culture and organisations, the 'individualism-collectivism' dichotomy has received considerable attention as a

---

3   The literature distinguishes between tacit and codified knowledge, the former being disembodied know-how acquired through informal absorption of learned procedures and behaviour. The latter, also referred to as explicit knowledge, is defined as knowledge that can be produced in the form of blueprints, manuals, documents, or operating procedures.

4   According to Lundvall (1992) other forms of learning include simple, isolated and individual imprinting of immediate experiences on memory, rote learning and feedback.

determiner of the form and operations of business enterprises. Although Hofstede does not cite Mbiti's (1969) famous summary of the African viewpoint – 'I am because we are.' – it is not difficult to see its relationship to the 'collectivist' end of the 'individualism-collectivism' continuum. A collectivist society is one in which the interest of the group prevails over the interest of the individual (Hofstede, 1997:50). The 'we' group, or what Hofstede terms the 'in-group' is the major source of identity and the individual's only secure protection against the hardships of life. The first – both in time and usually in importance – 'we' group is the family.

In most collectivist societies, the family consists of a number of people of different generations, including parents, children, grandparents, uncles, aunts, and other more distant relatives. Children growing up in such an extended family learn from an early age that they are part of a 'we' that is much larger than themselves. This sense of 'we' is then carried over into other groups, such as the school and the workplace (Hofstede, 1997:61-67), though the family usually remains the most important group.

This centrality of the family, in which all values are determined by reference to the maintenance, continuity and functioning of the family group, has been captured by the term 'familism' (Kuada, 1994: 72). The family limits, influences, and, in some situations, determines the individual's activities in society. This means that every worker and every business person has both a claim on his/her family and obligations to it. In countries with large numbers of poor households, those with more have a moral obligation to help less advantaged family members (Kuada, 1994: 73). This may mean paying for the education and training of relatives, finding them jobs, covering their health care, and providing them with other necessities. The contributions themselves are often collective as when, for example, several members of an extended family pool their resources to send a high-achieving young person for higher education. The recipients of such benefits have corresponding social obligations to provide similar assistance to others once they are in a position to do so.

Family structure is important for understanding how both African and Asian families operate in business. The most significant feature of the African family is the importance of the larger kin group (Kayongo-Male and Onyango, 1984). Marriage is viewed as linking two families rather than two individuals. Most ethnic groups are patrilineal and patrilocal, and most have systems of responsibilities, control, and distribution of resources based on age and gender. The group of elders make major decisions, often after consultation with others in the community.

The Asian traditional family structure appears similar, but there are important differences. The typical family is multi-generational, with parents, married sons and their children occupying a single large dwelling. The Asian family, like its African counterpart, is patriarchal, patrilineal, and patrilocal, and assigns roles and responsibilities, control and distribution of resources by age and gender. In the Asian family, however, total authority rests with the eldest male member of the family. The most important relationship is the father-son, which is marked with deference and an element of formality (Kashyap, 2002; Bharati, 1965).

The realities of urbanisation have modified both Asian and African family structures. It is not always possible for the extended family to reside together, though among Kenyan Asians, this practice is still common. Urban families tend to be smaller, and, among Africans, polygamy has become less common. What may prove to be important for the Kenyan business system is that both Asian and African business people come from collectivist societies for whom their own families are central. Although this means that both workers and managers bring an appreciation of collective values to the workplace, it also means that the workplace is likely to be a distant second in terms of importance to those for whom it has no connection to family.

Ethnicity

One can hardly discuss business in Africa without reference to ethnicity. Ethnicity refers to the shared sense of cultural identity within a society or group of people based on such things as language, religion, customs, and origin. A key feature of ethnicity in the African context is the association of ethnic groups with territory (Kimenyi, 2003). "Home" is very important, and can rarely be other than in the traditional home place. This aspect is, of course, more pronounced among indigenous communities than among immigrants, for whom ties to the traditional home are more difficult to maintain.

Most of the Asians who immigrated to East Africa came from the western side of the sub-continent. The Gujarati-speaking Hindus who form the majority, are not a single group, but are further subdivided by caste into the Lohanas, Patels, and other small groups. In addition, the Asians include Gujurati Muslims, Sikhs, Jains, and Goans who differ by religion as well as place of origin (Gregory, 1993). Indigenous Africans are similarly diverse. Kenya alone has over 40 African ethnic groups.[5] In East Africa, both immigrant and indigenous peoples tend to identify strongly with their ethnic groups and to find their primary social bonds within those groups (Bharati, 1965; Gregory 1993). This creates social networks that can, under certain circumstances, be transformed into supportive business networks.

According to many observers, it is these networks that are the main link between ethnicity and business (Ghai, 1965; Gregory, 1993; Himbara, 1996; Fafchamps, 2002a; 2002b). The mixing of co-ethnics in weddings, funerals, religious ceremonies, and informal social gatherings provides opportunities for network building that can be mined for business purposes. The chief product of such networks is access to information, which can lead to access to other resources, such as credit, supply and product markets, skilled labour, and public goods (Fafchamps, 2002a; Kimenyi, 2003). The linkage is, of course, not automatic. As Fafchamps (2002a) rightly observes, a Kenyan Asian cannot walk into another Asian's shop and obtain supplier credit without a referral. Nevertheless, because the two Asians are likely to have some common acquaintance, obtaining a referral may not be difficult. Such referrals and the networks that underlie them are one reason for the

---

5 These were enumerated in the 1989 Population Census. The published version of the 1999 census has omitted ethnic data.

continuation of ethnic concentration in business, especially in settings where the resources needed for business are difficult to access through formal institutions.

Gender

As can be deduced from the discussion of family and ethnicity, gender is a critical variable in the African context. Both African and Asian societies are patriarchal and both have strong institutions that divide rights and obligations as well as duties, opportunities, and societal expectations between men and women, boys and girls.

As has been observed elsewhere in the context of small enterprise, such institutions affect the way businesses are formed and operated (McCormick, 2001a). In Kenya, women's businesses tend to be smaller than men's, to be less profitable, and to grow more slowly (Parker, 1994; Daniels et al., 1995; CBS et al., 1999). Three factors appear to account for most of these observed differences: education, capital investment, and time investment (McCormick, 2001a). Each of these can, in turn, be linked to the institutions of gender in Kenyan society. Cases in point are the inheritance practices and restrictions on women's access to credit that reduce the capital available to women, and the typical gender division of household labour gives men more time to spend in business. Similar factors may also play a role in the formation and operations of larger enterprises.

Gender is also important in labour markets. Gender disparities in labour market participation, nature of work done, and compensation paid are common phenomena in both industrialised and developing countries. An additional factor has been identified in some developing countries. The gap between men's and women's wage rates is larger for countries that have adopted export-oriented trade and industrialisation policies. This appears to result from the downward pressure applied to wages in production for global markets (Gupta, 2002).

THE BUSINESS SYSTEM

A System of Institutions

Here, we have taken the intellectual position held by those whom the literature refers to as 'cultural and institutional relativists' who regard differences in moral codes, rationalities and conventions so strong across societies that they bring forth distinct forms of specific business practice and organisations[6] (Whitley, 1992). These combine and interact to create a business system. The interaction can be complementary or antagonistic. Institutions can reinforce one another, or they may be in opposition. However they relate, their interaction is boiling pot that produces a set of institutionalised conventions governing how business is conducted in a particular setting. Understanding the system requires examination of a large set of individual institutions. But study of individual institutions is not enough. It is critical that any attempt to understand a business system include careful study of the

---

6   This position contrasts with economic rationalism that vaunts market determinism and argues that social institutions are generally irrelevant.

interactions among various institutional groupings. To facilitate this analysis, we propose a simple graphic device.

Although defined and described as distinct groupings, the twelve sets of institutions discussed above can be viewed as occupying quadrants of 'institutional space' divided by horizontal and vertical axes (see Figure 2.1).

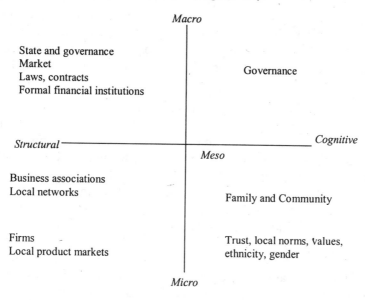

Figure 2.1: Institutions Relevant to Business

Adapted from Grootaert and Bastelaer, 2002

The horizontal axis ranges from the structural to the cognitive. In the left-hand quadrants, therefore, we find institutions such as state and government, markets, laws and contracts, formal financial institutions, firms, business associations, local networks, and local product markets whose rules are embodied in structured organisations. In the two right-hand quadrants are found institutions that are mainly cognitive. Trust, local norms and values, ethnicity, and gender are at the far right, indicating that they exist mostly at the cognitive level. Family and community, which are often supported by some structures, are placed toward the left of this quadrant.

The vertical axis ranges from micro to macro. Institutions in the top half of the diagram operate at the macro level of the economic and political environment, while those in the bottom half manifest themselves at the micro level of firms, households, individuals, and local networks. In between, at the meso level, are those institutions straddling the macro and the micro, such as associations and regional groupings that link their members with government and wider markets.

The diagram provides a rough framework for analysing a business system. It allows the analyst to see at a glance where the institutions included in the analysis fall and to identify gaps. Too much emphasis on either the structural or the cognitive, for example, would lead to an incomplete picture of the system. Similarly, an analysis including only micro or macro institutions without recognising the complementarity between these two groupings risks painting a distorted picture.

A description of a business system is implicitly comparative i.e., each business system differs from others because some elements of their institutional environments differ at least spatially and socially. Such comparison is, however, not about which business system is better than another but about such other considerations as which one is more supportive of industry as opposed to commerce, more likely to encourage innovation and increases in productivity and so on.

As argued by Whitley (1992), a comparison of business systems is an analysis of different ways of organising economic activity. It is more exacting than a cross-national analysis of micro-organisations. Since economic agents vary between societies, and the roles of firms differ according to the way they are legally defined, comparisons of business systems have to rely on more than the formal means of identifying important units of economic activity. The importance of groups and networks of relationships between firms that are otherwise independent complicates the identification of economic agents for purposes of comparison.

Variety of Business Systems

There are three broad areas of comparing and contrasting business systems. The first one is the nature of firms and the specific ways in which they compete and develop as distinctive components of a business system. The second is the sort of connections that firms in the same industry or market develop, and their connections across difference sectors. These connections are related to the firm-specific skills and capabilities and generate specific market organisation patterns. The third area relates to the control and coordination of skills and activities within the firm. These three elements are interwoven and each business systems can be viewed as a 'systematic interrelated response to the three foundational issues of any market based system. These are: first, what sorts of economic activities are to be authoritatively integrated and coordinated toward what competitive priorities? Second, how are market relations of competition and co-operation to be organised and firms' activities connected? Third, how are economic activities to be managed in authority hierarchies? ' (Whitley, 1992)

The evolution of capabilities and competences by different firms critically depends on their institutional contexts, so that as the literature suggests, it is impossible to talk about the multinational firms. Rather, it is more appropriate to talk about American multinational, British multinational, Japanese multinational and so on. This avoids falling in the trap of stereotypes such as the global firms. These firms are forced to internalise, so that actions that were suitable in the home-based institutional contexts are challenged as firms venture into new institutional contexts in host countries (Morgan and Whitley, 2003). The result is a hybridisation of multinationals with imposition and rejection of some of home-country practices, negotiation and adaptation of others in the new host country institutional context.

This argument on how multinational fair in host countries makes the point about differences in business systems that are shaped by differences in institutional contexts.

Asian Business Systems

Connections and state support are important components of the business system in South East Asia (Whitley, 1992). The system therefore demonstrates specific connections between type of firms, inter-firm relations and structure of authority. In Japan, an important feature of these relations is the existence of widespread networks of mutual obligations and interdependence between different actors such as large firms, banks and other financial institutions, and sub-contractors. The incidence of mutual dependence between firms relates to the narrow variety of activities coordinated through authority hierarchies. Similarly, there are high levels of mutual dependence between employers and core employees in large managerial hierarchies. Employment practices are long term and internal labour markets are more important than external ones.

Unlike in the West, external recruitment of senior managers is rare in Japan as managers and core workers stay in same employment until retirement. Women leave employment upon marriage or birth of children and, due to a positive correlation between work experience and wages, women earn less than men. But the general relationship between employers and employees is of mutual dependence. Recruitment procedures are highly selective and employees subjected to extensive indoctrination and socialisation. Core workers exploit the internal market in large corporations to move up the grades during their working lifetime. The management in Japanese firms facilitates group performance rather than direct workers and decision-making is collective.

These attributes of the Japanese business system are generally shared by the systems in other countries in East Asian region. In South Korea, large conglomerates are controlled by either founders or members of families of the founders. Control is centralised around founding families. Labour turnover in South Korea is greater than Japan and unions are under state control. The state is dominant and therefore more important in the South Korean business system.

Subcontracting and small firms are less important than they are in Japan. There is also greater willingness to hire senior managers externally, and South Korean corporations frequently recruit retired financiers, civil servants and military officers to senior management positions. Reliance on debt financing is more widespread and has helped maintain family ownership. Many senior management positions in the corporations in Korea are held by close relatives of founders[7] and corporations are more self-sufficient than in Japan.

Employer's commitment to workers' welfare is weaker in South Korea than in Japan. Even among managers, mobility across large corporations is greater. Unions

---

7   There is a saying reported in the literature that founders of South Korean corporations create subsidiaries for each family member to manage.

are not important and although loyalty is rewarded, such rewards are not systematically built into remuneration system as they are in Japan.

Striking differences abound in the business systems in Taiwan and Hong Kong. The dominant feature here is the strong family control, extensive sub-contracting and small and declining size of most firms. There are also dense networks of exchange relationships between firms used for mobilising funds, market information and subcontracting different parts of manufacturing process. The small sizes of firms are outcomes of what the literature refers to as a 'patrimonial management style' and the business ideology of 'entrepreneurial familism' (Whitley, 1992: 53). The role of the family is so central in Hong Kong and Taiwan that enterprises are occasionally perceived as part of the property of the family rather than separate administrative entities. This distinction is reflected in the further distinction made between managerial and entrepreneurial responsibilities. While the former can be delegated to non-family professional, the latter are the preserve of the family and its trusted partners.

Formal educational qualifications play a limited role in Hong Kong and Taiwan and although higher education is widespread especially in Taiwan, it does not play a filtering function in the high paying industrial jobs to the same extent as elsewhere in East Asia. Unionisation is higher in both Taiwan and Hong Kong than in Korea, lower than in Japan and Western countries. Labour unions in Taiwan enforce workers discipline, ensure political support and administer workers services than represent workers demands. Intermediating agencies between owner-managers and their workers threatens personal control and personal loyalty to the firm owner and are therefore not acceptable. Formal organisation is therefore fluid and managers hold multiple responsibilities that are prone to sudden change at the owners' whims and fancies.

Western European and America Business Systems

For a long time, banks in Germany have been more important sources of capital for starting and sustaining firms than bond markets and equities, and have also played a more crucial role in exercising stock voting rights for the large firms (Hollingsworth, 1997). One outcome of this state of affairs is that bank officers in German serve in the boards of other non-bank large firms, creating long term relationships between banks and firms. This made possible for German firms to maintain a longer term view of their financial needs, giving them more incentive for undertaking long-term product development. More recently, this historic importance of banks in shaping the Germany business system has been declining for two reasons. First, accumulation of retained earnings allowed firms to increase independence from banks. Second, a significant proportion of the market for industrial lending has been captured by savings and large regional banks.

Bargaining is supported by the state, shapes distribution and influences the international competitiveness of German products. While unions are responsible for collective bargaining and participation, elected work councils pay attention to the working conditions in firms and ensure that employment protection laws are obeyed. Workers and their representative are also heavily involved in the supervision of firms. These arrangements reduce conflicts between workers and employers and enhance intra-firm productivity. Rigidities resulting from well-organised unions and work councils create incentives for firms to develop the skills of their workers and create a peaceful environment that in turn leads to a flexible social productive system, which is the key to Germany's high degree of export competitiveness. Furthermore, German firms are forced by the institutional set up to develop a highly skilled labour force and high quality products.

In the United States, progression towards a social system of production has been undermined by existing educational system, financial system and industrial relations[8]. Manufacturing employment is more job-specific, workers less broadly trained, internal labour markets more rigid, and employers have less incentive for developing their workers' skills. The USA has had a very flexible external job market so that American workers find it easier to hop from one job to another than in other countries where there is long-term job security. Weakly developed trade unions and business systems have shaped industrial relations systems. The complexity and large size of the American market, compounded by the working class's racial, ethnic and religious diversity means an heterogeneity of interests among capital and labour, so that collective action is difficult. Limited ability to take collective action places severe limitations on the USA to progress towards establishing a social system supportive of flexible production.

Capital markets in the USA encourage firms to engage in short-term profit maximisation, which reduces the incentive for firms to develop employee skills. Equity markets were already institutionalised by the end of First World War. As a result, large firms hardly depend on commercial banks for financing. On the other hand, non-financial corporations depend on liquid financial markets to raise capital. Corporate managers are dependent on the strategies of stockholders and bond owners. One outcome of this state of affairs is a reduction in the time horizon of large firms, reducing prospects for developing long-term stable relationships between employers and employees. Such relationship is a prerequisite for a broadly trained, highly skilled workforce and a diversified social system of production.

The structure of financial system is conducive to the development of small new firms. This is because while banks are reluctant to finance new firms based on new technologies and new ideas but without a track record, the venture capital markets in the USA increase the availability of capital for such new, risky ventures. This contrasts with countries such as Japan and Germany that rely on banks for capital and end up with poorly developed venture capital markets and therefore few new start-ups. External labour market flexibility and the innovativeness of new start-ups are supported by university research. There is synergistic relationship between such universities and business firms and some of the dynamic sectors of the American economy tend to be located near leading American universities to promote exploitation of this synergy. The government promotes this synergy by funding

---

8   The material on the United States of America draws heavily from Hollingsworth (1997).

research that targets development of technology. There are also networks that draw participation from university scientists, government departments and agencies, and firms. Such networks are especially common during the early development of products and technologies.

Evans' (1995) review of the IT industry in Brazil is a window to how policies shape a business system. From an official backing beginning in 1977, the Brazilian microcomputer industry created a market reserve in which local firms fought for a share. Some of the firms forged ahead and made local improvements and some grew from innovation and enhanced performance. Others benefited from opportunities for free-riding and foreign technology without the knowledge of even the foreign firms. The market reserve created an arena through which new industrial skills could be forged. There were no opportunities for exploitation of scale economies due to the small size of the market. Brazilian firms struggled to establish local suppliers for technologically simple devises such as fans and power supplies while other countries shopped in the global markets for bargains.

The IT policy favoured hardware and treated the software market as a by–product of hardware sales. This meant a preoccupation with indigenous operating systems rather than development of local applications. By 1990, the multinational firms still controlled more than 65% of the software market. Export performance was also disappointing. This precipitated a policy shift that was to lead to a dismantling of what considered a 'greenhouse', putting many corporations and skilled workers into jeopardy.

The African Business System

The African business system is an agglomeration of different business sub-systems. There is a history behind this state of affairs. Most African countries were colonised and had to fight for political independence. They therefore share the same pre-colonial social structures, colonial rulers, patterns of settlement, post-independence industrial policies and development paradigms, as well as deep involvement of donors (Pedersen and McCormick 1999). For these reasons, their business systems have evolved in similar ways, and their production and distribution systems share the same distinctive segments, namely, a formal large-scale private sector dominated by subsidiaries of multinational firms; a parastatal segment, a non-indigenous segment owned by immigrant minorities such as the whites in Zimbabwe, Asians in East Africa and Lebanese in West Africa; and an informal, small scale African dominated sector.

The formal private sector in Africa has been a sub-system of multinationals minority — originally expatriate – communities that networks intensely and developed into highly concentrated and integrated systems of manufacturing, services and trading activities. They also controlled key sections of wholesale and export-import business. In some African countries, the dominance of minority immigrant groups in large formal private sector benefited from political leadership intolerant to budding indigenous industrialists who became objects of state harassment[9]. Post-independent policies also targeted the monopolist tendencies of this segment of the African business system.

Africa's informal sector is a mixture of micro-and small-scale enterprises operating outside state regulation. Some of the activities are illegal, and those that are legal neither use licences nor pay income taxes. They operate from back streets where they squat on public or other peoples' land and have limited access to formal credit, public utilities and infrastructure. Still, these activities occupy market niches out of the reach of the formal sector, often utilising human, financial and other inputs not particularly useful to the formal sector. A high and rising share of industrial employment is in the small enterprise sector, which also has close links with agriculture and is more labour-intensive and promotes more equitable income distribution. The informal micro and small scale sector is therefore an important segment in the African business system.

REFERENCES

Bennett, Robert J. 1998. "Business Associations and Their Potential Contribution to the Competitiveness of MSEs". *Entrepreneurship and Regional Development* 10: 243-260.

Bharati, A. 1965. "A Social Survey." In Ghai, Dharam P. (ed.). *Portrait of a Minority: Asians in East Africa*. Oxford: Oxford University Press.

Central Bureau of Statistics (CBS), International Centre for Economic Growth (ICEG), and K-Rep Holdings Ltd. 1999. *National Micro and Small Enterprise Baseline Survey, 1999*. Nairobi: K-Rep Development Agency.

Chibber, Vivek. 2002. "Bureaucratic Rationality and the Developmental State." *American Journal of Sociology* 107 (4): 951-89.

Coase, R.H. 1937. "The Nature of the Firm." *Economica* 4: 386-405

Coleman, James S. 1990. *Foundations of Social Theory*. Cambridge, MA: The Belknap Press of Harvard University Press.

Daniels, Lisa.; Mead, Donald C. and Musinga, Muli. 1995. "Employment and Income in Micro and Small Enterprises in Kenya: Results of a 1995 Survey." *GEMINI Technical Report* No. 92. Bethesda: Development Alternatives, Inc.

Evans, Peter. 1995. *Embedded Autonomy: States and Industrial Transformation*. Princeton: Princeton University Press.

Fafchamps, Marcel. 1996. "The Enforcement of Commercial Contracts in Ghana." *World Development* 24 (1): 427-448.

---

9 This was common in countries were incumbent governments progressively lost legitimacy and became ostensibly frightened of individuals that showed signs of gaining financial independence.

Fafchamps, Marcel. 2002a. "The Role of Business Networks in Market Development in Sub-Saharan Africa". In Masahiko, Aoki and Yujiro, Hayami (eds.). *Community and Markets in Economic Development*. Oxford: Oxford University Press.

Fafchamps, Marcel. 2002b. "Ethnicity and Networks in African Trade." Centre for the Study of African Economies (CSAE) WP 2002-20. Oxford: Oxford University.

Fine, Ben. 2001. *Social Capital versus Social Theory*. London: Routledge.

Ghai, Dharam P. 1965. "An Economic Survey." In Ghai, Dharam P. (ed.). *Portrait of a Minority: Asians in East Africa*. Oxford: Oxford University Press.

Gregory, Robert. 1993. *South Asians in East Africa: An Economic and Social History, 1890-1980*. Boulder, CO: Westview Press.

Grootaert, Christian and Bastelaer, van Theirry (eds.). 2002. *Understanding and Measuring Social Capital: A Multidisciplinary Tool for Practitioners*. Washington DC: The World Bank.

Gupta, Nabanita Datta. 2002. "Gender, Pay and Development: A Cross-Country Analysis." *Labour and Management in Development Journal* 3(2). Available at: http://ncdsnet.anu.edu.au.

Hart, Oliver. 1995. *Firms, Contracts, and Financial Structure*. Oxford: Clarendon Press.

Himbara, David. 1996. *Kenyan Capitalists, the State, and Development*. Nairobi: East African Educational Publishers.

Hofstede, Geert. 1980. *Culture's Consequences: International Differences in Work-Related Values*. Beverly Hills: Sage.

Hofstede, Geert. 1997. *Culture and Organisations: Software of the Mind*. New York: McGraw Hill.

Hollingsworth, J. Rogers. 1997. "Continuities and Changes in Social Systems of Production: The Cases of Japan, Germany, and the United States". In Hollingsworth, J. Rogers and Boyer, Robert (eds.). *Contemporary Capitalism: The Embeddedness of Institutions*. Cambridge: Cambridge University Press.

Hollingsworth, J. Rogers and Boyer, Robert. 1997. *Contemporary Capitalism: The Embeddedness of Institutions*. Cambridge: Cambridge University Press.

Kashyap, Lina. 2002. "Asian Families in Transition." Plenary Presentation at the CIF International Conference, Goa. See www.cifindia.org/conference (Accessed in Jan 2004).

Kayongo-Male, Diane and Onyango, Philista. 1984. *The Sociology of the African Family*. London: Longman.

Kimenyi, Mwangi. 2003. "Ethnicity, Governance, and the Provision of Public Goods." Paper presented at the African Economic Research Consortium's Biannual Conference, November-December 2003, Nairobi, Kenya.

Kimuyu, Peter. 2000. "Institutions Relevant to Commerce and Industry: Moral Norms, Social Capital, the State and the Law". Discussion paper No. 021/2000. Nairobi: Institute of Policy Analysis and Research.

Kuada, John. 1994. *Managerial Behaviour in Ghana and Kenya: A Cultural Perspective.* Aalborg: Aalborg University Press.

Langlois, Richard N. and Robertson, Paul L. 1995. *Firms, Markets, and Economic Change: A Dynamic Theory of Business Institutions.* London: Routledge.

Lundvall, Bengt-Åke. 1992. *National Systems of Innovation.* London: Pinter.

Mbiti, John S. 1969. *African Religions and Philosophy.* London: Heinemann.

McCormick, Dorothy. 2001. "Gender in Small Enterprise Development in Kenya." In Samanta, Purna C.and Sen, Raj Kumar (eds.). *Realising African Development: A Millennial Analysis.* Kolkata, India: CIADS.

McCormick, Dorothy. 2001b. "Value Chains and the Business System: Applying a Simplified Model to Kenya's Garment Industry." *IDS Bulletin* 32(3): 105-115.

McCormick, Dorothy; Mitullah, Winnie; and Kinyanjui, Mary Njeri. 2001. "Enhancing Institutional Capacity for Policy Development, Dialogue, and Advocacy: Role of Associations and Other Community Based Organisations". Unpublished. Institute for Development Studies, University of Nairobi.

Mkandawire, Thandika and Soludo, Charles C. 1998. *Our Continent our Future.* Ottowa: IDRC.

Morgan, Glen and Whitley, Richard. 2003. 'Introduction' *Journal of Management Studies* 40:3.

Nabli, M.K. and Nugent, J.B. 1989. "The New Institutional Economics and Its Applicability to Development." *World Development* 17(9): 1333-1348.

Nelson, Richard R. and Winter, Sidney G. 1982. *An Evolutionary Theory of Economic Change.* Cambridge, MA: The Belknap Press of Harvard University Press.

Noland, Marcus and Pack, Howard. 2003. *Industrial Policy in an Era of Globalisation.* Washington: Institute of International Economics.

North, Douglass C. 1990. *Institutions, Institutional Change and Economic Performance.* Cambridge: Cambridge University Press.

Olson, Mancur. 1971. *The Logic of Collective Action: Public Goods and the Theory of Groups.* Cambridge, MA: Harvard University Press.

Ongile, Grace and McCormick, Dorothy. 1996. "Barriers to Small Firm Growth: Evidence from Nairobi's Garment Industry". In McCormick, Dorothy and Pedersen, Poul Ove (eds.). *Small Enterprises: Flexibility and Networking in an African Context.* Nairobi: Longhorn Kenya.

Parker, Joan. 1994. "Micro and Small-Scale Enterprises in Kenya: Results of the 1993 National Baseline Survey." *GEMINI Technical Report* No. 75. Bethesda: Development Alternatives, Inc.

Pedersen, Poul Ove and McCormick, Dorothy. 1999. "African Business Systems in a Globalising World." *Journal of Modern African Studies* 37(1): 109-135.

Penrose, Edith T. 1959. *The Theory of the Growth of the Firm.* Oxford: Basil Blackwell.

Platteau, Jean-Philippe. 1994. "Behind the Market Stage Where Real Societies Exist – Part I: The Role of Public and Private Order Institutions." *Journal of Development Studies* 30 (3): 533-577.

Ricketts, Martin. 1994. *The Economics of Business Enterprise: An Introduction to Economic Organisation and the Theory of the Firm.* 2nd edition. London: Harvester Wheatsheaf.

Sachikonye, Lloyd. 1993. "Structural Adjustment, State and Organised Labour in Zimbabwe". In Gibbon, Peter (ed.). *Social Change and Economic Reform in Africa.* Uppsala: Scandinavian Institute of African Studies.

Schmitz, Hubert. 1999. "From Ascribed to Earned Trust in Exporting Clusters." *Journal of International Economics* 48: 139-150.

Selznick, Philip. 1966. "Leadership in Administration." In Golembiewski, Robert T.; Gibson, Frank and Cornog, Geoffrey Y. (eds.). *Public Administration: Readings in Institutions, Processes, Behaviour.* Chicago: Rand McNally and Company.

Standing, Guy. 2002. *Beyond the New Paternalism: Basic Security as Equality.* New York: Verso.

Streeck, Wolfgang and Schmitter, Philippe C. 1991. "Community, Market, State - and Associations? The Prospective Contribution of Interest Governance to Social Order." In Thompson, G.; Frances, J.; Levacic, R. and Mitchell, J. (eds.). *Markets, Hierarchies and Networks: The Coordination of Social Life.* London: Sage Publications.

Sverrisson, Arni. 1993. Evolutionary Technical Change and Flexible Mechanisation: Entrepreneurship and Industrialisation in Kenya and Zimbabwe. Lund Dissertations in Sociology 3. Lund: Lund University Press.

Weiss, Linda. 1998. *The Myth of the Powerless State.* Ithaca, NY: Cornell University Press.

Whitley, Richard. 1992. *Business Systems in East Asia: Firms, Markets and Societies.* London: Sage.

Whitley, Richard. 2003. "How National are Business Systems? The Role of Different State Types and Complementary Institutions in Constructing Homogeneous Systems of Economic Coordination and Control." Paper presented to the workshop on National Business Systems in the New Global Context, Oslo, 2003.

Williamson, Oliver. 1985. *The Economic Institutions of Capitalism*. New York: The Free Press.

Zucker, Lynne. 1986. "Production of Trust: Institutional Sources of Economic Structure, 1840-1920." *Research on Organisational Behaviour* 8: 53-111.

Chapter 3

Policies and Regulations for Business Development in Kenya

Walter Odhiambo and Winnie V. Mitullah

INTRODUCTION

Potential and existing business operators in any economy are usually concerned about their business environment as it has a direct effect on their operations. Generally, unfavourable business environments add unduly to the operating costs of firms, increase risks and uncertainty and constrain growth of entrepreneurship and investments. The business environment includes all those institutions, policies, laws, and regulations that impact on the performance of private firms. These include: competition laws and policies; the financial system; the legal and regulatory system; tax administration; labour laws; tariffs and customs, the quality of infrastructure such as roads, power, telecommunications, water supply and sanitation, and ports; health; and education of the workforce.

Business environments are dynamic and are shaped by a number of factors both domestic and international. At the local level, economic, social and political factors are at play and these inevitably affect enterprise behaviour. In Kenya, the business environment is a product of many factors including the country's colonial history, resource endowments, regional economic relations, foreign investor and donor perceptions, the prevailing socio-political and economic environment, as well as the general policy environment. The policies of the government are particularly important in that they are key in defining the environment for doing business as well as providing specific incentives to entrepreneurs.

At the international level, globalisation has in the last decade emerged as one of the most powerful forces shaping the economic and social environment in which enterprises operate. Globally, there has been a remarkable increase in cross-border interdependence of markets and factors of production. This has made national borders more permeable with the results that even enterprises focusing on domestic markets face competition from foreign enterprises. The conclusion of a number of international trade agreements under the World Trade Organisation (WTO) and the mushrooming of regional trading blocks has created a new and more competitive global environment. Kenya, like all other countries, has been part of these processes and has no doubt been affected in different ways.

One of the main objectives of government as far as the business environment is concerned is to design and implement appropriate policies for its development. This is particularly important now with the realisation that successful economic development depends largely on private initiative of entrepreneurs and firms. To improve the business environment, a government may decide to regulate some activities of private firms because of market failure, including externalities (e.g. pollution) and information asymmetries (e.g. inability of consumers to judge the safety and quality of products). Governments can also offer incentives to investors, both local and foreign, in order to attract investment. However, in many parts of the world, Kenya included, the policy and regulatory environments are at times, not favourable to enterprise growth and development, particularly for the micro and small enterprises. Policies can therefore be an incentive or disincentive to business development.

Thus, the aim of this chapter is to provide insights into policies and regulations for business development that Kenya has pursued since independence and how they have affected the overall business environment.

POLICIES AND THE BUSINESS ENVIRONMENT IN KENYA

Policies that affect the business environment in Kenya can conveniently be grouped into four broad categories: macro-economic policies; incentive policies; institutional policies and infrastructural policies. *Macro-economic policies* include measures that are meant to influence the overall economic and business environment in the country. Examples include monetary and fiscal policies. *Incentive policies* are aimed at stimulating the development of specific sectors of the economy e.g. policies related to public sector enterprises, tax incentives and access to inputs. *Institutional policies* relate to the legal and regulatory systems in place including licensing, labour laws and property rights. Lastly, *infrastructural policies* are those policies that the government uses to promote the development of basic infrastructure including water, electricity, transport and communication. For each of the broad policies, the government uses specific instruments to achieve its broad policy objectives. These policies are articulated in various policy documents in Kenya including the National Development Plans, the Poverty Reduction Strategy Paper (PRSP), and the Economic Recovery Strategy (ERS) for Wealth and Employment Creation (Republic of Kenya, 2003). Table 3.1 summarises the broad policies and the key instruments used to achieve the objectives in Kenya. A discussion of each of the broad policies and instruments follows below.

Table 3.1: *Policies Affecting the Business Environment in Kenya*

1. Macro-economic policies	1.1 Monetary policy • Inflation and money supply policies • Interest rate policy • Exchange rate policies • Credit policies 1.2 Fiscal policies • Business income taxes • Income based taxes • Capital based taxes • Taxes on inputs (labour, power, equipment and utilities) • Government expenditure on utilities • Government expenditure on business assistance and support
2. Incentive policies	2.1 Trade policies • Exchange rate policies • Industrial policies • Foreign exchange control • Import control (quotas, tariffs, licenses) • Export taxes and subsidies • Investment and tax incentives 2.2 Financial Sector Policies • Financial liberalisation • Banking and financial laws • Requirements on collateral and security
3. Institutional policies	3.1 Regulation and control policies • Registration requirements • Licensing • Regulation on activities (Company Act) • Insolvency regime • Health and environmental standards • Product standards and certification 3.2 Labour laws • Wage/employment policies • Labour legislation/trade unions
4. Infrastructure policies	4.1 Utility development policies 4.2 Land policies

Source: Authors

MACRO-ECONOMIC POLICIES

The objective of macro-economic policies has been to maintain the overall macro-economic stability. Macro-economic policies affect the business environment directly or indirectly in various ways. They affect the level of prices of inputs and outputs for firms, the interest rates firms pay when borrowing capital as well as the exchange rates businesses transact at. Instability, particularly high interest rates has a corrosive effect on contracting and discourages savings and investments. While some shocks are unavoidable everywhere, prudent monetary and fiscal policies are key to the development of a sound environment for doing business. The maintenance of a stable and credible macro-economic environment supports private sector development by reducing uncertainty from large fluctuations in relative and domestic prices.

Monetary Policies

Despite serious macro-economic challenges, Kenya has since independence strived to achieve stability in the key macro-economic fundamentals, namely, the rate of inflation, the exchange rate and the level of interest. Monetary policy in Kenya has evolved over the years. Before 1986, the primary objective of monetary policy was maintaining price and fostering liquidity, solvency and proper functioning of a stable market based financial system. During this period, the authorities relied on official direct instruments of monetary control, namely cash reserve requirement on commercial banks; a liquid asset ratio applied on both commercial banks and Non Bank Financial Institutions (NBFIs) and a system of credit ceiling.

Around 1991, the country found it self in a financial crisis which generated a new episode in monetary policy. An abusive use of the rediscount facility at the Central Bank caused a historic loss of monetary control. This was characterized by high inflation, near collapse of the shilling, instability and lasting macro-economic setbacks for the economy. To avert the crisis, the Central Bank gradually introduced indirect instruments. In 1991, the government decontrolled interest rates and began the use of open market operations (OMO). Due to macro-economic pressure, the government also resorted to the use of treasury bills to redress economic disturbances. However, because of the lack of a vibrant secondary market for treasury bills in the country, interest rates remained high throughout the 1990s. For most of the period, the government dominated the treasury bills market to draw funds for its own operations. Lately, the primary objective of monetary policy in Kenya has been attaining price stability. Because changes in the level of prices is affected more by the amount of money stock in circulation, CBK has focused on loosening and restricting money stock consistent with the desired price level and the economic growth targets.

An appropriate exchange rate policy is crucial for the development of a stable and predictable business environment. The real exchange rate is a measure of international competitiveness, which determines foreign investments. Like monetary policy, Kenya's exchange rate policy has undergone various regime shifts over the years driven largely by economic events. Up to 1974, the exchange rate for

Kenya was pegged to the US dollar but was later changed to the special drawing rate (SDR). Between 1974 and 1981, the movement of the nominal exchange rate relative to the US dollar was erratic resulting in the depreciation of about 14%. Towards the end of 1982, the exchange rate regime was changed to a crawling peg, which lasted until 1990 when a dual exchange rate regime was adopted. In 1993, the official exchange rate was abolished.

Figure 3.1 shows trends in the key macro-economic indicators since independence. It is evident that the country's exchange rate depreciated considerably in the 1980s and 1990s. The country's inflation rate was also fairly erratic over the period. By the mid 1990s, inflation had stabilised somewhat, with annual rates below or just above 10 per cent. It is significant, however, that the level of interest rate in the country rose considerably especially between 1990 and 2000. By 2000, the level of interest rates in the country was too high, and so was the interest rate spread relative to both domestic and global economic activity.

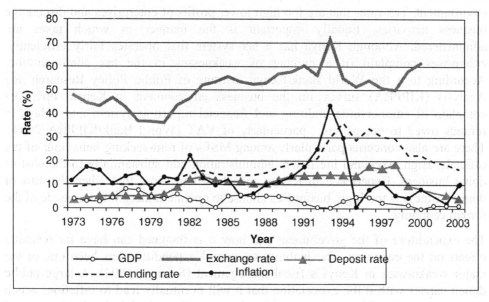

Figure 3.1: Trends in Key Macro-economic Variables in Kenya (1973-2003)

Source: Kenya, Republic of; Economic Surveys, various Issues

As is evident above, the economic reforms, which were aimed at reducing distortions in the economy, led to increased macro-economic instability. The instabilities have no doubt been harmful to the private sector in Kenya. For instance, the cost of borrowing increased considerably in the reform as evidenced by the rise in the lending rate. The Micro and Small Enterprises (MSEs) sector, given their limited options to ride over instabilities, has particularly been affected.

Fiscal Policies

Fiscal discipline is crucial in creating a sound business environment in any country. This discipline depends on the fiscal policies being implemented by the government and its prudence. When the government uses its powers to alter the disposable incomes of persons through changes in the level of taxation, transfers or influencing total spending by directly changing its purchases of goods and services, we have fiscal policy. On the revenue side, the government uses various taxes to influence economic activity in the country.

In Kenya, the tax system comprises five different types of taxes: personal taxes; value added tax (VAT); excise taxes; import and export taxes; and corporate taxes. Personal taxes, VAT, trade and excise taxes are by their very nature, consumption taxes which affect the demand for goods and services. These only have indirect effect on enterprises. The tax that affects business directly is corporate tax. This particular tax is levied on business profits made by corporate organisations. The rate in Kenya varies between resident and non-resident companies. Companies that are listed in the Nairobi Stock Exchange are also taxed at a lower rate to encourage listing.

The level of taxes plays an important role in shaping the overall business environment. Tax rates that are too high lower profits of enterprises and discourage business activities. Equally important is the manner in which taxes are administered. Although Kenya has a tax system that operates fairly efficiently, enterprises complain of a number of weaknesses in the tax administration. According to a the World Bank/Kenya Institute of Public Policy Research and Analysis (KIPPRA) survey on the business environment in Kenya, operators complain of cumbersome auditing and financial reporting system and delays in refunds owed to tax payers, particularly of VAT (World Bank/KIPPRA 2004). There are also concerns particularly among MSEs of rent-seeking behaviour of tax officials. High taxes and inefficient administration add substantially to the cost of doing business. Experience in Kenya and elsewhere show that when the cost of doing business is too high, businesses choose to operate underground, outside of the formal economy.

The expenditure of the government and how it is financed can have far reaching effects on the economy. The inability to control expenditure has been one of the major weaknesses in Kenya's fiscal management (Swamy, 1994). A large public deficit carries with it the expectation that it will eventually lead to inflation, which can be devastating for private sector development. Kenya's debt burden has soared considerably in the last few years. Although Kenya's foreign debt is larger, domestic debt has become more and more important. By December 2002, the accumulated domestic debt of the government stood at Kshs 252.5 billion compared to an external debt of about Kshs. 377.7 billion as at June 2003. With such a huge debt burden, debt servicing forms a large part of government spending, leaving little for consumption and investment. Heavy domestic borrowing, as has been the case in Kenya, also pushes up interest rates, which increase the cost of capital for investment. This in turn affects savings and investments. It is also important to note that government expenditure can be complementary to private sector activities especially where the expenditure is on say, infrastructure, security and utilities. This is discussed later in the chapter.

INCENTIVE POLICIES

A part from the macro policies, the government of Kenya also uses incentives policies to shape the business environment. Trade, industrial, investment and financial policies are by far the most important incentive policies that determine the level and structure of private sector activity.

Trade Policies

Trade policies affect the business environment by encouraging or discouraging domestic production of goods and services. Over the years, the government has made a variety of trade policies with varying objectives. At independence, the government embarked on an import substitution strategy for industrial development. This involved the local production of goods hitherto being imported from other countries. To realise the objectives of this strategy, the government relied on a variety of policy instruments including an overvalued exchange rate, high tariff barriers, import licensing, foreign exchange controls and quantitative restrictions.

The import substitution strategy had mixed results in Kenya. On the positive side, the strategy led to the growth of certain industries particularly those that enjoyed some level of protection. Industries that recorded rapid development during this period included processing of plastics, pharmaceuticals, steel rolling and galvanizing, electrical cables, paper, vehicle assembly, industrial gases, rubber ceramics, and batteries manufacture. Some of these industries expanded from a few establishments into industries with a wide range of products (Coughlin, 1988). The strategy, however, also had serious weaknesses. It was generally biased against the agricultural sector as it directed resources disproportionately to the manufacturing sector (Sharpley and Lewis, 1988). The strategy also created too few jobs as many of the industries used inappropriate capital-intensive technologies at under capacity (Coughlin, 1988).

The weaknesses of the import substitution forced the government to shift gears to adopt an outward oriented strategy in the mid 1980s. In 1986, the government published Sessional Paper No.1 of 1986 on Economic Management for Renewed Growth. The subsequent National Development Plan for the period 1989-1993 formed the basis for Kenya's trade policy shift – the phasing out of import substitution and pursuance export promotion. Trade reforms in Kenya had three main components: rationalization of the tariff code, reduction of the average tariff rate and the reduction of tariff bands. Due to lack of commitment to reforms as evidenced by episodes of relapse, the impact of trade reforms in Kenya became noticeable only after.1991. Trade reforms led to significant reduction in the average and maximum rates but also the dispersion of rates among industries were significantly reduced (Siggel et al, 2000). Since the onset of liberalisation, the top rate has been reduced from 170% to 35%. The other liberalisation measure has been the reduction in the number of tariff bands.

Kenya's current trade objectives include moving towards a more open trade regime and increasing its participation in international trade. The country has pursued this policy objective both on the domestic and international fronts. Domestically, Kenya embarked on unilateral liberalisation by among other measures dismantling its quantitative restrictions and eliminating price controls. At the international level, Kenya has actively engaged itself in unilateral and bilateral organisations and participated in the multilateral trading system. Currently, Kenya is a member of the Common Market for Eastern and Southern Africa (COMESA) and the East African Co-operation (EAC). The country is also active in the African Union (AU) (formerly the Organisation of African Unity (OAU) and in the Inter Governmental Authority on Development (IGAD). These arrangements are particularly attractive for investors looking for larger markets

The overall impact of trade reforms in Kenya has been mixed. On the one hand, the reforms have impacted positively on firms that relied on imports for production. This is because importation became relatively easier in the country after the reforms. On the other hand, the reforms did not benefit exporters in any appreciable manner as the industrial sector remained fairly uncompetitive (Ikiara et al, 2004). Part of the reason for this failure had to do with the slow manner in which the reforms were implemented and the lack of effective export promotion policies. Liberalisation has also exposed local producers just emerging from protected market, to severe competition from more efficient producers in other countries. The MSE sector has been particularly affected since the adoption of open trade policies in Kenya. One of the most affected sub-sectors in Kenya has been the textiles sector. The importation of ready-made garments, including second-hand clothes has posed a severe challenge to firms in the garment industry in general and those in the MSE sector in particular (see Chapter 9).

Industrial Policies

Industrial policies form an important part of the incentive structure that governments put in place for the development of the private sector. In 1997, the Kenya government produced Sessional Paper No.2 of 1996 on 'Industrial Transformation to the Year 2020'. This document highlighted some of the major constraints to industrial expansion in Kenya and proposed a broad strategy for industrialization in Kenya. Although the Sessional Paper was never quite effected, it reflected the government's broad thinking about industrialization.

As already indicated, the government approach to industrialization at independence was through import substitution. The country's first development plan, (1966-70), laid emphasis on import substitution as the main approach. This was to be achieved through inward looking trade policies such as the use of tariff and non-tariff barriers, exchange controls and import licensing. In the late 1970s and 1980s, the government's policy statement started to emphasize the need to reduce protection to domestic industry and to promote manufactured exports. In 1974, the government enacted a compensation plan under the Local Manufacturers (Export Compensation) Act of 1974. Under this scheme, exporters of eligible goods could claim export compensation. Eligible goods were mainly manufactured goods with high domestic value added. Natural resources and agricultural produce were excluded. This programme was phased out in 1993 and replaced with the duty and

VAT exemption scheme. The new programme was to provide incentives to manufacturers primarily servicing the domestic market. The program, which was executed by the Export Promotion Programs Office (EPPO) in the Ministry of Finance, offered duty and VAT exemptions to imported inputs used in the production of exports. To attract further foreign investment, an Export Processing Act was passed in 1990 for the development of exclusive export zones under the Export Processing Zones Authority (EPZA). The enactment of the Act was followed by the establishment of a number of zones mainly in Nairobi and Mombasa. The government also introduced export-processing zones (EPZs) in 1996 mainly to attract foreign investment.

The government's effort to promote exports from the country through a variety of export incentives has only met limited success. According to Glenday and Ndii (2001), the customs and excise legislation for drawing back the import duty content of manufactured exports failed because of the cumbersome administrative requirements of the drawback program. Similarly, Manufacturing Under Bond (MUB) and the EPZ platforms designed for processing of exports have also had very little impact in terms of export and employment growth. Although the situation changed somewhat in the EPZ with the African Growth and Opportunity Act (AGOA), the scheme's impact remains limited. Its greatest weakness perhaps has been its inability to promote domestic investment as it has so far mainly been attractive to foreign investors. Micro and small enterprises (MSEs) have so far not participated in the program.

MSEs are an integral part of the industrial sector in Kenya. Although the government recognizes the importance of the sector in industrial development in the country, MSEs face a myriad of problems that have inhibited their development. Policies and regulations are among the major bottleneck in the development of MSEs in Kenya. Policies have either been lacking, inappropriate or too restrictive. In cases where appropriate policies exist, implementation has been poor with regulatory framework full of punitive and corrupt practices. In some cases, the regulatory measures taken contradict existing policies.

Majority of MSEs operate within Local Authorities (LAs) whose functions are outlined in the Local Authorities Act, Cap 265. Section 145 on miscellaneous powers, offers an opportunity for local authorities to provide sites or put aside land for markets. While the operations of MSEs have existed for decades, there has been no deliberate attempt by local authorities to set aside land for their development. On the contrary, LAs have the option of allocating land to any purpose they deem necessary without any preference to MSEs. This legal provision has been used to harass the MSEs, especially street traders. A Task Force charged with the review of the Act recently observed that while obstruction of public places should not be encouraged, the law should be modified so as to accommodate trading activities of MSEs, especially hawkers (Kenya, 2001). It is significant that some local authorities such as Nairobi City Council have begun allocating spaces and back street lanes to street traders.

Investment Policies

The government's investment policy is outlined in various sessional papers and development plans. The objective of the government investment policy is to encourage investment that will produce foreign exchange, provide employment, promote backward and forward linkages and transfer technology. Since independence, the government has actively encouraged investments particularly from foreigners into virtually all the key sectors of the economy. The only exceptions are those sectors which the government still thinks are strategic and are therefore still dominated by state corporations. These are mainly in the area of infrastructure (e.g. power, telecommunications and ports). Even in these sectors, there have been substantial changes in the recent past largely due to economic reforms. For instance, there are currently six independent private sector power producers in the country. There are also plans to fully liberalise the telecommunications sub-sector.

To promote foreign investment, the government in 1986 created the Investment Promotion Centre (IPC), now the Kenya Investment Autority (KIA). IPC acted as a one-stop office for investors. The functions of IPC were: (a) promoting investments in Kenya by local and foreign business enterprises; (b) assisting business enterprises in implementing the approved projects; (c) advising the government periodically on changes in policies, strategies and administrative procedures necessary for the promotion and enhancement of investments in Kenya. KIA estimates that it facilitates about half of the new foreign direct investments to Kenya. Slightly more than a third of the investment KIA approves translates to actual investment. Thus, although the government provides incentives in form of tax holidays, accelerated registration and lower duties on inputs, the incentives provided have not attracted many investors. Investor confidence has been affected by several elements, including issues of governance, labour unrest, power shortages and high utility costs, and adverse weather conditions.

A major weakness of the investment policies in Kenya is their failure to provide sufficient incentives for domestic investors. Most investment incentives have traditionally been directed towards foreign investors. It is, therefore, not surprising that KIA has since its inception, facilitated only a handful of local investments. The EPZs, which also provide incentives for investors for export processing, have also not attracted a sizeable number of domestic investors. Currently, the EPZ authority in Kenya, EPZA, is considering starting an "incubator" program for local investors.

Financial Sector Policies

The financial sector plays an important role in the development of the private sector. This is because the sector intermediates between savers and investors thereby ensuring the latter's access to credit. Without credit, the growth of firms is restricted to their retained earnings and the capital they can attract from investors. To play the role of intermediation effectively, there is need for the regulation of the financial sector by the government. However, excessive regulations of the sector in the past, as has been the case in some countries, can be detrimental to the sector. It is imperative that government finds an appropriate balance between financial liberalisation and regulation and supervision.

Kenya has a well-developed financial sector. Besides the Central Bank and 49 commercial banks, there were four non-bank financial institutions, two mortgage finance, four building societies, eleven insurance companies, three re-insurance companies, 6 Development Finance Institutions (DFIs) and building societies by the year 2003. These institutions offer a wide range of services to foreign and local enterprises including savings and fixed deposits, commercial loans, purchase and sale of shares and securities, fund transfers, export and import finance, and commercial letters of credit. Starting from the 1990s, the financial and capital markets in Kenya have undergone considerable reforms. Apart from the liberalisation of the interest rates and exchange rates, specific measures were also undertaken to further develop the Nairobi Stock Exchange (NSE) to widen its base, increase competition and to facilitate greater inflow of foreign capital. In addition, the government in 1989 established the Capital Markets Authority (CMA) to guide the overall development of the capital market in the country.

In spite of the relative development of Kenya's financial sector, access to finance for investment still appears to be restricted to larger well-established companies with a long history of borrowing from the formal institutions. Opportunities to obtain long or short-term capital for small companies with good business ideas, entrepreneurial vigour but little capital are extremely limited. Many firms in Kenya fail to raise the capital they need. MSEs are particularly disadvantaged in this regard. The limited access to credit by firms has been attributed to high collateral requirements. Most banks in Kenya insist on collateral, which in most cases, is twice the loan being sought. Due to the problems associated with accessing bank credit facilities, a large proportion of Kenyan firms rely mainly on self-financing through retained earnings and supplier credit facilities. Successive Regional Programme of Enterprise Development (RPED) studies in Kenya and the recently concluded World Bank/KIPPRA business climate study have shown that over a third of the firms in Kenya rely on retained earnings. Studies have also shown that in Kenya, as in many other countries, business start-ups in the MSE sector are financed from personal savings and from relatives and friends.

INSTITUTIONAL POLICIES

The government has an important role in defining the institutional environment within which business operate. Two important aspects of the institutional framework are the legal and the regulatory systems in place.

The Legal System

The formal legal system is a crucial determinant of the overall business environment in as much as it affects the behaviour of firms. The existence of laws is crucial in protecting private property and enforcement of contracts which are important for the development of the private sector. Recent work, for example, by Hall-Dreimeier *et al* (2003) has demonstrated that in an environment of arbitrary and discretionary policies, investors invest less, withhold commitments and generate lower rates of economic growth. Where there is a well-established legal system, investments are likely to thrive. For firms to operate efficiently, they need to be able to make contracts with customers and suppliers, acquire new technology and receive financing. If contracts are not easily enforced through the judicial system, less trade takes place and the firms grow slowly since financiers are unwilling to supply capital.

Kenya's legal code contains some important laws that are considered necessary for a fully functional market economy. This includes laws governing exit and entry to the market, property rights, labour laws, monopolies and competition policy. Accessing justice from the country's legal system is however fraught with all kinds of difficulties characterised by long delays, coupled with an atmosphere of mistrust in the ability of the system to deliver justice. The result is that potential investors and existing business operators have little confidence in the judicial system. Businesses suffer a great deal when there are delays and subjective interpretation of laws and rules. Table 3.2 below shows comparative figures for procedures and duration for enforcing contracts in Kenya and other countries in the region. It is evident that enforcement of contracts is less cumbersome in Uganda and Zimbabwe than it is in Kenya. The situation is however worse in Tanzania.

Table 3.2: *Comparative Time for Enforcement of Contracts (2003)*

Country	Number of Procedures	Duration in Days	Cost (% GNI per capita)
South Africa	26	207	16.7
Uganda	16	99	10
Botswana	22	56	..
Zimbabwe	13	197	39.5
Tanzania	31	372	61.2
Kenya	25	255	49.5

Source: *http:/rru.worldbank.org. Doing Business/explore economies*

Business Registration

The process of business registration is important because it determines how long potential entrepreneurs take in incorporating businesses. In many developing countries, Kenya included, it takes a long time to register a business and this acts as a disincentive for investment. In some cases, entrepreneurs who find registration processes cumbersome prefer to establish business in the informal sector. Cumbersome processes are not only expensive in terms of time and costs but are also punitive. A recent survey by Foreign Investment Advisory Services (FIAS) estimate that it takes about 61 days and about US$195 (about Kshs.15,210) to start a business in Kenya. The process involves 11 steps as outlined in Table 3.3 below. According to the study, Kenya compares unfavourably with other countries in the region such as Uganda where it takes 36 days, Tanzania 35 and South Africa 38 days.

Table 3.3: *Entry Procedures in Kenya for an Average Small and Medium Size Business Enterprise*

Nature of Procedure (2003)	Duration (days)	Cost in US$
Pay stamp duty	10	61.46
Reserve company name	3	0.63
File with registrar	30	37.40
File for taxes	1	0
File for VAT	1	0
Register as employer	3	0
Apply for operational licenses	8	63.49
File with NSSF	1	0
Register with NHIF	1	0
Register for PAYE	1	0
Make a seal	2	0
Total	*61*	*31.74*

Source: FIAS, 2004

The principal legislation governing the operation of companies, including registration and liquidation of firms in Kenya, is the Company's Act Cap 486 of 1962. This Act restricts members of private companies to between 2 and 50 shareholders while limiting the minimum of shareholders in a limited company to 7. Registration under the Companies Act means that the business is incorporated, with its own legal status, separate from the rights and duties of its members. Most companies in Kenya are incorporated with limited liability status limiting the liabilities of the owners to their contributions to the business. Registration as a limited liability company encourages entrepreneurs to take risks with the knowledge that their personal assets are protected. It also facilitates the pooling of resources brought in by the different owners.

The Companies Act has, however, a number of limitations that makes it a bottleneck to the development of enterprises in Kenya. Kenya's Companies Act is based on the 1948 UK Companies Act designed to regulate big public companies. In Kenya, the vast majority of companies are small, owner-managed enterprises. Currently, firms are bound by strict rules relating to capital structures of capital and capital maintenance. The Companies Act, for example, has requirements for a company seal, for two shareholders and a formal procedure for the company meetings. All these requirements may not be necessary for small owner-managed enterprises in Kenya. For most companies in Kenya, therefore, the rules as embedded in the Companies Act are complex, technical, and inappropriate (FIAS, 2004).

Property Rights

Property rights have a profound effect on incentives, resource allocation decisions and economic performance. The desire for profits is the primary motivating factor for most, if not all business enterprises. Opportunity to earn and use profits as they wish motivates enterprises to make business decisions that maximize profits. A credible and efficient property rights system is thus an integral component of a good business environment.

Kenya's legal systems provide for the protection, acquisition and disposition of all property rights including land, buildings and mortgages. The country's constitution explicitly provides for the protection of private property rights. At the same time, there are subsidiary laws governing title issues. These include the Physical and Planning Act (1996), Government Land Act (Cap 280), Registration of Titles Act (Cap 281), Land Titles Act (Cap 282), Land Consolidation Act (Cap 283), Land Adjudication Act (Cap 284), Registration of Documents Act (Cap 285), Land (Group) Representatives Act (Cap 287), Trust Land Act (Cap 29)). Other important legislation governing property rights are Equitable Mortgages Act (Cap 291), Way Leaves Act (Cap 292), Distress for Rent Act (Cap 293), Trespass Act (Cap 294), Land Acquisition Act (Cap 295), Rent Restriction Act (Cap 296), Survey Act (Cap 299), Registered Land Act (Cap 300), Landlords and Tenants (Shops, Hotels & Catering Establishments) Act (Cap 302), and Land Control Act (Cap 302).

Lack of property rights is no doubt a challenge for the development of the private sector in Kenya. It is even a bigger challenge for the MSE sector where indications of instability of property rights are real. The numerous laws and regulations governing property rights in Kenya make it appear that the country's legal system protects and facilitates acquisition and disposition of all property rights including land, buildings and mortgages. In practice, however, securing and registering these rights is a cumbersome and sometimes a very expensive process. For instance, obtaining title to land in Kenya can be difficult and fraught with corruption. The process is often complicated by improper allocations to third parties of access and easement. Thus the real problem is not the inadequacy of property laws but lack of their implementation.

Intellectual property rights are also important for sound development of the private sector in Kenya. This has been realized and the country has put in place mechanisms to ensure respect for property rights. Kenya is a signatory to the WTO Trade-related Intellectual Property Rights (TRIPs) and is in the process of conforming its legislation to the agreement. The government also, through an Act of Parliament, enacted the Industrial Property Act (IPA), CAP 509, establishing the Kenya Industrial Property Office (KIPO) in 1990. The office, whose main function is to examine, grant and register industrial property rights, is mandated to implement two Acts of Parliament, namely, the Industrial Property Act and the Trade Marks Act Cap 506. The main mission of KIPO is to 'protect and promote inventive and innovative activities in Kenya effectively and efficiently in order to enhance technological, industrial and socio-economic growth'. Since its establishment, KIPO has received a total of 177 patent applications of which 89 were granted. The statistics show that 62 patents were granted to foreigners while 27 went to Kenyans. It is significant that many of the applications for patents from Kenyans are from MSEs and particularly, the *Jua Kali* sector.

Although much has been achieved in putting the relevant property rights systems in place, protection of intellectual property in Kenya remains largely inadequate. There is for instance rampant piracy of audio and videocassettes. Copyrights in Kenya are the responsibility of the Attorney General's Office which is guided by the Copyright Act. The main problem as relates to copyrights is that the Copyright Act provides very lenient penalties for infringement and it has never been strictly enforced. It is hoped that the revised Copyright Act (2001) will afford better protection for intellectual property.

Competition Law

Kenya has undergone a gradual change from a controlled economy to a free market based economy. This has been quite evident since the country embarked on the Structural Adjustment Programmes (SAPs) whose primary objective is letting market forces play a greater role in determining economic outcomes in the country. This shift has implied a commitment by government to rely less on instruments of direct control and more competitive element in the economy. The law that governs competition in Kenya is the Restrictive Trade Practices, Monopolies and Price Control Act, Cap 504 of the Laws of Kenya. The objective of this law is to encourage competition in the domestic market by prohibiting restrictive trade practices, controlling trade monopolies, and concentration of unwarranted economic power and prices.

The overall responsibility for ensuring competition in Kenya is in the hands of the Minister for Finance. The Commissioner for Monopolies and Prices advises the Minister on matters of monopolies and pricing. The Commissioner acts as a watchdog of the entire commerce in the country and carries out enquiries and analysis to determine the nature and extent of any anti-competitive practices in the country. The Commissioner has responsibilities for the efficient administration of and the enforcement of competition laws in Kenya. The Commissioner has also some responsibilities in protecting consumer rights in the country, largely by providing information and promoting competitive and responsible supply, a role that has hardly been performed.

Although the country has an elaborate competition law, there are some inherent constraints and bottlenecks, which have made its implementation difficult. The Monopolies and Prices Commission (MPC) has no prosecutorial powers under the current law. It can thus, only investigate and recommend action to a prosecuting body. This problem is made worse by the non-existence of provisions in the statutes spelling how MPC relates with the Attorney General and the Department of Police in criminal prosecution. The MPC also lacks operational and financial autonomy to carry out its mandate. The provisions contained in the laws are sometimes contradictory with sectoral laws. The law is also biased in favour of the large enterprises and neglects crucial aspects of MSEs.

Labour Laws and Relations

The principal source of institutional framework for industrial relations in Kenya is the labour code that comprises the country's labour laws. This includes the Trade

Disputes Act (Cap 234), the Trade Union Act (Cap 236), Workmen's Compensation Act, the Factories and Other Places of Work (Cap 514) and the Employment Act (Cap 226). The laws cover policy issues and regulations such as wage guidelines, pensions and other post retirement benefits. The laws and regulations also provide for acceptable working conditions including occupational safety at work, compensation for injuries during or in the course of official work, and settlement of trade disputes, among others. It is important to note here that these laws relate mainly to formal firms registered under the Companies Act. While most of these Acts are impressive in terms of what they provide for and set out to do, the problem is one of enforcement. The machinery for implementation of these laws is often ineffective. In addition, some of these laws are outdated, having been crafted in the colonial period to serve the interests of foreign firms. Some of the labour laws have not kept pace with changes and dynamics of the labour market and labour situation, both locally and internationally.

For most of the post-independence period, Kenya has had a highly regulated labour market (Siggel et al, 2000). Since the early 1970s, the country imposed wage guidelines that restricted wage awards that trade unions could negotiate with employers. For this reason, coupled with the ineffectiveness of trade unions, the real wages in the country declined substantially especially in the early 1990s. From the early 1990s, considerable liberalisation of the labour market in Kenya took place as part of the structural adjustment programmes that saw, among other things, the relaxation of the wage guidelines and the review of the redundancy and other laws. Currently, the Kenyan labour market is relatively free and open compared to other countries in the region (Siggel et al, 2000).

Despite its liberalisation, a number of labour market constraints have worked against the development of a conducive business environment in Kenya. The first problem relates to foreign work permits which are not only difficult to obtain but also shrouded with fraud. This has had the effect of denying deserving applicants even where there is clear justification and economic benefits to Kenya. Part of this problem has to do with lack of communication and clear division of responsibilities between the Ministry of Labour and Human Resources and the Immigration Department. A second problem relates to the recent amendments to the Employment Act (Cap 226), the Regulations of Wages and Conditions of Employment Act (Cap 229) and the Trade Disputes Act (Cap 234) which have made dismissal through redundancy contestable and contrary to international labour conventions. The end result has been that dismissals through redundancy have ended up as trade disputes. Another worrisome trend especially in the last few years is the growing labour unrest in the country. This has mainly been in EPZs where enforcement of labour laws is wanting.

A major weakness of the labour laws in Kenya is that they do not recognize those operating within the informal economy as workers. These workers are no different from any other workers except that they perform their work in unregulated and unprotected conditions. It is well known that a large number of people are engaged in the informal sector. In Kenya, such workers have no single pillar of decent work for all as set by the ILO: employment opportunities, workers rights, social protection and representation (ILO, 2002). This implies that those operating within the informal economy of Kenya have a deficit in decent work that has to be addressed if poverty is to be reduced in line with Kenya's stated policy. There is need to review the labour laws to improve flexibility and reduce compliance costs and paperwork on the part of enterprises.

Insolvency Regime

Insolvency is the state of being unable to pay one's debts. Governments establish insolvency regimes as a way of legally managing personal and corporate insolvency. An effective insolvency system regime is of particular advantage in that it supports the domestic banking system by enabling banks to curtail the deterioration of the quality of their claims. Kenya's insolvency regime is contained in three pieces of legislation: the Bankruptcy Act (Cap 53), The Deeds of Arrangement Act (Cap 54) and the Companies Act (Cap 486). The three Acts stipulate the procedures to be followed in the event that firms and individuals become insolvent. Insolvency regimes provide the only way an unsecured creditor may get access to debtor's assets.

Kenya's insolvency regime has a number of weaknesses that work against the interest of both creditors and debtors. First, the regime does not contain satisfactory mechanisms for troubled but viable companies to save their businesses, rather than put into liquidation. This implies that the probability that a firm under receivership bounces back to business is very low. Second, the insolvency regime provides very restrictive powers to creditors to seize the assets of the debtors. This means that creditors in Kenya are disadvantaged. Thirdly, the insolvency procedures in Kenya are lengthy and costly by international standards. Comparative data for the time involved in bankruptcy process for Kenya and other countries is shown in the Table 3.4. It is clear from the table that the insolvency process in Kenya is not only lengthy but costly as well, compared to other countries in the region.

Table 3.4: *Comparative Time and Cost of Bankruptcy (2003)*

Country	Actual time (in years)	Actual Cost % of estate
South Africa	2.0	18
Uganda	2.0	38
Botswana	2.2	18
Zimbabwe	2.3	18
Tanzania	3.0	8
Kenya	4.6	18

Source: http://rru.worldbank.org. Doing Business/explore economies

Business Regulation

Government regulations are also important in defining and shaping the business environment in a country. The rationale for regulation is to ensure that firms and other actors adhere to the laid down procedures and regulations. One advantage of regulation is that by laying down standards directly, one can avoid complexity and be seen to be fair. However, bad regulation can also create problems in the business environment, which can take the form of higher costs, wasted time and energy, restrictions on choice, stifling of initiative, and missed opportunities. Regulations can also be inflexible and expensive to monitor and enforce.

Licensing

Business licensing has its origin in regulation although governments see it more in terms of revenue. Traditionally, licenses have been used to regulate firms on ground of public health and order, to limit the number of competing traders and to protect consumers. Licensing in Kenya is also done for more or else these reasons. While licenses are necessary for ensuring that the business does not put in danger the health of its employees, the local community and the environment, they may also be associated with externalities including excessive time and costs.

Business licensing in Kenya dates back to the colonial period. The country's licensing policy is articulated in the Trade Licensing Act (Cap 497). The Act confers on the local governments the powers to license firms in their jurisdiction. Prior to the licensing reforms in the country in 1999, each local authority had its own tariff structure for licenses designed according to the type of businesses. In addition to the local authority, the Central Government also issued business licenses through different ministries and departments (e.g., Ministry of Trade and Industry, the Office of the President, Ministry of Tourism and Wildlife, Ministry of Energy, the Police Department, Ministry of Health, Ministry of Agriculture, Ministry of Environment and Natural Resources, Ministry of Finance, Ministry of Transport and Communication). The obvious difficulty with so many licensing agencies is that it creates confusion and makes the process of licensing costly and unnecessarily bureaucratic.

In a bid to simplify the licensing system in Kenya, the government in 1999 embarked on a programme of reforming business licensing in the country. The reform, which saw the introduction of the Single Business Permit (SBP), had the two objectives. Firstly, to enable Local Authorities (LAs) to collect more revenue, significantly and secondly, to reduce the compliance burden on businesses. The new system provides a standard tariff for all LAs but still allows LAs discretion over the actual tariff rates. The introduction of the SBP was accompanied by measures to improve local administration of the system. This included a simplified and standard registration forms and computerization. The system is simpler and has reduced the cost on businesses of complying with LA regulations. However, some MSEs still find the cost of the permit prohibitive, and choose not to register their businesses.

Standards and Certification

As part of its regulatory framework, the government also has set standards for goods to be sold in the domestic market. Firms are also being forced to meet international standards to remain competitive. There are a number of institutions in Kenya that are responsible for setting and enforcing standards. The main one, the Kenya Bureau of Standards (KEBS), is a national government agency established under the Standards Act (Cap 496) and charged with standards development and implementation, certification of products and firms, testing and metrology. KEBS has established about 1,000 standards for processed agricultural and manufactured commodities. Most KEBS standards are based on international standards, which are either adopted without change, or adopted to allow for local conditions. Another important institution is the Kenya Plant Health Inspectorate Services (KEPHIS). KEPHIS is a parastatal within the Ministry of Agriculture that was established in 1997 and derives its powers from the Plant Protection Act (Cap 323); Agriculture Produce (Export) (Cap 319); the Seed Act (Cap 326) and the Pest Control Products Act (Cap 326) of the laws of Kenya. KEPHIS is charged with the plant health aspects including overseeing the health of plant materials in exports and imports. Finally, the Ministry of Health is in charge of food and safety standards.

Environmental Regulation

Environmental sustainability is an important defining characteristic of a sound business environment. Kenya faces a serious challenge especially in dealing with the effluents from industries and other production entities. This is symbolized by the country's inability to dispose solid waste such as polyethylene and plastic generated waste. In an attempt to address some of these problems, an environmental legislation, the Environment Management and Coordination Act (2000) was enacted. Since it was enacted, the Act has created a state of flux in Kenya's environmental management legislation and policy as it represents a watershed that encompasses completely new administrative structures as well as specific standards. The Act establishes an elaborate institutional framework at all levels, among them, the National Environment Management Authority (NEMA); the Standards Review and Enforcement Committee; the Public Complaints Committee and the National Environment Tribunal. The Act also calls for the review of all policies and laws touching on environmental management as well as the development of Environmental Standards and Environmental Impact Assessment (EIA) guidelines and regulations.

The major implication of the environmental Act on business in Kenya is that existing and new enterprises must conform to the regulations and standards set out. Save for the costs of compliance, meeting the standards might not be a big challenge to large and well-established enterprises. It is, however, a big problem to the smaller enterprises that lack the requisite capital and the technical-know how to be compliant.

INFRASTRUCTURE

Infrastructure is a crucial component of the environment in which businesses operate. All businesses require reliable and efficient transport, water supply and energy to operate. Information must also be easy to obtain. Several recent studies show that inadequate and poorly maintained infrastructure in Kenya is a major impediment for business development in the country. The World Bank/KIPPRA business climate assessment noted that inadequate infrastructure and the poor quality of physical infrastructure such as frequent power outages and inadequate roads, causes frequent disruptions and delays with adverse effects on productivity (World Bank/KIPPRA, 2004).

The failure to effectively provide essential infrastructure directly affects investment and profitability of enterprises. One of the consequences of this failure is that a large proportion of enterprises are forced to engage in costly self-provision of various facilities. For example, to cope with frequent power outages, 70 % of the firms own one or more generators (World Bank/KIPPRA 2004). It was estimated that in 2002, firms met 14.5% of their electricity requirements with these generators. Previous RPED surveys in Kenya have also shown that a growing number of firms provided own waste disposal, water supplies and security. This has obvious implications on profitability and investment.

Roads and Rail

An important element of infrastructure is the road network. Kenya's road policy has evolved a great deal since independence (Wasike, 2004). In the first decade of independence, the government emphasised the development of infrastructure, especially in the rural areas, to uplift living standards. Thus, the government embarked on the development of rural access roads using cess funds from rural output. In the second decade, the emphasis was on the rural access and minor roads in the rural areas. In the third and fourth decades, and in response to the realities of the period, emphasis shifted somewhat to reform in the development of roads in the country.

The reforms in the roads sector culminated in the establishment of key institutions such as the Roads Board and the introduction of a road levy. The period also saw bold attempts from the government to enforce axle-loads limits throughout the country. Although it is not explicitly stated, it would appear that the policy of the government has been geared mainly towards increasing accessibility and less towards achieving economy. The latter involves getting good value for money which requires sound maintenance. The creation of the Roads Board in the reform period was an attempt to achieve integration, i.e. ensuring that all decisions in the roads are taken in an integrated manner.

Recent developments in roads include the establishment of a fuel levy which assures domestic funding for maintenance, the adoption of the Roads 2000 Maintenance Strategy, decentralization of funds to Districts Roads Committees and the implementation of the Axle Load Control, thereby reducing overloading and damage to roads. The government also plans to concession the management and maintenance through the Northern Corridor Transport Improvement Project. The Northern Corridor is the most critical transport corridor, not only for Kenya but also for Uganda, Rwanda, Burundi, DRC and Ethiopia.

The importance of the railway as a mode of transport has declined considerably in the last ten years. Freight traffic has been declining and financial performance of the Kenya Railways Corporation has been poor. The Company is unable to service its long-term debt (more than Ksh. 10 billion is owed to the government). In a bid to reform this mode of transport, the governments of Kenya and Uganda have jointly handed over the management of the Kenya-Uganda railway to a strategic private investor under a concession arrangement. . This, it is hoped, will resuscitate railway transport in the country.

Electricity and Telecommunications

Electricity is one of the most important utilities in industrial production; it is also the most problematic. Kenya electricity generation system is predominantly hydro-based, thus, exposing the country to power shortages in times of drought. In the World Bank/KIPPRA study, sample firms reportedly experienced 33 outages in the year 2002. The study estimated the average value of lost production due to power outages or surges, as a percentage of total annual sales, at 9.3%. In addition, 64.4% firms experienced damage to or, complete loss of equipment due to power fluctuations or outages. There have also been concerns that the cost of power in Kenya is high compared to competing countries. According to the study, the cost of electricity per kilowatt-hour (Kwh) is about 7.8 Ksh. (or 0.10 cents US).

Current government thinking for addressing the difficulties in the power sector revolves around making power generation and distribution more efficient. As a first stem, the government plans to restructure the state-owned and run Kenya Power and Lighting Company, (KPLC). The intention is to first restructure the company and then enable a public-private partnership to be created, which will mobilize the investment needed for expanding generation. The government has also plans to strengthen the institutional capacity of the Electricity Regulation Board (ERB), the Kenya Power Generation Company (KenGen) and KPLC.

Telecommunications has also emerged as an important defining component of any business environment. Improvements in telecommunication and the emergence of the Internet have in the recent years changed the way business is conducted throughout the world. Despite the importance of Information and Communication Technology (ICT) for business development, the government is yet to enact a comprehensive policy on the same. In adequate and inefficient telecommunications in Kenya has contributed to the high cost of doing business in the country. To address these constraints, the government has plans to restructure in order to fully liberalize the telecommunications sub-sector including VSAT services. There are also plans to develop a master plan for e-government in Kenya.

SCIENCE AND TECHNOLOGY

To guide science and technology in the country, the government enacted the Science and Technology Act (Cap 250) in 1977. This Act established the National Council of Science and Technology (NCST), a statutory body, to focus on science and technology policies. The main function of NCST is to advise the government on all aspect of science and technology, and more importantly, on how to utilize technology to enhance the economy. An important component of the technological development in the country is in the area of Information Technology (IT). NCST is directly involved in the formulation and implementation of sub-sectoral policies in informatics. However, the country has yet to formulate an integrated national informatics policy. This can be attributed to political and legal, as well as technical difficulties.

ACCESS TO LAND

Land is without doubt an important factor of production. Investors, whether local or foreign, require adequate land to locate their activities and for future expansion. Two important considerations are crucial for investors when acquiring land for production: the cost, including time for acquiring the land and securing property rights. In Kenya, most land that is of high potential for investment is either government land or private (FIAS, 2004). Trust lands are generally less attractive to investors because they are often remote, arid and with inadequate infrastructure. Freehold and leasehold land in Kenya is readily available in the market as there is an active market for these types of land. Through estate agents, investors can get information on pieces of land being sold in the market. Transactions are also possible between private parties without resorting to estate agents.

Government land is available mainly for long-term leases under the Government Lands Act (Cap 280). According to the Act, investors can use government land on a leasehold basis for a period of up to 99 years. This period is reasonably long and provides sufficient assurance to investors. The investors are also free to transfer the land to other parties at the market rates subject to certain conditions. One such condition is that before the land is transferred, it must be developed to a certain level.

Foreign investors willing to invest in Kenya generally have reasonable access to land. Although the Lands Controls Act prohibits the Land Control Boards from consenting to any transaction in land to non-citizens, investors have found ways of acquiring land in the country. This they do by forming non-private companies which are not subject to the Land Control Boards. Foreign investors who go through Investment Promotion Council (IPC) get assistance in obtaining land in the country. Access to land by small investors is, however, problematic. Not only do such investors lack the political clout to influence allocation of land, but they also lack the resources to acquire them. The MSEs are particularly disadvantaged in this respect. The situation is even worse if the entrepreneur involved is a woman. This is because of the dominance of patriarchal property ownership traditions, which have historically worked against women.

Land tenure is an issue for many MSEs. According to data collected in 1999, only one quarter (23.8%) of all MSEs own or lease the land their business occupies.[1] More than half (59.6%) of the enterprises rent their premises, hold temporary occupation licences, or simply use available space. The remainder (16.6%) are mobile businesses without fixed premises. Urban businesses that operate on unused land, streets or roadsides not set aside for trade are especially vulnerable because they are often in conflict with urban authorities and provincial administration. Even

---

1   This is according to our own calculation from data collected by the Central Bureau of Statistics for the 1999 Baseline Survey of Micro and Small Enterprises.

those who operate from licensed stalls also feel insecure as outdated by-laws are indiscriminately applied. Temporary Occupation Licenses (TOL) require MSEs to remove any structure and vacate a site as soon as LA gives notice that the site is to be developed for the initial use for which it was intended. While this is a good planning provision that maximises land use, it has been abused by councillors and chief officers of LAs. In the past regime, councillors and chief officials of LAs colluded with individuals to sell such parcels of land at throw-away prices in order to keep their patron-client linkages. In such incidences, the MSEs would be thrown out without an alternative option. An accommodative policy would give the MSE operators an option of either purchasing the land or continuing to hold a TOL.

Land as a resource has another important function especially for enterprises owners. Land is often used as collateral for borrowing capital from financial institutions. Enterprises, both large and small, however, face a number of problems in using land as collateral in Kenya. One of the problems is that banks in Kenya do not readily accept land titles as collaterals because many of them do not have confidence in the titles. The lack of confidence has been occasioned by the perceived erosion of the credibility of the land registration process in Kenya. This has been made worse by the fact that banks find it difficult to sell land held as collateral in the event that the borrower fails to pay. Court decisions on land matters have been quite erratic and have in many instances, discouraged financiers.

CONCLUSIONS

This chapter sought to review government policies and regulations for business development in Kenya and their effects. It is clear from the review that the country has, over the years, put in place a number of policies and regulations that have affected the Kenya business environment in different ways. Generally, the policies and programs pursued by the government have been supportive of business development in the country. However, some of the programs, policies or interventions designed to help the private sector have actually impeded the development of the private sector in Kenya. This is largely due to the poor quality of government institutions, the high level corruption, and in certain cases, poor implementation of policies and programs. Some of the regulations are also quite cumbersome and add substantially to the cost of doing business in Kenya.

Finally, despite recognition of its important role in the economy, the MSE sector continues to operate in an unfavourable business environment. A number of policy and institutional constraints still inhibit the development of the sector. Key among them are the general failure in the targeted policy formulation and implementation, mismatch between policy pronouncement and resource allocation, and an inhibitive legal and regulatory environment.

REFERENCES

Alchian A. A. and Demsetz H.1973. "The Property Rights Paradigm". *Journal of Economic History, 33: 16-27.*

Bienen H. 1990. 'The Politics of Trade Liberalization in Africa'. *Economic Development and Cultural Change* 38 (4): 713-731

Coughlin P. 1988 "Toward a new Industrialization Strategy in Kenya'. In Coughlin P. and Ikiara G. K. (eds.). *Industrialisation in Kenya: In Search of a Strategy.* pp 275-303. Nairobi: Heinemann (K).

Devas, N. and Kelly R. 2001. "Regulations or Revenues? An Analysis of the Local Business Licences, With a Case Study of a Single Business Permit Reform in Kenya in Public Administration". *World Development* 21: 381-391.

Foreign Investments Advisory Services. 2004. "Kenya: Accelerating Reforms to Improve the Commercial Legal Frame and Remove Administrative and Regulatory Barriers to Investment". Final Draft Report, Nairobi.

Global Labour Institute. 2002. *Workers in the Informal Economy: Platform of Issues.* Geneva: Global Labour Institute.

Glenday G. and Ndiii D. 2000. "Export Platforms in Kenya" African Economic Policy Discussion Paper No. 43, USAID.

Hallward-Driemeier, Wallsen S.and Xu, L. C. 2003. *The Investment Climate and the Firm: Firm-Level Evidence from China.* Washington D.C.: World Bank.

Holden, P. 1996. The Firm and the Business Environment; Lessons from Latin America for South Africa. In Maasdorp, G. (ed.). *Can South and Southern Africa Become Globally Competitive Economies?* London: Macmillan.

Ikiara, G. K.; Olewe-Nyunya, J. and Odhiambo, W. 2004. "Kenya: Formulation and Implementation of Strategic Trade and Industrial Policies". In Soludo, C.; Ogbu, O. and Chang, H. (eds.). *The Politics of Trade and Industrial Policy in Africa: Forced Consensus.* Ottawa: IDRC.

ILO. 2002. *Decent Work and the Informal Economy.* Geneva: International Labour Office.

Kenya, Republic of. 2001. "Ministry of Local Government: Review of Local Government Act Workshop". Nairobi: Pan Afric Hotel, April.

Kenya, Republic of. 2002. *National Development Plan, 2002-2008.* Nairobi: Government Printer.

Siggel, E.; Ikiara, G.K and Nganda B. 2000. "Policy reforms, Competitiveness and Prospects of the Kenya's Manufacturing Industries: 1984-1997". Eager Project Report. HIID.

Sharpley, J. and Lewis, S. 1988. "Kenya's Industrialization, 1964-1984" Discussion Paper No 242. Institute of Development Studies, University of Sussex

Swamy, G. 1994. "Kenya: Patchy, Intermittent Commitment". In Hussain, I. and Faruque R. (eds.). *Adjustment in Africa: Lessons from Case Study Countries*. Washington: World Bank.

World Bank/KIPPRA. 2004. "Enhancing the Competitiveness of Kenya's Manufacturing Sector: The Role of the Investment Climate." Africa Private Sector Group. Washington and Nairobi: The World Bank and Kenya Institute for Public Policy Research and Analysis.

Wasike, S.K.W. 2004. "Road Infrastructure Policies in Kenya: Historical Trends and the Current Challenges". Working Paper No. 1. Nairobi: Institute of Policy Analysis and Research.

Chapter 4

Kenya's Socio-Economic Environment

Mary Omosa and Joseph Onjala

INTRODUCTION

According to the Business Systems theory, the socio-economic environment of a place shapes the business environment and this in turn determines the type of opportunities that these businesses portend. In other words, a country's socio-economic environment is an outcome of the interaction between the people's socio-economic and political beliefs and what their immediate environment is able to offer. In Kenya, a multi-ethnic country with a diversity of cultural practices and beliefs, the business operations and practices are highly influenced by this socio-economic environment. Hence, it is important that we examine Kenya's growth performance, demographic trends, rural-urban linkages and the distribution and magnitude of poverty, human capital, physical infrastructure and the natural resource base in order to understand the nature of the Kenyan business system.

DEMOGRAPHIC CHARACTERISTICS AND TRENDS

Kenya's population has almost tripled since the first post-independence National Housing and Population Census of 1969. According to this Census, there were 10,942,705 people in Kenya, of who over 50 percent were men. A further breakdown shows that slightly more than half of the population (5,526,509) was below 18 years of age. Ten years later, Kenya's population had grown by 40 percent to become 15,327,061 people, with slightly more women than men. At the same time, with the rapid growth, there was a substantial movement of people from high population concentration areas to the low-density parts of the country and urban settings. By 1989, Kenya's population had more than doubled over the 1969 figure and was dominated by women and youth.

The 1979 Census revealed that Kenya had one of the highest population growth rates in the world (3.8%). This growth rate had a number of perceived negative effects, especially on access to basic services, physical facilities, and employment opportunities. However, by 1993, the country's population growth rate had dropped to less than 3 percent and fertility had declined from an average of 7.7 to 4.7 children in 1999 (Kenya, 1999). The country's population, according to the 1999 Census, now stands at 28,686,607 people.

These demographic changes have not, however, been accompanied by a significant or sustained increase in per capita income. Instead, the country has been characterised by increased unemployment in both absolute and productive terms. For instance, per capita income dropped from US $340 in 1991 to a mere US $260 by 1994 (Kenya, 1995).

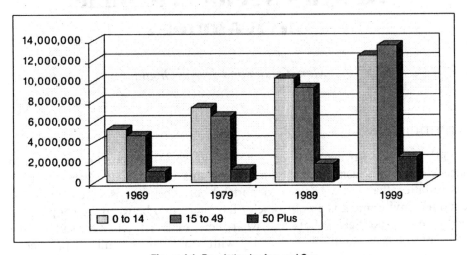

Figure 4.1: Population by Age and Sex

Source: Kenya population Census 1969-1999

At the regional level, most of the country's population is concentrated within the Rift Valley Province followed by Eastern and Nyanza Provinces and this has been the case since the first post-independence Census of 1969. However, Nairobi area has grown most dramatically from just 509,286 people in 1969 to over 2 million inhabitants in 1999. The capital city has the highest density of 3,079 people per sq. km followed by Western, Nyanza and Central Provinces with 406, 350 and 282 persons per sq. km, respectively. Although these densities are a reflection of potential economic opportunities, the actual location of industry and other economic activities have not depended on population density.

The changes in population dynamics at the regional level are attributed to migration, almost invariably, from rural to urban areas. The implied growth in urban centres is associated with certain attractions including wage employment and a cosmopolitan lifestyle. No matter the driving force, these changes have an impact on both the rural and urban areas of the country especially in the area of commerce and industry; access to basic facilities and infrastructure; and agricultural development.

Table 4.1: *Population by Province (1969-1999)*

Region	1969	%	1979	%	1989	%	1999	%
Nairobi	509,286	4.7	827,775	5.4	1,324,570	6.2	2,143,254	7.5
Central	1,675,647	15.3	2,345,833	15.3	3,111,255	14.5	3,724,159	12.9
Coast	944,082	8.6	1,342,794	8.8	1,825,761	8.5	2,487,264	8.7
Eastern	1,907,301	17.4	2,719,851	17.7	3,768,689	17.6	4,631,779	16.1
North Eastern	245,757	2.2	373,787	2.4	371,391	1.7	962,143	3.4
Nyanza	2,122,045	19.4	2,643,956	17.3	3,507,160	16.4	4,392,196	15.3
Rift Valley	2,210,289	20.2	3,240,402	21.1	4,917,551	22.9	6,987,036	24.4
Western	1,328,298	12.1	1,832,663	11.9	2,622,397	12.2	3,358,776	11.7
Total	*10,942,705*	*100*	*15,327,061*	*100*	*21,448,774*	*100*	*28,686,607*	*100*

Source: *Kenya Population Census, 1969 – 1999*

Recent trends further suggest a change in the demographic structure of this population (Kenya, 1999c). For instance, Kenya's population growth rate dropped from almost 4 percent in 1979 to about 2 percent in 1998. Although life expectancy increased from 45 years in the 1960s to over 61 years in the 1990s, this has reverted to about 40 years. Similar reductions in gains made are evident in infant mortality rates and general morbidity. The country's socio-economic environment is further challenged by stagnation in other sectors of the economy. For example, per capita income levels have continued to drop largely because of a decrease in gainful employment.

The above trends in population dynamics and composition suggest that Kenya's population is unevenly distributed and urban centres and high potential regions of the country tend to have higher densities. In general, therefore, we expect that these demographic trends will impact on investment patterns and the quality of life in general. The question is, however, to what extent have investments in the country taken these demographic variations into account? And, at the national policy level, has the structure of the country's population guided resource allocation and general planning?

SETTLEMENT PATTERNS AND RURAL-URBAN LINKAGES

One key feature of the Kenyan population is its ethnic composition. There are about 40 ethnic groups, a number of whom share cultural practices and a common history. The size of some ethnic groups vary from 20 percent of the population in the case of the Kikuyu to less than one percent in the case of many others such as the Teso, Suba, and Garbatula. Indeed, the Kikuyu, Luhya, Luo, Kalenjin, and Kamba alone constitute more than 50 percent of the country's population.

Each of Kenya's ethnic communities has since pre-colonial time largely occupied a particular territorial location that for the most part has recognised boundaries or frontiers. These are the boundaries that the colonial administration formally and clearly marked out in the course of establishing administrative districts and provinces that essentially became ethnic enclaves. Indeed, segmentation contributed to the formation of new ethnic identities for ease of administration by grouping a number of otherwise substantially diverse ethnic groups into larger ones to which a new identity was assigned. Matters like place of work, place of residence, or where to go to school were largely influenced by these settlement patterns.

Currently, the Kikuyu occupy predominantly, Central Province, Metropolitan Nairobi and parts of Rift Valley Province, particularly Nakuru District. The Luhya dominate Western Province; while the Luo are found mainly in Nyanza; the Kamba in Eastern; the Kalenjin in Rift Valley; the Kisii in parts of Nyanza, the Meru in parts of Eastern, and the Mijikenda in the larger part of the Coast Province. Most ethnic groups occupy exclusive districts with the exception of a few 'settlement' districts especially in the former White Highlands. This settlement pattern has both political and economic implications, especially with regard to possible potentials for self-enhancement. In Kenya, therefore, ethnicity is geographically specific and culturally distinct.

Similarly, the nature and strength of linkages between rural and urban Kenya is historical, largely rooted in the colonial wage labour policy. Prior to independence, migration labour laws necessitated the continued existence of fairly firm ties between the rural and urban areas of this country (Hay, 1976). At independence, development was perceived to be modernisation and was therefore deemed to be synonymous with urbanisation, leading to a mushrooming of urban centres. Some of the policies that have engendered the urbanisation process include pegging the development process to industrialisation, although the latter is yet to take off. However, the unprecedented expansion of these urban areas occasioned the call for a balance between the rural and the urban areas of the country. This was championed by the introduction of the *District Focus for Rural Development Strategy*. This sought to even out the distribution of economic activities and the establishment of linkages between these two spheres of life. Espoused in the spatial dimension of development, this approach aimed at the type of development that would achieve a rural-urban balance through an even dispersion of economic and development activities in all parts of the country (Kenya, 1994-96, p.73). Some of the areas where balance was sought include size of the population, infrastructure and related facilities.

Generally therefore, Kenya has exhibited a fairly rapid growth in urbanisation, both in terms of the number of urban centres and size of settlement. For instance, the urban population rose from 1.08 million in 1969 to 4.17 million in 1990, 5.65 million in 1996 and 7.44 million in the year 2000. Projections now suggest that the urban population will grow even more rapidly to reach 11.5 million people by the year 2010 and this will account for over 26 percent of the total population (Kenya, 1999c).

Similarly, the number of urban centres increased from 48 towns in 1969 with a population of about 1.08 million people to 117 towns in 1979 with over 2.3 million people. By 1994, there were 135 towns with an estimated 4.9 million people. The majority of these people are found in Nairobi and Mombasa. These two cities and other towns that have attracted large populations are faced with pressing needs for food, employment, physical infrastructure, and other basic services. Related to the above are problems of informal settlements, insecurity and violence, environmental degradation, and deterioration of public health standards. Nevertheless, the majority of the Kenyan population remains rural based, currently estimated at 76 percent having dropped from 80 percent in 1995 and 82% in 1990 (Kenya, 1999c; Kenya, 1999a; Kenya, 1999b). In spite of this, most rural areas are characterised by limited employment opportunities, low incomes, and high incidences of poverty, all of which have continued to contribute to a desire to migrate to urban areas.

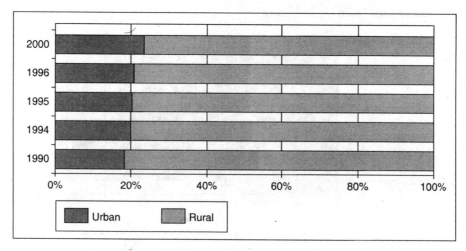

Figure 4.2: Urban and Rural Populations (Millions)

Source: Kenya 1999c

Some of the concerns arising from emerging rural-urban linkages relate to the apparent imbalance, both in facilities and population size. Government policies have, over the years therefore, endeavoured to reverse rural-urban migration by making rural areas equally 'attractive'. Some of these attractions have aimed at availing employment opportunities within rural settings and smaller towns. This is, however, yet to be fully realised. Instead, the evident disparity between the rural and urban areas of this country continues to disadvantage sections of the population. For instance, current estimates show that women constitute about 51 percent of the rural dwellers (Kenya, 2002: p.21) and in effect, therefore, are the most disadvantaged with regard to access to resources and basic facilities.

HUMAN CAPITAL

The development of human capital is key to sustained business activities. However, the quality, structure and productivity of human capital have remained key constraints in Kenya. After the high enrolment of the two post-independence decades, there has been a reversal at the pre-primary, primary and secondary levels of education characterised by low enrolment, high levels of drop-outs, and low completion and transition rates. However, gains have been made at the tertiary level where enrolments and the demand for learning opportunities have increased. The decline in the primary and secondary education has been attributed to the high cost of education, which has had a negative impact on access, retention, equity and quality of education.

Enrolment in the various levels of the educational system is characterised by gender, income, and regional disparities. While female representation in 2000 was 49.1 percent at pre-primary and 49.4 percent at primary level, this dropped to only 46.2 percent at secondary, 29.2 percent in national polytechnics and 31.7 percent in public universities. Females are also grossly under-represented in the post-secondary school science, maths and technology based courses and other post-school institutions (Kenya, 2002:54).

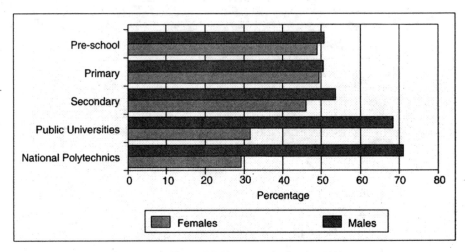

Figure 4.3: Enrolments by Gender, 2000

Source: Kenya National Development Plan, 2002

With regard to quality and relevance of education, concern continues to be raised regarding the failure to satisfactorily inculcate a modern scientific culture, and imbue learners with desirable social skills and values. This is attributed to inadequacies in the provision and maintenance of essential physical facilities, instructional and research materials and human resource capacity (Kenya, 2002:55).

In the past, development of human resources especially through education, training and capacity building have not been demand driven (Kenya, 2002:18). The training system is skewed in favour of technologists. The current ratio of technologists to technicians to craftsmen is 1:3:12 as compared to an optimal ratio of 1:5:30. The imbalance of professionals in the labour force is thought to impact negatively on research and development, which is a crucial element towards industrialization (Kenya, 2002:56).

Yet, a total of 500,000 persons enter the labour market annually while the economy only generates between 250,000 to 330,000 jobs in the urban formal sector (Kenya, 2001). Generally, unemployment has soured and productivity has fallen over time.

NATURAL RESOURCES

Kenya's economic fortunes depend on the availability and management of natural resources. Its main economic activities – agriculture and tourism – depend directly on a diversity of bio-productive resources. The natural resources that are critical to the survival of most Kenyans include: land, forests, water, energy, wildlife, fisheries, and minerals.

Land Resources

Kenya has a diverse land tenure system with individual private property, group private property, state-owned land and land held in trust by the state. Only 20 per cent of Kenya's land is suited for agriculture. About 80 percent of the total land surface is arid and semi arid. The arid and semi arid lands support 25 percent of the human population and 50 percent of Kenya's livestock population (Kenya, 2002: 41). On the other hand, 50 percent of the Kenyan population is supported by the 20 percent of Kenya's agricultural land, implying low productivity for much of the land. The low productivity is the biggest source of pressure on land resources. The rapidly growing population is putting more pressure on all regions. Coupled with changes in the social modes of production, limited growth in the corresponding technological knowledge and skills to manage the ecological base, lack of a clear land-use policy has contributed to unsustainable land-use practices in Kenya (Kenya, 2001:45). Land administration and planning policies have a bearing not only on the management and development of the resource, but also on the productivity of the owners. Unfortunately, these are the issues that have remained unresolved in Kenya for many years.

Forests

Kenya is endowed with forest ecosystems that include moist highland forest, dry forest, tropical rain forest, coastal forest, and river line and mangrove forests. The total area of gazetted forest reserves is 1.64 million hectares of which 1.24 million hectares consist of indigenous forest. Forests cover about 2 percent of Kenya's total land surface. About 40 percent of large mammals, 30 percent of birds, 35 percent of butterflies, and over 50 percent of threatened mammals in Kenya are found in these forests (Kenya, 2002). The local communities, particularly in the rural areas, depend on forests for provision of timber, fuel wood and non-wood products for their livelihoods. Forests contribute about 95 percent of the total rural domestic energy (Kenya, 2001). Forests also provide the raw materials for the timber and paper industries. The domestic production of wood and paper is estimated at US$100 million per year. Over 100,000 people are employed in wood-based enterprises. However, the unsustainable rate of depletion of the forests base means that Kenya's capacity to cope with adverse climatic conditions, such as drought and flooding, has been significantly reduced. For instance, the 1999-2000 two-year drought had deeper negative impacts on national social and economic well-being than other longer and more acute spells that have been experienced previously (Kenya, 2001:44).

Water Resources

There are various sources of fresh water in Kenya. These include surface water in rivers, reservoirs and ponds and groundwater that has been developed through the use of shallow wells and boreholes. Surface water resources account for 86 percent while ground water accounts for the balance (14%) of Kenya's water resources. The potential annual renewable water resource in Kenya is about 24.3 billion m^3. The main factor responsible for water availability is climate of which rainfall is the most important element. Effective rainfall (where rainfall is greater than evaporation) occurs in the central highlands and the Coastal region (14%), while nearly 86 percent of the remaining part of the country receives less than 750mm per annum. The climatic conditions imply that water resources in Kenya are marked by both gross and temporal variability.

The scarcity of water has intensified competition among various water users. Furthermore, the poor quality of the available water in urban areas remains a major concern as it is sometimes untreated. The provision of clean water has been supplemented by the private sector, local authorities and NGOs. Historically, the provision of water as a basic necessity has either been done free or at very subsidized prices (Onjala, 2003). Sustaining this policy has been difficult. Hence, a majority of Kenyans lack access to clean water. This problem has been compounded by the poor management of the existing water works and the non-existent or poor sewerage systems (Kenya, 2001). The water supply situation in rural areas has deteriorated over the years to a point where demand cannot be sustained with current systems. Access to piped water has not increased since 1989 and those accessing water from other sources have increased from 14 to 29 per cent of rural households over the same period (Kenya, 2001:41).

Energy

The three main sources of energy in Kenya are wood fuel, petroleum and electricity accounting for 70, 21 and 9 percent respectively of all energy consumption (Kenya, 2001:50). Currently, demand for wood fuel outstrips supply. The lack of adequate and reliable energy hampers the attraction of additional investments into the economy.

Kenya has no known reserves of fossil fuels but exploration activities undertaken have shown potential for commercial oil discovery. Petroleum accounts for 20 percent of the energy consumed in the country while coal contributes about one percent. The current domestic demand for various petroleum fuels on average stands at 2.5 million tones a year, which is equivalent to Kshs.54 billion imports in a year. The discovery of oil, if commercially viable, will greatly alleviate the pressure created by oil importation (Kenya, 2002:89). Petroleum exploration in the country started in 1954, and to date, 30 oil exploratory wells have been drilled. Some of these wells have shown some positive geological results, which give continued hope for oil discoveries.

Wildlife and Biodiversity

Wildlife remains the dominant land-use activity within the Kenyan rangelands. Kenya has 59 wildlife parks covering about 8 percent of the total land area under the protected area system managed by the Kenya Wildlife Service (KWS). Over 70 percent of terrestrial wildlife is found outside the protected areas for most of the year, contributing to human-wildlife conflicts and to rural poverty, mainly in the arid and semi-arid lands. About 70 percent of gross tourism earnings in Kenya and 5 percent of total GDP are attributed to wildlife. The sector is estimated to account for a tenth of total formal sector employment, over half of trade, restaurants and hotel sector earnings, and contributes over a third of total annual foreign exchange earnings.

Kenya has over 35,000 identified species of animals, plants and micro-organisms. But overtime, the country has lost some of her biodiversity resources mainly due to habitat destruction, desertification, over exploitation of species and conversion of wetlands into agriculture and settlement areas. Population growth is a major reason for this; but then this problem is compounded by limited functional mechanisms for monitoring and regulating importation into the country of alien invasive species. Currently, there is no comprehensive policy on biotechnology and legislative framework to regulate access and exploitation of genetic resources. Furthermore, enforcement of environmental regulations is still at infancy, having enacted the Environmental Coordination Act (EMCA) only in 2000.

Fisheries

Kenya's fishery resources are important sources of food, employment and foreign exchange. In 1999, the sector contributed 3 percent of total GDP and 2 percent of total export earnings. The fisheries industry employs over 48,400 artisanal fishermen and 500,000 persons engaged directly or indirectly in fish processing and trade. Lake Victoria accounts for about 98 percent of total inland fish production. The coastline and the 200 miles Exclusive Economic Zone (EEZ) are highly productive but remain relatively un-exploited due to lack of appropriate technology and adequate funding.

Mineral Resources

Kenya has substantial mineral deposits, which have been documented and are earmarked for exploitation. Hence, most of the minerals are yet to be exploited, or are not found in economic quantities. The Ministry of Environment and Natural Resources (MENR), through the Department of Mines and Geology, has the responsibility of undertaking geological surveys, geo-scientific research, coordination and regulation of the activities of the mining sector. The private sector on the other hand is involved in mining and mineral exploration throughout the country. Below is a summary table of the quantities and values of the main mineral activities in Kenya between 1997 and 2002.

Table 4.2: *Quantity of Mineral Production, 1997-2002 in Tonnes*

Minerals	1997	1998	1999	2000	2001
Soda Ash	257,640	242,910	245,680	238,190	297,780
Fluorspar	68,700	60,854	93,602	100,102	118,850
Salt	6,280	21,742	44,886	16,359	5,664
Limestone Products	32,668	32,000	32,000	32,000	32,000
Crushed Refined Soda	392,000	370,000	335,230	382,556	207,647
Other	10,934	9,823	10,682	8,323	13,552
Total	*768,222*	*737,329*	*762,080*	*777,530*	*675,493*

Source: *Department of Mines and Geology, Economic Surveys - Various*

PHYSICAL INFRASTRUCTURE

The physical infrastructure examined here is composed of transport, communications, buildings and construction, water and sanitation, and energy. An efficient network of the infrastructural facilities is paramount for the smooth operation of business. Poor infrastructure leads to increased production and transport costs, and reduced competitiveness.

Transport System

Kenya's transport system consists of a single commercial sea port at Mombasa; a single track rail network consisting of a main line and a few branch lines; an oil pipeline connecting the port to the capital city, Nairobi, and extending to Eldoret and Kisumu. There is also a classified road network and three international airports, namely: Jomo Kenyatta International Airport (JKIA) in Nairobi, Moi International Airport (MIA) in Mombasa, and Eldoret International Airport (EIA). The government currently owns and operates the port, railways, airports and pipeline as public corporations. The government is also responsible for the road network while the private sector dominates road transport and general aviation. Transport activities are concentrated along the main section of the Northern Corridor from Mombasa to Nairobi. The corridor facilitates transit transportation to other countries in East and Central Africa. It therefore, constitutes Kenya's major transit transport artery and sea-access route for the landlocked countries such as Uganda, Rwanda, Burundi, the Eastern Democratic Republic of Congo (DRC), and Southern Sudan (Irandu, 2000).

Roads

Kenya's road network consists of over 63,000 km of the classified road system and about 87,600 km of unclassified road system. The classified road network has grown by 51 percent from 41,800 km at independence, to 63,291 km in 2000, with the tarmacked road length increasing from 1,811 km to 8,937 km over the same period. The road transport in Kenya currently accounts for over 80 percent of the country's total passenger and 76 percent of freight traffic (Wasike, 2001). The development of the road network during the colonial period tallied closely with major business centres in Kenya. The regions that are served by relatively good road network are the ones enjoying booming business activities. The urban road network has been characterized by heavy traffic congestion during peak hours, overloaded passenger transport, stiff competition for limited road space, few packing spaces and inadequate supply of public transport. These factors have deteriorated transport and have given rise to economic and social problems. In Nairobi, peak hours travel time are 50 per cent higher than travel time during off-peak hours resulting in waste of time and fuel, and a large number of road accidents (Kenya, 2002).

Railway Transport

The total railway network consists of 2,765 kilometres and the system has an annual capacity of more than 6 million tones. The Kenya Railway Corporation, however, operates only on about 1,500 kilometres and handles between 2.4 and 3.2 million tones per year. The railway's efficiency and reliability is important for international trade and transit traffic to neighbouring countries and also, in supplementing road transport, reducing road damage and road traffic. Due to operational and financial constraints, and slow development of container capacity, the Corporation is unable to rehabilitate and modernize locomotives, railway line, wagons and other equipment.

Marine Transport

Marine transport consists of port facilities in Mombasa and minor ports along the coast, and in Kisumu at Lake Victoria and inland container depots in Nairobi, Kisumu and Eldoret. The Mombasa Port serves the hinterland countries of Eastern and Central Africa. The efficiency of the port operation remains low due to: high management turnover, poor and near obsolete equipment, inadequate maintenance of equipment and weak links to the hinterland as a result of poor performance of Kenya Railways and the state of the road networks.

Air Transport

Kenya is strategically placed to serve as the hub for East, Central and Indian Ocean areas. The country offers transit and refuelling facilities for North/South and East/West air Traffic. The volume of passengers handled at the airports rose from 2.77 million in 1994 to 4.0 million in 2000. Freight handled rose rapidly from 23,000 in 1994 to 145,400 in 2000. The Government has reduced its direct participation through the privatisation of Kenya Airways, commercialisation of airport operations and de-linking the Directorate of Civil Aviation from the civil service.

Telecommunications

The indicators of potential for telecommunications traffic are telephone exchange connections, public call boxes, e-mail and mobile telephony. The number of telephone exchange connections increased from 261,000 in 1996 to 321,000 in 2001. During the same period, the number of public call boxes increased from

5,932 to 8,346. There has been an overwhelming subscription for mobile phone services after the commissioning of two mobile phone service providers. Consequently, the number of mobile phone subscribers increased from 3,000 in 1996 to 85,000 in 2000; 668,000 in 2001; and about one million in 2002. Coverage of mobile telephony has expanded to cover urban and rural areas as well as major highways in the country, beyond what landlines can conceivably achieve. Nevertheless, only about 1.2 percent of Kenyans have own telephone services. The number of telephone exchange connections has been rising steadily over the last decade by 3 percent annually. The total telephone exchange capacity is expected to increase from 446,302 in 2001 to 943,000 in 2008, an average annual growth of 9 percent. The total number of exchange connections was also anticipated to increase at 9.9 percent in the same period. The number of public payphones is expected to increase by 27 percent to 24,600 by 2008. These developments are expected to raise the telephone density from 1.07 to 2.16 lines per 100 people over the same period. The status of fixed and target network is provided in Table 4.3.

The problem of telephone access has been addressed in recent years by opening a number of market segments to the private sector. These include licensing mobile phone operators. Mobile telephone services are being offered by Safaricom Limited and Kencell Communications Limited (now Celtel). By June 2001, the Communications Commission of Kenya (CCK) had licensed 66 Internet Service Providers. However, of these, only 30 are operational, serving about 50,000 users the majority of who are based in Nairobi (Kenya, 2002).

Table 4.3: *Status of Fixed Telephone Network*

	Actual	Target Growth						
	2001	2002	2003	2004	2005	2006	2007	2008
Capacity (000's)	446	466	545	627	709	787	865	943
Connections (000's)	321	373	436	502	567	629	692	755
Tele-Density	1.09	1.24	1.41	1.58	1.75	1.89	2.03	2.16
Automation (%)	97	97	97.5	98	98	98	98	98.5
Manual (%)	3	3	2.5	2	2	2	2	1.5
Digital (%)	66	67.3	68.7	70.0	71.4	72.9	74.3	75.8
Analog (%)	31	29.7	28.8	28.0	26.6	25.1	23.7	22.7
Payphone	8,938	10,500	12,200	14,300	16,500	18,600	21,000	24,600

Source: Kenya, Republic of, Various Development Plans

Telecommunication costs remain high for both international and local calls and, in most cases, totally unavailable in the rural areas. Kenya is still lagging behind in liberalisation of telecommunications and companies in this sector continually come into conflict with the government's desire to control electronic communication. Telkom Kenya has the monopoly in providing gateway services and telephone lines. These services have proved inefficient and costly thus curtailing the development of the Internet and telecommunication service. The State Corporation exhibits serious incompetence and inefficiency in service delivery. The waiting list of customers seeking services has remained long, especially in urban areas. Its coverage of the rural areas can only be described as a token service. In spite of government unease with privatisation and liberalisation of the telecommunications sector, the private sector continues to grow and develop new services and clients.

GROWTH AND PERFORMANCE OF THE ECONOMY

Kenya's growth performance has substantially varied over time. The macro-economic performance of the Kenyan economy since independence is best understood in the context of the external shocks and internal challenges that the economy has had to adjust to. Four phases are clearly identifiable: a rapid growth phase (1964-73); an era of external shocks dominated by oil price shocks and a coffee boom (1974-79); a period of stabilization and beginning of the structural adjustment in the 1980s; and an era of liberalisation and declining donor inflows from 1990 to 2002 (Onjala, 1999; Mwega and Ndung'u, 2002).

The overall effect of the changing circumstances has been a declining trend in economic performance (see Table 4.4). In the first decade of independence (1964-73); the economy performed relatively well with an average GDP growth rate of about 6% per annum. This was due to increased agricultural output; expansion of the manufacturing sector supported by the adoption of import substitution strategies, rising domestic demand, expansion of the regional market and substantial inflows of foreign aid. From the mid-1970s, there has been a persistent downward trend in the per capita growth rate, with the rate turning negative over the 1990s.

Table 4.4: *Average Annual Growth Rates of Real GDP (%)*

Sector	1964-73	1974-79	1980-89	1990-95	1996-2002
Agriculture	4.6	3.9	3.3	0.4	1.1
Manufacturing	9.1	10.0	4.8	3.0	1.3
Finance, Real Estate	9.8	12.4	6.7	6.6	3.6
Government Services	16.9	6.5	4.9	2.6	1.0
Private Household	3.5	14.5	10.0	10.3	5.6
Others	6.1	8.8	7.7	3.6	2.3
Total GDP	*6.6*	*5.2*	*4.1*	*2.5*	*2.0*

Source: Onjala (1999); Mwega and Ndung'u (2002)

A series of exogenous factors, compounded by an inadequate macroeconomic policy response reversed the impressive economic growth of the first decade. The first oil crisis of 1973 brought an abrupt halt to the rapid growth. Consequently, the growth rate decelerated to below 4 percent for much of the 1970s except for 1976/77 when the unexpected "coffee boom" saw the GDP growth rate rising to 8.2 percent in 1977. The collapse of the East African Community in 1977, and the second oil crisis of 1979 contributed to a further deceleration in economic performance.

The drought experienced in the early 1980s, world recession and the international debt crisis worsened the domestic economic situation. In addition, misaligned real exchange rates, the fixed interest rate regime, as well as poor commodity pricing undermined macroeconomic stability. Balance of payment problems induced the country to seek conditionality finances from the Breton Woods institutions. Substantial donor-driven reforms were therefore introduced in the late 1980s that covered nearly all sectors of the economy including liberalisation of the foreign exchange market; trade and payments system; domestic financial and capital markets; and privatisation and commercialisation of public corporations.

Even though the 1980s was marked by economic reforms through the structural adjustment policies, the controversy surrounding these policies tended to mask the broad goals and benefits, mostly due to the conditionalities that were attached to them and the vested interests in the pre-reform organisations. In the end, due to their slow implementation (and at times reversals), these reforms did not achieve their intended goals and they do not seem to have worked well, especially for the key markets. On the other hand, a mixed implementation of these reforms led to a resurgence of growth, which averaged 5 percent over 1986-1990 period.

In the 1990s, poor economic performance was mainly as a result of declining donor support; poor weather and infrastructure; insecurity; and depressed investments. Consequently, Kenya faced declining tourism activities and poor performance in the manufacturing sector. In the first half of 1990s, there was a worsening of the economic environment, with an average growth rate of 2.5 percent. Some of the contributing factors were: a drought in 1991/1992, the increase in oil price following the Gulf War, compounded by galloping corruption that led to the aid embargo of 1991-93, and the "ethnic clashes" of 1992. In the second half of the 1990s, economic growth declined further to an average of 1.9 percent, with the period characterized by an aid embargo in 1997-2000, "ethnic clashes" in the run-up to and after the 1997 elections, bad weather conditions (*el nino* rains of 1997/1998 followed by a major drought leading to power rationing in 2000). Overall, the GDP growth declined further to 2.5 percent between 1990 and 1995, and to 2 percent between 1996 and 2002.

Table 4.5: *Distribution of GDP by Productive Sector (%)*

	1964-73	*1974-79*	*1980-89*	*1990-95*	*1996-2002**
Agriculture	36.6	33.2	29.8	26.2	24.5
Manufacturing	10.0	11.8	12.8	13.6	13.3
Public Services	14.7	15.3	15.0	15.7	14.8
Other Services	38.7	39.7	42.4	44.5	47.4
Total	*100.0*	*100.0*	*100.0*	*100.0*	*100.0*

Source: Muga and Ndungu (2002)

Thus, the Kenyan economy has undergone a structural transformation over the years as shown in Table 4.5 above. There has been a gradual decline of the share of agriculture in overall GDP from one third in the decade after independence to just one quarter over the 1996-2002 period. The share of manufacturing has only grown slowly and actually stagnated at less than 14 percent of the GDP during the 1990s. The share of public and other services has also stagnated at about 1 percent while public services have increased from 39 percent to almost 47 percent of the GDP.

DISTRIBUTION AND MAGNITUDE OF POVERTY

In Kenya, as in other African countries, poverty alleviation strategies have generally been organised around different assumptions and these have changed over the years. In the 1960s, poverty alleviation was seen as synonymous with raised incomes. These were perceived as a natural outcome of investment in industry, human resource development and improvement in export earnings. The major assumption here was that once the economy prospered, benefits would trickle down to all Kenyans and rid them of poverty, ignorance and disease (Kenya, 1966:7). Subsequent plans, however, noted that in spite of commendable growth in the economy, the expected trickle-down failed to take place. Instead, average incomes were still very low and poverty levels were on the increase. The fact that poverty alleviation still pre-occupies policy level and academic discussions in Kenya suggests that poverty has become both elusive and diffuse.

According to the 1997 Welfare Monitoring Survey (WMS III), over 2.5 million households in Kenya live below the poverty line. In other words, almost one in every two Kenyans is poor and three quarters of these live in the rural areas of the country (Kenya 2001). In the urban areas, majority of the poor live in informal settlements, which are characterised by inadequate or low quality services such as unclean water, limited access to quality schools and health facilities, and general unhygienic living conditions. Most of the urban poor do not have a job or income and this results in them being caught in a vicious cycle of poverty.

In money terms, absolute poverty in Kenya is pegged at Kshs. 1,239 per person per month in the rural areas and Kshs. 2,648 per person per month for the urban areas of the country (Kenya, 1997a; CBS *et al.* 2003). Some of the characteristics of the poor include having large families, being engaged in subsistence farming, and lack of a source of cash income. According to the country's second Welfare Monitoring Survey, the poor devote a higher proportion of their incomes to the purchase of food. They also have limited access to health facilities and formal education; lack access to clean water and safe sanitation; have low agricultural productivity, and lack access to household amenities (Kenya, 1994a).

It is further noted that poverty is multi-dimensional and diversely distributed between genders and within geographical areas and economic sectors (Ayako and Katumanga, 1997; Kenya, 1999a). Generally, women are more vulnerable to poverty than their male counterparts. This is attributed to the inequitable access to the means of production, limited access to economic goods and services and low participation in remunerative employment. For instance, 69 percent of the active female population in Kenya work as subsistence farmers as compared to only 43 percent among the males. Moreover, only 25 percent of the adult women population are engaged in formal employment as compared to over 40 percent among their male counterparts (Kenya, 2001:16).

Further analysis, however, suggests that poverty trends are dynamic. For example, in 1994, poverty was most prevalent in North Eastern Province (58%) followed by Eastern (57%) then Coast province (55%) while both Nyanza (42%) and Central (32%) provinces had the lowest incidences of poverty. However, by 1997, poverty had increased rapidly and its distribution had also changed. Nyanza province recorded the highest prevalence level of 63 percent followed by Coast province with 62 percent (Kenya, 1997a).

In terms of occupation, incidences of poverty are most prevalent among farming communities and those engaged in the informal sector. Subsistence farmers (47%) and farmers engaged in food crop production (46%) have the highest proportions of poor people as compared to groups engaged within the public (16%) or formal private (31%) sectors. These disparities are explained in terms of the fact that the agricultural sector is over taxed, poorly financed, under remunerated and subject to the vagaries of weather. The informal sector presents a considerable proportion of poor people because it is just as unpredictable a source of livelihood as rain-fed agriculture (Omosa, 2002).

Poverty is also a seasonal phenomenon (Kenya, 1999a:12). For instance, in the rural areas, lean food periods coincide with limited job opportunities and slacked social support. And in the urban areas, the mid-month is a period of scarcity for salaried workers; this too affects traders, especially those engaged in petty businesses (Omosa, 2002:6). The poor are therefore characterised by lack of jobs or job security, few assets if any, limited or no access to health and educational facilities, inability to plan their lives, and large families (Kenya, 1997b:15).

However, Bahemuka *et al.* have argued that attempts to conceptualise and measure poverty in Kenya and elsewhere have lacked consensus due to the magnitude and complexity of poverty as a concept and the diversity in strategies aimed at poverty alleviation (Bahemuka *et al.*, 1998). Generally, indicators of poverty tend to vary with differences in conception and this has continued to characterise the type of interventions that governments and individuals put in place to avert or alleviate poverty. Nevertheless, most of the interventions have focussed on income as a primary indicator of poverty, in contrast to the major shift towards the social conception of poverty (Ikiara, 1999:301). The latter draws from the argument that the best approach is one that looks at what available incomes can do, rather than the quantities of these incomes (cf. Omosa, 2002).

According to the 2001 Poverty Reduction Strategy Paper (PRSP), economic growth is no longer a sufficient condition for a reduction in poverty. Instead, the PRSP puts emphasis on the need to integrate sector-based priorities so as to ensure that they are consistent with spurring economic growth and poverty reduction. The Paper further states that it will adopt a participatory approach with the primary aim of putting in place a people-centred set of policies and priorities, all geared towards achieving growth and a reduction in poverty levels (Kenya, 2001). This strategy is based on a new realisation on the part of government – that poverty is not just about being hungry and malnourished, lacking adequate shelter and housing or being illiterate. It is also about being exposed to ill-treatment and being powerless in influencing key decisions that affect one's life (World Bank, 2000; Kenya, 2001). In other words, because the poor lack voice, power and representation, they become more vulnerable to ill health, illiteracy, unemployment, disasters and violence. Accordingly, overcoming these vulnerabilities involves 'facilitating sustained and rapid economic growth, improving governance and security, increasing the ability of the poor to raise their income levels, improving the quality of life of the poor, and improving equity and participation' (Kenya, 2001:5).

CONCLUSION

We set out to provide an overview of Kenya's socio-economic environment. The foregoing discussions show that Kenya's socio-economic environment has been characterised by a general decline in economic performance. The structure of the economy has changed gradually with agriculture's contribution to GDP declining while the sector continues to dominate economic activities in rural Kenya. However, the rapid demographic changes occurring between 1960s and 1990s and lack of sustained increase in per capita income have impacted rather adversely on both the rural and urban areas of the country. Access to basic facilities, infrastructure and pressure on natural resources (including land and forests), and the slow response by the government to initiate radical reforms has created an uncertain environment for trade and commerce.

REFERENCES

Ayako, A. and Katumanga, M. 1997. *Review of Poverty in Kenya*. IPAR Special Reports Series. Nairobi: Institute of Policy Analysis and Research.

Bahemuka, J.M.; Nzioka, C.B.K. and Nganda, P. 1998. *Poverty Revisited: Analysis and Strategies Towards Poverty Eradication in Kenya.* Nairobi: UNESCO.

Hay, M.J. 1976. "Luo Women and Economic Change during the Colonial Period". In Hafkin, N.J. and Bay, E.G. (eds.). *Women in Africa: Studies in Social and Economic Change.* Stanford: Stanford University

Ikiara, G.K. 1999. "Economic Restructuring and Poverty in Kenya". In Ng'ethe, N. and Owino, W. (eds.). *From Sessional Paper No. 10 to Structural Adjustment: Towards Indigenising the Policy Debate.* Nairobi: Institute of Policy Analysis and Research.

Irandu, E. M. 2000. "Improving Railway Transport in Kenya: Policy Options and Achievements to Date". Regional Trade Analytical Agenda implemented by Technoserve –Kenya and ARD.

Kenya, Republic of.1966. *Development Plan 1966-70*. Nairobi: Government Printer.

Kenya, Republic of. 1969. *Population Census*. Nairobi: Ministry of Planning and National Development.

Kenya, Republic of. 1979. *Population Census*. Nairobi: Ministry of Planning and National Development.

Kenya, Republic of. 1986. *Sessional Paper No. 1 of 1986 on Economic Management for Renewed Growth*. Nairobi: Ministry of Planning and National Development.

Kenya, Republic of. 1989. *Population Census*. Nairobi: Ministry of Planning and National Development.

Kenya, Republic of. 1993. *Economic Survey*. Nairobi: Ministry of Planning and National Development.

Kenya, Republic of. 1994a. *Welfare Monitoring Survey II*. Nairobi: Central Bureau of Statistics, office of the Vice-President and Ministry of Planning and National Development.

Kenya, Republic of. 1994b. *Economic Survey*. Nairobi: Ministry of Finance and Planning.

Kenya, Republic of. 1995. *Economic Survey*. Nairobi: Ministry of Planning and National Development.

Kenya, Republic of. 1997a. *Welfare Monitoring Survey III*. Nairobi: Central Bureau of Statistics, office of the Vice-President and Ministry of Planning and National Development.

Kenya, Republic of. 1997b. *The Second Participatory Poverty Assessment Study*. Volume I. Nairobi: Ministry of Planning and National Development.

Kenya, Republic of. 1999a. *National Poverty Eradication Plan 1999-2015*. Nairobi: Government Printer.

Kenya, Republic of. 1999b. *Sessional Paper No. 3 of 1999 on National Poverty Eradication Plan 1999-2015*. Nairobi: Ministry of Planning and National Development.

Kenya, Republic of. 1999c. *Population and Housing Census*. Nairobi: Ministry of Finance and Planning.

Kenya, Republic of. 2000. *Second Report on Poverty in Kenya, Volume I ad II*. Nairobi: Ministry of Finance and Planning.

Kenya, Republic of. 2001. *Poverty Reduction Strategy Paper for the Period 2001-2004. Prepared by the People and Government of Kenya. Volume I*. Nairobi: Ministry of Finance and Planning.

Kenya, Republic of. 2002. *National Development Plan 2002-2008. Effective Management for Sustainable Economic Growth and Poverty Reduction*. Nairobi: Government Printer.

McCulloch, N. and Ota, M. 2002. "Export Horticulture and Poverty in Kenya". Working Paper No. 174. Sussex: Institute of Development Studies.

Mwega, F. and Ndung'u, N. 2002. "Explaining African Economic Growth Performance: The Case of Kenya". Draft Final Report Prepared for the AERC Collaborative Project on Explaining African Economic Performance. May 2002.

Omosa, M. 2002. "Export Horticulture and Livelihood Strategies: A Focus on the Opportunities and Constraints Facing Smallholder Farmers in Kenya". Sussex: Institute of Development Studies.

Onjala J. 1999. "Economic Growth and Development in Kenya since Independence". In Ng'ethe N. and Owino W. (eds.). *From Sessional Paper No.10 to Structural Adjustment: Towards Indigenizing the Policy Debate.* Nairobi: Institute of Policy Analysis and Research.

Onjala, J. 2003. *Managing Water Scarcity in Kenya: Industrial Response to Tariffs and Regulatory Enforcement.* Copenhagen: Institute for International Studies.

Wasike, S.K. Wilson. 2001. "Road Infrastructure Policies in Kenya: Historical Trends and Current Challenges". KIPPRA Working Paper No. 1, April 2001. Nairobi: Kenya Institute for Public Policy and Analysis.

World Bank. 2000. *Attacking Poverty: World Development Report 2000-2001.* Oxford University Press.

Chapter 5

Essential Services – Electricity and Water: The Challenges and Options for Business in Kenya

Joseph Onjala

INTRODUCTION

Infrastructure services are a basic ingredient to the business activities that promote growth and social development. According to the 1994 *World Development Report*, infrastructure capacity grows in concert with economic output. Other studies have also shown the close links between infrastructural costs and the overall production costs among businesses. For example, manufacturers can pay a high cost for intermittent and "dirty" electricity, and unreliable water supply. The adequacy of infrastructure helps determine one country's success and another's failure – in diversifying production, expanding trade, coping with population growth, reducing poverty, or improving environmental conditions. Good infrastructure raises productivity and lowers production costs, but it has to expand fast enough to accommodate growth (World Bank, 1994).

Providing infrastructure services to meet the demand of business, households, and other users is one of the major challenges of economic development. The availability of infrastructure has increased significantly in developing countries over the past several decades. However, because of low levels of access, infrastructure in developing countries is still driven primarily by issues of supply instead of demand. Furthermore, the full benefits of investments are not being realized, resulting in a serious waste of resources and loss in business opportunities. Creating the institutional and organisational conditions that oblige suppliers of infrastructure services to be more efficient and more responsive to the needs of business and other users is clearly a challenge.

In recent years, three converging forces have opened a window of opportunity for fundamental changes in the way infrastructure is provided. First, a consensus is emerging on a larger role for the private sector in infrastructure provision. Second, greater concern now exists for environmental sustainability and poverty reduction through provision of infrastructure services. Third, changes in the regulatory environment of infrastructure services have created new scope for participation of businesses in the provision of infrastructure competitively. Alongside these changes are new perceptions on the role of government in infrastructure provision. Despite these changes, access to physical infrastructure remains a critical challenge to business in many developing countries.

In this chapter, we examine the current state of Kenya's power, water and sanitation infrastructure. Even though the challenge of limited infrastructural support in Kenya cuts across many issues such as marketing, finance, technical information, quality and legal systems, this chapter focuses on the most prominent physical services, electricity and water. We begin by posing a number of questions: Does Kenya have adequate electricity and water services to stimulate and support the needed level of business activities? What are the challenges faced in the provision of these services? How can the requisite flow of these services be developed and what are the options for businesses in Kenya? Our conclusion is that, despite reforms in recent years, Kenya is still at a crossroads with regard to orientation of water and electricity services provision.

KENYA'S ENERGY SECTOR PROFILE

Kenya's energy sector is largely dominated by imported petroleum for the modern sector and wood fuel for rural communities, the urban poor and informal sector. The current domestic demand for petroleum fuels accounts for about 25.7% of the total import bill. In terms of energy supply, wood fuel provides about 68% of the total energy requirements, petroleum energy 20%, electricity 10% while other alternative sources account for 2% (Kenya, 2002:88). Compared with other parts of the world, traditional energy consumption stands out above that of Sub-Saharan Africa which averages 62.9 per cent and the World 8.2 per cent as shown in Table 5.1. Both the electricity consumption per capita and GDP per unit of energy use are also low compared to the same regions.

Table 5.1: *Access to Energy, 2000*

	Traditional Fuel Consumption	Electricity Consumption per capita (kilowatt hours)		GDP per Unit of energy use PPP US$ per kg of oil equivalent	
	1997	1980	2000	1980	2000
Kenya	80.3	92	106	1.0	1.9
Sub-Saharan Africa	62.9	463	457	-	2.9
World	8.2	1,442	2,156	2.1	4.5

Source: UNDP, Human Development Report, 2003. Millennium Development Goals: A Compact among Nations to End Human Poverty.

Alternative sources of energy in Kenya include solar, wind, power alcohol, biogas and bagasse. Though abundant, they are grossly under exploited, and currently contribute only a small fraction of the country's total energy requirements. The main challenge lies in their development and utilization on a wide scale. Petroleum exploration in the country started in 1954, and to date, 30 oil exploratory wells have been drilled. Some of these wells have shown some encouraging geological results, therefore, giving momentum for continued work in the fields.

THE STRUCTURE OF THE ELECTRIC POWER SECTOR IN KENYA

Electricity Supply

Kenya derives its electric power from hydro, thermal and geothermal sources. Electricity is supplied at 240 volts, 50 cycles single-phase and at 415 volts, 50 cycles three-phase. Other commonly used sources of power include solar power, biogas and wind energy. Hydro sources account for 624.5 MW (62%) of the total installed capacity while geothermal, thermal and imports from Uganda provides 57 MW (5%); 410.8 (35%) and 30 MW (3%) respectively. The effective capacity under normal hydrological conditions is 1000 MW. A breakdown of the trends in the structure of electricity supply is provided in Figure 5.1 and Table 5.2.

Independent Power Producers (IPP's), produce 10% of the electric power sold by Kenya Power and Lighting Company (KPLC). Currently, there are four licensed IPP's, namely: IberAfrica Power (Kenya) Ltd., Westmont Power (Kenya) Ltd., OrPower4 Inc and Tsavo Power Company. The first two have a combined capacity of 88 MW, with IberAfrica operating a diesel plant in Nairobi while Westmont operates a gas turbine plant in Mombasa. OrPower4 Inc., whose 64 MW plant is under construction, is the first IPP to develop a geothermal plant. Tsavo Power Company is currently developing a 74 MW diesel plant in Mombasa. The current installed interconnected capacity are Hydro[1] (60.8%), Thermal (34.3%), Geothermal (4.8 %) and Wind (0.0%).

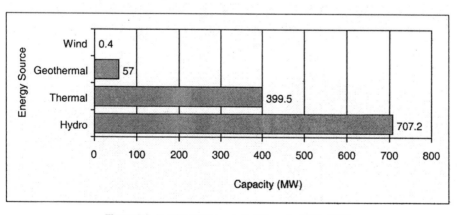

Figure 5.1: Installed Interconnected Capacity (MW), 2002

Source: Economic Survey, 2004

---

1   This includes the non-firm 30MW imports from Uganda.

Table 5.2: *Trends in Installed Capacity and Generation of Electricity 1997 – 2003*

Year	Installed Capacity in MW[1]				Generation in GWH[2]					
	Hydro	Thermal Oil	Geo-Thermal	Total	Hydro[3]	Thermal	IPP	Geo-Thermal	Wind	Total
1997	598.5	216.7	45.0	860.2	3,373.4	459.9	186.8	369.0	-	4,389.1
1998	594.5	217.2	45.0	856.7	3,497.6	280.8	391.4	388.6	0.2	4,558.6
1999	594.5	290.7	45.0	930.2	3,062.5	716.0	420.1	383.0	0.2	4,581.8
2000	674.5	427.9	58.0	1,159.4	1,793.8	1,201.1	816.7	367.1	0.2	4,178.9
2001	677.2	407.0	58.0	1,142.1	2,031.0	652.6	1,312.8	455.6	0.1	4,452.1
2002	677.2	407.0	58.0	1,142.2	3,070.9	279.8	887.5	447.2	0.4	4,685.8
2003	677.2	407.0	58.0	1,142.2	3,233.3	248.1	682.5	498.4	0.4	4,662.6

Includes generation for industrial establishment with generation capacity of over 100 KVA and Emergency Supply of 99MW by contracted generators
[1] *1 megawatt = million watts = 1,000 kilowatts.*
[2] *Gigawatt hour = 1,000,000 kilowatt hours.*
[3] *Includes imports from Uganda.*

Source: Various Economic Surveys

In addition to the interconnected system capacity by the principal power stations, there are a number of embedded generating plants mainly in the sugar belt (co-generating using bargasse). Kenya also has 9MW isolated generating capacity providing about 20GWh of energy to the off-grid towns of Garissa, Lamu, Lodwar, Mandera, Marsabit and Moyale.

Though Kenya presently has the largest installed hydro-electricity power resource base in East Africa, future implementation of large-scale hydro projects will not be as simple as it was in the past. First, there are few appropriate large scale hydro sites. Secondly, modern hydropower projects require much greater attention to environmental questions – and significantly, higher financial investments than in the past. As well, much attention must be paid to the social impacts – The Tiomin Project and Sondu Miriu's slow progress has shown how "social impacts" of large projects can affect implementation timetables. Finally, as the experience of the last few years has shown, hydropower availability is greatly decreased during extended periods of low rainfall. New investment to augment lines and transformer systems is needed. Kenya needs to shift its electricity base away from over-dependence on hydro sources to Geothermal and alternatives such as solar and wind power that are less prone to variability.

Transmission of Power

Kenya's electricity transmission network comprises 132 and 220 kV systems with total circuit lengths of 2,032 km and 885 km respectively as at June 30, 2001. For the corresponding period, the distribution network comprised 576 km for 66kV; 126 km for 40 kV; 4,639 km for 33 kV; and 10,397 km for 11 kV. Low voltage supply is at 415/240 volts. Losses within the distribution system are the major part of the problem and at 20 % on average, compared to only 8% in the Organisation for Economic Cooperation and Development (OECD). Part of the problem is technical, requiring new investment to augment lines and transformer systems. By far, the greater part of transmission losses has been due to business and metering problems with substantial theft of electricity. There have also been delays in the necessary investment to reduce transmission and distribution system losses. Another reason for the poor performance is the length of the transmission axis at low voltage (132kV) that leads to instability. End consumers also suffer from this deterioration in standards since fuel costs are passed through directly to them. It is conceivable that KPLC could reduce the level of overall system losses to 7.5%, the energy loss level that was the original target set in the 1996 Energy Sector Management Assistance Programme (ESMAP) study for the distribution systems where the major loss occurs. If this is done, it could reduce annual power purchase costs by as much as shs.3.0 billion (Mwangi, 2003).

Technical performance in generation and transmission of power remains generally weak, and in several respects, adversely affected by the operating environments. For example, performance has been hindered by low population densities and low loads. Performance at the distribution level, especially commercial and financial results have been disappointing. For example, system losses are relatively high. Much of this is attributable to a range of non-technical difficulties – thefts of power, problems with billing, metering, and recording. Losses within the distribution system are the major part of the supply problem as 20 % on average are lost every year.

The Structure of Energy Demand

Like many developing countries, Kenya has quasi dualistic economy: one part is modern and the other traditional. This dualism is an important determinant of Kenya's energy demand matrix. Wood fuel is the predominant energy source in the traditional (rural) sector. The modern sector (commerce, industry and urban consumers) depends largely on fossil fuels and electricity and constitutes the largest energy user. Transport is the second largest energy end-user in the Kenyan economy, and the largest single user of petroleum products. The manufacturing sector is the third largest energy end-user in the Kenyan economy. Over 60 per cent of the energy consumption in the manufacturing sector is accounted for by only two sources: wood fuel and residential fuel oil. On average, the proportion of energy used by this sector stood at about 14 percent of the entire economy's consumption in the second half of the 1990s. The commercial sector is the smallest energy-using sector in the economy, accounting for only about 5 per cent of the country's consumption. Demand for electricity is outgrowing available supplies in Kenya and the region.

Access to Electricity

As at 30 June 2001, Kenya had 537,079 electricity consumers comprising 465,365 KPLC customers and 71,718 Rural Electrification Fund customers. This translates to about 10% of the population who have taken up supply of electricity and an estimated 15% of the population with access to electricity. Figure 5.2 shows electricity access by region and economic status.

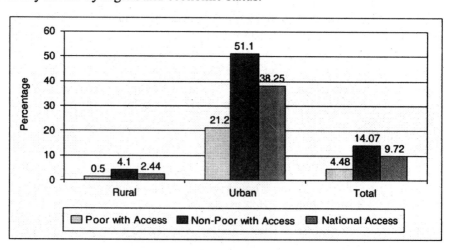

Figure 5.2: Households with Access to Electricity for Lighting, 2000

Source: Kenya, 2000

The provision of electricity in the rural areas is undertaken through the Rural Electrification Program (REP). Rural Electrification Program (REP) was initiated in 1974 to supply electricity to the rural areas of Kenya. It was motivated by the need to provide electricity where households are more dispersed than in urban areas, hence comparatively higher costs of electrification. The aim was to spur industrial processing and other forms of off-farm income generation activities that would hopefully impact positively on agriculture through capital flows and adoption of improved farming technologies. Since its inception, about KES 5 billion in capital has been spent on the program (Kenya, 2001).

At issue is the weak commitment of the KPLC to expand access in rural areas. Since 1998, partial funding for the REP has been drawn from a levy on consumers of electricity of 5% of units consumed. The KPLC is responsible for collection of the levy. The KPLC also acts as managing agent for the Government in the implementation of REP schemes. The REP operates as a subsidy on capital costs and consumption since the government subsidizes operating costs and has a uniform national tariff policy. Rural electrification presents particular problems to grid-based utilities because investments in grid expansion for low population density areas represent large financial risks. Moreover, investments in areas that are unsupported by industrial or commercial activity also increase the risk of the utility. It is not surprising therefore that the KPLC has a bias towards electrifying high population density areas with significant amount of economic activity.

Kenya's rate of electrification can be put into perspective by comparing it with those achieved in other countries/regions given in Figure 5.3. As at the end of 2001, South Africa is reported to have 66% electrification, a level achieved with connection of 2.5 million households since 1995 under ANC's Reconstruction and Development Programme following the country's independence. By the year 2001, Ghana had achieved 80% electrification, well above the average for Sub Saharan Africa of 20%.

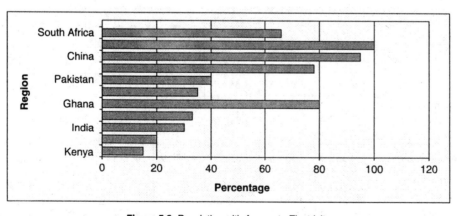

Figure 5.3: Population with Access to Electricity

Source: Kariuki (2003)

Kenya's current level of access to electricity can at best be described as meager and at the current rate of electrification (6-7%), it is unlikely that a significant proportion of the population will access and take supply of electricity in the near future. In order to enhance electrification in Kenya, alternative approaches to grid extension and off-grid systems must be considered. New renewable technologies would be expected to play an increasing role. Nevertheless, serious legal, policy issues e.g. taxation, tariffs, subsidy, etc., remain to be overcome. Other issues that remain to be overcome are technical and institutional (Kariuki, 2003).

The need to expand access to power beyond the currently low levels is obvious. However, rural and peri-urban electrification is typically not commercially attractive. Lack of electricity power sources for rural energy implies that farmers cannot add value to their crops, industries cannot develop, small towns cannot grow and economies are stifled due to lack of modern power sources i.e. electricity for commerce and institutions. Without electricity, there can be no computers, internet, televisions, and adequate lighting. How are the businesses to thrive or compete with those in the major towns?

Demand for Electricity

Table 5.3 provides details of trends in electricity demand in Kenya. Most of the consumption is by commercial and industrial establishments, institutions and households. Large and medium consumers have the highest electricity demand. This is followed by domestic, small commercial and small industrial consumers.

Table 5.3: *Electricity Energy Supply and Demand Balance, 1997-2002 (Million KWH)*

Demand	1997	1998	1999	2000	2001	2002	2003
Domestic & Small Commercial, small industrial	1,165.8	1,212.6	1,256.8	1,065.6	1,282.2	1,262.9	1,283.0
Commercial Industrial (large)	2,261.4	2,137.3	2,180.8	2,061.8	2,181.3	2,277.9	2,305.0
Off-peak	89.2	86.7	84.9	59.8	57.5	60.5	59.0
Street Lighting	11.2	10.1	10.7	8.8	5.4	6.4	7.0
Rural Electrification	144.1	155.1	152.0	124.7	128.4	134.3	153.2
Total	3,671.7	3,601.8	3,685.2	3,320.7	3,654.8	3,742.0	3,807.2
Transmission losses & unallocated demand	717.4	956.8	896.6	858.2	683.6	943.6	855.1
Demand = Supply	4,389.1	4,558.6	4,581.8	4,178.9	4,338.4	4,685.6	4,662.3
Imports from Uganda	149.5	138.9	149.6	220.5	113.7	238.4	189.4
Net generation	4,239.6	4,419.7	4,432.2	3,958.4	4,224.7	4,447.2	4,472.9

Source: Kenya Power and Lighting Company

On the end-use side, Figure 5.4 shows six major industrial activities. The leading energy consumer is cement manufacturing, which takes about 70 per cent of the energy used in industry. Thus, the key characteristics of energy use in Kenyan industry are: (i) industry are dependent on a wide range of energy sources; (ii) the sector is the only consumer of coal; (iii) the end-user activities are considerably diverse; and (iv) cement manufacturing accounts for 70 percent of the industrial energy used.

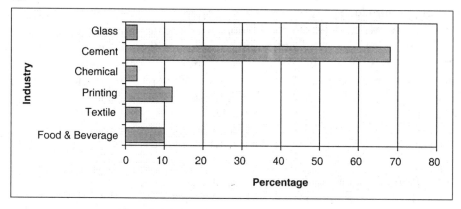

Figure 5.4: Industrial Eenergy Consumption in Kenya

Note: Glass includes clay and potter metal, and metal fabrication, non-metal and miscellaneous; printing and publishing, pulp and paper, chemical and fertilizers, rubber and plastic. Source: Nyoike, (1993).

Power demand is expected to grow from 843 MW in 2002/03 to 1202 MW in 2007 while energy demand is estimated to rise from 4,632 GWH to 6,713 GWH representing a 6.4% mean growth per annum. To meet the growing demand, additional generating projects, namely, Olkaria II (64MW), Olkaria III (36MW) and Sondu Miriu (60MW) are to be completed and commissioned, adding a total capacity of 160MW to the national grid. The number of customers under the REP grew by 9.9 percent from 61,436 in 1998/99 to 67,542 in 1999/2000, to 77,060 in 2001 and 91,069 in 2003 (Kenya, 2004).

The REP has had little impact partly because of high capital costs. Other rural electrification programmers are sub-sector or commodity based, mainly funded by donors. There are three on-going donor funded projects under the rural electrification programme including the Coffee Factories Rural Electrification Programme (COFREP) which is funded by the stabilization of exports (STABEX) Fund from the European Union. This program aims to increase the total number of coffee factories served with electricity. By end of 2003, out of the targeted 168 factories under the first phase of COFREP, 84 factories were electrified at a cost of Kshs. 230 million. A further 60 coffee factories were declared ineligible on account of being on electricity supply. There are 24 factories that have not been electrified. The end of these projects is expected to usher in the implementation of additional projects under Phase II of USD 10.3 million. Besides, the government is currently exploring a new rural electrification strategy that proposes the creation of an autonomous agency to increase efficiency and speed of electrification in the rural areas.

THE POLICIES AND STRUCTURAL CHANGES IN ELECTRIC POWER SECTOR

The Kenya Government policy is to provide electricity to all parts of the country in order to cover as many people as possible. Reform efforts in the electricity sector has sought to introduce private sector participation and at the same time entrenched the main state owned generation and transmission enterprise at the centre of the power sector. Also, the state entities are the sole purchaser of privately generated electricity under long-term power purchase contracts with exclusivity clauses. As a result, the state remains central and dominant in the electricity sector. Below is a table summarizing significant changes in the power sector in the last ten years.

Table 5.4: *A Chronology of Significant events in Kenya's Power Sector*

Period	Events
October, 1996	The energy sector is liberalized
December, 1997	• *The Electric Power Act (Cap 314),* and *The Electric Supply Lines Act (Cap 315)* are repealed. • *The Electric Power Act,* 1997 is enacted. • The Electricity Regulatory Board established by law.
Jan/Feb, 1999	ERB commences operations.
Mar-May, 1999	Long rains fail resulting in minimal recharge; hence hydro-generation derived mainly from dam storage
June, 1999	Application by KPLC for a general upward adjustment of tariffs
July, 1999	ERB holds public hearings on objections to upward tariff adjustment, but grants KPLC's application.
August, 1999	Revised tariffs come into effect.
Sep/October, 1999	Short rains fail necessitating greater conservation of dam storage.
November, 1999	Partial rationing of electricity instituted countrywide.
Mar-May, 2000	Long rains fail yet again greatly reducing hydro-generation.
May, 2000	Electricity rationing intensified as the hydrology conditions deteriorate into a national emergency.
Jan 2003	In its effort to accelerate system losses reduction, KPLC appointed a System Reduction Team in 2003.
June 2003-2004	The Ministry of Energy has initiated the process of preparing a new National Energy Policy covering the period 2004-2023. The policy document, which is in the final stages of preparation, is expected to provide a more investor friendly fiscal, regulatory and legal regime of the energy sector. This is aimed at attracting private investors, lowering costs of production, increasing exploitation of indigenous resources and providing access to energy.

Adapted from Nyang (2000)

The Electric Power sub-sector has been restructured, among other things, to attract private investment and improve operational facility. A competitive environment is also being created to enable improvement of efficiency through private sector participation in power generation on the basis of what is commonly known as build-own-operate (BOO) arrangements. In the late 1990s, the Kenya government split Kenya Power and Lighting Company (KPLC) into three entities: a power generator (KenGen), a distributor (KPLC) and a regulator – the Electricity Regulatory Board (ERB) – to regulate retail tariffs and approve power purchase contracts between KPLC and producers. The government also licensed two independent power producers to sell electricity to the grid. Although KenGen appears to be a model of technical expertise and energy generation, non-payment of bills and accounts by the Kenya government and KPLC have adversely affected the operations of all entities, particularly KPLC.

Following enactment of a new electricity law by Parliament in 1997, the Government appointed the Electricity Regulatory Board. The new Electric Power Act (1997) provides an effective legal and regulatory framework within which both the regulatory body and economic players in the sub-sector will operate. The reforms in power sub-sector since 1997 have seen entry of five Independent Power Producers (IPPS) with current capacity of 187.5 MW. Four IPPS namely, Ibera Africa, Westmont, Mumias Sugar Company and Tsavo Power Company, are in thermal generation while the fifth one Orpower4 is exploiting geothermal energy. As a result, total installed capacity has expanded since the reform process started. Despite reforms in recent years, Kenya is still at a crossroads with regard to access and efficiency in the provision of water and electricity.

THE ROLE OF NEW RENEWABLE TECHNOLOGIES IN ENHANCING ELECTRIFICATION IN KENYA

Although New and Renewable Technologies do not feature in Kenya's electricity generation plans, these technologies have potential for complementing the conventional sources of generation, thereby enhancing electrification. Considering that in many cases grid electrification is simply uneconomical in some parts of the country, the potential role of new renewable technologies in off-grid electrification can be substantial. The new renewable technologies with potential for production of electric power include biomass, small (mini and micro) hydro, wind, municipal waste, landfill gas and solar photovoltaic.

Small Hydro Plants

Small hydro systems (mini and micro) capture the energy in flowing water and convert it to electricity. Systems can be either run-of-the-river or with pondage. Micro hydropower is not new in Kenya. Prior to the 1960s, micro hydro was used to power grain mills. These outdated systems were quickly outpaced by the diesel engine for milling grain. Today, improved technology makes micro hydropower economically viable in many situations.

Box 5.1: Micro Hydro Unit in Kirinyaga District

One case example of a micro hydro power plant in Kirinyaga district, was built by a retired policeman in his rural home, which located close to a small waterfall. Water was diverted from the main waterfall into a small reservoir (dug-out hole), and channelled through a wooden tunnel to drive a wooden water wheel. The plant was locally manufactured and the estimated cost of setting up the plant was about US$ 400. The water wheel provides both motive and electric power. A number of business activities have been initiated using the motive and shaft power provided by the hydro plant – they include wood sawing, lathing, grinding, carpentry, battery charging, welding and running a posho mill.

The micro hydro plant has contributed to business expansion not only for the owner, but for the surrounding community. Additional financial and technical support is however required, in order to scale-up the activities that can be undertaken, as well as ensure proper construction, and maintenance of the plant.

AFREPREN Newsletter No.36 May, 2004 p. 2

Accordingly, unless with significant pondage, the output of these plants vary widely and low (of the order of 30%) load factors are common-place. It is therefore important that adequate data on hydrology be gathered. Like wind turbines, small hydro plants are connected on weak networks, and therefore raise similar concerns on power quality.

The Intermediate Technology Development Group – East Africa (ITDG-EA), worked closely with the Tungu-Kabiri community in developing and carrying out the micro hydropower scheme. About 200 members of this 300-household community came together to form a commercial enterprise. The Ministry of energy provided technical support. As a result, the micro enterprises already benefiting include shops, battery charging, a welding unit, and beauty salon.

Biomass Power Plants

Biomass utilizes the energy content of agricultural residue, wood waste, animal wastes or energy crops. These materials are either combusted in boilers to produce steam and/or heat, or converted into combustible gases and subsequently used to generate electricity. An example of application of this technology in Kenya is the combustion of bagasse to generate electricity in the sugar belt. When well structured, bagasse projects can provide competitive power. "Mumias Sugar Factory is contributing a capacity of 2MW to the national power grid and has the potential for expanding production." The other Sugar Factories with similar electricity potential from bargasse that are waiting to be tapped include Muhoroni, South Nyanza, Miwani and Chemelil Sugar Factories. Out of the bagasse produced from these industries, only 54% is utilized per year as fuel for the generation of steam for the milling processes. The power sector is not fully liberalized so as to attract investments in power generation by sugar companies as profitable venture. It will be necessary to change the current legal framework to allow the sugar companies to invest in power generation.

Solar Photovoltaic Generation

Solar photovoltaic energy is widely used for provision of electricity in off grid rural areas for low power generation. It is estimated that 4 MW of photovoltaic power is installed in the country (Kenya, 2004). Kenya has an active commercial Solar Home Systems (SHS) market, with cumulative sales in excess of 150,000 units and current sales of over 20,000 systems per year. To date, more than 3.2 MW of amorphous and crystalline silicon have been installed and the PV industry is worth US$ 6 million new installations per year (500kW/year). There are hundreds of PV businesses in terms of manufacturers, vendors, installers, and after-sales providers active in the market (Agumba and Osawa, 2004).

The demand for PV has grown exponentially since the mid 1980s courtesy of private entrepreneurs. More than 15 companies based in Nairobi currently supply the market through scores of agents based in the rural areas that market, install and maintain the systems. Amorphous silicon systems currently dominate the market with an overall average system size of 25Wp. Potential demand is estimated at 25 MWp and is predominantly SHS. Market constraints include lack of favourable policies, missing credits lines, lack of enforceable standards, low quality Balance of Systems Components and low consumer awareness. PV systems can potentially electrify 40% of rural households in an economical way. Technical support and strategic financing are key to strengthening PV infrastructure and reaching rural households. Below are the Salient characteristics of the market (Agumba and Osawa, 2004):

- All solar modules are imported. There is no local manufacture. These come with varying warranties.

- Average system size stands at 25Wp with an average purchase expenditure of US$418.

- More than 50 % of the systems use a-Si modules with a majority of the systems undersized for their loads.

- Over 90% of the a-Si systems do not use charge regulators.

- Over 90% of the systems use locally manufactured SLI or modified SLI ('solar') batteries.

- Of all the 'Solar and TV" batteries sold to rural Kenya, 30 % are SLI, while 70% are modified automotive batteries.

- All battery manufacturers currently offer a one-year warranty.

- Over 85 % of the systems power black and white TVs, 84% power lights, while 70% power radios/cassettes.

- Users are from a wide range of backgrounds, but most have regular incomes. The majority of users buy systems to run B&W TV, lights and radio together, as opposed to lights only.

- Customers save up to $ 10 monthly on kerosene, dry cells and battery charging expenditures.

THE STATUS AND MAIN FEATURES OF WATER SUPPLY IN KENYA

Kenya is mainly an agricultural country with an expanding economy whose basic element for development is water. Kenya is facing a complex situation water resources supply and use because of three legacies (Mogaka et al, 2003).

First, there is a natural legacy: an extremely limited per capita endowment of freshwater resources and high hydrological variability, both temporally and spatially. The annual quantity of renewable fresh water resources is estimated at 20.2 billion m^3 comprising 19.59 m^3 of surface water and 0.62 billion m^3 of ground water. The amount of water actually available for utilisation in any one year (among other factors) depends on the rate of run-off, the aridity of the catchment area and the methods of interception at various points in the hydrological cycle. Given the country's population of over 29 million people, per capita supply is approximately 696 m^3 /person per year, which makes Kenya a water scarce country since the global benchmark is 1,000 m^3 /person per year.

Secondly, Kenya has a management legacy from the recent past which is characterized by, on the one hand, rapidly growing demand for water for most sectoral uses and, on the other hand, diminution of natural storage capacity (wetlands, catchments and aquifer recharge areas) and a lack of development of artificial storage capacity (dams and reservoirs) to meet demand. Third, the country has a colonial legacy whereby national boundaries were drawn without regard for geographic or social realities. Consequently, Kenya shares over half of its rivers, lakes, and aquifers with neighbouring nations.

Precipitation across parts of Kenya is exceptionally variable and unpredictable, and runoff is exceptionally low (varying from near zero in the north-eastern part of the country to over 1600mm/yr in the western part of the country). The consequence of these two features is endemic drought in large parts of the country. Throughout Kenya, even within the same districts, there is an enormous variance in water amounts. Because of pronounced differences in average annual rainfall, evapo-transpiration, and hydrogeology, there is high variability within the same season, between different seasons i.e. twelve-month period, and over several years. Existing studies have used "water collection time" to characterize rainfall variability across the country (Kenya, 1996). Figures 5.5, and 5.6 illustrate the temporal variations of water nationally, in rural areas and urban areas respectively. The illustration in figure 5.5 shows that for consumers who spend 5-30 minutes to fetch water, their proportion decreases during dry season. On the other hand, for consumers who spend more than 30 minutes to fetch water, the proportion increases during dry season. This suggests an upward shift in the proportion of Kenyans who switch from 5-30 minutes time range to over 30 minutes collecting water.

In the rural areas, a large number of homesteads are still far from water points, especially those in the low - potential areas where rivers are mainly seasonal. On the other hand, groundwater resources are either limited or undeveloped. Although ample water resources may exist, the patterns of use and accessibility may be a serious problem. The level of coverage goes down as low as 20 per cent during the dry seasons when seasonal water sources often dry up, making distances to water long and often exceeding 5 kilometres (Kenya, 1996).

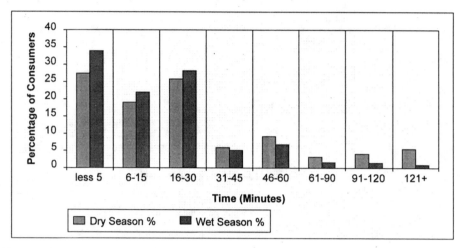

Figure 5.5: Temporal Variations in the Availability of Water in Kenya: Dry and Wet Season Time Shifts, 2001

Note: Graphs derived from the Welfare Monitoring Survey II, 1994, Basic Report. Central Bureau of Statistics, Office of the Vice-President and Ministry of Planning and National Development - Kenya, May 1996.

Within the urban areas, the main reasons for shifts in time taken in sourcing water are;

(i) the low service coverage and inability of the local water authorities to sustain supplies of piped water to all segments of the towns where there is reduced supply pressure in dry season. Hence, more consumers have to fetch their piped water from alternative sources and often-contaminated locations,

(ii) in some of the towns, there is increased concentration of piped water users to inferior alternative sources (such as boreholes, nearby rivers) even during wet seasons, due to unreliability (caused by bursts etc) of piped water supply.

The hydrological variability causes significant economic losses. Kenya lacks the buffering capacity to deal with the shocks of too much or too little rainfall. Kenya has not considered investments in buffering capacity as a strategic part of its development planning. Impacts of past and recent droughts and floods have been so severe that, within a few months, they have undone years of economic growth, devastated and possibly contributed to increased poverty. Kenya has not invested adequately in the water storage capacity needed to meet increasing demand and provide a buffer against floods and droughts. Consequently, Kenya's per capita total water storage for all uses in now extremely low by the standards of other countries that are subjected to variable climate.

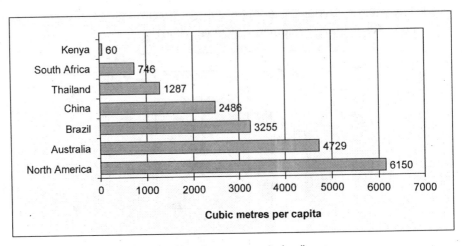

Figure 5.6: Water Storage per capita for all uses

Source: Mogaka et al., 2003

Access to Water

Results from Multiple Indicator Cluster Survey (MICS) and Kenya Demographic and Health Survey 1989, 1993 and 1998 show that there has been no improvement in access to safe drinking water in the past decade. Most of the Kenyan population drink unsafe water from unprotected wells, springs, etc. However, access to safe water is more a rural than an urban problem. The 2000 MICS reports an overall rural access rate to improved water source of 44% compared to 90% in urban areas. At the national level, in 2000, only 48% had access to improved water source (Kenya, MDG Report, 2003).

Current estimates indicate that about 65% and 30% of Kenya's urban and rural populations respectively have access to but declining safe drinking water. According to a World Bank Survey in 2001, there were approximately 742,000 water connections in about 680 piped systems in Kenya (World Bank, 2001)[1]. In addition, there were over 350 community run water schemes in Kenya, though, a good percentage of the connections were inactive due to poor maintenance. There were 1,800 water supplies that were operational out of which about 1,000 were public operated schemes. Non-Governmental Organisations, Self-help Groups and communities ran the rest. There existed about 1,782 small dams and 669 water pans of which 1,183 were operational and 1,168 silted but operational; 100 had dried up or had been abandoned. In addition, there existed about 9,000 boreholes, the majority of which require rehabilitation or replacement. The demand for water supply and sewerage facilities has been outstripping the development of the same.

1　In this context, access to improved water sources refers to the percentage of the population with reasonable access to an adequate amount of water from an improved source, such as household connection, public stand-pipe, bore hole, protected well or spring, and rainwater collection. Reasonable access is defined as the availability of at least 20 litres per person a day from a source within one kilometre of dwelling.

In all regions of Kenya, piped water, wells and boreholes, rivers and springs have been the main sources of water used by the majority of the households. A survey conducted in 1988 (Kenya Demographic Health Survey, 1989), showed that about 30.7 percent of the population used piped water as their main source of water compared to 32.1 percent in 1994. Another 36.8 percent used rivers in 1988 compared to 24.9 percent in 1994. About 37 and 25 percent of Kenyans obtained their water directly from rivers in 1988 and 1994. The 31 and 32 percent who used piped water in 1988 and 1994 obtained it directly from rivers. In total, about 68 and 67 percent of Kenyans obtained their water from rivers either directly or indirectly in 1988 and 1994 respectively. These figures illustrate the importance of surface water as the main source of clean water to Kenyans. There are significant regional variations in access to water resources. In some regions, only a mere 9% of the population has access to piped water while in Nairobi, more than 90% have access to piped water.

Compared to other regions of the world, access to water in Kenya is slightly lower than that of Sub-Saharan Africa, though the above average is higher. Table 5.5 details these comparisons.

Table 5.5: *Access to Water and Sanitation, 2000*

	Population with sustainable access to an improved water source					Urban population with access to improved sanitation	
	Rural (%)		Urban (%)		Total		
	1990	2000	1990	2000	2000	1990	2000
Kenya	31	42	91	88	57	91	96
Sub-Saharan Africa	39	44	86	83	57	75	74
World	-	71	-	95	82	-	85

Source: UNDP, Human Development Report, 2003. Millennium Development Goals: A Compact among Nations to end human poverty.

Sanitation

The results of 2000 MICS showed that 81.1% of Kenyans had sanitary means of excreta disposal (flush toilet and pit latrine), comprising a high 94.8 per cent in urban areas and 76.6 percent in rural areas. Even though a simple or traditional pit latrine is typically not acceptable in urban areas, if traditional pit latrine was not retained in urban areas as an improved category of sanitation, the urban coverage of improved sanitation in Kenya will fall to 47 per cent (Kenya, 2003). Thus, about 11 million people have no access to decent sanitation services in Kenya (Pricewaterhouse Coopers, 2003)2. About 2 million people in urban areas are

---

2   Considered to be excreta disposal facilities, private or shared that can effectively prevent human, animal and insect contact with excreta

connected to 35 sewerage systems (about 145,000 connections), with the remainder of the population relying mostly on pit latrines and septic tanks.

Industrial / Commercial Water Demand

In the total use of public water in Kenya, the industry is still a minor user, only consuming 4% of the public water supply. The relatively small industrial water use however masks substantial differences in the industrial water consumption and its impact on the water resources. In all the urban areas, the manufacturing industry consumes 13% of the public water and in the large urban centres, the industrial consumption is much higher i.e. in Nairobi (39%), Nakuru (26%), Kisumu (22%), Thika (23%), and Eldoret (17%) as the illustration in Figure 5.7 shows (Onjala, 2002c). However even these figures underestimate the impact of the industrial/commercial water use because in addition to the public water, many of the large industries consume large amounts of water from the rivers and private boreholes (about half of the industrial firms use water from rivers and own boreholes). Secondly, many industries send polluted effluents into the rivers thereby degrading water resources on which the population downstream is dependent.

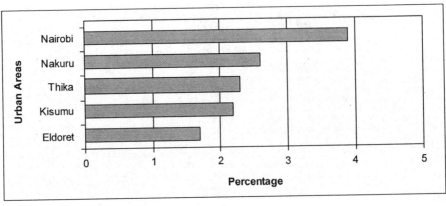

Figure 5.7: Water Consumption by Industries in Selected Urban Areas (Kenya)

Source: Onjala, (2002c)

Institutional and Regulatory Arrangements

The Ministry of Water Resources Management and Development, the National Water Conservation and Pipeline Company (NWCPC), and the local authorities are the main players in the WSS sector. The ministry runs approximately 630 piped systems (280,000 connections), while the NWCPC runs 40 piped systems (approximately 230,000 connections). Ten municipalities (Nairobi, Nakuru, Kisumu, Eldoret, Kericho, Nanyuki, Nyeri, Kitale, Thika, and Nyahururu) are responsible for a further 230,000 connections, over 160,000 of these in Nairobi. The Ministry is responsible for overall policy formulation and currently, has the main regulatory roles. The policies were reinforced by the enactment of the 2002 Water Act. The Act provides for a Water Services Regulatory Board to be established as the national regulator, Water Services Boards (WSB) to be set up with responsibility for the provision of WSS in defined areas, Water Service Providers to act on a delegated agency basis for the WSBs and a Water Appeals Board to provide dispute resolution between various parties.

THE CHALLENGES OF PROVIDING WATER AND SANITATION SECTOR

Provision of water and sanitation services remains a major challenge in Kenya largely due to inadequate provision and poor management of existing facilities. A particularly important area that has suffered from inadequate budget allocation is the water resources assessment. Flow monitoring stations have been severely neglected during the 1990s because of lack of funds for maintenance. Even where the stations were operational, there were insufficient funds to obtain readings. By 2001, 78 per cent of the registered stations were not operational (Mogaka et al, 2003). This general neglect of the hydro-meteorological data network makes it impossible to carry out meaningful water resources planning, design, and management. Consequently, water allocation and abstraction decisions and investment decisions are based on inadequate data, exacerbating the conflicts over water use and access.

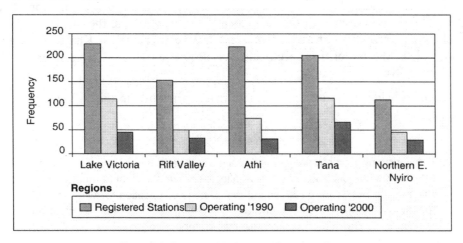

Figure 5.8: Operational Hydrometric Stations in Kenya

Source: Mogaka et al., 2003

While most urban centres in Kenya have functional facilities, the level of service has not been as expected and most of these systems are in dire need of rehabilitation and augmentation to meet the rising demands. There are still quite a number of urban centres that require development of new sanitation facilities, as the existing ones can no longer cope up with the demand. The Sessional Paper No. 1 of 1999 on National Policy on Water Resources Management and Development currently guides water resource management. The overall goal of the national water development policy is to facilitate provision of water in sufficient quantity and quality and within a reasonable distance to meet all competing uses in a sustainable, rational and economical way. The declining public resources for investment in new water projects, operation and maintenance have diminished the role of the public sector in the provision of water. These have been exacerbated by cyclical droughts that have plagued the country in the past three decades.

Unreliable and Low Service Coverage in Urban Areas

The urban water utilities are able to meet only a small portion of the total water demand within their jurisdiction. The range varies between 39-88% and the rest of the consumers have to go without adequate water or find alternative water. Nevertheless, Nairobi City, in spite of its inability to account for nearly 50% of its water is still able to service 88% of the residents in formal settlements (Onjala, 2002b). Water supply remains a problem for residents of informal settlements who do not have water directly connected to them. A majority of these dwellers get their water from the private water providers, while other sources of water include boreholes, rain water and river water (Kiura, 2005)[3]. In other parts of Nairobi there are private water companies responsible for supplying water (example of Runda Water Company supplying Runda Estate).

Urban Water Demand in Kenya: The Delicate Balance

There are two delicate scenarios that necessitate balancing of the urban water provision in Kenya today. First, traditionally, urban water supply entails imports of large volumes of water from the rural areas. For many years, the need to balance development in both rural and urban areas has been critical in Kenya. The rural sector, where the majority of Kenyans live, is the agricultural base which is the backbone of Kenyan economy.

The need to balance rural-urban water transfers arise due to the following factors (Onjala, 2002a).

A major problem confronting policy makers in Kenya is that growth of urban areas has so far occasioned water re-allocation from the rural to urban areas. The existing pattern of development that implies competition for water would appear to undermine the long-term development goals of creating rural-urban balance since the rural areas themselves do not have adequate supplies of clean water.

The challenge of balancing water allocation between urban and rural constituencies remains real for Kenya. For example, while water transfers across competing uses create positive externalities in the urban areas to which water is being moved, the negative externalities in the source areas include reduced water supplies for other water right holders, diminished economic activity, lower river flows and groundwater tables, and consequent degradation of water quality, wildlife habitat, and recreation opportunities.

---

3 Kiura C. Munene (2005). New Ecosystems Approaches to Human Health Program Initiate, Nairobi City Report. Prepared for International Development Research Centre (IDRC).

Box: 5.2 Competing Water Usage in the Economy

Kenya's water resources balance carries significant social, economic (business), and political risks. Growing water demand over a limited endowment of water generates competition and causes conflict over water use, posing considerable social risks to the poor and communities without adequate representation in the allocation decision making. The boom in Kenya's horticulture industry – cut flowers and vegetables – has been attributed to many factors, including favourable market conditions for the outputs, entrepreneurship and a very aggressive approach at harnessing and utilizing water. What is less recognized is that this has often been at the expense of other uses and users of water through unsustainable water allocation practices.

.Mogaka et al, 2003.

ELECTRICITY AND WATER IN KENYA: THE NEED FOR BUSINESS ORIENTATION IN SERVICE PROVISION

Electricity and water must be conceived of as "service industry" providing goods that meet business needs. Such a commercial orientation contrasts sharply with the situation in Kenya where water and electricity utilities suffer from multiple and conflicting objectives. Service providers have little motivation to satisfy business needs or to achieve a reasonable efficiency in order to minimize transaction costs for business. Typical services provision are subject to unreliable service flow, long queues in paying bills and slow response in dealing with consumer complaints. There is lack of well-focused performance objectives conducive to business activities.

Affordability and Reliability of Electricity

The cost of electrifying rural areas where households are more dispersed than in urban areas is comparatively higher. Part of the high electricity tariffs are due to high transmission losses attributed to technical and commercial losses and accounting for 20-30% of the energy costs. Consumers in Kenya also experience high customer tariffs due to a levy to help pay for generation from petroleum based imports, a rural electrification levy that has not worked, and small consumers have been charged for large consumers who have not paid their bills. Even in areas where electricity has been supplied, there are still problems of frequent breakdowns due to a surge in power demand. These frequent power failures affect the industries and small enterprises especially. In the years 1999 and 2000, Kenya faced an unprecedented power shortage, the immediate cause of which was the reduction in hydro-generation as a result of low water levels in the reservoirs. The country had experienced low rainfall for three consecutive seasons starting with the 1999 failed long rains. The reduced hydro-generation capacity compelled KPLC to implement a lead shedding program from November 1999, which was intensified in May 2000 due to persistent drought. The electricity power shortage is, however, not entirely due to poor hydrology. The country's inability to attain the planned installed capacity has been due, among other things, to the withholding of donor support between 1991 and 1998, and the power deficit exacerbated by the growth in demand for electricity.

Problems of Water Management

A number of problems afflict the institutional environment for industrial water management in Kenya. The physical conditions and the challenges highlighted introduce complexity in the institutional arrangement required to manage water service delivery. These factors compound the high transaction costs and uncertain conditions imposed upon business firms by the water authorities through flawed regulatory measures. Efforts have been made to regulate surface and groundwater withdrawals through licensing restrictions for wells or through spacing norms to maintain ecological sustainability. However:

- Issuance of surface and ground water permits is lengthy, involving lengthy processing of applications. This often takes months and in some cases years, thereby frustrating the industrial applicants.

The borehole completion records currently filed in the Groundwater Section of MENR would be the basic data for future groundwater resources management. Of the nearly 10,000 boreholes in Kenya, only 11% have some water quality data logged on the MENR database. Most of the data represents those tested at the time of initial drilling, but no testing has been undertaken for most of the boreholes since then. The scarcity of existing data makes it quite difficult to meaningfully assess the groundwater quality in the country.

Efficiency in water service delivery has serious bearing on productivity and corporate profitability of firms. Deficiencies in the public water supply and sanitation force more and more households, commercial enterprises and industrial units to make their own arrangements. The nature of the urban water problem in Kenya is such that, there are many seasonal shortages and cuts and the areas in which business are located (far from residential areas) are the hardest hit. The absence of clean water, and the exclusionary practices through which such water systems result, can undermine business environment and compromise the quality of services provided by businesses.

As noted earlier, all the water utilities are able to meet only a small portion of the total water demand within their jurisdiction. The Local Authorities are characterised by high unaccounted-for water (UFW). About 40-70 per cent of the water produced is lost during transmission and distribution as a result of old pipes that are neither properly maintained nor replaced; and illegal connections. There is high (inverse) correlation between water service coverage and unaccounted for water. This implies that most water authorities could improve service coverage by minimizing unaccounted-for water (UFW).

Table 5.7: *Comparison of Water Sector Performance in Sub-Saharan Africa*

	Kenya		C'D'Ivoire	Senegal	Ghana	Uganda
	NWCPC	Nairobi				
1990 GNP per Capita	360	360	710	510	390	320
Unaccounted for Water	40%	50%	18%	25%	55%	47%
Staff/1000 connections	6.2	16.2	3.3	5	17.7	30
Tariff level (US$/m3)	0.40	0.40	0.50	0.56	0.27	0.73

Source: World Bank Kenya Review of WSS Sector 2001

MEETING THE CHALLENGES OF ESSENTIAL SERVICES FOR BUSINESS IN KENYA

We have examined the challenges posed to business by electricity and water services in Kenya. The inability of the public sector to provide an adequate level of these services has forced individual firms to devise their own coping mechanisms. In the case of Small and Medium Enterprises (MSE), the scope for adopting these mechanisms may be seriously constrained due to the level of capital required. Furthermore, even though self-provision may be an option to ensure service reliability, it often implies higher production costs for business. Thus business firms may not entirely be able to safeguard against electricity and water service malfunctioning.

For sometime, the Kenya government has had the objective of increasing private participation in the water sector so as to reduce the fiscal load on the Government and other agencies such as Local Authorities. The constitution has previously been interpreted to require that the provision of electricity and water services was an inherently state-based public service. Consequently, private participation is being pursued only gradually through institutional reforms that involve the state retaining or ultimately attaining ownership of the relevant physical assets. The scope for private participation through self-provision of services by industries and other businesses so far appears to be limited as private participation is still geared towards mass production and distribution of electricity and water.

Business in Kenya

Table 5.8: *Summary of Performance Indicators by the Water Authorities in Kenya*

Indicator	Nairobi	Eldoret	Kisumu	Nakuru	Nyeri	Thika	NWCPC	MENR*
Urban Pop	2100000	300000	400000	500000	100000	149448	1170000	3400000
S. Ratio (%)	88.2	58.3	56	60	40	80	81.2	39.4
Connections	158000	8776	13653	17317	5848	4260	53500	124000
Staff Employed	1870	202	302	599	187	146	1617	7600
Staff per 1000 connections	12	23	22	35	32	34	30	61
Water production (M3/day)	347000	29668.3	18000	28164	6545	24000	79452	1700000
UFW (%)	51	52	69	45	40	47	36.2	74.35
CE	39.2	51	39	62	35	76.4	50	41.2

*Water Development Department;

CE = Collection Efficiency;

N. connections = Number of connections;

NWCPC = National Water Conservation and Pipeline Corporation;

UFW = Unaccounted For Water;

UP = Urban Population Served;

S. Ratio = Service Ratio (% of population served).

MENR = Ministry of Environment and Natural Resources
(or Ministry of Water).

Source: Onjala, 2003a

Case studies highlighted in this chapter suggest, however, that opportunities for expanding these services via, say, micro schemes, is massive with huge prospects for reaping benefits in the form of increased employment and livelihoods. Possibilities of localised investment on micro projects entailing production, distribution and re-selling of water and electricity by entrepreneurs and individuals are the new opportunities which businesses are being challenged to accept. There is also need for the Government to create an environment that is supportive of private sector participation. The appropriate legal structures, such as stipulations on power and water tariffs that enable viable private operations, need to be put in place. Enhanced private participation will have the advantage of increasing efficiency in the delivery of services since it will provide existing businesses with an exit option.

REFERENCES

AFREPREN Newsletter No.36 May, 2004: 2.

Agumba, M. and Osawa, B. 2004. *Kenya's PV Market*. Mimeo: Solar Energy Network and Energy Alternatives Africa Ltd.

Kariuki, K.K. 2003. Enhancing Electrification in Kenya: The Role of New Renewable Technologies. Mimeo.

Kenya, Republic of. *Economic Surveys*. Various Years. Government Printer.

Kenya, Republic of. 1996. *Welfare Monitoring Survey II, 1994, Basic Report*. Nairobi: Central Bureau of Statistics, Office of the Vice-President and Ministry of Planning and National Development.

Kenya, Republic of. 1989. *Kenya Demographic and Health Survey Report 1989*. Nairobi: Office of the Vice-President and Ministry of Planning and National Development.

Kenya, Republic of. 1999. *National Poverty Eradication Plan, 1999-2015*. Nairobi: Government Printer

Kenya, Republic of. 2000. *Second Report on Poverty in Kenya, Volume I and II.* Nairobi: Government Printer.

Kenya, Republic of. 2001. *Poverty Reduction Strategy Paper for the Period 2001-2004*. Nairobi: Government Printer.

Kenya, Republic of. 2002. *National Development Plan, 2002-2008*. Nairobi: Government Printer.

Kenya, Republic of. 2004. *Economic Survey*. Nairobi: Government Printer.

Kiura, C. Munene. 2005. "New Ecosystems Approaches to Human Health Program Initiative. Eco-Health Research in Slums and related Issues in Sub-Saharan Africa". Nairobi City Report prepared for International Development Research Centre (IDRC).

Mogaka H.; Gichere, S.; Davis, R. and Hirji, R. 2003. "Impacts and Costs of Climate Variability and Water Resources Degradation in Kenya". A World Bank Report Vol. I and II. May, 2003.

Mwangi E. 2003. *Strategic Options for Energy Sector Regulation and Privatization of State Owned Public Utilities.* Nairobi: Kenya Leadership Institute.

Nyang, F.O. 2000. "Administering a Two-Tier Tariff System under Conditions of Rationing: A Case Study of Kenya's Electricity Regulatory Board". Paper presented at the 8th International Training Program on Utility Regulation and Strategy, June 12-13, 2000, Gainesville, Florida.

Nyoike, P.M. 1993. "National Industrial Energy Conservation Perspectives from Kenya". In Karekezi S. and Mackenzie G. (eds.). *Energy Options for Africa: Environmentally Sustainable Alternatives.* London and New York: Zed Books Ltd.

Onjala, J. 2003. "Bridging the Urban Waters – Public or Commercial?: Early Lessons from Institutional Changes in Kenya". Mimeo.

Onjala, J. 2002a. "Regulating Industrial Wastewater in Kenya: Towards an Appropriate Institutional Arrangement". CDR/IIS Working Paper No. 02.8, July 2002. Copenhagen: Centre for Development Research.

Onjala, J. 2002b. "Good Intentions, Structural Pitfalls: Early Lessons from Urban Water Commercialization Attempts in Kenya". CDR/IIS Working Paper 02.2 January 2002. Copenhagen: Centre for Development Research.

Onjala, J. 2002c. "Managing Water Scarcity in Kenya: Industrial Response to Tariffs and Regulatory Enforcement". Unpublished Ph.D Dissertation, Department of Environment, Technology and Social Studies. Denmark: Roskilde University, January 2002.

PriceWaterHouse Coopers. 2003. "Water Supply and Sanitation, Building Kenya Together". Conference on Private Sector Participation in Kenya's Infrastructure, 15th May.

United Nations Development Programme. 2003. *Human Development Report on Millenium Development Goals: A Compact among Nations to End Human Poverty.* New York: UNDP and Oxford: University Press.

World Bank. 2001. Kenya Review of Water and Sanitation Sector. Washington D.C.: World Bank.

World Bank. 1994. *World Development Report on Infrastructure for Development.* Oxford: University Press.

Chapter 6

Production and Trade

Mary N. Kinyanjui and Paul Kamau

INTRODUCTION TO PRODUCTION AND TRADE ISSUES

Production comprises all those activities that provide goods and services, which people want and for which people are prepared to pay a price. Production is the process of converting resources into goods and services for consumption by economic agents. It takes place through a series of activities that are chained together and involve many actors. At each stage of the chain, value addition and power builds among different actors. A production process is not complete until commodities produced reach final consumers. Therefore, consumption is the final stage of any production process. Trade on the other hand is an institutional arrangement that facilitates economic agents to exchange goods and services. Through trade, economic agents acquire what they do not produce, sell what they produce and in the process make economic gains (exchange process). This chapter examines how trade and production systems in Kenya have changed between 1963 and 2004, with a view to providing some broad historical developments. Secondly, the chapter discusses some of the institutions that facilitate production and trade in Kenya, and finally examines the role of labour markets, technology and foreign aid in production and trade processes in Kenya.

Production and trade all along played a central role in the Kenyan development discourse, to the extent that they are referred to as the engine for facilitating economic growth and development (Kenya, 2003). Other than providing employment to millions of Kenya, they also facilitate integration of the Kenyan economy in the global world. For them to continue playing this facilitative economic role more effectively there is need for stable economic, political, and social environment that is inherent in the business system theory production (McCormick, 2001; UNDP, 2004). The approach taken to examine how production structure has changed in this chapter is to analyze the contribution of the six major sectors to the Gross Domestic Product (GDP) over the period 1963-2004. Literature suggests that GDP is the best measure of a countries production capability, and therefore an analysis of how different sectors contribute to it is offers a better approach to understanding production.

The analysis of trade follows the broad categorization identified from the literature. This entails domestic (internal) trade which is mainly the exchange of goods and services within the national boundaries and also the export (external) trade which is the exchange of goods and services between Kenya and other countries of the world. One of the common features of the two different types of trade is the paradigm shift in the 80s from one that state had so much control to a more liberal one. Therefore, as pointed by Onjala (2002) and Kimuyu (1999), trade liberalization policy aimed at ensuring that 'State' played a more minimal role (of facilitation) and that market forces of supply and demand effectively determined the market price of goods and services. In addition, trade liberalization was expected to enhance productivity, efficiency, as well as better resource utilization for economic development. Hence, the last two decades have witnessed significant policy shifts towards a more liberalized and globalised environment.

PRODUCTION IN KENYA

Kenya is predominantly an agricultural based economy in which agricultural based activities dominates in production and trade. As such most of the economic activities revolve around the agricultural sector which is the mainstay of the economy (Kenya, 2003). Agricultural alone accounted for nearly a third of the GDP through the period 1963-2004. At independence, Kenya inherited a fragmented production system based on race whereby the colonial settlers dominated the well-developed, western-based modern agriculture and livestock farming. The settlers operated large-scale farms that produced primary commodities such as coffee, tea, pyrethrum and cotton for export. They were also involved in manufacturing activities comprising first stage agricultural products processing (Ikiara, 1991). The Asians were involved in small scale retail trade and manufacturing activities geared towards domestic consumption. The other fragment was the African peasant and small-scale farmers. With possession of relatively small piece of land, they grew food crops mainly for meeting their local needs, such as maize, potatoes, beans, and sorghum. Just a few of them were however involved in growing of tea and coffee, which they marketed through cooperative societies. Micro and small enterprises also emerged as constituents of this fragmented production system.

Immediately after independence, the Government committed itself to addressing the fragmentation that existed in the economic structures. The first approach was to promote rapid economic growth through public investment, encouragement of smallholder agricultural production, and incentives for private (often foreign) industrial investment. It was expected that this would create a cohesive and unitary production system which would reduce race differentials.

The other approach was the 'Africanisation' in all sectors of the economy, which done through actions aimed at promoting indigenous ownership in economic activities[1]. A number of parastatals were established to promote the ideology which included Agricultural Finance Corporation (1964), Development Finance Company of Kenya (1963), Industrial and Commercial Development Corporation (ICDC), and Industrial Development Bank (1973)[2]. Their mandate was mainly to finance agricultural, trade and manufacturing activities in the country (Himbara, 1994; McCormick, 1999). As a result of these affirmative actions, GDP grew at an annual average of 6.6% from 1963 to 1973. Equally, agricultural production grew by 4.7% annually during the same period, stimulated by redistributing estates, diffusing new crops strains, and opening new areas to cultivation. Other sectors of the economy performed comparatively well during this period. Table 6.1 presents the percentage contribution of the six most significant sectors of the economy to the GDP in the last 4 decades.

Table 6.1: *Percentage Contribution of Main Sectors to GDP by Selected Activities 1964-2004*

Year	Agriculture	Manufacturing	Building & Construction	Wholesale, Retail & Hotels	Business Services	Transport, Com. & Storage
1964	38.9	10.4	2.7	9.9	2.9	7.4
1968	34.7	9.9	4.3	9.7	3.9	9.1
1974	32.4	12.5	2.9	7.7	3.9	7.9
1980	32.8	13.4	5.6	10.8	6.1	5.9
1986	29.9	13.1	4.9	11.1	7.6	11.1
1990	28.2	13.3	4.9	11.0	7.9	5.9
1995	25.0	13.5	4.2	11.8	9.8	6.1
2000	24.1	13.1	4.0	12.6	10.6	7.5
2001	24.1	13.0	4.0	12.6	11.4	7.4
2002	24.0	13.8	3.9	12.7	11.9	7.2
2003	24.6	13.5	3.2	10.0	11.8	7.3
2004	23.7	13.6	3.6	11.2	11.4	7.7

Source: *Economic Surveys, (Various Issues)*

Agricultural Production

The agricultural sector has remained as the backbone of Kenya's economy during the last four decade. Its percentage contribution to the GDP has remained relatively higher than all the other sectors. As indicated in Table 6.1, in 1964, it accounted for the highest proportion of the GDP at almost 39%. This can be attributed to the fact

---

1   The Sessional Paper No. 1 of 1965 on 'African Socialism and its application to Planning in Kenya' was the first policy document that spelt these strategies. Subsequently, the National Development Plans concretised these philosophies into actions.

2   The Industrial Development Corporation was the first development finance to be established in Kenya in 1954 with an objective of assisting and financing medium and large-scale investment in the industrial sector. In 1963, IDC was changed to Industrial and Commercial Development Corporation (ICDC) (Grosh: 1991: 91).

that other sectors at that time were less developed having received special attention during the colonial era. Through the Government intervention and support, the sector contribution to the GDP declined slightly and by 1968 it accounted for almost 35% of total GDP, but obviously taking the lead. In 1974, this sector accounted for 32% whereas in 1980, it accounted for 33%. Thereafter, the sector contribution to the GDP fell below 30%, a share that has been maintained all through. The prominence of the agricultural sector is evidenced by the higher proportion of the Kenyan population that deriving their livelihood from this sector. It is estimated that close to 70% depend either directly or indirectly on the agricultural for their income.

The agricultural sector is quite diverse in terms of activities, structure and markets. Broadly, agricultural activities comprise cash crop, food crop and livestock farming. In terms of the structure, large scale farming has co-existed along side the small scale farming and in both cash crops and/or food crops activities are undertaken (Kenya, 2002). The market diversity refers to whether products end up in the domestic or export market. In most cases, cash crop farming includes tea, coffee, horticultural crops, pyrethrum, pineapples, tobacco, cotton and sisal are destined for export market, while food crop farming that includes maize, beans, vegetables, wheat, rice, potatoes, bananas, millet, among others are mainly for domestic consumption. Finally, livestock farming which is a significant component of the agricultural sector entails dairy, beef and poultry farming which could be destined for domestic and/or export markets. In the early years of independence, the practice was that cash crops and livestock were practiced in the large-scale farms, this has gradually changed due to declining land availability such that today there is enough cash crop farming being undertaken on small-scale size of farms (see the Omosa's chapter on tea, in this volume).

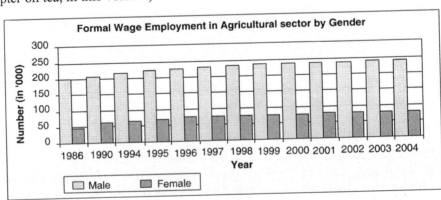

Figure 6.1: Gender Distribution of Employees in Commercial Agricultural Sector

Source: Economic survey (various issues)

This sector is undoubtedly a major employer in Kenya as it accounts for a large share of formal and informal employment. Gender disparity is quite common in this sector with majority of female workers being in the rural, informal agriculture, while their male counterparts are largely in the formal agriculture more often than not found in urban areas. Moreover, female workers constitutes majority of workers in small-scale agriculture (McCulloch, 2001). Women also work as farmhands in the flower farms and they also pick tea and coffee in the rural areas. In contrast, employment figures in the formal employment within the commercial agriculture depict male workers as the majority. Figure 6.1 illustrates the gender disparity in the Kenyan formal wage employment within the agricultural sector for the period 1986-2004. We observe that in all these years, the male workers are more than double of the female workers, and that the growth rate for female workers appear to be significantly lower than that of male. According, to the Economic Survey (2005), female workers in the formal wage employment are generally fewer than the male in all the major sectors of the economy. Elsewhere, analysis of gender status shows that the proportion of female to male workers in wage employment nationally remains low at only 29.2% (UNDP, 2005:29). Even then, most of the female workers are clustered in the middle and lower cadre of wage employment and their upward mobility is highly constrained.

The agricultural sector has had its ups and downs during the last four decades. While in the first decade it experienced impressive performance, the period 1974-93 was generally difficult for the sector. This originated first from the macroeconomic instability caused by the oil crises in 1973-74. Additionally, the agricultural policies adopted in the first decade were inappropriate as they were designed to work in the ideal situation which changed after 1973. Inadequate credit and poor international terms of trade contributed to the decline in the agricultural production. In mid-1980s, the Government adopted the so called economic adjustment programmes (ESAPs) which in part required the 'State' to withdrawal most of agricultural sector supports. As a result the sector experienced a major set backs. Some of the services that the government provided previously were all privatised including the extension services and marketing services. The period 1990-93 was particularly bad as the sector for the first time experienced a production decline of 3.9%. The marketing boards which were overseeing the sale of produce were unable perform efficiently following the liberalization of the sector. In the coffee industry, this was more acute as the marketing boards abandoned farmers. They not only paid them low for their produce but also payments were in most cases late. As a result small-scale coffee farmers discarded coffee farming to try their luck in other crops (see Kanyinga, in this volume for detailed analysis). Although tea was affected by the liberalization in 1980s, the impact was not as severe as in the coffee industry. The tea industry was boosted by the fact that tea prices in the world market were on the rise; and that Kenya Tea Development Agency (KTDA) that took over the marketing responsibility offered farmers better and prompt payments for their produce. The demand for Kenyan tea has remained relatively high in the traditional markets of the EU, Egypt and Pakistan. It is this turn of event that reversed the trend whereby tea became the leading exchange earner surpassing coffee which had dominated most of the first two decades of independence[3]. Even though the tea market seems to be performing better more recently as compared to coffee, the quantity of tea

---

3 For details on foreign exchange earnings from tea and coffee during the liberalization period, see Table 6.4 as generated from various issues of Economic Surveys.

exported has grown just slightly. This is due to the fact that, tea continues to be produced mainly by small-scale farmers who ill-afford the high cost of inputs. In addition, tea is sensitive to climatic conditions.

Livestock farming is an important component of agricultural production because of its potential for domestic as well as export markets. Livestock includes domestic animals which are kept for use or profit such as cattle, sheep, goats, pigs, bees, and poultry. Given this importance, the Government has since independence encouraged farmers to engage in commercial livestock farming (Kenya, 2003). Beef and dairy farming are perhaps the most widely practiced livestock activities in Kenya. In beef farming, it is estimated that close to 90% is in the hands of pastoralists and subsistence farmers. The rest is in large-scale farming and ranches. Influenced by the rainfall pattern and climatic condition, most of beef farming is practiced in the Rift Valley, Central and Coast Provinces. The Kenya Meat Commission (KMC), established in 1950, was originally intended to buy, slaughter and process meat at low and competitive costs from all over the country[4]. It was to play a central role in the promotion of the beef industry by ensuring that the marketing system operated efficiently and that farmers were not loosing to brokers. Its mandated during the colonial time and independent was to process and market livestock meat in both the domestic and export markets. For almost four decades (1950-1987), KMC dominated the marketing chain of meat products in the country. However, in 1975, for the first time local abattoirs were allowed to operate and compete with KMC owing to the complaints by farmers that KMC was not serving them well. By then KMC had become so inefficient and notorious of taking livestock and delaying payments to farmers, which were apparently low (Kenya, 2003). The KMC was unable to compete with private abattoirs and eventually collapsed in 1987. The collapse of KMC contributed to the decline of meat production since private abattoirs could not buy all livestock from farmers. For instance, between 2000 and 2004 beef farming declined from 7.6 million to 5.6 million animals (Economic Survey, 2005:154). Although KMC was set to re-open by April 2006, livestock farmers were still apprehensive about its efficiency.

Dairy farming just like the beef is practiced in most parts of the country mainly by small-scale holders who account for nearly 80% of total milk production. Regionally, most of dairy faming is practiced in Nyandarua, Nakuru, Kericho, Laikipia, Uasin Gichu, and Kwale Districts. More recently, some dairy farmers have shifted into the zero-grazing of dairy cattle particularly in Central and Eastern Provinces. The Kenya Cooperative Creameries (KCC), established in 1925, was for a long time the largest dairy marketing institution in Kenya and more widely in Africa. It was the oldest cooperative in the processing and marketing of dairy products. KCC has a well developed network of milk collection centres throughout the country to ensure that milk is delivered economically. In mid-1990, the dairy industry started experiencing difficulties owing to the effect of liberalisation. For

---

4   KMC in collaboration with Livestock Marketing Department (LMD) acted as the buyer of last resort during times of drought when it would buy livestock from drought stricken areas keep them in holding areas and eventually take them to the market.

the first time milk products from other countries (notably South Africa) started getting into the country. Coupled with the emergence of private milk processors such as Brookside Dairy, Limuru Dairy, Aberdare and Spin Knit, meant that KCC was facing steep competition. By then KCC was facing liquidity and management related problems that it was unable to face competition. Farmers delivered their milk to KCC but their payments were delayed. The entry of privately owned processors was a big blessing to dairy farmers as they were able to get their payments promptly. Due to increased competition and internal inefficiency, KCC closed down in 1996. In 2000, KCC was sold to private companies and a small clique of farmers at a cost of Kshs. 400 million which was way below its capitalization and its name was changed to KCC 2000. In 2003, the NARC Government challenged the sale of KCC to private individuals and offered to refund the owners of KCC 2000 Kshs. 547 million (Kenya, 2005; 2003). In addition, the government committed itself to reviving KCC and renamed it New KCC which began operation again in 2005. Farmers are now enjoying higher and prompt payment for their milk, thanks to NARC government and the processing factories in many parts of the country have also been rehabilitated to ensure that milk all parts is collected, handled and processed by KCC more efficiently.

Manufacturing Production

Since the time of industrial revolution, manufacturing has been regarded as the main engine for growth and for transforming the economic structure of poor countries. It is a catalyst for shifting from simple, low-value activities with poor growth prospects to high productivity, increasing returns and strong growth potentials activities. Historical experience throughout the world has shown that a country's objective of achieving rapid and sustained economic growth cannot be achieved in the absence of industrialization (UNIDO, 2002a). Industrial success among the Newly Industrialised Countries (NICS) in Asia clearly shows how industrialisation facilitates development. In general, industrialization provides means for accelerating economic development. This realization among developing countries has triggered an enormous interest in promoting growth of their manufacturing sectors. In Kenya, the Sessional Paper No. 2 of 1996 on Industrial transformation to the year 2020 spell out how industrial sector plays a central role towards the realization of national economic goals.

The manufacturing sector remained the engine of growth even at the worst times in Kenya. At independence in 1963, manufacturing accounted for about 10% of the GDP. As demonstrated in Table 6.1, this sector has not changed much over the years at its contribution to the GDP has on average oscillated between 10% and 13 % per annum. In 1974, this sector accounted for 12.5% of the GDP, which increased marginally to reach 13% in 1980s and 1990s. It is only in the last 3 years, that this sector has shown impressive performance. Nonetheless, it is worth noting that the sector has also evolved in terms of the structure during the last four decades.

Statistics show that the manufacturing sector provide employment to a majority of Kenyan population as it accounts for almost 20% of total wage employment in the private sector and approximately 5% in the public sector per year (see Kenya, 2005). Elsewhere, it is argued that this industry also employs approximately 400,000 people in the formal sector and more than 3.7 million in the informal sector (UNDP, 2005; Kenya, 2003). In addition, the sector on average accounted for over 40% of Kenya's total export earnings (Onjala, 2003). The sectoral composition of manufacturing activity is fairly broad and diverse. Some of the dominant sub-sectors include food processing, paper and paper products, printing and publishing, plastic products, clay and glass products, electrical equipment, transport equipment, and petroleum and other chemicals. Other sub-sectors include textiles and clothing, leather and footwear, wood and furniture, as well as beverage and tobacco[5]. In terms of employment, food processing and metal, each account for 25%; textiles and clothing (17%); leather and wood (12%); and chemicals petroleum and plastics (8%).

The manufacturing sector appears to have thrived well during the import substitution industrialization (ISI) regime compared to the export oriented industrialization (EOI) era[6]. During the ISI regime the sectoral output was that food and beverages accounted 42%, chemicals, petroleum and plastics 23%, and metal, machinery and equipment 13% (see UNDP, 2005; McCormick, 1999, Kimuyu, 1999). During the EOI (1996-2004), the output was food processing 57%, chemicals, petroleum and plastics 20%, and metal, machinery, and equipment 13% (UNDP, 2005). The textile and clothing industry which was not featuring among the main sub-sectors of the manufacturing became significant during EOI era, accounting for 16% of the total manufacturing employment.

Ownership Structure of Manufacturing Enterprises and MSEs

Ownership of industrial enterprises varies greatly with size in terms of gender, race and ethnicity, and legal status of ownership. In general, the smaller the size of an enterprise, the more likely it is to be female-owned, African-owned, and a sole proprietorship. Most of the manufacturing enterprises are locally owned even though there is a minority which are foreign-owned or joint ventures. There are also a few enterprises owned by the government. Kenyans of Asian origin dominate in the manufacturing sector, majority their enterprises being family businesses which are registered as either partnership or private limited companies. Some of these Asian-owned enterprises are being run by second generation having been established soon after independence (Himbara, 1994; Ikiara, 1991). Majority of the foreign owned manufacturing firms are either Multinational Corporations (MNCs) or more recently, the Export Processing Zone (EPZ) firms[7].

---

5   See Economic Survey 2005:179 for more details.

6   See McCormick, 1999, Kimuyu, 1999 and Onjala, 2002 for detailed analysis of the ISI and EOI strategies in Kenya.

7   See the Chapter by McCormick, Kimuyu and Kinyanjui on textile and clothing for a detailed analysis of the EPZ programme.

Majority of the micro and small enterprises (MSEs) are sole proprietorships or partnerships; and as the size increases, sole proprietorships decline while partnerships and limited companies form of ownership increases. Within the MSE sector, gender distribution in terms of ownership is fairly distributed between male and female, however, male dominate in manufacturing and construction while female tend to dominate in textile and clothing activities (McCormick, 2004). Again as the size of the firm increases, male ownership becomes dominant. As such the medium and large-scale manufacturing activities are predominantly male, even though some firms count women among their partners or shareholders.

Broadly speaking, MSEs which cover a wide range of establishments employing 1-49 workers form an important component of the Kenyan industrial sector as well as the business system. Found in almost all productive sectors of the economy, the MSEs are involved in production, trade or service provision activities. According to the MSE Baseline Survey, Kenya had 1.3 million MSEs in 1999 and approximately 2.5 million people depended on MSEs for their income (CBS, 1999). Projections estimated that by 2004, the number of MSEs had risen to 2.2 million enterprises, translating to one MSE for every four households (Kenya, 2005). Additionally, it was estimated that more that 5 million Kenyans depended on MSE. Existing studies argue that trade accounts for nearly two thirds of all MSEs in which case retail trade dominates. Services is the next dominant MSE activity which include, hotels, bars, repairs, transport, real estates, professional services and other various types of personal services accounting for abut 20% of all MSEs (McCormick, 2004, CBS, 1999). In addition, about 13% of the MSEs are engaged in manufacturing, while only 2% are in the construction activity. Majority of the MSEs operate in small sheds or in the open spaces under the hot sun hence, the term *Jua Kali*. In most cases, make goods on orders, with their market being mainly domestic and few exceptions for the export market.

Almost all MSEs start small and just a handful of them grow vertically to get to medium and large scale enterprises. There has been a concern among scholars as to why MSEs do not grow and also experience high death rates (See Kinyanjui and Khayesi, 2005; McCormick, et al., 1997). MSEs have been found to rely heavily on social capital particularly in the provision of labour where family labour is dominant. In addition, since MSEs tend to cluster in specific areas, they are able to develop close networks. Among the issues that have been suggested to support the growth of MSEs include, long life education, and formal training, over and above the provision access to finance.

By way of summarising this section, the performance of manufacturing activities has been constrained by a number of factors, that make business environment in less conducive. Some of the factors that affect business environment include the macroeconomic factors, governance issues, infrastructure, labour cost, and insecurity just but to mention a few. As already mentioned, macroeconomic environment changed drastically following the economic liberalization in early 1990s, which to al large extent exposed the Kenyan manufacturing enterprises to competition from imports. While cost of production is arguably high in Kenya, the manufacturing firms have been unable to face this competition and are in most cases classified as inefficient. The fact that the GDP growth rate has been low for most part of the last decade implied that the local market for which the manufacturing sector relied on previous was gradually not expanding. Subsequently, firms found themselves with excess production. Infrastructure is an integral part of the business environment, but the truth of the matter is that in the last two decades the transport system deteriorated to the worst levels since independence (Kimuyu, 1999). This implied that manufacturers had to spend more in transporting raw materials as well as their products to the market. Other infrastructural services such as water, electricity and communication were not efficiently provided. For some of these services, under-provision has been compounded by managerial excesses, rent-related service stretching, mismanagement and corruption. The result has been a steady deterioration in both the quantity and quality of these services (Onjala, 2002; Kimuyu, 1999). Another major concern among the manufacturers has been the high cost of labour in the country which is closely related to the high cost of living. On average most firms argue that they spent approximately 40% of the operation costs on labour force which somehow impedes their competitiveness in both the domestic and export markets. Equally, the high level of political uncertainty and the general insecurity in the country constraints the business environment in Kenya more so to the manufacturing sector.

Building and Construction

Development of infrastructure is an important prerequisite in creating and supporting business environment that facilitates private sector investment, growth and employment creation (Kenya, 2003). The government policy on building and construction has been to encourage participation of private sector in the development of the sector by providing a conducive investment climate. An efficient infrastructure network in both urban and rural areas is a priority towards achievement of investment in the country. The government involvement in this sector has been more of facilitative and the private sector has been at the centre of operations. Broadly, activities of this sector include housing and roads construction.

The contribution of this sector to the GDP has been low during the last four decades of Kenya's independence, which annual average has 4.1%. From Table 6.1 we observe that at independence in 1963, this sector accounted for merely 2.7% of the GDP. There was a slight growth between 1964 and 1968 when the percentage share increased to 4.3%, but again declined and by 1974 it only accounted for 2.9%. The highest contribution of this sector to the GDP was recorded in 1980 which was at 5.6%. There after, it was under 5%. This low contribution to the GDP could perhaps be attributed to the fact that most of the construction taking place (especially in the housing) is informal and therefore not captured in the official statistics. In addition, the high costs of building materials, coupled with lack of finance have contributed to the poor performance of the formal building and construction industry.

Transport, Communication and Storage

The contribution of transport, communication and storage sector has fluctuated over the years as indicated in Table 6.1. The highest contribution of this sector to the GDP was 1986 when it accounted for 11.12%. Between 1990 and 1995, the contribution declined to approximately 5.9% and 6.1% respectively. After the year 2000, the sectors proportionate share to the GDP increased to about 7% and has remained more or less at that level. While this contribution to the GDP may appear low in comparison to the other sectors of the economy, it is important to note that this sector is basically a service based whose contribution to the GDP is not direct. According to the United Nations (2006), this contribution of this sector compares well with other countries such as the US, Europe, and Africa whose contribution was 6.7%, 6.6% and 7.3% respectively in 2004. It is, however, important to note that transport system in Kenya is in poor state making it costly to produce goods in Kenya (see the Chapter on Transport in this volume).

The communication industry has perhaps undergone the most significant changes in the recent times. First, this is due to the embracing of information and communication technology (ICT) in almost all the other sectors of the economy. This has witnessed a transformation of the production operation during the last one decade. Providers of ICT services have also emerged increasing the level of production in this sector. Secondly, and related to the first one is the transformation of communication process. Following the sale of mobile phone licences to private companies in 2000, the use of mobile phones has increased dramatically. It is currently estimated that more than 5million Kenyans are connected to a mobile phone. The Government has made a commitment to encourage use of ICT by lowering, and some case eliminating all value added taxes on ICT components. Similarly the number of private TV and radio station has increased tremendously in the last decade. Nonetheless, the monopoly of TELKOM in the provision of internet connection through the JamboNet has made cost of internet communication services to remain relatively high.

Wholesale and Retail Trade and Hotels

The wholesale and retail trade and hotels forms a significant portion of the Kenya's production activities. While wholesale and retail trade are important for domestic economy, hotels and restaurant is driven by tourism which is mostly an international activity. However, the contribution of this sector to the GDP has been moderate throughout the period 1964-2004. From Table 6.1, we observe that the average annual contribution has been 10% of the GDP. The lowest value was recorded in 1974 when the sector accounted for only 7.7%. More recently, the sector has registered impressive growth as reflected in its contribution to the GDP between 2000 and 2004.

Turning to the hotel and restaurant industry, we observe that its growth has been driven by tourism main the international one. The expansion of hotel industry relies heavily on tourism. As such the terrorist attack on Kenya in 1998 and 2001 followed by travel bans on the US and the UK citizen had adverse impact on the industry. Although the figure is not shown in the Table 6.1, the general performance of the sector was low in 1999. The best indicator of the performance of this industry is the rate of bed occupancy shown in Table 6.2. From Table 6.2 one can see that 1994, the bed capacity was about 12 million of which only 43% was occupied. While bed occupancy displayed high rates between 1994 and 1997, this drastically reduced in 1998 and 1999 following the Nairobi terrorism attacks, with the occupancy declining to 35% and 34% respectively. The bed capacity in 2004 which stood at 10 million is a clear indication to the fact that several hotels closed down between 1994 and 2004. The lowest bed availability was recorded in 1998 and 2003 representing approximately 8 million. It is not surprising to note that during this period, bed occupancy was similarly low, standing at 2.8 million and 2.6 million respectively.

With regard to wholesale and retail trade, we observe that its structure had changed significantly since independence. In the first two decades of independence, the structure was that wholesale trade played a key role in proving goods to retailers. However, following trade liberalization, wholesaler gradually found their role being taken over by emerging supermarkets. Similarly, retailers have had a difficult time in the liberalization period as supermarkets are being started in almost all urban and rural areas. Importantly, trading MSEs have managed to adjust so as to fit in the new trading structure. They have particularly become more specialised so as to compete with supermarkets by dealing with cereals, groceries, and fruits. Main supermarkets include Uchumi, Nakumatt, and Tusker Matt (see Odhiambo, *et al.,* in this volume).

Table 6.2: *Hotel Bed-nights Occupancy 1994-2000 '000 persons*

Year	Bed Occupancy	Bed Available	Occupancy Rate %
1994	5,109.7	11,908.9	43.1
1995	5,054.8	11,562.2	43.7
1996	5,061.2	11,354.5	44.6
1997	4,910.3	9,516.6	51.6
1998	2,813.0	7,975.7	35.3
1999	2,951.0	8,711.4	33.9
2000	3,687.8	9,382.3	39.3
2001	3,354.9	8,327.8	40.3
2002	3,436.8	8,182.7	42.0
2003	2,605.9	7,765.7	33.6
2004	3,791.5	10,030.7	37.8

Source: Economic Survey (various issues)

Business Services

Business services sector consist of financial, real estate, rents and insurance services. In the early years of independence business services contribution to GDP was rather low ranging between 2.9% and 3.9% in 1964 and 1974, respectively. As indicated in Table 6.1, after the 1980, this sector began to experience impressive growth, starting at 6% of total GDP in 1980, 8% in 1986, and 10% in 1995. Between the year 2000 and 2004, the contribution of this sector on average has been 11%. The financial sector has been the major beneficiary of economic liberalization as it operated in a very controlled environment. As a result, the number of commercial banks increased, as well as those of all other financial intermediaries. As at 2004, the financial system consisted of the Central Bank, 45 commercial and development banks, 39 Insurance companies and 95 foreign exchange bureaus. At the apex of insurance industry is the Commission for Insurance, which is a government agency that regulates policies of the industry. In addition there are 39 insurance companies, 212 insurance brokers, 2,004 insurance agents, 8 risk managers, 17 loss adjusters, 29 insurance surveyors, and 208 loss assessors.

THE SIZE AND STRUCTURE OF TRADE IN KENYA

As already mentioned earlier, the agricultural sector dominates in both production and trade in Kenya. This is due to the fact that the agriculture is the mainstay of the economy. Agricultural trade contributes significantly in both domestic and external trade (Kenya, 2003). The Ministry of Trade and Industry (MTI) is in charge of coordinating all matters relating to both internal and external trade. The Kenyan trade agenda since independence has been geared towards increasing economic activity, creating employment and getting fair deal for Kenyan in the global market in order to increase welfare of all Kenyans.

Internal Trade

The domestic trade in Kenya is divided into four main categories for the purposes of management within the MTI. These are: Hotels and Restaurants; Wholesalers; Retailers; and Small-scale industries. The Department of Internal Trade (DIT) in the Ministry facilitates and coordinates operation of this trade in conjunction with local authorities. The DIT is responsible for facilitating orderly development and growth of domestic trade by formulating and implementing appropriate policies and strategies. Domestic trade is significant for economic growth and enhancing social economic development in Kenya. In addition to formulating policies, DIT issues trade licences, gather trade information and collaborate with private sector to ensure that business environment in the Kenya is more conducive.[8] The actual contribution of domestic trade to GDP cannot be estimated due to lack of comprehensive statistical data in the country, which has also made it receive low attention in research.

Regulation of domestic trade is based on the Trade Licensing Act (CAP. 497) of 1968 that require all businesses operating in the country to obtain trade license. The issuing of licence was considered crucial for monitoring and regulating trade activities in the country. However, according to Himbara, (1994) the trade licence

---

8 Some of these organizations include the Kenya National Chamber of Commerce and Industry; Kenya Association of Manufacturers, and many other financial institutions.

requirement was designed as a way of preventing Asian from doing trade business in the country during the 'Africanisation' process. To operate a business, one required a trade licence from the MTI and also from the local authority all at a fee. However following the Finance Bill of 1997, all fees that the MTI used to charge for trade licences were scrapped as from January 1st 1998. Otherwise, the MTI was expected to continue issuing the licenses free of charge, whereas local authorities charged for their trade licenses arguably to use the revenue collected to boost their activities. Since then the collection of trade licenses by the businesses declined and this has adversely affected the potential of MTI to collect useful statistical data on domestic trade.

External Trade

Most studies have echoed the important role that external trade plays in development process. Among the many reasons advanced for the importance of external trade include its provision of foreign exchange required to import capital equipment and inputs. It also expands the market size especially in developing countries where the markets are fragmented; it is also a sound measure of the sustainability of overall balances; finally, it links an economy to the global world (Todaro, 1990; World Bank, 2000; Kenya, 2002; McCulloch, et al., 2001 and Riddel, 1990). External trade can be classified as bilateral, regional or multilateral. Given the crucial role that external trade plays in the development process, countries are in constant negotiations either bilateral regional or multilateral with a view to trade between or among them. As such Kenya has since independence placed great importance to her external trade relations. This is clearly demonstrated by the Kenya's active participation in regional bodies and in the WTO where most of the trade agreements are negotiated. Within these negotiations, Kenya has constantly expressed the need to have fair trade especially in the agricultural products.

The Kenya's external trade policy has all along been linked to the industrialization policies pursued. For instance, during the ISI policy, the general practice in the external trade was highly inward looking. In essence tariff and non tariff barriers were commonly used to control the level of imports. As noted by Kimuyu (1999) measures to promote export during this regime were minimal as a lot of attention was given to controlling imports. The assumption then was that as efforts were consolidated in providing for the domestic market, firms would eventually grow and begin to export but this was far fetched idea. In reality domestic firms as a result of protection became more inefficient, rigid and used low technology. As a result demand for imports in the domestic market continued to increase. By mid 1980s, it was obvious that the ISI policy would not facilitate economic development as earlier thought. Coupled by the pressure from the country adopted the EOI policy whose main objective was to relax trade restriction measures and at the same promote an industry with export bias (See for example McCormick, 1999; Onjala 2002; and Ikiara, 1991). The effect of trade liberalisation and increased Globalisation was a mix increased competition, erosion of trade preferential treatments and increase in total trade. Although Kenya has strong presence in the region, its dominance has gradually been eroded.

Table 6.3 demonstrated how the structure and value of external trade in Kenya changed between 1964 and 2004. One of the major observations is that external trade balance was in deficit as import exceeded exports during this period. Secondly, the coverage ratio which indicates the proportion of imports that is covered by exports was on a declining trend from 90% in 1964, to about 60% in 2004. The lowest coverage ratio was recorded in 1990 when it stood at only 49%. Finally, the total value of external trade increased more substantially following the trade liberalization. The second decade of independence was particularly tough for the Kenyan external trade due to the rising costs of energy emanating from oil crisis, the collapse of East African Community in 1977 as well as the changing pattern of global economy. The latter part of the last decade saw a number of policy programmes that revived the external trade. These entailed the creation of the WTO in 1995 which tried to harmonise trade restrictions applying to all member countries. The other one was the enactment of the US-AGOA in 2000 which allowed market access for several products made in Kenya.

Table 6.3: *External Trade Performance 1964-2004 (Kshs. Mln)*

Year	Exports	Imports	Balance of Trade	Total Trade	Cover Ratio (%)
1964	1,588	1,758	(170)	3,346	90.32
1968	1,786	2,542	(756)	4,328	70.26
1974	4,368	7,328	(2,958)	11,696	59.61
1980	10,314	19,180	(8,866)	29,494	53.77
1986	19,737	26,758	(7,021)	46,495	73.76
1990	24,880	50,913	(26,032)	75,792	48.87
1995	97,339	155,168	(57,829)	252,507	62.73
2000	134,527	247,804	(113,277)	382,331	54.29
2001	147,590	290,108	(142,518)	437,698	50.87
2002	169,283	257,710	(88,427)	426,993	65.69
2003	183,154	281,844	(98,690)	464,998	64.98
2004	214,791	364,205	(149,415)	578,996	60.12

Source: Economic Surveys (Various Issues)

Agricultural products form the bulk of Kenya's export as they constitute the lion share of the export revenue. These products include coffee, tea, horticultural, pineapple, cotton, pyrethrum and sisal. Others non agricultural products include metal, cement, tinned fruits, and clothing. Table 6.4 presents the value of major export products from Kenya between 1964 and 2004. While coffee dominated the export trade during the first two decades of independence, it was overtaken by tea, which took the lead as from 1990-2003. Currently, tea which is mostly produced by small-scale farmers is the second main foreign exchange earner after horticultural

Table 6.4: *Value of Selected Export Commodities (Current Kshs. Million)*

Commodity	1964	1968	1974	1980	1986	1990	1995	2000	2001	2002	2003	2004
Coffee	153	256	704	2,163	3,891	4,420	13,004	11,707	7,460	6,541	6,286	6,944
Tea	61	200	458	1,160	3,267	6,290	16,882	35,150	34,485	34,376	33,005	36,072
Cotton	-	60	71	32	1	-	76	-	-	-	-	-
Pyrethrum	16	29	147	181	193	877	1,378	704	993	798	813	943
Metal	-	39	14	9	33	-	-	153	123	98	147	208
Meat	21	60	96	32	4	112	125	-	-	-	-	-
Sisal	12	61	108	177	198	379	663	606	728	792	906	1,119
Cement	18	23	107	203	197	251	1,618	1,358	1,031	1,479	1,976	1,959
Iron &Steel	-	-	-	-	-	-	-	2,605	3,673	4,122	4,047	7,532
Textile & Clothing	4	7	6	45	72	194	1,040	1,091	1,116	1,196	1,450	1,625
Horticulture	18	9	28	177	484	3,198	10,626	21,216	19,846	28,334	36,485	39,541

Source: Economic Survey (Various issues)

products, which took the leadership only in 2003. Kenya imports mainly industrial machinery, crude petroleum, motor vehicles and transport equipment, minerals, iron and steel, chemicals and other manufactured products. These products are generally supplier driven in that the exporting countries more often than not fix their prices and Kenya as a developing country has little room for bargaining. In contrast, the prices for Kenyan exports are fixed at the world market; and again Kenya is only a price taker, hence terms of trade have been poor for Kenya.

Analysis of the export destination reveals a unique case of Kenyan exports, Table 6.5. During the first two decades of independence, the European market was the dominant destination of the Kenyan exports, specifically between 1964 and 1986. The African market was ranked second in terms of absorbing Kenyan exports. However, it is important to highlight that the products destined for these two different markets were completely different. Whereas, the EU market absorbed agricultural products, the African market was geared towards manufactured output. However, after 1986, the African market somehow became the leading destination of Kenyan exports, a position it has retained until 2004. For instance, between 1996 and 2000, the African market absorbed about 46% of Kenya's total exports, while European market absorbed 31%. Of the African market, Tanzania and Uganda are the two major destinations of Kenyan exports. For the period 2001-2004, these two countries absorbed an average of 27% of the Kenyan exports per year. The dominance of African market as a major export destination is associated with the relatively high level of industrial development in Kenyan.

Table 6.5: *Proportion of Kenyan Exports by Destination 1964-2004 (Percentage)*

Region / Year	EAC	Africa, less EAC	Europe	USA & Canada	Asia, Middle East, Far East & Australia	Other Regions	Total
1964	-	5.1*	49.5	6.6	24.8	14.0	100
1968	-	12.6	43.9	8.8	8.9	25.8	100
1974	22.1	9.3	36.4	5.2	12.2	14.8	100
1980	13.9	13.4	39.5	4.2	16.9	12.1	100
1986	10.1	11.3	50.8	9.7	14.2	3.9	100
1990	7.7	13.9	50.6	4.3	16.6	7.3	100
1995	28.6	20.1	34.3	3.5	13.9	1.1	100
2000	26.2	19.8	31.1	2.7	16.9	3.3	100
2001	29.5	19.6	28.8	2.9	17.8	1.6	100
2002	26.7	22.4	29.2	2.4	15.6	3.7	100
2003	24.7	21.5	29.1	2.1	15.5	7.1	100
2004	25.6	21.9	27.8	2.8	16.1	5.8	100

Source: *Economic Surveys (Various Issues), Pedersen, et al., 1999*

* *The figure includes the East African Community (EAC) i.e. Tanzania and Uganda*

Within the European market, United Kingdom is the largest importer of the Kenyan products and has remained relatively stable (see Pedersen and McCormick, 1999 for a detailed analysis). Exports to the Far East and Middle East were high in 1964 when they accounted for 24%. However, this declined to between 12% and 16% for the period 1974-2004. Surprisingly, exports to North America (Canada and the US) have remained significantly low accounting for less than 3% of total export trade between 2000 and 2004. This is certainly not withstanding the recent effort to promote trade between the US and Kenya through the enactment of AGOA in 2000. We therefore conclude that the trade between the Kenya and the North American region is constrained by measures that the US and Canada have taken to protect the agricultural sectors through subsidies and tariff barriers.

INSTITUTIONS THAT FACILITATE PRODUCTION AND TRADE IN KENYA

Cooperative Movement and Business Systems in Kenya

The history of the co-operative movement in Kenya goes back to the beginning of the century, when European settler farmers established the first society to market their agricultural produce and distribution farm inputs. The cooperative movement remained essentially non-African until 1945, when the Co-operative Societies Ordinance made it possible for African smallholder farmers to form co-operatives primarily to market subsistence crops such as maize and millet. When African farmers were for the first time allowed to grow cash crops in 1950s, the cooperative movement gained momentum. At independence, there were about 693 registered societies with membership of 200,000 (Kenya, 1987:29). Since then, the number of co-operative societies has grown at an annual average rate of 5.2% per annum.

One of the outcomes of the economic liberalization polices was the drastic increase in the number of co-operative societies registered between 1996 and 1998 as clearly demonstrated in Figure 6.2. Today, the cooperative movement has evolved to become one of the most well-established institutional arrangements for conducting business.

The cooperative movement's democratic structure, full involvement of people and its coverage of both rural and urban sectors fit well in the development strategy. '*A co-operative is defined as an association of persons who have voluntarily come together to achieve common economic goals through a democratically controlled organisation with equitable contribution to capital and sharing of risks and benefits*' (Kenya, 1987; UNDP, 2003). As business organisation, a co-operative society is established with a spirit of service in order to achieve self-help through mutual help. It is based on the principal of voluntary membership, democratic administration, and equity distribution. The cooperative movement was particularly fundamental in the indigenization of the economy.

The main contribution of the cooperative societies lies in their impact on rural development and on the welfare of workers in urban areas (Alila, 1991; UNDP, 2003; Kenya, 1987). Throughout the period 1964-2004, the agricultural based co-operatives were the majority, followed by the saving & credit cooperative organisations (SACCOs) (see Figure 6.2). According to the UNDP Human Development Report (2003), in 1999, 46% of co-operatives were agricultural based, 38% were SACCOs, and the 'others' were only 16%. However, beginning the year 2003, the number of SACCOs surpassed that of agricultural based, such that in 2003 and 2004, the SACCOs accounted for 40% and 42% respectively. During the same period, the agricultural based cooperatives accounted for 39%. Between 1994 and 2004, the overall number of co-operative societies increased by more than 60% from 6,276 to 10,642, respectively. Indeed, by 2003, it was estimated that more than 2.5 million people in Kenya derived their livelihoods either directly or indirectly from cooperative movement (Kenya, 2003). The other two categories of cooperative societies 'Other non-agricultural' and Unions have been few throughout the period accounting for approximately 16% of the total registered societies.

As an institution, cooperative movement plays an important role in Kenya's economic development. For instance, within the agricultural sector, the movement enhance production and marketing commodities, while in the financial sector, it has helped to mobilize savings and channel them to productive investment (Alila, 1991; Kenya, 2003). The movement also offers an innovative form of combined savings and insurance to members.

The dominance of agricultural based cooperatives again points to the fact that agriculture plays a key role in the economy. It is in the agricultural sector that the first cooperative society was established, and over the years, the agricultural cooperative societies have been involved in production, primary processing and marketing of agricultural and livestock commodities. More generally, cooperative societies have played a critical role in mobilising rural and urban savings.

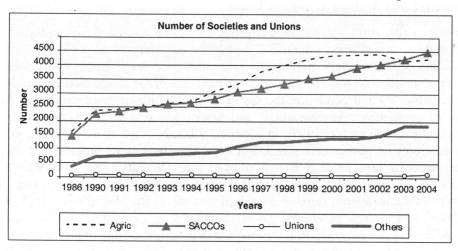

Figure 6.2: Growth in the Number of Cooperative Societies
Source: Economic Survey (Various Issues)

Before 1998, co-operatives enjoyed more protection from the State. However, things changed with the amendment of the Cooperative Act that removed that protection.[9] Although this legislation was expected to make them more efficient, the reality was inefficiency in most of them was exposed and as a result many of them became insolvent due to wrangles and mismanagement. In the year 2003, the NARC Government re-established the Ministry of Co-operative Development, which had been scrapped for over a decade. Prior to 2003, it operated as a department within the Ministry of Agriculture. The revival of this Ministry has brought a new meaning to the lives of many Kenyans (see, Kenya, 2003, 1997). There is however a dire need   for training and awareness creation in the cooperative movement.

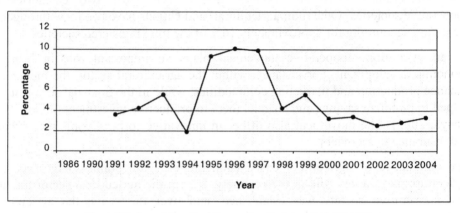

Figure 6.3: Annual Growth of Cooperative Societies 1991-2004 (%)

Source: Economic Survey (Various issues)

Parastatals and Business Systems in Kenya

Parastatals also known as public enterprises are not new in the Kenyan production and trade activities. First established during the colonial rule as a mechanism for providing certain services, particularly those that were not provided by the private sector, they grew to become significant institutions in the production and trade in the country. At independence, the Government established more parastatals as a way of promoting 'Africanisation' and arresting inequity in regional income distribution (McCormick, 1999). In addition, public enterprises were established to serve as tools for government investment in the industrialisation process. It is one of those colonial legacies that Kenya adopted (see Himbara, 1994; Pedersen and McCormick, 1999, and Yoshida, 1984). Today, parastatals are found in almost all sectors of the economy ranging from agricultural, financial, transport, trade and industry. *"A public enterprise or a parastatal is defined as an institution established by the government to be involved in a particular line of activity with the government support either to make profit or to provide a service that private sector may not be willing to undertake. Alternatively, it is a form of business established in which government owns at least 25% of total capital".*

---

9   For more details, see Kenya (1997) Sessional Paper No 6 of 1997 on "Cooperatives in a liberalized economy."

The colonial government established many parastatals because they were believed to be the most efficient mechanism for providing certain services that private sector would not find profitable to engage in[10]. During this period, most parastatals were in crop marketing organised to benefit European farmers in marketing their products. At independence, the government adopted similar arguments and undertook to establish more parastatals in other sectors such as banking, transport, wholesale, and manufacturing (Pedersen and McCormick, 1999:5). Table 6.6 shows when selected parastatals (public enterprises) were established, their core business and the status of privatization process. The dominance of the agricultural based parastatals is also evident in Kenya (see Grosh, 1991). In a snap shot, from Table 6.6, one can see that Coffee Board of Kenya, Cotton Lint & Seed Marketing Board, Kenya Tea Development Authority, Mumias Sugar Company, Pyrethrum Board of Kenya, Sugar board of Kenya, National Cereals and Produce Board and Horticultural Crops Development Authority (HCDA) are all agricultural based.

Table 6.6: *Establishment of Selected Parastatals in Kenya*

Parastatal	Year Established	Core Business	Privatised
Kenya Railways	1903	Transport	NO
Coffee Board of Kenya	1920	Coffee	YES
Kenya Cooperative Creameries	1925	Dairy	YES*
Kenya Meat Commission	1950	Meat	NO
Pyrethrum Board of Kenya	1950	Pyrethrum	NO
Kenya Airways (East African Air)	1950	Air Transport	YES
Kenya Commercial Bank	1970	Finance	YES
Cotton Lint & Seed Marketing	1955	Cotton	NO
Kenya Tea Development Authority	1963	Tea	YES
Agricultural Development Corporation	1964	Finance	NO
Horticultural Crops Development Authority	1967	Horticulture	NO
Mumias Sugar Company	1973	Sugar	YES
Kenya Power & Lighting Company	1973	Energy	YES
National Cereals & Produce Board	1980	Cereals	NO

Source: *Grosh, 1991; Kenya, 1998, Kenya, 2003*

It was privatised but in 2000 was repossessed by NARC government in 2003

According to the literature, public enterprises performed during the first decade of independence when their contribution to the GDP rose from 11.2% in 1963 to

---

10 The colonial government considered it undesirable to leave monopolies in private hands because of the exploitation that would have resulted, an argument the Kenyan independent government also used to establish more parastatals at independent in 1963. For details see Yoshida 1984, Gross 1991, and Himbara, 1994.

14.4% in 1971. Thereafter, most of them started performing poorly to the extent that they were for most part sustained by the exchequer. At the dawn of economic liberalization some of the parastatals became redundant as the services they provided could efficiently be provided by the private sector and couple with mismanagement most of them could not compete. It is for this reason that in 1991, the Government established a parastatals reform committee to implement the privatization process[11] . This was followed by a policy paper on Public Enterprise Reform and Privatization, declaring that the Government would sell its equity in 207 parastatals classified as non-strategic and retain some shares in 33 strategic ones[12]. Since 1992, however, the privatization process has moved very slowly. In 2003, soon after the present Government came to power, the process has began moving somewhat faster again. According to Kenya (2003:16), the Government pledged its commitments to divesting from commercial ventures that can be performed more efficiently and effectively by the private sector.

Privatization process in Kenya has had mixed results as can be observed from Table 6.6. While some of those parastatals privatised were able to turn around their poor performance into profit making, others actually went under. The most successful ones include the Kenya Airways, Mumias Sugar, Kenya Tea Development Authority, Kenya Commercial Bank and the Kenya Power & Lighting Company Ltd. Those that have not had a success story include, the National Bank of Kenya, Coffee Board of Kenya and Uchumi Supermarket. Similarly, for some of the parastatals which are not financially sound, effort to privatize them has been unsuccessful.

Foreign Aid in Production and Trade

Foreign aid represents an important source of investment and production finance in most of the developing countries where it supplements low savings, narrow export earnings and thin tax revenue. Kenya is by no means an exception and has received development assistance since independence. In 1960s and 70s, the average annual gross external aid inflows was 5.8% but then increased to 9.9% in 1980s. However, in the 1990s, the gross annual aid inflows as a proportion of GDP again declined to 5% per annum. Kenya needs foreign aid to supplement its limited domestic resources in the development process. It bridges the gap between the gross domestic savings and gross national investment needs. Foreign aid is critical in two ways (1) it acts as a means of supporting policies and programmes which lead to improved economic performance, and (2) it facilitates the implementation of planned programmes in order to enhance economic development. Studies have established that foreign aid opens up inaccessible areas of the economy, taps, new resources

---

11 Privatization is a generic term often used to describe a range of policy initiatives designed to alter the mix of ownership or management away from the Government towards the Private sector. The main objective of privatization is to improve efficiency and spread of capital through wider shareholding (UNDP, 2005:15).

12 Non –strategic parastatals are those enterprises undertaking business activities that can easily be provided by the private sector whereas the strategic ones are those considered to be undertaking crucial business which private sector many not undertake adequately (Kenya, 1997).

and helps in augmenting regional imbalances (White, 1992; Njeru, 2001). More importantly, if well managed, foreign aid raises national productivity, incomes and employment, which in the long run leads to a better standard of living in the recipient country.

Foreign aid also known as the Official Development Assistance (ODA) is defined as all those resources channelled into the country through the government or non-government systems, whereby the Government is held at least partially responsible or accountable for the management of such resources. ODA which include both grants and loans from bilateral and multilateral official agencies, are considered as important sources of funds especially for capital expenditures (World Bank, 2000). ODA therefore consists of grants or loans that a government or a international organisation such as the World Bank, International Monetary Fund (IMF), International Finance Corporation, give to another country to in order to promote recipient's economic development and welfare.[13] Ordinarily, grants are given without any payment obligation, while grants are repayable but on concessional terms mostly negotiated and agreed upon before the disbursement. These concessional terms include lower than market interest rates, longer repayment period and a longer grace period. A loan is said to be 'tied' if the recipient country has to purchase some goods or services from the country giving out the loan. The fact that foreign aid creates debt obligation especially when the loan component is high, then it is important that ODA is utilized in an optimal way so as not to crowd-out future investments.

There are different reasons why ODA is given to a country ranging from development programmes to military support. Literature suggests that productivity impact on the national economy will depend strongly on the reasons. In other words, foreign aid given for different purposes has different effects on development process of the recipient country. For example, foreign aid designed to foster economic reforms or improve production methods is likely to have a greater impact on development than military assistance, which aims at building a stronger armed forces in the recipient country. In the long run, both development and military ODA influence the development process either directly or indirectly. Military ODA impact on the development indirectly because it enables the recipient country to devote a greater percentage of its resources to development programmes than it would otherwise do if it had not received the military assistance.

Foreign aid has remained a major source of development finance in Kenya. In the early years of independence, foreign aid was considered important for the reconstruction of the economy, land settlement schemes, and budget deficit financing in which case the British Government took the lead. Other major donors then included Germany, Netherlands, Japan, Sweden, Denmark, USA and Norway.

---

13 The World Bank was created in 1944 to provide aid mostly for infrastructure projects in countries that could not attract private capital on their own. On the other hand, IMF is an international organization of 184 member countries. It was established to promote international monetary cooperation, exchange stability, and orderly exchange arrangements; to foster economic growth and high levels of employment; and to provide temporary financial assistance to countries to help ease balance of payments adjustment.

The World Bank and IMF also contributed immensely towards development assistance (Kenya, 2003). It is argued that development assistance played a significant role in enhancing economic growth during the first two decades of independence.

In the 1990s, foreign aid started to dwindle as donor community became more stringent about fiscal discipline and governance policies. The period 1990-2002 was the worst hit by declined foreign aid when most of multilateral donors withheld their assistance to Kenya. Initially, the withholding of ODA was to pressurize the government to embrace a more democratic political system and also to meet ESAP commitments made earlier to the IMF on governance reforms. With suspension of ODA, the Kenyan government resulted to domestic borrowing which led to crowding-out private investments.

When the NARC Government took power in 2003, it began an ambitious economic reform programme and resumed its cooperation with the World Bank and the IMF with a view to reviving the ODA programmes.[14] Currently, besides the World Bank and IMF, other major donors at bilateral level include Japan, Germany, Finland, USA, UK, Denmark, European Union and Canada (Kenya, 2005). The effectiveness of foreign aid in Kenya has been constrained by poor governance, lack of an overall framework for management of external aid, poor accountability mechanisms and high aid-transaction costs. A major evolution in the bilateral ODA more recently has been the increased reliance on the donors' development agencies in the disbursement and monitoring of foreign aid. Some of these agents include Japan International Corporation (JICA), United States Agency for International Development (USAID), Swedish International Development Agency (SIDA), Canadian International Development Agency (CIDA), Department for International Development (DFID), and Danish International Development Agency (DANIDA) in case of Japan, the US, Sweden, Canada, Britain and Denmark, respectively.

Role of Technology Development in Production and Trade

The definition of the term 'technology' is very easy to come by, but generally, it is accepted that technology is more than just a collection of physical products of science. It can be vague defined as the relationship of society and its tools. Technology as a practice, means not only that new tools change, but also that human beings can change the practice. Therefore, we loosely define technology as one of the means by which mankind changes and expand its living conditions. It embraces a combination of four constituents namely, technique, knowledge, organisation and product. Technology in a modern definition covers the production technique; product design and organisational methods, which are inherent in production and trade process (Dahms, 2001; UNIDO, 2002b). Technological development is therefore a necessary and sufficient condition for a country to become industrialized.

The last decade has witnessed increased global concern regarding technological acquisition; more so in developing countries. The concern stems from the fact that, most developing countries are not able to meet their demand for technology as they lack qualified as well as skilled human capital to innovate and maintain the required level of technology. Innovation is defined as a process that allows firms to improve on their methods of production is an integral part of the technology which manifests itself in new products, and new processes (Dahms, 2001). Therefore, innovation and indeed technology forms a major component of business systems. For example, firms create competitive advantage by discovering new methods of conducting business. Similarly as firms try to adjust to government's regulations in areas such as product standards, environmental controls, restriction of entry, and trade barriers, they acquire more advanced technology. On the other hand, trade has been identified as an important channel through which technological transfer and innovation can take place.

Given the low technological level available in Kenya, the country has for a long time been relying on technology developed in the developed world mainly the US, Europe and so some extent Asian. The recent policy trend has been to enhance technological transfer from the North by allowing foreign investors in the country. For along time, this followed the approach of Multinational Corporations (MNCS) (Lall, 1992; UNDP, 2004). Unfortunately, the success in technology transfer was limited because the linkage between the MNCs and local firms was weak (Kimuyu, 1999). The creation of export processing zones in 1990 was to among other things foster technology transfer into the country through backward linkages to local firms. Literature argues that the newly industrialized countries such as Korea and Singapore invested heavily in technological acquisition during the initial years of industrialization process. UNIDO (2002b) notes that with Globalisation and liberalization on the rise, countries must be internationally competitive to survive and grow. Kenya must embrace new technology in order to compete in the world market.

Kenya's effort towards technology acquisition and development has come a long way. In the beginning, there was a need to establish institutions responsible in facilitating technological advancement. Towards this goal, the Kenya Industrial Research Development Institute (KIRDI), was established in (1979) under the Science and Technology Act whose primary objective is to facilitate acquisition of industrial technology (Kenya, 2002). Additionally, the National Council for Science and Technology (NCST) was established for the purpose of processing and formulating a technology policy capable of building local technological capacity and culture. It was also established to enhance institutional linkages between private and public institutions in the area of technology. The Kenya Industrial Property Institute (KIPI) was also established in 2003 with a mandate of protecting innovations in the country through patents. It was expected to work closely with KIRDI and NCST. Another institution in area of technology is the Kenya Bureau of Standards (KEBS), established through the Standard Act of 1974 to verify quality and standards for all commodities being consumed in the country whether locally produced of imported.

Labour Markets Issues Relating to Production and Trade in Kenya

Labour economics underscores the need to understand the functioning of the labour market and dynamics of labour. The labour markets function through the interaction of workers and employers and the subject matter looks at the suppliers of labour services (workers), the demanders of labour services (employers), and attempts to understand the resulting patterns of wages and employment. At micro level, the issue is to examine the role of individuals in the labour market, while at macro level the concern is the interrelation between labour market, the goods market, money market and trade. To most countries the attainment of full employment by reducing unemployment is the ultimate goal for the obvious reasons that unemployment is a problem that affect development directly. Therefore understanding the labour market is a prerequisite for informed discussion of issues surrounding unemployment and growth.

There has been a tendency for some people to think of the labour as similar to other markets (selling goods) whereby supply and demand forces interact to jointly determine the price. However, the labour market differs from ordinary markets in several ways. The main difference is in the function of supply and demand in setting price and quantity. In the ordinary market, if the price is high there is a tendency in the long run for more goods to be produced until the demand is satisfied. With labour, overall supply cannot be effectively manufactured because people have a limited amount of time in a day and people are not manufactured. Therefore, a rise in overall wages will not result in more supply of labour: it may instead result in less supply of labour as workers take more time off to spend their increased wages, or it may result to no change in supply. Unlike other markets which have a geographical connotation, labour markets do not have this. Given these dynamics analysis of the labour markets needs to be considered in as a special case. However, in more general terms a labour market is said to be 'tight' if demand exceeds supply and 'loose' if supply exceeds demand.

Labour markets in Kenya like in other developing countries are highly fragmented such that the flow of information is highly asymmetrical. Furthermore, they are characterised by surplus labour, leading to high unemployment rate. In order to address the unemployment there is need to promote investment and growth of labour intensive industries.

Table 6.7 provides a sectoral distribution of formal employment in Kenya between 1990 and 2004. One of the observations is that public sector (Community, social and personal services) account for almost half of the total wage employment followed by agricultural sector. Secondly, employment in the manufacturing sector was low for most of the period under the analysis meaning that industrial sector is yet to grow to a level that it can absorb extra labour force. The electricity and water as well as the building and construction sectors appear to have experienced minimal growth in terms of wage employment during the period 1990-2004. Whereas trade restaurant and hotels employment was high in 1990s, this seems to have declined in the period 2000-2004 perhaps due to the decline in the tourism industry in the latter part. Finally, transport and communication appear to have gained significantly between the year 2000 and 2004, arguably due to the growth of ICT and mobile-phone service industry.

Table 6.7: *Wage Employment by Industry and Sector 1990-2004 in 000's*

Industry	1990	1995	2000	2001	2002	2003	2004
Agriculture & Forestry	276.9	298.7	312.2	312.5	313.6	316.1	320.6
Manufacturing	187.7	204.3	218.7	216.6	229.8	239.7	242.0
Electricity & Water	22.4	22.9	22.8	21.4	21.3	21.1	20.8
Building & Construction	71.4	76.4	76.8	76.8	76.5	76.6	77.4
Community, Social & Personal Services*	600.3	662.2	733.1	719.6	726.9	734.9	745.8
Trade, Restaurant & Hotels	113.9	134.9	85.0	83.8	83.2	83.8	85.1
Transport & Communications	74.5	79.1	66.2	84.3	85.5	86.8	98.3
Total	1,409.4	1,332.6	1,182.6	1,677.1	1,699.5	1,727.3	1,763.7

Source: Economic Surveys, (Various Issues)

* This includes, Public Administration, Educational services and Domestic services

There is no doubt that the informal sector is an important sector in the country harbouring millions of Kenyans. It provides employment and income to a big proportion of the Kenyan population. It is a significant part of economic, social and political life in Kenya. Furthermore, due to high population and urbanization growth rates, the informal economy tends to absorb most of the growing labour force. Nonetheless, the information relating to this sector is not captured in the official statistics. Employment in the informal economy relates the estimated number of persons employed in the informal economy to the total number of employed persons. Therefore, the wage employment figures presented in Table 6.7 underestimates the employment situation in Kenya.

CONCLUSION

This chapter has reviewed the structure and the size of trade and production in Kenya since independence in 1963 with a view to linking their structure to business environment. We find that trade had grown in volume, value and structure a reflection of changing development needs in the country. In particular, we have demonstrated external trade plays a central role in development by linking the country to the global world and also facilitating backward linkages to other sectors of the economy. Production structure appears to have changed over time as reflected in the percentage contribution of different sectors to the GDP. Nonetheless, production output has experienced moderate growth as reflected in the GDP growth rates. Although the percentage contribution to agriculture has declined, from about 39% at independence to about 24% in 2004, its dominance both in production and trade is worth mentioning. Manufacturing sector has more or less remained stagnant with its contribution to the GDP oscillating between 10% and 14%. The service sector (both business services and hotels) which appear to have gained prominence over the last decade offers Kenya a new development approach. Jointly these two sectors account for more than what agriculture contributes to the GDP, implying that there is higher potential in these sectors than in the traditional ones.

By discussing the structure of production and trade, this chapter provides a strong link to the sectoral chapters of this book. In particular, we have provided an overview of how agricultural commodities such as tea and coffee have evolved in terms of production and trade as well as some of the institutions governing their operations. In regard to manufacturing, this chapter has indicated how metal, textile and clothing sub-sectors anchor on both domestic and external trade. We have also demonstrated how trade and trade services are structured in Kenya. Finally, the chapter highlights in brief role played by different the institutions and their impacts on production and trade. The list is long but most notable ones include cooperative societies, parastatals, donor community, international organizations and government departments.

REFERENCE

Alila, P.O. 1991. *Evaluation of the Support to Co-operatives in Rift Valley under the Kenya/Nordic Co-operative Development Programme.* NORDIC Centre.

Central Bureau of Statistics, International Centre for Economic Growth, and K-REP 1999. *Kenya's National Micro and Small Enterprise Baseline Survey.* Nairobi: K-Rep Development Agency.

Dahms, M. 2001. "No Cause for Afro-pessimism: A Study of Technical Innovation in Sengerema District, Tanzania". In Muchie, M.; Gammeltoft, P. and Lundvall (eds.). *Putting Africa First: Making of African Innovation Systems.* Aalborg: Aalborg University Press.

Grosh, B. (ed.) 1991. *Public Enterprises in Kenya: What Works, What Doesn't and Why.* London: Lynne Reiner Publishers.

Himbara, D. 1994. The Failed Africanisation of Commerce and Industry in Kenya, *World Development, 22:3,* pp 469-482

Ikiara, G. K. 1991. "Policy Changes and the Informal Sector. In Coughlin, P. and Ikiara, G.K. (eds.). *Kenya's Industrialisation Dilemma.* Nairobi: Heinemann Kenya.

Kenya, Republic of. 2005. *Sessional Paper No. 2 of 2005 on Development of Micro and Small Enterprises for Wealth and Employment Creation for Poverty Reduction.* Nairobi: Government Printer.

Kenya, Republic of. 2003. *Economic Recovery Strategy for Wealth and Employment Creation 2003– 2007*. Nairobi: Government Printer.

Kenya, Republic of. 2002 *National Development Plan 2002-2008*. Nairobi: Government Printer.

Kenya, Republic of. (Various Issues) *Economic Survey*. Nairobi: Government Printer.

Kenya, Republic of. 1998. *Policy Paper on Public Enterprises Reforms and Privatization*. Nairobi: Government Printer.

Kenya, Republic of 1997. *Sessional Paper No. 6 on Co-operatives in a Liberalized Economy*. Nairobi: Government Printer.

Kenya, Republic of. 1996. *Sessional Paper No 2 of 1996 on Industrial Transformation to the year 2020*. Nairobi: Government Printer.

Kenya, Republic of. 1987. *Renewed Growth Through the Cooperative Movement, Sessional Paper No. 4 of 1987*. Nairobi: Government Printer.

Kenya, Republic of. 1965. *Sessional Paper No. 10 of 1965 on African Socialism and its Application to Planning in Kenya*. Nairobi: Government Printer.

Kimuyu, P.1999. "Structure and Performance of the Manufacturing in Kenya". In Kimuyu, P.; Wagacha, M. and Abagi, O. (eds.). *Kenya's Strategic Policies for the 21st Century: Macroeconomic and Sectoral Choices*. Nairobi: Institute of Policy Analysis and Research.

Kinyanjui, M. N. and Khayesi, M. 2005. *Social Capital, Micro and Small Enterprises and Poverty Alleviation in East Africa*. Addis Ababa: OSSREA.

Lall, S. 1992. "Technological Capabilities and Industrialisation". *World Development* 20(12):165-186.

McCormick, D. 2004. *"Micro and Small Enterprises: Backbone of Kenyan Business"*. Unpublished Research Paper.

McCormick, D. 1999. "Policies Affecting Industrialization: 1964-1994". In Ng'ethe N. and Owino W. (eds.). *From Sessional Paper No. 10 to Structural Adjustments: Towards Indigenizing the Policy Debate*. Nairobi: Institute of Policy Analysis and Research.

McCormick, D. 2001. "Value Chains and the Business System". *IDS Bulletin* 32(3):105-115

McCormick, D.; Kinyanjui, M. N. and Ongile, G. 1997. "Growth and Barriers to Growth among Nairobi's Small and Medium-Sized Garment Producers." World *Development* 25(7): 1095-1110.

McCulloch, N.; Winters, L.A. and Cirera, X. 2001. *Trade Liberalisation and Poverty: A Handbook*. London: Centre for Economic Policy Research.

Njeru, J. 2001. "Impact of Foreign Aid on Public Expenditure in Kenya". Research Report submitted to the African Economic Research Consortium, Nairobi.

Onjala, J. O. 2002. "Total Factor Productivity in Kenya: The Links with Trade Policy." AERC Research Paper No. 118. Nairobi: African Economic Research Consortium.

Pedersen, P. O. and McCormick, D. 1999. "Globalisation and Regionalisation of Kenya's Foreign Trade and Production". CDR Working Paper No. 99.9. Copenhagen: Centre for Development Research.

Riddel, R. C.1990. "Introduction". In Riddel R. C. (ed.). *Manufacturing Africa: Performance and Prospects of Seven Countries in Sub-Saharan Africa*. London: James Currey.

Todaro, M. P. 1990. *Economics for a Developing World*. London: Longman Publishers.

UNDP. 2005. *Fourth Kenya Human Development Report: Linking Industrialization with Human Development*. Nairobi : UNDP.

UNDP. 2004. *Third Kenya Human Development Report: Participatory Governance for Human Development*. Nairobi :UNDP.

UNDP. 2003. *Second Kenya Human Development Report*. Nairobi: UNDP.

UNIDO. 2002a. *Industrial Development Report 2002/2003: Competing Through Innovations and Learning*. Vienna: UNIDO.

UNIDO. 2002b. *Integrate Industrial Development Programme in Kenya*. Vienna: UNIDO.

UNIDO. 1996. "Kenya: Paving the Road to Newly Industrialised Country". *Industrial Development Review Series*. Vienna: UNIDO.

United Nations. 2006. National Account Main Aggregates Database, United Nations Statistics Divisions. Available at: *http://unstats.un.org/unsd/snaam*. Accessed on 6th February, 2006.

World Bank. 2000. *Can Africa Claim the 21st Century?* Washington D.C.: World Bank.

White, H. 1992. "The Macroeconomic Impact of Development Aid: A Critical Survey". *Journal of Development Studies* 28:163-240.

Yoshida, M. 1984. *Agricultural Marketing Intervention in East Africa: A Study in the Colonial Origins of Marketing Policies 1900-1965*. Tokyo: Institute of Developing Economies.

Chapter 7

The Financial System

Patrick O. Alila and Rosemary Atieno

INTRODUCTION

The key role of finance in the development process is universally well recognized, especially in the developing countries where a great deal of emphasis has been on capital accumulation, with particular concern over savings, and the need to raise the level of investment. The understanding and acceptance of the role of finance can be traced back to early thinking on economic development in which land, labour and capital were identified as the key factors of production.

In a fundamental sense, and central to business development, capital is commonly viewed as the provision of funds for investment. This should be a pointer to two functionally related dimensions of finance namely, savings and credit. It is through savings that credit or funds to invest become available. This applies to, direct foreign investment and or donor funds which are products of foreign savings, government investments that are likewise products of public savings domestically mainly from taxation and, thirdly self-finance whereby individuals or firms invest own funds which in effect are savings from past incomes or savings. The implication is that the Siamese twin type relationship of sorts between credit and savings needs to be sustained for meaningful economic development and growth to be realized.

It is for the basic purpose of nurturing, regulating and above all, to sustain the co-existence of credit and savings that a financial system is created and developed. The financial system, like any system, broadly consists of interlinked parts that comprise components that are interdependent and functioning together as a whole. The components consist of financial institutions, viz. money market, bonds market, and stock market; financial instruments or claims, viz. currency, cheques, credit cards, bonds, equities, etc. It should be noted that while the foregoing financial instruments are mostly written or electronic evidence of debt, stock shares and guarantees, there are cases also of verbal contracts or promises sustained by solidarity and mutual trust in informal financial markets (Ouma, 2002: 21-2; Alila, 2001). The financial system is therefore made up of institutions whose basic components are (a) financial rules of engagement in the exchange for goods and services for consumption and investment and (b) financial organisations, both formal and informal, having set social, economic and even political objectives.

Financial institutions, in a market economy, through the sale of financial instruments or claims perform the task of financial intermediation. Through intermediation, economic units having surplus resources and those with deficits are brought together in a financial market(s). The overall process is one of mobilization of surplus resources in the form of savings from savers or lenders and the allocation of such resources to investors or borrowers in the form of credit.

Within the business systems, financial institutions can be seen as part of a system of support for business enterprises. Institutions, however, affect the functioning of such support systems and hence their effectiveness. Weak institutions that result in imperfect information and the related high transaction costs affect the process of financial intermediation (Besley, 1994; Stiglitz and Weiss, 1981). Weak institutions also lead to imperfect contract enforcement in the financial system, which often leads to difficulties in enforcing loan repayment. This argument has been used to explain the existence of fragmented markets, notably, the dichotomy between formal and informal financial markets in Africa. Due to the failure of contract enforcement in the formal sector, informal financial markets use social sanctions to ensure repayment. The result is that the different segments of the financial markets use different enforcement systems and penalties (Besley, 1994). Weak institutions and structures especially in Africa have been seen as being the major causes of financial market fragmentation and market failures, hence undermining their role of financial intermediation (Braverman and Guasch, 1986).

This chapter provides the necessary premise for a proper understanding of business and finance relations, and aid analysis of the overall business development. The focus is on the establishment and evolution of financial systems in Kenya. The discussion highlights financial sector reform effort, blossoming of Micro Finance Institutions (MFIs) and the consequence of Micro and Small Enterprises (MSEs) and, finally the implications overall for the growth of business systems in Kenya.

FINANCE AND DEVELOPMENT: SOME THEORETICAL CONSIDERATIONS

Financial systems play an important role in development by facilitating both the accumulation and mobilisation of capital for investment and the supply and access to working capital. As development takes place, credit for instance helps the resource poor entrepreneurs to take advantage of the emergent entrepreneurial opportunities (Hossain, 1988:20). In many developing countries, financial market involvement, especially borrowing for small firms is limited. This, however, differs with respect to firm size, with larger enterprises generally receiving more loans and displaying higher indebtedness in contrast to smaller. The failure by small enterprises to apply for loans may be a reflection of their unwillingness to incur transaction costs and lack of the necessary collateral (Bigsten et al., 2000). The role of finance in business development, especially factors explaining firm access to credit, is worth examining within the relevant theoretical context in order to have a sound basis for business systems analysis.

A well functioning financial sector is important in the process of industrialisation by facilitating investment in real capital, smoothening of expenses and income flows, as well as financing working capital. At the aggregate national level, financial sector development is integral for economic growth. Where unstable macro economic environment and institutional factors like imperfect information and inefficient legal systems hinder efficient financial intermediation, industrial sector growth and overall economic development may be compromised (Isaksson, 2004). It is argued that lack of external finance in many African countries can explain the significantly longer time it takes for manufacturing exports to catch up with opportunities provided by relative changes that favour international competitiveness (Isaksson, 2004)[1].

In many African countries, financial systems are characterised by fragmentation, and this affects their functions. Informal finance is widespread, but generally self contained, and isolated from those of the formal sector. Integration of the different segments of the financial markets could facilitate economic development by effectively mobilising resources and improving their flow to enterprises. The main institutional features that result in fragmentation are: imperfect information on creditworthiness and differences in the costs of screening, monitoring and contract enforcement among lenders; limited information flow due to poor communication and high cost of information gathering; inadequate legal structure that affects the costs and risks of contract enforcement, which affects lender's willingness to enter into contract and the type of security they are willing to take; and lack of well functioning insurance markets to offset the risks of default.

An increasing body of analytical work has attempted to explain the functioning of credit markets mostly following from the pioneering work of Stiglitz and Weise (1981). These works have explored the implications of incomplete markets and imperfect information for the functioning of credit markets in developing countries and, notably, access to credit.

It is argued that, for example, interest rates charged by a credit institution has a dual role of sorting potential borrowers (leading to adverse selection), and affecting the actions of borrowers (leading to the incentive effect). Adverse selection occurs because lenders would like to identify borrowers most likely to repay their loans since the banks' expected returns depends on the probability of repayment. In an attempt to identify borrowers with high probability of repayment, banks are likely to use the interest rates that an individual is willing to repay as a screening device. However, borrowers willing to pay high interest rates may, on average, be worse risks takers, thus as interest rate increases, the riskiness of those who borrow increase, reducing the bank's profitability. The incentive effect occurs because as

---

1   Collier and Gunning (1999) give a general description of how financial issues are related to economic performance in Africa.

interest rate and other terms of the contract change, the behaviour of borrowers is likely to change since it affects the returns on their projects (Bigsten et al., 2000). Interest rates thus affect the nature of the transaction and do not necessarily clear the market. Both effects are seen as a result of the imperfect information inherent in credit markets.

Banks are not able to control all actions of borrowers due to imperfect and costly information, and will formulate the terms of the loan contract to induce borrowers to take actions in the interest of the bank and to attract low risk borrowers. The result is an equilibrium rate of interest at which the demand for credit exceeds the supply thereby forcing banks to ration out borrowers. Other terms of the contract, like the amount of the loan, and the amount of collateral will also affect the behaviour of borrowers and their distribution, as well as the bank returns. Raising interest rates or collateral in the face of excess demand is always not profitable, and banks will deny loans to certain borrowers. The result is credit rationing in the credit markets, which refers to two situations: (1) among loan applicants who appear to be identical, some receive and others do not, with those who don't having no chance of receiving a loan even if they offered to pay higher interest rates. (2) there are identifiable groups of people who at a given supply of credit, are unable to obtain credit at any interest rate, but with a larger supply, they would (Stiglitz and Weiss, 1981; See also Bigsten et al., 2000:2).

FINANCIAL MARKET CHARACTERISTICS AND ACCESS TO CREDIT

A number of factors explain access to and the nature of participation in financial markets especially by borrowers. These factors emanate mainly from the loan rationing behaviour of lenders and the inadequate supply in the market, resulting in credit market imperfections. Among the possible factors, which would stop firms from applying for credit is the inability to meet collateral requirements and the high costs associated with loan applications. Factors affecting collateral include assets, outstanding debt, and opportunities for collateral substitutes like ethnicity, networks, legal status, ownership structure, firm age and links with the financial sector. The foregoing factors also affect transactions costs and imply that there will be firms that would prefer but avoid application for external financing. Such firms are considered constrained. Equally constrained are those firms, which apply for but do not receive credit (Bigsten et al., 2000, p.15).

A number of credit market characteristics like inter-temporal risk, information asymmetry, and enforcement problems are important in determining access to credit (Aryeteey and Nissanke, 1995), since they determine the amount of lending that takes place. In most cases the access problem, especially among formal financial institutions is one created by the institutions mainly through their lending policies. This is displayed in the form of prescribed minimum loan amounts, complicated application procedures, and restricting credit for specific purposes, which eventually lead to credit rationing (Schmidt and Kropp, 1987:58-60). In the case of small-scale enterprises, reliable access to short term and small amounts of credit is more valuable and emphasising it may be of greater relevance in credit programmes aimed at such enterprises (Adams and Von Pischke, 1992).

The characteristics of the lending institutions are therefore of critical importance especially for small firms, most of which, like other smallholders, demand specific types of credit (See also Ouma, 2002:116). This kind of access problem is more difficult to avoid since conceptually, it raises the problem of how loans can be tailored to the needs of specific borrowers. Financial institutions, therefore, need to expose actual and latent demand for credit through their programmes. However, even if the needs are known, not all institutions will be capable of providing credit with the desired conditions because they lack the necessary resources. The emerging dominance of Micro Finance Institutions (MFIs), providing credit through targeted programmes to MSEs can therefore be seen as a response to special type of demand for credit. In Kenya, credit rationing is an important characteristic of financial market mainly because of poor information and contract enforcement (Atieno, 2004). This calls for the need to address the credit problem from the lenders perspective.

Governments and development aid agencies have for long used credit as a tool for promoting development. A major assumption of development programmes based on such premise has been that credit markets are not functioning well and intervention is therefore necessary to facilitate increased economic activity and growth. However, due to the risky nature of credit markets, the cost of information and enforcement are generally vast and affect the outcome of such programmes negatively. The borrower is therefore constrained to either borrow money at a higher interest rate to cover monitoring and enforcement costs, or be rationed out by not being allowed to borrow at the existing interest rate. In the end, less borrowing takes place (Bigsten et al., 2000:2). MSEs in particular are known to be rationed out due to their failure to meet the lending terms and conditions set by the formal finance institutions. However in most African countries, there is a dearth of evidence on the nature and actual scope of credit market imperfections while at the same time, their consequences on economic activity are not fully understood.

In many developing countries MSEs have become the target of an increasing number of development programmes whose main component is credit. It has been argued that these programmes resemble earlier attempts to assist small-scale farmers through credit programmes with generally unfavourable outcomes (Adams and Von Pischke, 1992:1463). The discussions regarding the negative experience with credit aside, there is a general consensus among development specialists that finance can make an important contribution to development especially for MSEs and may be the only type of MSE assistance that can be provided sustainably (CBS et al., 1999:81). It is due to the perceived role of MSEs in combating poverty and unemployment that they have become a focus of development policies. Alila (2001:330) observes that there is a major focus on MSEs in Kenya as an entry point for development initiatives mainly due to the development crises that have plagued the country and witnessed in virtually the whole of African continent. On a wider context, credit initiatives and arrangements can be seen as a form of institution building. This is key in fostering long term development since credit institutions act like development catalysts through the dissemination of new ideas, and eventually, providing avenues for participation by people in the development process.

FRAGMENTATION OF CREDIT MARKETS

In the African situation, credit markets are largely fragmented with different segments serving clients with distinct characteristics. Credit markets in Africa have mainly been characterised by the inability to satisfy the existing demand for credit especially in rural areas. In any case, whereas for the informal sector the main reason for this inability is the small size of the resources it controls, for the formal sector, it is difficulties in loan administration like screening and monitoring, high transaction costs, and the risk of default (Aryeetey, 1996). A significant consequence of this is that lending units are unable to meet the needs of borrowers interested in certain types of credit.

Fragmentation of financial markets has underlying policy and structural institutional explanations. Two main theoretical paradigms have been advanced to explain the existence of this fragmentation: the policy based explanation and the structural institutional explanations (Aryeetey et al., 1997). According to the policy based explanation, fragmented credit markets in which favoured borrowers obtain funds at subsidised interest rates, while others seek funds from expensive informal markets develop due to repressive policies which raise the demand for funds. Unsatisfied demand for investible funds forces credit rationing using non interest rate criteria, while an informal market develops at uncontrolled interest rates. Removing these restrictive policies should therefore enable the formal sector to expand and thereby eliminate the need for informal finance.

According to the structural institutional explanations, imperfect information on creditworthiness cost of screening, monitoring and contract enforcement among lenders result in market failure due to adverse selection and moral hazard, which undermine the operation of financial markets. As a result, lenders may resort to credit rationing in the face of excess demand, thus establishing equilibrium even in the absence of interest rate ceilings and direct allocations. Market segmentation then results. Market segments that are avoided by the formal institutions due to institutional and structural factors are served by informal agents who use personal relationships, social sanctions and collateral substitutes to ensure repayment. An extended view of this explanation is that structural barriers result in monopoly power, which perpetuates segmentation.

Among the questions, which arise out of this fragmentation scenario, is that of access to financial services from both sources. In a fragmented credit market, what explains borrowers' decision to borrow at all, and whether to borrow from any specific segment of the market? In a study of credit constraints in manufacturing enterprises in Africa, Bigsten et al. (2000), find a diversity of financial institutions, ranging from private to government ones. In terms of firms' involvement in credit markets, the study finds that the percentage of firms receiving loans is small and most lending is collateralised, with most non-collateralised loans having alternative guarantee and conditions attached. In most cases, the value of collateral is on average higher than the loan value.

FORMAL AND INFORMAL FINANCE

Another view has attempted to explain the existence of informal finance as simply residual finance, satisfying only the excess demand by those excluded from formal finance. According to this view, informal sector finance develops in response to the formal sector controls. Structural and institutional barriers across segments perpetuate segmentation by providing opportunity for monopoly power. A further explanation is that fragmentation exists due to inherent operational characteristics of the markets. Looking at the role of informal financial sectors in Ghana, Aryeetey and Gockel (1991), attempted to investigate factors, which motivate the private sector to conduct financial transactions in the informal financial sectors. They argue that the informal sector derives its dynamism from developments in the formal sector as well as from its own internal characteristics. An important cost of segmentation is that funds fail to flow across groups of individuals and firms despite benefits in doing so. According to Besley (1994), this kind of segmentation may also be reinforced by government regulations.

The fragmented nature of the financial markets leads to the loan rationing behaviour of lenders, limiting access to credit from some segments, and resulting in a credit gap, affecting mainly firms, which want to grow. MSEs fall within this category. As firms expand, their credit needs exceed the amounts that the informal sector can provide. However, they still do not qualify for the formal sector credit due to the lending terms and conditions by such institutions.

Financial markets in African countries are therefore characterised by imperfect and costly information, risks and market segmentation, resulting in credit rationing. This is one of the underlying factors for the co-existence of both formal and informal credit markets serving the needs of the different segments of the market. In contrast, policy based and structural institutional explanations attempt to explain the coexistence of formal and informal segments of the market as outcomes of the policy and structural institutional rigidities.

Imperfect information emerges as an important explanation for credit rationing due to information asymmetry. Loan terms and conditions are used which affect the behaviour of borrowers. There is evidence also showing that the assumption that formal interest rates are the reason why borrowers do not use formal credit is not necessarily correct. Rather, the unique characteristics of credit services explain segmentation in the credit market. For instance, lack of effective contract enforcement and the consequent default risk are also important considerations in loan rationing.

FINANCIAL SYSTEM IN KENYA

Background and Origins

The origins of Kenya's financial institutions are rooted in the country's historical past of a colonial economy while their growth has mainly taken place in the organisational framework of a mixed economy during the post independence period, in the last four decades. The institutions in broad groupings comprise banks, non-bank financial institutions, mortgage finance companies, foreign exchange bureaus, building societies, micro-finance institutions, development finance institutions etc. The government in the colonial era established and/or had control over institutions in the financial and virtually all other sectors of the economy and society. The principal mechanisms for government influence was control over money supply and credit, for instance, directing allocation exclusively to white settler cash crop farming for export while perpetuating subsistence food crop production in the African native reserves.

In the post independence era mixed economy, there has been more of government participation together with private enterprise in strategic sectors of the economy, notably banking. The private sector in such arrangements has considerable scope for independent development but subject to government controls, for example, over credit and transactions with other countries. However, of significance is the major growth, both in numbers and type of financial institutions, resulting in diverse forms of the components of the financial system especially in the past decade (Kenya, 1965; 1986).

The financial system understood to deal essentially with money matters, in terms of asset ownership, distribution and use, socio-economic mobility and generally wealth creation and accumulation, had structures set up in Kenya prior to independence in 1963. Banks were started, beginning with the National Bank of India subsequently becoming National and Grindlays Bank; Standard Bank of South Africa and the National Bank of South Africa, which came into the scene soon thereafter (Anjichi). There was a lapse before the setting up of the current leading bank, Barclays Bank (Dominion, Colonial and Overseas), through a merger of the National Bank of South Africa and the Anglo-Egyptian Bank. It was thereafter not until the 1950s that the banking sector witnessed a significant entry of foreign continental Europe and Asia banks, all of which still operate in Kenya, although some changed business names (Kenya, 1983).

There were only two non-bank financial institutions, specifically hire purchase houses, prior to the attainment of independence and building societies were five. The same regulations under the Money Lenders Ordinance and Banking Ordinance applied to banks and finance houses, except that the latter could not maintain chequer accounts and dealt with specialized activities. Kenya, Uganda and Tanzania were members of the East African Currency Board. However, the board operated a passive monetary policy lacking discretionary powers to influence or regulate the activities of commercial banks and non-bank financial institutions in the three countries. This is evidenced by the foreign commercial banks operation of a "gentleman's club" with respect to interest rates on deposits and loans/advances and commissions and charges on various services offered until a few years after independence.

POST INDEPENDENCE GROWTH AND DEVELOPMENT OF FINANCIAL STRUCTURES

Growth of Financial Structures in the Country

The evolution of the financial system, involving fast growth and expansion following independence, is mainly due to the pursuit of economic development goals. These included striving to achieve high economic growth, employment generation, foreign exchange earnings and economic stability. A principal means used by the government towards achieving the foregoing goals is the control over money supply and credit and thereby influencing the direction of the economy. This is the fundamental rationale for the strong desire favouring independent monetary and financial authorities in Kenya, Uganda and Tanzania even before the break up of the E.A. Community. In essence, this meant power over the direction of allocation of money to priority sectors or particular forms of credit and influence of those particular sector's growth and credit by the government.

The control over money supply and the volume of credit is through the central bank, commercial banks and non-bank financial institutions. Thus, Kenya established a Central bank in 1966 to add to the already existing financial institutions around the time of independence comprising of six commercial banks, three hire purchase houses, insurance companies, building societies, savings and loan associations and various other finance and investment companies. The banks and non-bank financial institutions have all had tremendous growth and expansion over the years reflected in the current diversity.

The financial sector grew steadily in the 1990s as indicated by the growth of the sector's share in GDP and assets of the banking system. The number of commercial banks increased significantly in 1980s, from 16 in 1981 to 26 in 1990 and 48 in 1997, and reaching 55 in 1998. The Non Bank Financial Institutions (NBFIs) also experienced rapid growth over the same period, more than doubling from 23 in 1981 to 54 in 1988, before declining sharply after that to 24 in 1997 and 16 in 1998 (CBK 1998). This growth in the number of these financial institutions was due to regulatory framework in which entry requirements were deliberately relaxed as deliberate government effort to promote the growth of locally owned financial institutions.

As at December 2001, the number of banks dropped to 47 from 50 in 2000, and the NBFIs down to three. There was a case of a bank under Central Bank management and another placed under liquidation but the banking sector remained fairly stable. The commercial banks, however, significantly reduced their branch network from 512 to 465 reasoning that this was to reduce their operating costs. A related and contrasting development was that liquid assets of commercial banks increased by nearly 10 per cent in 2000/2001, reflected in a rise in their liquid ratio which was interestingly attributed to low demand for credit by the private sector (Kenya, 2002). Moreover, the profitability of the sector increased substantially, more than doubling to reach Kshs.8.6 billion, and two multinational banks accounting for 86 percent of the profits.

It should be recalled that banks in Kenya at the time of independence were either foreign owned or foreign controlled and foreign domination has persisted as clearly evidenced by the lion's share of the profits. There are, in any case, three major developments in terms of indigenous population participation in the banking sector that need highlighting. First was the enacting of the Banking Act in 1968 aimed at harmonising the Central Bank Act and older Banking Act to establish a foundation for the future expansion of the banking industry by notably assigning the Central Bank an inspection responsibility. The Act made a distinction between a bank and a non-bank financial institution and made a provision for minimum capital required to open either one, which has been amended from time to time. Also relevant were others such as Companies Act, Building Societies Act, Hire Purchase Act and the Exchange Control Act.

Secondly, because the existing foreign banks at independence lent very little to Africans, and mostly chose to invest surplus funds abroad, the government was motivated to participate in the financial sector to make it more responsive to borrowing need of indigenous Kenyans. The government, therefore, entered the banking sector by way of setting up the Cooperative Bank of Kenya (1965) to look after the interests of the cooperative movement. For other national interests, Kenya Commercial Bank (1970) and the National Bank of Kenya (1968) were established. In the same vein, the Housing Finance Company of Kenya (HFCK) was set up and accepted deposits for onward lending for mortgages.

Thirdly, around the mid 1970s Kenya nationals started venturing into banking through non-bank financial institutions comprising finance houses and building societies. There was a marked rapid increase of these institutions by a colossal 300% between 1978 and 1987, most of them belonging to Africans. The increase was a result of deliberate government policy of low capital requirements, which subsequently led to problems and eventual closure for some of them. Specifically in the period 1985/86, these institutions faced severe insolvency problems which led to loss of confidence and panic in the banking system resulting in a shifting of funds to the longer established commercial banks.

Financial Sector and Business Development

It is largely argued that Kenya's financial sector is relatively developed due to the level of private sector participation and diversity of services offered (Kenya, 1997; Isaksson and Wihlborg, 2002). However, viewed against its ability to meet the particular credit needs of the different types of both urban and rural enterprise activities, Kenya's financial system displays a deficiency in the range of financial instruments and lack of coordination between different financial institutions and providers of different services.

One important aspect of the financial sector in Kenya, however, is that despite this growth of the sector, there has been no diversity in the type of institutions and products they provide as would be expected. The banking sector is dominated by a few large commercial banks, which control the largest share of deposits and focus on short term lending. The short-term nature of their lending and concentration on a small corporate clientele has meant that they are indifferent to the small-scale borrowers and savers, thus excluding a large number of investors from their services. The profitability in the banking sector has not led to increased entry and efficiency in the banking sector, pointing to the existence of barriers to entry in the sector. Despite the recent drop in the number of financial institutions, the banking sector's profitability increased substantially due to reduction in other banking costs (Kenya, 2002:85). Kenya's financial system also displays a deficiency in the range of financial instruments and the lack of coordination between the different financial institutions. Hence, among the major constraints faced by MSEs, are low capitalisation and lack of access to credit (UNDP, 2002).

Institutions that provide credit to the small and micro enterprise sector in Kenya include commercial banks, non-bank financial institutions, development finance institutions, non-governmental organisations, multilateral organisations, business associations and rotating savings and credit associations. In addition, financial transactions also take place between traders, friends and relatives, landlords, employees, as well as commercial moneylenders. Many financial institutions, especially commercial banks, rarely lend to small and micro enterprises since they emphasise collateral which most MSEs lack. Few enterprises are able to provide the marketable collateral and guarantee requirements of commercial banks, with the result that MSEs lacking such requirements have not been able to obtain credit from banks. Most of them, therefore, rely on their own savings and informal sources of credit (Oketch et al., 1995).

Financial institutions not under Central Bank umbrella but provide credit for enterprises, either directly or indirectly, include development finance institutions operating under their own character, Kenya Post Office Savings Bank, micro finance institutions and savings and credit cooperatives. The basic feature of these institutions is that they offer people a variety of financial assets to channel and keep savings. Thus, these are a diversification of financial assets and loan portfolios that spurs and strengthens the savings and investment initiatives.

These institutions are varied, some being in the public sector such as state corporations or even government departments. The functions are likewise multiple often including both savings and credit, but often going a step further to undertake promotion of ventures in agriculture, commerce, industry, housing etc. through financing policy, marketing, training and related activities. The financial institutions have been segmented in terms of economic activities, as well as sources of funding. Hence, commercial banks concentrated in short term loans, mortgage banks on residential loans, while development finance institutions concentrated on long-term loans.

The 1999 survey of MSEs observes that Kenya has about 150 organisations with credit programmes most of which are NGOs. However, attempts to estimate the credit supply to the MSE sector are constrained by the fact that commercial banks are under no legal obligation to report them, while some NGOs are reluctant to reveal their portfolios. This has meant that attempts to estimate credit supply to the sector do not cover all the sources (CBS et al., 1999:80), making it difficult to estimate the credit demand and supply. What is clear, however, is that available credit from formal and semi formal institutions is often not adequate to meet the credit needs of the MFIs, leaving them to seek credit from informal sources.

Commercial Banks

Commercial banks as a source of credit have the advantage of a wide branch network, which can reach several micro enterprises. They also operate savings accounts, which make it possible to monitor their clients closely. Most of them are, however, located in urban areas thereby making it difficult to provide services to those enterprises located in rural areas. Given the fact that up to 66% of the MSEs are located in rural areas, this is a major limitation on the extent to which commercial banks can serve them. Other limitations of commercial bank lending to the MSE sector in Kenya include the fact that they lack the appropriate savings instruments to mobilise savings to the MSEs, and the restrictions on withdrawals, which discourage savers who would like frequent access to their savings. Their locations away from many enterprises also imply high transaction costs which discourage most enterprises from using their savings and other services. For commercial banks, dealing with a large number of small firms also has implications for transaction costs. This is compounded by their lack of perfect information about borrowers, which often leads to the problem of moral hazard and adverse selection.

Development Finance Institutions

Development Finance Institutions (DFIs) notably AFC, ICDC, DFCK, IDB, EADB, KIE etc were the main sources of long term finance especially in the 1960s and 1970s post independence period. These were set up by the government to fill the gap for long-term credit. The funds were mobilised from development assistance and pooled together with funding from the government. The rationale for setting up the Agricultural Finance Corporation (AFC) and the Agricultural Development Corporation (ADC) was provision of finance to the average farmer on suitable terms. It was argued that the existing banks and financial institutions primarily "serve the Asian and European communities and so far conduct only a minority of their business with the African people" (AFC Statistical Digest, 1998).

The Industrial Commercial Development Corporation (ICDC), the Development Finance Company of Kenya (DFCK) and Industrial Development Bank (IDB) were set up to serve the industrial and commercial sectors. ICDC and DFCK have given loans and participated in equity in most sectors of the economy, notably textiles, agricultural processing (foods and beverages), engineering and instruction, trade and services. A subsidiary company of DFCK, Small Enterprise Finance Company (SEFCO) was incorporated for advisory services, expansion and rehabilitation of enterprises owned and managed by indigenous business people. In the same way, Kenya Industrial Estates (KIE), initially a subsidiary of ICDC, became an autonomous institution for promotion and financing of small scale industrial projects countrywide.

The Industrial Development Bank (IDB) was established to promote, establish and modernize medium and large scale manufacturing industries operating on the basis of banking principles. The East African Development Bank (EADB) was set up under the Treaty for East African Corporation (1967) with headquarters in Nairobi. It was mandated to foster regional development. EADB has supported several industrial projects, also through loans and equity participation. In a nutshell, the DFIs, as the service of long-term finance to the private sector is concerned, were key promoters of new investments that played a major role in the empowerment of African businessmen in particular. Furthermore, joint ventures between the government and foreign investors formed the backbone of the now fledging industrialisation strategy. The DFIs, however, never managed to gain their independence especially in sourcing for funds, and continued to rely on government funding, thus constituting a significant drain on budgetary resources. They also faced other constraints like unprofitable portfolios.

Micro-Finance Institutions (MFIs)

In the recent years, a number of non-governmental organisations (NGOs) have been involved in financing of micro enterprises. The onset of NGOs in the form of MFIs has improved access of MSEs to credit. Most of them operate tailor made credit programmes targeting specific activities. In most cases, they have targeted small-scale enterprises operated by women as groups. Most NGOs have, however, not had positive performance. Their inexperience in financial intermediation and limited financial resources have limited their potential. Their lending activities tend to have suffered from the cheap credit problem. There is little co-ordination among the NGOs, resulting in duplication of resources and activities. Most of them have high credit costs, are donor based and sponsored, lack adequate funding and are limited in their geographical coverage. They are also discriminative against small-scale enterprises who get rationed out by lenders since cheap credit creates excess demand for loanable funds forcing lenders to lend to large enterprises with collateral and perceived to be less risky. Since 2001, the Central Bank of Kenya has taken the responsibility of regulating the MFI sector, to provide a reliable alternative source of credit.

Rotating Savings and Credit Associations

Rotating Savings and Credit Associations (ROSCAs) are also an important source of credit for MSEs in the country. They are found in both rural and urban areas either as registered welfare groups or unregistered groups. They mainly provide credit to those who would not likely be legible to borrow from other sources. ROSCAs have developed mostly in response to the lack of access to credit by MSEs forcing them to rely on their own savings and informal credit sources for their financing. Their ability to integrate savings into their credit schemes enables them to mobilise savings from their members. The ROSCAs have also acted as an important link for MSEs to credit from NGOs which channel their credit through existing groups like ROSCAs. However, even for members of ROSCAs, not all their credit needs can be satisfied within the associations. This implies that there is some proportion of borrowing and lending that is not catered for by both the formal institutions and such associations. This is catered for by personal savings as well as borrowing between entrepreneurs and other forms of informal transactions.

ROSCAs, together with other lending institutions, and even some microfinance institutions also operate like clubs, where their credit facilities only benefit their members. Potential borrowers who are not members are automatically locked out from such programmes regardless the viability of their enterprises and their ability to repay the loans.

FINANCIAL MARKET REFORMS IN KENYA

During the first decade of independence, Kenya experienced rapid economic growth. However, during the 1970s, the country started experiencing structural distortions, which necessitated reforms to correct the situation. The first Structural Adjustment Lending (SAL), was received in 1979, and the second one in 1982. However, a comprehensive adjustment programme for the financial market was undertaken in 1989, with the main objective of improving the mobilisation and allocation of domestic resources. These reforms were mainly institutional and policy oriented in nature. The institutional reforms included strengthening the regulation and supervision of financial institutions as well as developing and implementation of specific restructuring programmes for weak and insolvent institutions (World Bank, 1992). Policy reforms involved, among other measures, the liberalisation of interest rates and improving the efficiency of financial intermediation by removing distortions in financial mobilisation (O'Brien and Ryan 2001). Some have argued that these reforms have led to further development of the financial sector (Isaksson and Wihlborg, 2002).

Interest rates were first reviewed in 1974 following the oil crisis that led to a rise in inflation. This made both the savings and lending rates negative in real terms. By 1979, a combination of factors like the fall in inflation, low interest rate offered by government securities and credit guidelines, which made asset portfolio reallocations inflexible, resulted in positive real lending rates. However, deposit rates were set at a low level and remained negative in real terms.

During what can be termed as the period of reforms (1980-1990), interest rates were reviewed several times in efforts to allow commercial banks greater flexibility to meet the needs of the customers, by narrowing the difference in interest rates between NBFIs and commercial banks. Since interest rates are also used as instrument of monetary policy, its adjustments were also made to contain inflationary pressure. During the late 1980s, further reviews were made following increased inflationary pressure due to increased money supply. Although savings rates increased to 13.5% in 1990, with high inflation rate, it remained negative in real terms. With the lending rate raised to 19% over the same period, the interest rate spread widened to 5.5% (O'Brien and Ryan, 2001).

The liberalisation of interest rates in 1991 was theoretically expected to result in an increase in interest rates. However, the minimum savings rate in the country declined from 13.5% in 1990 to 6.9% in 1995, while the maximum lending rate increased to a peak of 38.6% in 1993. The spread therefore assumed a rising trend. The expansionary fiscal policy further resulted in the lending rate going up while the low savings rate became negative in real terms in the first half of the 1990s.

During the second half of the 1990s, savings rates increased but never reached the levels recorded in the first half of the decade. On the other hand, lending rates declined but settled at higher levels compared with the periods immediately after liberalisation. As a result, the interest rate spread peaked in 1996 (Ngugi, 2001; Central Bank of Kenya, 1995:4-5). Other outcomes that have been attributed to financial liberalisation are the growth in the financial sector and the number of financial instruments available to the public. Although the foreign exchange market was liberalised and access to foreign exchange improved, the Kenyan financial market still remained segmented from the world markets (Isaksson and Wihlborg, 2002).

Despite reforms in the financial sector, efforts to introduce competitiveness did not achieve much as the banking sector gained more oligopolistic structure, with only a few banks controlling the banking sector. The high lending interest rates also discouraged borrowing from the banking sector. Ngugi and Kabubo (1998) observe that the prerequisite of financial market liberalisation were not put in place before the process was started. The result is that financial markets are still underdeveloped, and the central bank not independent in its operations. This has had implications for the development of business enterprises in the country.

FINANCING CONSTRAINTS IN THE DEVELOPMENT OF MSES IN KENYA

Access to financing can be a constraint to economic activity. This results from a number of factors, some of which are institutional. The existence of interest groups with political influence might lead to a credit allocation system whereby many firms with viable projects are left out while others get credit on favourable terms. Where the legal institutional framework for enforcement of financial contracts are weak, the consequence is that lenders have to either rely on self enforcement mechanisms, or not give loans (Isaksson and Wihlborg, 2002). In most cases, small firms are more affected by such biases than the large firms.

Access to financial services is mainly a constraint to the MSEs. Despite the increasing importance of MSEs in many African countries Kenya included, financial constraints remain one of the problems facing the sector. MSEs suffer from a general bias with respect to accessing financial services especially from the formal financial sector. Among the major reasons for closure of businesses, the shortage of operating funds has featured prominently (Daniels et al., 1995). The survey also showed that less than 10% of the MSEs used credit for start up capital. The limited use of credit by MSEs has meant that most of them depend on non-credit sources like personal savings, or donations from their families to start their businesses.

The problem of access to credit for most of the MSE is confirmed by a number of surveys on the sector in Kenya (Parker and Torres, 1994; Daniels et al., 1995, Oketch et al., 1995). The studies conclude that although there had been a steady growth in credit from the banking sector in the past, little of this credit had reached the MSEs, reflecting the general bias by the financial sector against the MSEs. According to the 1993 baseline survey, only 9% of the MSEs had received credit, with only 4% of this credit having been obtained from the formal financial institutions. The bulk of the MSE credit came from informal savings and credit associations. The 1999 survey of MSEs confirms that this situation has not changed much. The survey shows that only 10.4% of the MSEs have ever received credit from any source. The majority of the MSEs therefore, operate without credit (CBS et al., 1999:81). Limited access to credit has thus remained one of the constraints to MSE development in the country.

MSEs access to formal sector credit continues to be of major concern to policy makers and practitioners. The performance of formal financial institutions and credit programmes in Kenya in terms of alleviating the financial constraints of the smallholder sector has met with increasing criticisms, mainly due to their lending terms and conditions. Formal institutional credit has reached only a minimum of smallholders. The criterion of credit worthiness, delays in loan processing and disbursement, and the government approach to preferential interest rates, resulting in non price credit rationing, have all acted to limit the amount of credit available to smallholders and the efficiency with which the available funds are used (Atieno, 1994:124). This can be seen as an indication of the general inadequacy of the formal credit institutions in meeting the existing credit demand in the country.

A number of factors can be seen as explanations for the limited access. Government controls have played a role with respect to MSE access to credit. Although there is a strong private sector involvement in the financial sector in Kenya, and diversity in the services offered, some government controls still remain in place, despite the financial sector liberalisation, since the early 1990s. This limits lending to the various sectors of the economy. The study by Bigsten et al. (2000:12) shows that the percentage of firms receiving loans is very small, indicating a limited involvement in the financial markets in the form of borrowing. This is mainly because loans are collateralised, with non-collateral loans having alternative guarantees and conditions attached. However, the level of involvement varies with firm size. Most large firms have overdraft facilities, receive more loans, and have higher indebtedness and more access to trade credit than smaller firms. Small firms have less credit, although this does not mean that they are less constrained in the credit market (Bigsten et al., 2000:13). Small firms and by extension the MSEs, are therefore more constrained by the financial system than the large firms.

Existing evidence shows that the majority of the MSEs in the country get their loans from the informal financial sector, with limited use of the formal sector (CBS et al., 1999; Aleke Dondo, 1994; Alila, 1991; Atieno, 2001; Ouma, 2002). Ouma (1991) found that 72% of the sample surveyed saved with and borrowed from informal sources. Due to the limited supply of credit from the formal sector, firms respond by directing their demand for credit to specific market segments depending on the nature of their demand for credit. Different studies show that credit rationing exists among enterprises in Kenya (Atieno, 2001; Bigsten et al., 2000). Such credit market constraints restrict small firms from seeking credit especially from the formal sector, leaving most small firms to seek credit from informal sources. Bureaucracy in loan administration also adds the costs to MSEs in terms of missed opportunities, forgone earnings etc., which make small loans expensive for MSEs (Ouma, 2002:192).

The general picture is that few MSEs (less than 50%) used credit from any source. This was mainly due to lack of information about credit, lack of security and no need for credit. However, not all the MSEs who do not use credit are free from constrain. Their lack of application for credit can be interpreted to mean that they perceive their chances of success as very low. Hence, loan rationing, either by rejecting applications of those who need credit, or giving them amounts less than what they applied for, is an important characteristic of financial institutions determining access to credit by the MSEs in Kenya. Both formal and informal credit sources practise credit rationing to the MSEs. Therefore, although potential borrowers need credit and may have the ability to repay, the lending terms and conditions may prevent them from seeking credit.

Although more MSEs depend on informal sources for their credit needs, the amounts of credit from informal sources is inherently lower than those from the formal sources. This implies that whereas informal credit may enable MSEs to establish, it may not be adequate for those wanting to expand their activities. Hence, despite its relative accessibility compared to the formal sources, the informal credit does not satisfy the credit needs of a certain category of enterprises, which are too big for it, but do not meet the lending requirements of the formal credit market (Atieno, 2001:29). This conforms to the argument that credit markets in Africa result in a credit gap, which captures a certain category of borrowers. It also has implications for the growth and development of MSEs, which can use informal sources to start up, but as they grow, their credit needs exceed what they can get from the informal sector, while at the same, time they still do not qualify for the formal sector credit.

A study (Ouma, 2002) suggests that as MSEs grow, they slowly graduate to access different sources of credit. The study observes that majority of the MSEs fund their economic activities from their own resources, mainly personal savings. When the MSE activities are up and running they are able to attract a number of financial institutions like ROSCAs, Mutual Assistance Groups (MAGs) and NGOs to finance their activities. But even at this stage, loans and grants from relatives, friends, and neighbours still play a major role in financing these enterprises (Ouma, 2002:107). Such reliance on informal credit has meant that MSEs maintain strong links with their background in order to guarantee a source of finance for their businesses.

CONCLUSIONS

Finance or capital is important in the overall development process as one of the major factors of production, together with land and labour. In the same vein, it is one of the key inputs in the development and growth of business enterprises. Furthermore, in a business system, one of the reasons firms form linkages and relations with one another is for the purpose of access to financial capital (McCormick and Atieno, 2002). It's likewise, the case that in the overall process of development, financial markets in particular serve the broad purpose of mobilization of surplus resources or savings from savers/lenders, and their allocation to investors/borrowers, in the form of credit through transactions taking place in an organized financial system. In a nutshell, the financial system is therefore made up of institutions for savings and/or borrowing whose basic components are the financial rules of engagement in the exchange of goods and services for consumption and investment and financial organisations, both formal and informal that have set social, economic and even political objectives.

In Kenya, the financial arrangements established in the colonial economy have evolved overtime into a financial system which has played a major role in the national and international business transactions. The institutional elements of the financial sector include the regulatory framework revolving around the central bank, commercial banks, non-bank financial institutions, mortgage finance companies, foreign exchange bureaus, building societies, stock exchange, micro finance institutions, development finance institutions, etc. The indications in Kenya and Africa generally are the lack of financial services which has been one of the major constraints to the development of business enterprises. This raises the question of adequacy of the financial institutions to play an effective facilitating role in business ventures.

In this regard, it is useful to bear in mind that from early origins of the financial sector, government policies have not generally aided the appropriate evolution of the necessary institutions to help realize development goals in the various sectors, especially the business sector. The institutions continue to have an urban concentration and bias. They therefore lack a significant presence in the rural sector to be able to benefit the mostly rural based MSEs and the agricultural sector overall. There is also a major shortcoming of coverage in terms of size of firms which continues to work to the greater advantage of large firms than micro and small ones including tea and coffee smallholder farms.

The establishment of institutions to provide financial assistance to manufacturing industries, especially medium scale, can be taken as a demonstration of government political will to support industrial development. Similarly, participation in banking, initially intended to aid Africanisation and recent moves to regulate MFI sector to make it a reliable alternative source of credit are positive indications of government support for business development are encouraging moves. However, the problem of growing concern is that reliance on government sources has continued and to some extent has become a permanent feature of the financial system. This has largely contributed to the inability of the institutions in the system to respond effectively to the development in the demand for their financial services.

REFERENCES

Adams D. W. and Pischke J.D. Von. 1992. "Microenterprise Credit: D'eja Vu". *World Development* 20 (10): 1463-70.

Agricultural Finance Corporation. 1995. *Statistical Digest.*

Alila, P.O. 2001. "Micro and Small Enterprises: Policies and Development". In Alila, P. O. and Pedersen, P. O. (eds.). *Negotiating the Social Space: East Africa Enterprises.* Trenton: Africa World Press.

Anjichi, S.N. (n.d.). "Kenya's Financial Institutions and Markets". Unpublished.

Aryeetey, E.; Hettige, H.; Nissanke, M. and Steel, W. 1997. "Financial Market Integration and Reforms in Ghana, Malawi, Nigeria and Tanzania". *World Bank Economic Review* 11(2): 195-218.

Aryeetey, E. 1996. "Rural Finance in Africa: Institutional Development and Access for the Poor". World Bank Annual Conference on Development Economics 25-26 April, Washington D.C.

Aryeetey, E. and Gockel, F. 1991. "Mobilising Domestic Resources for Capital Formation in Ghana: The Role of Informal Financial Sectors". AERC Research Paper No. 3. Nairobi: African Economic Research Consortium Research.

Atieno, R. 1994. "Institutional Credit Lending Policies and the Efficiency of Resource among Small-scale Farmers in Kenya". Studien zur Landlichen Entwicklung No.46, LIT Verlag Munstaer-Hamburg.

Atieno, R. 2004. "Small Scale Enterprises in Kenya. How Important is Access to Credit?" In. Wohlmuth, K.; Gutowski, A.; Knedlik, T.; Meine M. and Pitamber, S. (eds.). *African Entrepreneurship and Private Sector Development.* Africa Development Perspectives Yearbook 2002/2003. LIT Verlag Munster.

Atieno, R. 2001. "Formal and Informal Institutions' Lending Policies and Access to Credit by Small Scale Enterprises in Kenya". AERC Paper Number 111. Nairobi: African Economic Research Consortium Research.

Besley, T. 1994. "How do Market failures justify Intervention in Rural Credit Markets?" *The World Bank Research Observer* 9(1): 27-47.

Bigsten, A.; Collier, P.; Dercon, S.; Fafchamps, M.; Guthier, B.; Gunning, W.; Soderbom, M.; Oduro, A.; Oostendorp, C.; Patillo, Teal F. and Zeufack, A. 2000. "Credit Constraints in Manufacturing enterprises in Africa". Paper presented at the Conference on Opportunities in Africa: Micro-evidence from Firms and Households, 9th-10th April Oxford University.

Braverman, A. and Guasch, J. L. 1986. "Rural Credit Markets and Institutions in Developing Countries: Lessons for Policy Analysis from Practice and Modern Theory". *World Development* 14 (10/11): 1253-1267.

Central Bank of Kenya. 1995. *Monthly Economic Review.* Nairobi: Central Bank of Kenya.

Central Bureau of Statistics, K-Rep Development Agency, International Centre for Economic Growth. 1999. *A National Survey of Small and Micro Enterprises in Kenya*. Nairobi: K-Rep Development Agency.

Collier, P. and Gunning, J. 1999. "Explaining African Economic Performance". *Journal of Economic Literature* (37): 64-111.

Daniels, L.; Mead, Donald C. and Musinga M. 1995. "Employment and Income in Micro and Small Enterprises in Kenya". Results of a 1995 Survey. K-Rep Research Paper No. 26, Nairobi.

Hossain, M. 1988. "Credit for the Alleviation of Rural Poverty: The Grameen Bank in Bangladesh". IFPRI Research Report Number 65.

Isaksson A. 2004. "Access to Formal Finance in Kenyan Manufacturing". In Wohlmuth K.; Gutowski, A.; Knedlik, T. ;Meine, M. and Pitamber, S. (eds.). *African Entrepreneurship and Private Sector Development*. Africa Development Perspectives Yearbook 2002/2003. LIT Verlag Munster.

Isaksson, A. and Wiglborg, C. 2002. "Financial constraints on Kenyan Manufacturing". In Bigsten, A. and Kimuyu, P. (eds.). *Structure and Performance of Manufacturing in Kenya*. Oxford: Centre for the Study of African Economies.

Kenya, Republic of. 1965. *Sesssional paper number 10 of 1965 on African Socialism and its Application to Kenya*. Nairobi: Government Printer.

Kenya, Republic of. 1983. *Kenya Official Handbook*. Nairobi: Colourprint.

Kenya, Republic of. 1986. *Sessional Paper Number One on Economic Management for Renewed Growth*. Nairobi: Government printer.

Kenya, Republic of. 2002. *Economic Survey*. Nairobi: Government Printer.

McCormick,m D. and Atieno, R. 2002. "Linkages between Small and Large Firms in the Kenyan Food Processing Sector". In Van Dijk, M.P. and Sandee, H. (eds.). *Innovation and Small Enterprises in the Third World*. Cheltenham: Edward Edgar Publishing.

Ngugi, R. W. 2001. "An Empirical Analysis of Interest Rate Spread in Kenya". AERC Research Paper No. 106. Nairobi: African Economic Research Consortium.

Ngugi, R. and Kabubo, J. 1998. "Financial Sector Reforms and Interest Rate Liberalisation: The Kenyan Experience". AERC Paper Number 75. Nairobi: African Economic Research Consortium.

O'Brien, F.S. and Ryan, T.C.I. 2001. *Kenya*. In Devarajan, S.; Dollar, D. and Holmgren, T. (eds.). *Aid and Reforms in Africa: Lessons from Ten Case Studies*. Washington D.C: World Bank.

Ouma, A.S. 2002. *Financial Sector Dualism: Determining Attributes for Small and Micro Enterprises in Urban Kenya. A Theoretical and Empirical Approach Based on Case Studies in Nairobi and Kisumu*. Aachen: Shake Verlag.

Ouma, A.P.S. 1991. "Informal Financial Sectors in Kenya: The Case of Siaya District". Unpublished M.A. Research Paper, Kenyatta University.

Oketch, H.; Abaga, A. and Kulundu, D. 1995. *The Demand and Supply of Micro and Small Enterprise Finance in Kenya.* Nairobi: K-Rep.

Parker, J. C. and Torres, T. R. 1994. *Micro and Small Enterprises in Kenya: Results of the 1993 National Baseline Survey.* Gemini Technical Report No. 75. Bethesda: Development Alternatioves,Inc.

Schmidt, E. and Kropp, E. 1987. *Rural Finance: Guiding Principles.* Eschborn: GTZ.

Stiglitz, J. and Weiss, A. 1981. "Credit Rationing in Markets with Imperfect Information". *American Economic Review* 71(3).

UNDP. 2002. *Kenya Human Development Report 2001.* UNDP: Nairobi.

World Bank. 1992. Kenya: Reinvesting in Stabilisation through Public Sector Adjustment. Washington D.C: World Bank.

Part II

Sectoral Perspectives

Chapter 8

Linkages and Business Competition in Kenya's Metal Products Sub-sector

Benjamin Okech, Rosemary Atieno and Winnie V. Mitullah

INTRODUCTION

Firms relate to each other and respond to changing business environments in different ways. These include forging linkages, and developing competitive behaviour. Institutions, as rules of the game, guide and determine the nature of linkages and competition. This chapter uses this thesis to discuses firm linkages and competition among firms in Kenya's metal products sub sector within the context of business systems. The analysis is done by firm sizes. Linkages between firms enable them access services, which they would otherwise not be able to access individually. It also enables them to tap markets, and even keep abreast with technological developments. Different forms of linkages are possible between firms. Contractual linkages allow firms to reduce their costs, reduce risks and even specialise, while associations provide settings for cooperation between firms.

The analysis in this chapter is based on data collected through a scoping exercise covering over 429 firms, a survey of 117 firms and an in-depth study of 15 firms in the metal product sub sector. The survey of the 117 firms was undertaken between September and November 2001. Follow up surveys were also carried out in the months of November 2002 to January 2003. The survey was done using a structured questionnaire. The firms studied included both formal and informal firms. The data collection process went through different stages which included a scoping exercise[1] followed by a survey of sampled firms.

---

1 The Scoping Study was a first step in the study. It was aimed at identifying firms and providing basic information on the nature and dynamics of the sub sector. The scoping exercises had four stages. The first stage involved classifying firms into three categories: manufacturers of furniture and fixtures, structural metal products and fabricated metal products using four different directories. The second stage involved listing of firms in the four sites according to the three categories. This generated a total of 429 firms, with no firm listed

The sampled firms, located in four urban centres in Kenya: Nairobi, Mombasa, Eldoret and Migori were divided by sizes into small (61), medium (35), and large (21) firms. These were further sub divided into 21 large formal, 32 formal and 3 informal medium firms, and 9 formal and 52 informal small firms. The formal firms were distributed by town and category of activity.

The data are used to present and discuss firm linkage with a focus on sub-contracting, associations, networks and institutional contracts. The chapter also examines competition and business rivalry before drawing conclusions about the nature of the business system, as seen from the perspective.

UNDERSTANDING FIRM LINKAGES AND COMPETITION

Overview

Firm linkages can be seen as part of a larger network of social relationships, which occur within a business systems environment. Firms interact with markets in a social, economic and political institutional context. Pedersen and McCormick (1999) have identified different elements in institutional environment. These include financial systems, social structures, process of socialization, educational systems, market structures, infrastructure and services, legal systems and enforcement, technological capabilities and innovation systems. All these elements function to influence business system.

Pedersen (1996) has argued that networks can be based on personal relations, trust and reciprocity than on pure market or power relations. The linkages can also be seen in a narrower sense, by considering them individually, in which case linkages are connections between persons or individual organisations. These can take different forms like market connections, contractual relationships, ownership ties or social bonds linking members of a family and workers among others. Linkages can be narrowed further, by limiting the linkages to economic transactions (Meyanathan and Munther, 1994).

Here, we do not limit linkages to the narrow focus of economic transactions, but see them as part of a larger network embedded in a fragmented business system. This is because economic activity is informal and affected by underlying social political and cultural systems as well as particular social relations. We therefore look at linkages between firms within the sector and with those outside the sector. Pedersen and McCormick (1999) have argued that countries in Africa have fragmented business systems that consist of several distinct segments: a parastatal sector, large-scale private sector and informal economy. This is demonstrated in the metal sub sector where large metal product firms co-exist with small scale *Jua Kali* firms, and a number of metal products firms operating as parastatals. Economic transactions

for one site (Migori). The third stage focused on identification of the 429 firms and enumeration of informal firms that were not listed in four directories. The enumeration relied on the District Trade Licensing records, local *Jua Kali* Associations, civil society organisations providing support services to informal firms and mapping of clusters of informal firms and identification of firms in respective sites. A total of 158 firms were identified through these processes. They formed the sampling frame from which a total of 117 firms discussed in this chapter were drawn.

and activities in these systems are affected by particular social relations in addition to the underlying social, political and cultural systems (McCormick and Atieno, 2002). Thus, we look at linkages in terms of contractual relations and associational life as part of a wider social network of firms and individuals.

Business systems can also be seen in terms of market orientation in which case the focus is on those producing for local markets versus those producing for exports. The existence of control regimes in most African countries for a long time restricted the development of international trade through a variety of instruments with substantial effects on growth (Collier and Gunning, 1999). Among the strategies for growth, manufacturing for exports has become a major element because of the advantages associated with outward oriented development policy. Increased international competition may enhance productivity of the firm, through pressure on domestic industry to reduce costs, thereby increasing growth. As markets grow, the exploitation of economies of scale may provide important spill over effects. Both of these potential benefits are associated with manufactured exports. The increased trade diversification resulting from manufactured exports has a stabilizing effect, reducing the vulnerability from market fluctuations (Graner and Isaksson, 2002). Exports are also expected to enhance growth because they concentrate investments in the most efficient sectors while access to foreign markets allows a country to gain economies of scale as the domestic market expands.

Firms relate for many reasons. These include the need to facilitate ease of access to inputs, expand markets, access finance, access market information, technology, address common concerns and subcontract specialised activities. Firms also cooperate to attain certain ends that would otherwise be difficult for individual firms to attain alone. This is particularly important in circumstances faced by firms in developing countries like poor infrastructure, lack of information, weak technological capabilities, lack of finance and weak/missing institutions. By linking together, firms can overcome some of the constraints in industrial development. In addition, the nature of the industry in terms of its production technology, input and output markets and its financing also determines the type of linkages that are likely to develop (McCormick and Atieno, 2002). Linkages between firms for the procurement of inputs may allow small firms to access different sets of supplies, which give the immediate gains. Firms can also link to tap a market, which individual firms cannot do alone. Technology is also another important area for linkages.

Types of Firm Linkages

Within inter firm linkages, different forms of relationships can be identified. These include interactions between large and small firms[2], which can be subcontracting, collaborations, informal contacts and associations. Here, we restrict ourselves to

---

2   The definition of micro, small and large firms adopted in this paper is that of the 1999 Micro and Small Enterprise Survey. The survey defines micro firms as those having up to 10 employees, small firms as those employing more than 10 up to 50, while medium and large firms employ more than 50 employees .

contractual linkages in the form of contractual arrangements, associations, networks and institutional contacts.

Linkages have various benefits to the firms. They improve firm performance through reducing market friction and costs, increasing flexibility among firms, improving skills and diffusion of skills as well as the facilitation of sharing information (McCormick and Atieno, 2002). In the Kenya metal products sub-sector, linkages are likely to be important in facilitating firms to overcome some of the constraints. But linkages also have risks. For small firms, it may also result in the loss of small firm autonomy. We discuss the relevant firm linkages in the metal products sub sector, their nature, and the advantages they have for the firms as well as the constraints related to them.

One important aspect in business performance is firm size. The discussion of firm linkages here is done according to firm sizes. Recent studies on the manufacturing firms in Africa show that labour productivity increases with firm size, and is higher among large firms across the manufacturing firms in Africa. This is attributed to the differences in capital intensity between large and small firms (Soderbom, 2000). Firm size also determines access to different services like finances, markets, technology and information among others. The effect of linkages is therefore likely to be different among the different firm sizes. We also analyse the specified types of linkages according to the firm sizes of small, medium, and large.

The definition of firm size here is based on employment size, where firms with 1-10 employees are categorized as small; 11-50 employees are medium, while those with over 50 employees are large. This definition is adopted from the GEMINI studies (Parker and Torres, 1994). It is, however, useful to note at this point that employment based definition of firm size may not always be appropriate. In other related works on the metal products, what firms say about their sizes is discussed. This shows that there is a divergence between what firms say about their sizes and the sizes according to employment (Okech et al., 2002; see also McCormick and Atieno, 1997 and 2002 for more discussion of the same).

Associational life or membership is multilateral. Business associations are groups of individuals and firms that come together for the purpose of fostering business activities. They provide structured setting for cooperation on specific issues facing the business (McCormick and Atieno, 2002). Here, we discuss membership to associations and informal networks and their benefits to members.

Competition

Owing to Kenya's industrialisation policy, which for a long time had been inward looking, competition among firms has been mainly confined to the domestic market. An important factor in competition is firm competitiveness. Competitiveness has been defined as the ability to compete effectively in the market place (UNIDO, 2003). It is largely determined by the industrialization policy and is a function of technical efficiency and hence productivity. This will determine firms' ability to respond to competition. In Africa, lack of productive capacity has been a major constraint in raising industrial competitiveness (UNIDO, 2003).

Many firms have their competitive position weakened by their small size and low production technology. Firm size appears important, with small firms facing more competition compared to large firms. For firms to survive and grow, they have to fulfil the needs of their owners, employees and organisations or individuals with which they deal (Beardshaw and Palfreman, 1986). This requires clear strategies for production, marketing and managing competition. Competition as an aspect of business varies from one situation where there are many firms to where there are very few firms or only one dominant firm monopolising the market. Business environment is never perfect and hence the prevalence of competition. Perfect markets with perfect or fair competition hardly exist in business environment. Perfect markets have many buyers and sellers and no one person can affect the market price through her/his own actions. Perfect markets are homogenous, have freedom of entry and exit to both buyers and sellers, and the two actors have perfect knowledge of the market and can buy and sell any amount of commodity at the market price. Such conditions hardly exist in conventional markets. Almost all markets are, to a greater or lesser extent, imperfect. This results in imperfect competition, chiefly, out of the different numbers of firms, which make up any particular industry and the consequent differences in market behaviour in the short run and long run (Beardshaw and Palfreman, 1986).

In Kenya, firms dealing in metal products face a number of problems of competitiveness and competition. Competition within the sub-sector is not restricted to firms of the same size but within the sector and across firms of different sizes. There is also global competition where large metal firms in Kenya compete globally both for raw materials and markets for their products. The level of competitiveness and competition among firms affects performance, and it is therefore, necessary to understand the nature of competition, as discussed here.

Another important factor in firm competition is the market orientation of the industry. The Kenyan manufacturing has mainly been inward looking which has meant that the main source of competition has been the domestic market. Among the factors that limit their competitiveness are small firm size and low productive technology. Size factor is important in competition since smaller firms operate in a more competitive environment and therefore face more competition. Large firms have costs and related advantages that ensure secure market share for them. The nature of competition also reflects the market stratification with smaller firms exposed to more intensive competition while large firms have immense market power. The Kenyan manufacturing has for some time, therefore, exhibited significant market power and limited internal competitive pressure except for the micro-and small scale enterprises (Ikiara et al., 2002).

OVERVIEW OF METAL PRODUCTS SUB SECTOR

The metal products sub-sector falls under the manufacturing sector, which has an important role to play in Kenya's economy especially with respect to the country's industrialisation strategy. The metal products sub-sector is one of the main sub-sectors in manufacturing after food beverages and tobacco, and chemicals, rubber and petroleum products. The manufacturing sector has been expected to be more dynamic in accelerating economic growth in the country through employment creation, linkages between firms and across regions, skill formation and export earnings (Kenya, 1997).

The products of the smaller firms in the sector are popular with consumers in the local market and have kept the metal sector thriving. Metal products from larger firms are also exported to neighbouring countries within the East African region, while other products are destined to COMESA countries. The sector is, however, highly import dependent on its raw materials mainly because Kenya does not have large deposits of iron ore or other metallic ores, which are the major raw materials in this sector. Here, we describe the major characteristics of the sub-sector, with the view to providing a benchmark for analysing the business system in the sector.

Sector Activities and Performance

The metal product sub-sector is characterised by diversity in both activities and products. The main activities of the sector include the manufacture of basic metals, furniture and fixtures, hand tools, and general hardware, structural metal products, fabricated metal products, railroads equipment, electrical machinery and appliances. The main products produced by the sector include ferrous metals including cast and wrought, iron and steel products, and non ferrous metals, like aluminium, antimony, cadmium, copper, led, zinc and tin. Others include manufacture of simple products such as *jikos* (charcoal cooking stoves), pans and fabrication of simple capital goods like storage tanks, farm implements, repair and maintenance of vehicles and processing machinery. The sector also has a wide range in the levels of technological sophistication. These range from simple products to the more sophisticated ones. Production units also vary from small shops to international production units. Many firms undertake simple engineering works based on sheet metal and repairs and use basic equipment and skills (Aguilar and Bigsten, 2002). Due to the diverse nature of the sector, this study focused only on three sub-sub-sectors namely, structural metal products, fabricated metal products and furniture and fixtures, primarily of metal.

The performance of the metal products sub-sector should be viewed in the context of the overall development policy for the manufacturing sector in the country. The manufacturing sector received support within the paradigm of the Import Substitution Industrialisation (ISI) Strategy, based on the perceived importance of the manufacturing sector for the structural transformation of the economy. The ISI strategy, however, failed to create the necessary dynamism within the sector. Hence, while the manufacturing sector grew by 8.5per cent during the 1960s and 1970s, it only grew by 4.8per cent between 1980-1989, and 3per cent for the period 1990-1995. This was hardly enough to absorb the surplus labour from the agricultural sector and generate linkages with the rest of the economy (ILO/EAMAT, 1999). The resulting inefficiency in the sector, and lack of competitiveness of its products, led to the review of the industrial strategy and investments incentive structure. The government adopted structural adjustment programmes (SAPs), with increased reliance on market forces.

The protection from external competition enjoyed by the sector during the 1970s resulted in inefficiencies and high capacity under utilisation (Coughlin, 1991). By the mid 1980s, the scope for ISI had been exhausted due to diminishing domestic opportunities for ISI. Due to the heavy protection, the inefficiencies in production and the accumulation of excess capacity, the sector's products failed to penetrate external markets. The production of the sub-sector, therefore, declined steadily in the 1980s. This changed gradually with the implementation of macro economic policy changes. The sector experienced improvements in performance since early 1990s mainly due to the availability of foreign exchange and the liberalisation of the economy. The removal of import restrictions, and stability of the shilling against other major currencies, resulted in liberalised stable economy. This provided the sub-sector with an easy and stable access to raw materials. The informal *Jua Kali* sector, which is a major user of metal products, also contributed to the good performance of the sector (Kenya, 1995). The result was in the sub-sector registering a growth in real output of 21.2 per cent between 1996 and 1997 (Kenya, 1998). During the year 2001, the performance of the manufacturing sector declined by 1.5 per cent, mainly due to the devastating effect of power rationing and the general poor economic performance in the country.

Other factors that have contributed to the poor performance of the sector include power rationing, high duty charged on intermediate goods, and lack of adequate technical and entrepreneurship skills. Competition from cheap substandard and counterfeit imports has also constrained the growth of industrial production in the country. Inadequate research and lack of awareness of intellectual property rights have further constrained technological advancement that are key to industrial development. The limited use of foreign licensing as a means of obtaining industrial technology is another factor contributing to the low performance of the sector. Ikiara et al., (2002) observe that licensing and technology assistance have very limited technological impact on the Kenyan manufacturers. Bigsten (2002) notes that growth in the manufacturing production has been due to increase in factor input rather than improvement in productivity.

The Sector's Contribution to the National Economy

The metal products sub-sector is an important contributor to the national economy. This is in terms of its contribution to Gross Domestic Product (GDP), employment generation, skill creation and linkages between firms and sectors. It also contributes to the generation of foreign exchange through the manufacture of products for export. This sub-section presents an overview of the metal product sub-sector's contribution to the national economy in terms of GDP and employment. The sector's contribution to GDP and employment largely reflects not only trends in its performance, but also its overall contribution to the economy.

Contribution to GDP

The metal industry has experienced a steady decline in its share in the manufacturing throughout the 1980s, 1990s and early 2000. This is despite the rising index in production over the same period (figure 8.1). Figure 8.1 shows the quantity index of manufacturing production for metallic products between 1990 and 2002.

Figure 8.1 show that the metal products experienced a steady increase in production between 1990 and 1997 except in 1992 and 1993 when it registered a decline. This is attributed to the sector being adversely affected by shortage of foreign exchange during this period. However, since 1998, there has been a general downward trend in production mainly due to the structural problems and weak demand in the economy. 1997 registered the highest growth in the sector. Among the issues in the sector contributing to the massive under utilisation of the installed capacity is tied aid for some donor-funded projects. Earlier studies have also identified this as one of the factors reducing the demand for various products that can be produced in the country (Coughlin, 1988).

The manufacturing sector, in general, and the metal products sub-sector in particular are expected to have a significant contribution to Kenya's industrialisation process through employment opportunities, savings of foreign exchange and creation of forward and backward linkages. It is also expected to attract and generate indigenous Kenyan entrepreneurs especially in the informal sector (Kenya, 1986).

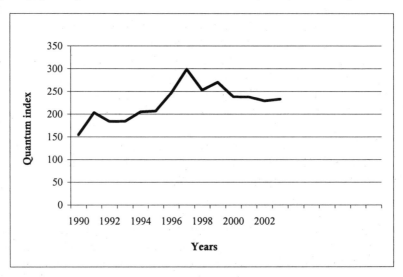

Figure 8.1: Quantum Index of Manufacturing Production: Metallic Products 1990-2002

Source: Kenya Republic of. Economic Surveys, various issues

Contribution to Employment

The metal product's sub-sector is recognised as having many possible employment creation potentials mainly due to its linkages with firms in smaller urban centres. It also has linkages with other sectors like construction and agriculture. This is mainly through the manufacture of simple metal products used in the different sectors. The sub-sector is one of the major contributors to employment in the manufacturing sector. Its share of employment in the total manufacturing, however, declined from about 25 per cent in 1980 to 20 per cent in 1997. Employment in the whole of the manufacturing sector remained depressed in the period between 1998 and 2001 mainly due to retrenchments and closures of factories.

Among the major contributors of the industry in terms of employment in 1980 was manufacture of fabricated products like machinery and equipment, contributing about 17.9 per cent and manufacture of structural metal products with 6.9 per cent. In 1990, the two sub-sectors were still among the top contributors, although manufacture of fabricated metal products contributed 3.7 per cent, and manufacture of structural metal products contributed 1.7 per cent. Manufacture of fabricated metal products remained the leading sub-sector in the metals industry together with the manufacture of railroad equipment between 1980 and 1990 (Departments of Economics, 1994).

It is, however, important to note that the sector's potential to generate employment has been largely determined by the overall industrial policy pursued immediately after independence. The ISI strategy followed to develop the manufacturing sector relied on capital-intensive production technology, which resulted in limited employment potential. The strategy also led to the sector heavily relying on imported raw materials. As a result, the sector developed little linkages with the domestic economy, thus limiting its potential to generate economic activities in other sectors, and therefore, employment (ILO/EAMAT, 1999).

A unique feature of the manufacturing sector in Kenya is the presence of the informal *Jua Kali* small and micro enterprises. The importance of this sector in employment creation and incomes has been recognised by the government as reflected in various policy documents (Kenya, 1986; 1992; 2003). During the last decade, the importance of the informal sector has increased significantly especially as a source of employment. As the formal sector employment has declined, the informal sector's share in total employment has risen steadily, reaching 70.4 per cent in 2000 (Kenya, 2000). However, the *Jua Kali* sector has suffered from a number of constraints, major among which have been poor policy and co-ordination issues as well as legal and regulatory environment (ILO/EAMAT, 1999).

Informal sector activities comprise small undertakings employing less than 10 workers. A large proportion of this output is directed towards satisfying basic needs. Despite the sector having had the potential to act as a spring-board for industrialisation, many producers in the sector seem to view their activities as a way of generating funds to use in other sectors like agriculture. Since 1999, the government has been re-examining laws and regulations affecting the operations of the informal economy in order to come up with enabling policies and regulations. Various government policy papers (Kenya, 2003; Kenya, 2002) lay emphasis on supporting the informal sector of the economy in order to create wealth within the economy.

FIRM CHARACTERISTICS AND ACTIVITIES

Firm Characteristics

This section presents the main firm characteristics from the empirical survey. These include gender, level of education, and nationality of the owner as well as types of ownership and size. Most of the individuals engaged in metal products sub-sector were found to be males. This trend has also been observed by Ikiara et al. (2002). This is largely characteristic of manufacturing firms, except for the lower levels where women work as support staff. Majority of those working within the sub-sector, especially in formal firms have high levels of education. This implies not only experience but also a wide scope of networks and linkages as well as ability to adopt new business skills and technology. Most firms had sole owners. Sole owners, followed by two person owners, owned over 50% of the firms.

Most of the firms (96%) are owned by Kenyans of both African and Asian origin. Kenyans of African origin owned 63% of the firms, while Kenyans of Asian origin owned 33%. However, it is important to note that most of the firms owned by Africans were small scale and/or informal, with a few others owning medium firms. Of the 55 informal firms, Africans owned 50 of them, while out of the 21 large firms, Kenyans of Asian origin owned 13 firms. The concentration of African entrepreneurs in micro and small scale enterprises can be attributed to their limited ability to mobilise financial and human resources. Nevertheless, a few of them have managed to penetrate the middle level and are owners of medium firms.

The indigenous local Africans seem to largely own small formal and/or *Jua Kali* informal firms, which are comparatively small in terms of total capital investment. An examination of the formal firms covered in this survey shows that majority of them are owned by Kenyan Asians and other foreigners. This trend is prevalent in most other large and medium scale-manufacturing firms in Kenya. A study by Ikiara et al. (2002), shows that males dominate manufacturing activities particularly, in metal fabrication.

The pattern of firm ownership in Kenya has drawn different observations from scholars. Bigsten (2002) notes that since the 1970s, a clear pattern of firm ownership emerges where large industries are dominated by parastatals and multinational cooperations, small to medium sized firms are owned by Kenyans of Asian origin and the micro and small scale enterprises are owned by Kenyans of African origin. Ikiara et al. (2002) further observe the race factor in enterprise ownership, confirming a similar trend where Africans own micro and small scale enterprises.

Firm Activities and Products

Firm activities and products were investigated to show the nature and structure of the sub sector as well as the diversity of both the activities and products. The main activities and products of the metal products firms at start of their business were fabrication of metal products, general mechanical repair services, electrical and mechanical works, furniture metal fixture works, manufacture of PVC products, sale of tools and equipment, general welding and repair services, welding machine and roof construction and structural metal works. Other activities included: bore hole drilling, production of mattresses, break bonding, general repairs for farm tools and equipment, wood joinery works, repair of injector pump, steel rolling, processing imported billets, grinding services for metallic tools, water supply, scrap metal moulding and battery charging.

This description gives evidence of great diversity in both activities and products of the sub sector. Table 8.1 gives the distribution of the type of activities undertaken by the firms covered in the survey.

Table 8.1: *Distribution of Activities by Firms*

Type of Activity	Number of Firms involved	Percentage of Firms involved
Fabrication of metal products	71	60.7
General mechanical repair services	11	9.4
Structural metal works	8	6.8
Furniture fixture works	8	6.8
Manufacture of electrical cables	5	4.3
Sheet metal fabrication and repairs	2	1.7
Others	12	10.3
Total	*117*	*100*

The fabrication of metal products appears to dominate the main activities, with (61%) of the firms being involved in the activity. This dominance of the fabrication of metal products seems to be an overall characteristic of the sector as was reflected in the sampling frame.

This diversity of activities extends to products, with many firms having a wide range of products. This is shown by the fact that only 12 firms (10%) out of the total sample had their main product constituting 100% of their total production. Most firms had their main products constituting 50% of their total production. The average proportion of the main product in total firm production was found to be 47.4%, the second major product constituted 22.9%, while the third major product was 14.6%. Table 8.2 gives the distribution of the proportion of main product in total production.

Over one third of the firms (43.7%) had their major product constituting less than 40% of their total production, while only 11.2% of the firms had their main products constituting over 80% of their total production. When looked at by the three sub-sectors, we find that the least diverse sub-sector was the furniture and fixtures, while the fabricated metal products had the greatest diversity in products. Diversity in both products and activities, therefore, appears to be a major characteristic of the sub-sector.

Table 8.2: *Distribution of Shares of the Main Product in Total Firm Production*

Proportion of main product in total production	Number of firms	Percentage of firms
5-20	24	20.5
21-40	27	23.2
41-60	30	25.7
61-80	18	15.4
81-100	13	11.2
Missing	5	4
Total	*117*	*100*

Explaining Diversity in Activities and Products

A review of the metal products sub-sector shows that it is characterised by diversity in both products and activities. Other studies confirm the diversity in the manufacturing sector. Ikiara et al. (2002) argue that diversification is an attempt by firms to spread risk. However, it does not provide opportunities to develop business enterprise. Improving the commercial environment of business would reduce some of the incentives to diversify and enable firms to specialise.

Diversity can be seen as a response by firms to market situations perceived by firms as risky. Diversification has been seen as a coping strategy in the face of risk and uncertainty and hence a way of searching for new income sources (Ellis, 2000). Here, we view diversification as a coping strategy by firms in response to changing business systems. In Kenya, the diversification of activity is more prevalent among the small and micro enterprises compared to large firms.

From the survey, one of the main reasons for diversity by firms was found to be response to the changing market conditions. As the demand for the specific products fluctuates, firms respond by diversifying products and activities to capture the emerging markets with less competition. It also enables them to continue using their existing facilities like labour and fixed capital. Instead of relying on one product whose market share is not certain, firms find it prudent to diversify into other products, thus spreading their risks. Another reason that emerged was that this diversity is inherent from the nature of the products. This was particularly true with firms in fabricated metal products. In this case, diversification provides the firm with opportunities to use the bi-products. Many firms also engaged in production activities cutting across sub sectors. For example, firms in fabrication were also engaged in manufacture of furniture fixtures of metal, and vice versa. This is a further sign of the high diversity among the firms.

There are a number of views on how enterprises react to changes in the incentive structure (Qualmann, 2002). According to the neoclassical approach, the new incentives after a shock are the main determinants of enterprise behaviour, with rational entrepreneurs seeking the most efficient allocation of resources. In the new institutional economics approach, institutional framework determines the kind of performance that will pay off in a social, and economic setting. In a situation of uncertainty, firms will organise transactions in a way to minimise risks and losses. Hence, transaction costs will be important in firm decision to change its structure, production lines and/or marketing modes. Such costs are high in environments of uncertainty, asymmetric information and low contractual enforcement. In the face of market uncertainty and lack of information, firms respond by diversifying their products to minimise their risks. These are constraints faced by firms especially the small and micro enterprises in Kenya, and to which some have responded by diversifying their activities.

FIRM LINKAGES

Firm linkages is considered as part of a larger network, since economic transactions and activities are affected by particular social relations in addition to the underlying social, political and cultural systems (McCormick and Atieno, 2002). We therefore look at linkages as part of a wider social network of firms and individuals. The type of firm linkages investigated here are subcontracting arrangements and associational lives of the firms.

Subcontracting

Subcontracting is a broad category of contractual linkage. Firms subcontract for different reasons like reducing risks, lowering costs, and the need to get specialised products or services that cannot be got in house. Firm linkages can be seen as part of a larger network of social relationships, which can be based on personal relations, trust and reciprocity than on pure market or power relations (Pedersen, 1996). The linkages can also be seen in a narrower focus, by considering them individually in which case, linkages are connections between persons or individual organisations. These can take different forms like market connections, contractual relationships, ownership ties or social bonds linking members of a family, workers, etc. The linkages can still be narrowed further by limiting them to economic transactions (Meyanathan and Munther, 1994).

Subcontracting are examined in this section in terms of whether they give out or receive subcontracts. Among the reasons for entering into contractual arrangements, firms may subcontract due to limited capacity, need for specialised work or reducing risks (McCormick and Atieno, 2002). From this survey, majority (68.4%) of firms were found not to sub-contract any of their activities. Among the formal firms surveyed, only 29% were sub-contracting some of their activities, while among the informal firms, 34% were sub-contracting any of their activities. The main activities subcontracted were fabrication works, furniture making, construction work, electrical works, manufacture of wooden drums, metal cutting and welding, food supply, bed making, block-line re-boring, welding, aluminium works, and installation of heavy machines. Subcontracting is, however, not common in the Kenyan manufacturing. Two studies have found that subcontracting is not common in food processing sector (McCormick and Atieno, 2002; Mitullah, 1999).

A comparison between formal and informal metal product firms shows that, while sub-contracting activities are spread in different areas among the formal firms, it is only concentrated in fabrication works, metal cutting and welding among the informal firms. A major observation is that, while most formal firms sub-contract work to *Jua Kali* firms, rarely do *Jua Kali* firms subcontract to formal firms. In the sample, only one *Jua Kali* firm was found to sub-contract work to a formal firm. In-depth surveys showed that both formal and informal firms view each other as competitors and only sub-contract work when there are gains to be made, like subcontracting work in order to reduce on the cost of production. Competition is intense between different players, at times manifested in suspicion between the different players. Firms mainly subcontracted to *Jua Kali* firms due to favourable subcontracting fees, and short-term requirements for orders. The lack of elaborate bureaucratic procedures by informal firms may be one of the factors attracting firms to subcontract to them. From this study, the main reasons for subcontracting can be summed as lack of capacity, work needing specialised skills, and seasonal increase in demand. The distribution of the types of subcontracts by firm size is summarised in table 8.3.

While large firms mainly subcontracted due to specialized products and seasonal demand, most small firms subcontracted due to inadequate capacity. Lack of capacity, therefore, appears not to be a constraint among the large firms unlike the small firms. A number of firms in the metal sub-sector study reported operating at excess capacity (Okech et al., 2002). It is, therefore, unlikely that they would subcontract as a result of inadequate capacity.

Table 8.3: *Types of Subcontracting Done by Firm Size*

Type of subcontracting	No. of Small firms	No. of Medium firms	No. of Large firms	Total No. of firms subcontracting
Specialised subcontracting	4	2	4	10
Seasonal subcontracting	4	3	4	11
Inadequate capacity	14	2	0	16
Total	22	7	8	37

NB: *The table shows the total number of firms that subcontracted from the different firm sizes. The percentage of firms that subcontracted from the total sample is 32%.*

Most firms, both small and large, subcontracted to *Jua Kali* firms. However, while small firms mainly subcontracted to *Jua Kali*, large firms also subcontracted to other large firms in addition to what they subcontract to small firms. A comparison of the size of firms subcontracted shows that 50% of the small firms, which subcontracted, did so to firms smaller than themselves, while only five firms subcontracted to firms larger than themselves. All medium firms, which subcontracted, did so to firms smaller than themselves, while large firms subcontracted to both smaller and larger firms.

The distribution of firms according to whether they subcontract or not did not differ between the different firm sizes. Among the small firms, 22 (36%) subcontracted while 39 (63.9%) did not subcontract. Among the medium firms, only seven (20%) subcontracted, while 28 (80%) did not subcontract. Among large firms, eight (38.1) subcontracted while 13 (61.9%) did not. Across the different firm sizes, the firms, which did not subcontract exceeded those, which subcontracted. A number of reasons are used to explain the lack of subcontracting by firms (Table 8.4).

Table 8.4: *Distribution of Reasons for not Subcontracting by Firm Size*

Reasons for not subcontracting	Small firms	Medium firms	Large firms
Adequate resources to meet demand	17 (27.1)	14 (40)	9 (42.9)
Not much work to subcontract	14 (23)	6 (17)	2 (9.5)
Specialised firm, dealing in standard products	-	4 (11.4)	1 (4.8)
Lack of trust in other firms	2 (3.3)	-	-
Increased staff to meet the increased demand	4 (6.6)	1 (2.9)	-
Management policy not to subcontract	-	-	1 (4.8)
No response	1 (1.6)	3 (7.6)	-

Note: The percentages are out of total sample in the category, and not only those who did not subcontract.

Adequate resources (personnel and machinery) to meet the demand was the dominant reason across the different firm sizes for not subcontracting. Other firms also did not have much work to subcontract, while others increased staff to meet demand. Other reasons included firm specialisation, lack of trust on other firms, stiff competition, firm policy not to sub-contract, and additional machines and tools hired when demand is high. The reasons seem to vary by firm size, but adequate resources is the most dominant explanation among the three categories of firm sizes. Only medium and large firms gave specialization and standard products as a reason for not subcontracting. The observation that most firms had adequate resources to meet the production requirements may be an indication that the domestic market is not adequate for the full utilisation of the existing installed production capacity in the sector. A similar case was found in a study of fish processing industry (Mitullah, 1999).

It would, therefore, appear that firms have different ways of responding to market conditions and subcontracting out extra work is only one of them. The ability of small firms to increase staff to meet increased demand for production indicates the level of flexibility among small firms as opposed to large and medium firms.

Subcontracting relationships do not only involve giving out subcontracts, but firms also receive subcontracts. Firms covered in the study also received sub-contracts. Up to 50% of the sample received subcontracts. The major sources of sub-contracts ranged from *Jua Kali* firms, construction industry, mechanical engineering firms, assemblers/dealers, hotel/food industry, textile industry, tourism, textile, and oil industries, furniture makers, farm machinery and manufacturers, ship builders and repairers, illustrating the fact that the metal products sub sector has linkages with other sectors. Viewed by firm size, the results show that it is only among the small firms where more firms received subcontracts than those who did not, confirming the earlier observation that most firms subcontracted to smaller firms. For both the medium and large firms, those who did not receive subcontracts exceeded those who received (table 8.5).

Table 8.5: *Distribution of Firms Receiving Subcontracts by Firm Size*

Receive sub contracts	Small firms	Medium firms	Large firms
Yes	33 (54)	17 (48.6)	9 (42.9)
No	28 (45.9)	18 (51.4)	11 (52.4)
Total	61 (100)	35 (100)	(100)*

 * No response = 1 (4.8)

A number of reasons were given for receiving subcontracts. For small firms, these included many firms being in similar areas, reduced product demand, lack of trust among small firms, and competition from other firms. For the medium firms, the main reasons were small firm size, reduced demand for their products, not yet approached by any firm, and not engaged in piecework. For the large firms, the reasons were reduced product demand, firm policy to specialise in its own products, and competition from other firms.

Firms therefore received subcontract from a variety of industries and firms both within and outside their sector. The sources of subcontracts also differ with firm sizes. Most small firms received from the *Jua Kali* unlike the medium and large firms. Although most medium firms received subcontracts from construction industry and vehicle assemblers, they also receive sub-contracts from other industries. The large firms received from a wide range of industries. Subcontracting arrangement therefore exists in the metal product sub sector and while this can be seen as a response to changing business environment, it is also a reflection of the nature of the sector, which is characterised by diversity.

Associations, Networks and Institutional Contacts

Associational life, networks and institutional contacts are other forms of linkage explored in this chapter. Membership in associations, networks and institutional contact have benefits to firms, since there are a number of tasks, which individual entrepreneurs of firms cannot effectively undertake on their own. It also enables them to access services or resources, which they would otherwise not be able to access individually.

Associational Life

The study on the metal products sub-sector (Okech et al 2002) showed that equal numbers of firms either belong or do not belong to any association. Among those who belonged to associations, majority were members of Kenya Association of Manufacturers (KAM), Federation of Kenya Employers (FKE), Kenya National Chamber of Commerce (KNCC) and Migori *Jua Kali* association[3]. Apart from the latter association, most of the other associations are well known national associations, which look after business issues concerning formal firms.

Most of the major associations with national out look, support their members in various ways. These include sensitisation of the membership on government policies, lobbying to influence government policies, engage government on policy discussions, updating members on new technological development, providing advisory services, monitoring illegal importation of goods, and offering product quality control services. They also address issues on security, maintenance, and upgrading of infrastructure.

Some small firms belonged to Intermediate Technology Development Group (ITDG) an organisation that supports small-scale enterprises in the area of technology and provides tools and machinery for hire. This enables small-scale firms to hire relevant tools for manufacturing and processing their products.

Jua Kali Association covered in the survey of firms are small local level associations, which take care of the interests of small Scale *Jua Kali* enterprises. Such associations mainly look into social welfare matters of members. This includes assisting members meet funeral expenses and offset medical bills. In some cases, they offer soft loans to members, solve disputes among members, assist in accessing working sites, dealing with harassment by urban authorities, sharing business information and tools, training members, and undertaking advocacy on behalf of members. Few *Jua Kali* associations deal with issues similar to those handled by well-known national associations

An analysis of the metal products sub-sector study further probed associational life of firms by firm size. Among the small and medium sized firms, those who did not belong to any association exceeded those who belonged (table 8.6). In both cases, more than half of the firms did not belong to any association. This is in contrast to the large firms where over 80% of the firms belonged to associations.

Table 8.6: *Distribution of Association Membership by Firm Size*

Association Membership	Small firms	Medium firms	Large firms
Yes	27 (44.3)	13 (37.1)	18 (85.7)
No	33 (54.1)	22 (62.9)	3 (14.1)

Given the reasons for firms not belonging to associations, the fact that more of the large firms belonged to associations compared to small firms may imply that more

---

3 Migori *Jua Kali* Association is one of the four *Jua Kali* associations covered by the study. In Migori town, there were no formal firms therefore only informal firms were covered. Most of these belonged to the Migori *Jua Kali* Association. In contrast, while informal sector firms were covered in the other towns, most of them did not belong to the *Jua Kali* associations registered in their towns. The Migori *Jua Kali* association therefore features more prominently in the discussions in this chapter than the others.

large firms benefit from associations than the small firms, including *Jua Kali* firms. This can be explained by the comparatively better governance of associations with membership drawn from medium and large firms. Such firms are more productive, able to support their associations, including an efficient secretariat that most small firms cannot sustain.

Table 8.7: *Relationship Between Association Membership and Performance: Production Volume*

Total Sample				
	Belonged to Association	Did not belong to Association	X^2	Significance level
Production decreased	41.9%	55.8%	14.8	0.063*
Production increased	52.5%	47.5%		
Small firms				
Production decreased	14.8%	26.2%	7.868	.446
Production increased	24.6%	24.6%		
Medium firms				
Production decreased	20%	20%	9.729	0.045**
Production increased	34.3%	8.6%		
Large firms				
Production decreased	9.5%	4.8%	1.264	0.738
Production increased	66.7%	9.5%		

We further investigated the relationship between membership in associations and firm performance. As already mentioned elsewhere in this chapter, the performance indicator used in the study was production volume. Table 8.7 gives the results of cross tabulations between association membership and firm performance in terms of production volume. The results show that for the total sample, among those who reported a reduction in production volume, about 42% belonged to associations while 56% did not belong to an association. For those who reported an increase in production, 53% belonged to associations while 48% did not. The relationships were significant, implying that in some ways, associations may help their members to increase their production. We further probed this relationship by firm size, and the relationship was only significant among the medium firms, with small and large firms showing no significance. There is no immediate or obvious explanation for this observation. However, from the results of this study, it can be concluded that although the number of medium firms that belonged to associations was fewer than those who did not, associations are useful for those who belong to them. Association membership should, therefore, be encouraged among this category of firms.

Among the small scale and informal firms, association membership may not be as yet well entrenched. Most of the *Jua Kali* associations did not exist in Kenya until the 1992 Sessional Paper No 2 on Small Scale Enterprises and *Jua Kali* Development in Kenya was published (Kenya, 1992). In the paper the government outlined its commitment to support small-scale enterprises. This was further affirmed by Sessional Paper No. 2 of 1996 on Industrial Transformation to the year 2020 and subsequent Development Plans. It was these policies, which resulted in the promotion and growth of *Jua Kali* associations. Most informal sector firms, however, still operate outside these associations, which are largely de-linked from the membership.

While small-scale enterprise associations have been in existence for a long time, most of the associations, which use the concept *Jua Kali* association, owe their origin to the mobilisation of the artisans to form associations by the then Ministry of Research Technical Training and Technology (MRTT&T). This was done in anticipation of expected funding from international agencies such as the World Bank, UNIDO and ILO (McCormick et al., 2001). While the idea of associating is key in contributing to policy development and promoting enterprise development, associations form an important political constituency which most governments wish to control, and engage in their politics, sometimes to the detriment of associational life (McCormick et al, 2001). This has affected the performance of *Jua Kali* associations, especially their umbrella organisation, the National Federation of *Jua Kali* associations (NFJKA). This association should handle issues similar to those handled by the known national associations such as KAM, and FKE. However, the association has been entangled in politics and leadership wrangles and has not managed to perform.

Our survey of the metal products sub-sector firms showed that half of the firms interviewed are not interested in associational life, with a significant percentage (15.5%) indicating that majority of associations are mismanaged. The lack of interest in associational life is problematic to the development of the metal products sub-sector. Research in other sectors, for example, the construction sector, has shown that associations cushion firms and provide support in the areas of finance and supplies, including favourable credit conditions, especially during hard times (Kinyanjui and Mitullah, 1997). The same has been demonstrated among the fish processors and exporters (Spencer and Mitullah, 2004). Associations provide legal advice on regulations, settle labour disputes, provide financial support and expand business opportunities for members.

In a study conducted on the role of associations and other community based organisations in four districts in Kenya, it was revealed that both social and business organisations participate in business development through loan provision, buying stock for business and giving money on rotational basis. The benefits members get were listed as welfare, financial support and savings. However, the area of advocacy, which is viewed as key, was found to be hardly a focus of associations. In very isolated cases associations were found to undertake advocacy on campaigning for better services, protecting members from harassment and lobbying for sites of operation (McCormick, 2001).

The inability to address issues of advocacy and policy influence on matters relating to business operation seem to be prevalent among associations of small scale non manufacturing enterprises. The metal products study showed that over 50 per cent of firms, which are members of respective associations, engage in issues relating to policies, especially in ensuring that reasonable taxes are charged; and also update members on technological development. Individual firms cannot effectively manage these aspects. Umbrella organisations such as KAM and FKE and KFJKA are best placed to deal with such issues.

Networks and Institutional Contacts

Another way by which firms can develop linkages is through networks and contacts with institutions or systems of support as well as organisations. Support systems can help firms meet their different needs like information, skills, finance as well as technology. Relationships with such institutions of support may enable firms to influence or determine support mechanisms like policies, regulations, infrastructure and legislations (McCormick and Kimuyu, 2003). We investigated networks and institutional contacts in terms of the type of organisations that they related to in the course of their activities. The results show that firms related to different types of institutions. Viewed by firms size, the results show that up to 38 (62.3%) of the small firms did not relate to any institution. Those who related did so with polytechnics, schools, businesses, ITDG, agricultural companies like flower firms, and tea estates, and micro-finance institutions. Among the medium firms, about one half (51,4%) did not relate with any institutions, while those who did, related with polytechnics, schools, banks, Kenya Bureau of Standards (KEBS), missionaries, and civil society organisations. For the large firms 47.6% did not relate with any institution. The rest related with institutions like KEBS. The nature of the relations for the different firm categories involved financial assistance, student attachment, trainings, quality control, research and technology development and exchange.

The extent to which firms relate with other organisations appears to increase with firm size. Smaller firms appear to relate less. For those which related, the focus on institutions providing education and skills may be an indicator of the kind of constraints facing small firms like technology, skills and financial resources. Since these firms act as attachments, they provide important avenues for imparting skills and therefore their capacity needs to be strengthened if they are to contribute to the country's industrialisation.

Firms also turn to different institutions for support. However, most small firms (54.1%) did not turn to any institution for any support. The remaining turned to banks, friends, and micro-finance institutions. Among the medium firms, only 34% did not turn to any institution for support. The rest turned to banks, associations, and consultancy firms for financial help, general advice, and wage negotiations. Among the large firms, up to 50% turned to banks for financial support, while only four firms did not turn to any institution for support. Other forms of support involved technical support, legal advice, and provision of equipments. It therefore appears that most of the large firms turned to other institutions for support, while the majority of small and medium firms did not.

Firms, from small, medium and large categories indicated that they had benefited from the different forms of relationships. These were in the form of increased production, improved business performance, improved product quality, expansion of the firms and improved services to their clients. Hence, while relationships with other institutions have potential benefits to firms, many firms may not be realizing these benefits by not entering into these relationships. It is, therefore, necessary for policy to address reasons why firms do not relate with other institutions.

Within the context of business systems analysis, the nature of institutional contacts, and networks may raise the question of what determines such linkages. Firms which are limited in resources, like small firms, may be constrained from joining any networks or contacts due to the costs involved in such associations. This limited ability to join in turn limits the extent to which they can influence the support mechanisms like policies, legislations and infrastructure that affect their businesses. In reality, small firms face a number of constraints, which are institutional in nature. However, their weak organisational ability and limited or non existent linkages limits the extent to which they can address such constraints.

COMPETITION AND BUSINESS RIVALRY

Competitiveness of Firms

Before discussing competition between and among firms, it is necessary to briefly have an overview of competitiveness of metal products firms. The Kenya Association of Manufacturers (KAM), Metal and Allied Sector (2002) have isolated four factors, which affect the competitiveness of firms within the sector. They include: The cost of power, logistics, high finance cost and poor infrastructure.

The cost of power is relatively high in Kenya, and alternative solutions have to be found to ensure both local and international competitiveness for manufacturing firms. Most firms surveyed for the study indicated unreliable power supply and high cost of power as major problem of running business. Another problem, which affects the competitiveness of firms, has to do with logistics, especially those relating to port charges and transportation costs. Kenya Ports Authority (KPA) allows only 4 working days from the arrival of a vessel as rent-free period before charging a Late Documentation Charge (LDC) of US$ 1 per tonne per day.

The time period allowed is inadequate since some vessels, for example, for South Africa take only about 5 days to reach Mombasa, and it is often not possible to obtain original documentation to process customs documents. This results in importers of bulk consignment paying very heavy LDC. Those who import under Bond and have to process warehouse entries are worse off. Processing papers takes long, at least two days, and it is never possible to process documents within the rent-free period (KAM, 2002).

The port handling charges are also high, costing US$ 5 per Metric Tonnes (MT) in case of direct loading and US$ 12 per MT in case of normal loading. The profit margins in the steel industry have been noted to be very low and the high port handling charges reduce the level of competitiveness of firms in the global market. In addition, Kenya has a high finance cost, reflected in pre and post shipment costs and high interest costs. The poor infrastructure, insecurity and poor local service also add to the cost of operations. The roads are poor and rail services are at the verge of collapsing. All these factors increase cost of production, which in turn has led to high prices of finished goods (KAM, 2002).

Port handling charges and related issues affect large firms which rely on imports of raw materials and also export their finished products; while other issues such as power supply, transport, infrastructure and security affect all firms within the sector. Consequently, these issues need to be addressed by all parties concerned if the sector is to prosper and compete in both local and global markets.

Our study of 117 firms showed that one third of the firms receives incentives from the government. However, further probe revealed that the incentives are not adequate and should be improved. The respondents indicated that there should be: a reduction of tax levies, bank interest rates and protection from foreign firms. Respondents also indicated the need to improve infrastructure, government support in getting contracts, especially to local firms, restriction of importation of sub-standard goods, and revamping of the economy to raise domestic demand. Most of these issues, especially importation of sub-standard goods need policy intervention and close collaboration with stakeholders. All these factors affect the competitiveness of firms both in the domestic and regional markets.

Institutional linkages and contacts may be important factors in improving the competitiveness of firms. Poor organisational abilities and weak institutions however limit the extent to which firms can use such linkages to influence the direction of policies, regulations and other support mechanisms that affect their competitiveness.

Inter-firm Competition

Inter-firm competition within the metal sub-sector is dominant. In our survey of the sector, high competition ranked third to inadequate funds for expansion and low purchasing power respectively as problems facing the sector. Between the small medium and large firms, competition is dominant among small and medium firms, while the large firms have minimal local competition. The large firms face global competition in getting raw materials and marketing their products.

All steel manufacturers in Kenya are secondary steel producers, importing Primary Raw Materials from Japan, Europe, Korea, South Africa, Brazil, Argentina and other countries having integrated steel plants. Although steel smelters use locally available steel scrap and power, all other inputs like electrodes, alloying elements, among others, are imported along with precision spares. Cold rolling mills import hot rolled pickled and oiled coils of varying widths and grades based on the end use, while zinc for galvanizing and resins for colour coating are also imported.

Other imported products include: zinc, ferrosilicon, and ferromanganese along with other foundry accessories.

The large firms do not only compete globally but also compete locally and within the region. However, a number of large firms are managing local competition in a unique way. Some of these firms have subsidiary firms and local dealer network, which produce and market their products. One large firm noted that in terms of marketing, the local dealer network takes a high portion of products, followed by subsidiary firms and exports. Most of these large firms value the local market that accounts for over 65 per cent of their market with the rest divided almost equally between regional and international markets. The market is also affected by cheap imported metal and plastic products, which firms noted to be the source of unfair competition.

Our research showed that international competition is intense and firms operating internationally have to keep abreast with production technology, innovations, relevant information and expansion of market. Most of these firms achieve this by sending their personnel on exposure trips, including short training. A number of firms also work closely with foreign firms and have exchange programmes for personnel. In cases where firms acquire new technology, they often bring in those who are conversant with the technology to train their staff, or take their staff for training abroad. In addition, these firms lobby relevant bodies such as KAM and FKE to influence government to provide tax rebates. This is mainly prevalent among large firms and few medium firms. Large firms also introduce new product lines aimed at securing an exclusive market for their products by targeting specific clients. In some cases, there is also cutting down fixed costs.

Local competition between and among firms is quite intense and can be viewed at two levels: competition arising due to the advantages some firms have, and competition for the market. On advantages, our research revealed that some firms gain undue advantage due to poor law enforcement of legislation. Some firms, for example, do not pay Value Added Tax (VAT) and this results in what KAM refers to as unethical competition. Other firms use fake papers for exports and do not pay legitimate duties on commodities (KAM, 2002). These types of unethical competition arise due to loopholes in the government system. In some cases, the government officers are compromised through bribes thereby highlighting the role of corruption. KAM has indicated that better systems need to be put in place by the Kenya Revenue Authority (KRA) in order to eliminate loopholes that result in unethical competition. The association has further observed that a reduction of VAT on manufactured goods would discourage the evasion of VAT payment and peddling of fake papers. Restriction of sub-standard imports would also expand the market for firms, and thereby reduce the unethical competition used by some firms. At firm level, our findings show competition cutting across firms (Box 8.1).

Box 8.1: How Firms of Different Sizes Respond to Market Competition

Firm x in Mombasa, dealing in fabricated metal products and considering itself a large firm, faces competition from firms of different sizes in the same sector throughout the country. The firm has responded to this challenge by installing a new plant, which is more efficient, hence cost effective. This, it hopes will enable it compete better through reduced prices. The firm has also opened a service centre in western Kenya, to facilitate marketing of its products.

Firm Y, also located in Mombasa and dealing in steel fabrication but considering itself a small firm, views firms larger than itself, and the Jua Kali sector as its major competitors. The challenge with large firms is their connections with other large firms, which gives them advantage in accessing markets and technology. However, the firm considers Jua Kali firms as giving unfair competition because they do not pay many of the levies that a formal small firm like firm Y has to pay, and also makes products of inferior quality, thus able to charge less. The Jua Kali firms, in his words "thrive on imitating products, and pirating on their established clients". The firm has invested in a new machinery in order to expand its production line and cut down its fixed costs. This is expected to enable them establish and penetrate new markets. The purchase of the new machine was accompanied by technical training on its use and production of the new products.

Firm Z in Mombasa, dealing in structural metals, but considering itself medium, sees its main competitors as restricted to firms of the same size and the Jua Kali. This firm also considers the Jua Kali as giving unfair competition due to their low quality products. The firm has resorted to diversifying its activities, and turning to rental houses to complement its income from the business.

Firm A in Mombasa is a local branch of a multinational firm, and is large. It deals in fabricated products. It faces major competition from firms dealing in the same line of products in Mombasa and Nairobi. The firm responds to competition by using its link with the mother company to get advice on technology, innovations and market expansion. Currently, the firm is introducing new product lines aimed at securing an exclusive market for its products by targeting specific clients.

Firm B in Eldoret considered itself medium sized firm, but now considers itself small-scale due to the significant drop in its operation. It is using only 30% of its established capacity. It deals in fabricated metal products, with its main activity being fabricating machine parts and repair of machinery for the textile, tanning, milk industries and farming tractors. The collapse of these industries and the farming sector has therefore had very adverse effects on its operations. The firm faces the greatest competition from the Jua Kali sector, which also undertakes repairs of machinery spare parts at much lower charges, thus diverting their potential customers. Lack of market outlets for its products is, therefore, the major problem faced by the firm. The firm has not put in place any specific measures to counter this declining market trend. It is hoping that the situation will improve. It this does not happen, it will close down.

Source: Okech B., W.V. Mitullah, and R. Atieno (2002). Understanding Business Systems in Kenya: Firm Response to Changing Market Environment in the Metal products Sector. Draft Report presented at the regional workshop on Business Systems in Africa, 15-16 April, Nairobi, Kenya, April 2, 2002

The small firms undertake repairs of machinery spare parts at much lower cost, thus attracting customers, especially household and small organisations. Medium firms argue that the small firms compete unfairly since quality of their products is low and some of them do not pay any operational fees. While this blame may be founded, in most urban councils, the urban authorities are reluctant to charge any fees to firms, which are not formally registered. This fact has been exploited by such firms but at a cost. Instead of paying regular fees, the firms pay non-compliance fees (bribes). In most cases, this fee is higher than the regular compliance fees, further distorting the market (K'Obonyo et al 1999). At the same time, the inability to pay regular compliance fees results in harassment, especially by urban authorities. Harassment mainly affects the *Jua Kali* firms, which operate on road reserves, and other areas not planned for such activities.

Small firms also compete among themselves, and they have a unique way of dealing with competition. They diversify their activities, an option which seems problematic in terms of marketing and having a market niche. Most of these firms try to keep their customers and continue looking for markets. In most cases, competitors do not give each other supplies in case of shortage, but they reluctantly direct their customers to their competitors when they are not able to immediately satisfy their needs. In cases where they have to give goods to their competitors, they ensure that they make some profit.

Our research found out that competition is more dominant among formal retailers of metal products and the small scale *Jua Kali* traders of small metal products (pad locks, hinges and nails). The formal retailers deal with this competition by retailing products not sold by *Jua Kali* traders. Discussions with both *Jua Kali* traders and formal retailers revealed that the prices charged by *Jua Kali* are lower and they are conveniently located to customers, often close to formal firms.

Firms therefore employ different strategies to fight competition and ensure their survival. Diversification, either by expanding the product line, new activities or venturing into new markets, seems to be the main ways of responding to increasing competition and declining market demand.

Inter-firm Rivalry

Using in-depth discussions, firms were asked whether they have any cases of business rivalry, what dimensions it takes, the type of firms considered as main competitors in terms of locations, the consequences of such rivalry and how they address the different types of competitions. From the in-depth discussions, it emerged that competition was not restricted to firms of the same size, or in the same location.

The discussions showed that most metal products firms operate as single entities with limited linkages with firms in the sector. In almost all in-depth studies of firms conducted for this study, firms indicated that they had no association with other firms in the metal sub-sector. This is partly corroborated with a question asking the 117 firms interviewed to indicate whom they turned to for support whenever need arose. Over 60 per cent of the firms, indicated that they turn to nobody. The few who got support largely turned to banks, relatives and friends. A few others indicated that they turned to business associations, insurance firms and suppliers. Business associations such as KAM were largely used for lobbying government for lower taxes and infrastructure development.

Although business rivalry did not show itself explicitly, most respondents acknowledged that it existed. This was mainly so among firms producing same products. It mainly took the form of guarding against leakage of technology to a competing firm, and manifested itself to limited interaction between such firms. Firm visits and discussion of technical aspects of production between employees was restricted due to fear of "stealing" or copying each other's technology. A manager of a large firm in Mombasa producing structural metal products, confessed that due to fear of "stealing" each other's technology, employees of the firms can only interact outside the factory but cannot visit each other in the workplace. Business rivalry may therefore not be explicit, but is a major characteristic of firms in the metal products sub sector.

SUMMARY, APPLICATION OF BUSINESS SYSTEM AND CONCLUSIONS

Summary

This chapter has discussed firm linkages among small, medium, and large firms in the metal products sub sector of Kenya. The types of linkages discussed are subcontracting as a contractual relationship, and associational lives among the firms. The discussion is based on survey results of 117 firms, falling within small, medium and large firms.

The findings in this analysis show that most firms in the sector have sole owners, with nationality of owners being dominated by Kenyans of both African and Asian origins. While Kenyans of African origin mostly owned small and informal firms with a few owning medium firms, Kenyans of Asian origin mostly owned the medium and large firms. The firms in this sector displayed great diversity in both their activities and products. This was found to be mainly due to declining markets for their products and increasing competition from other firms. Firms, therefore, diversify in order to reduce their risks.

Subcontracting as a contractual linkage is prevalent within the sector with one-third firms engaged in it. The main reason leading firms to subcontract was urgent orders and inadequate capacity. Most small firms subcontracted due to inadequate capacity while large and medium firms subcontract mainly due to seasonal demand increases, and need for specialized skills. For firms which did not subcontract, the main reasons were adequate resources, and lack of extra work to subcontract. Firms also received subcontracts. However, a number of reasons inhibited many firms from receiving subcontracts. The main reasons were reduced demand for the products, lack of trust among small firms and firm policy not to receive subcontracts.

A significant number of firms operating within the sector belong to associations, while a few others do not belong to any association. The latter attributed their reluctance to join associations to mismanagement. When looked at by firm size, the results showed that among the large firms, more firms belonged to associations compared to the medium and small firms. It, therefore, appears that large firms benefit from the associations more than the small and medium firms. They are able to develop useful networks and lobby for various benefits, including lower tax and customs duty rates.

Networks and institutional contacts were also limited among these firms. For the firms, which had contacts, the nature of such contacts involved financial assistance, student attachments, training, quality control and research. Although institutional contacts had benefits for those who were involved in them, many firms may not be realizing such benefits by not entering into such relations.

The chapter also shows that the main factors, which affect firm competitiveness in the sector, are the cost of power, poor logistics and bureaucratic red tape, which significantly increases the cost of importing raw materials, interest rates on financial services, poor infrastructure and insecurity. All these increase the cost of production, which lead to high prices for the finished products.

Inter-firm competition is dominant, and firms respond by introducing new product lines, diversifying products and investing in new technology. Inter-firm rivalry was also found to exist implicitly, and was found to be largely responsible for the limited interactions between firms dealing in the same products. What the results of this study reveal cannot be described as a free market economy. There is no perfect information, no free entry and firms are not equal in their access to technology. Some activities, like manufacture of fabricated metal products are dominated by a few large firms, which are in themselves not similar in their characteristics. What results is inter firm rivalry, with each firm striving to outdo the other through efforts to use superior technology, modify their products to capture a specific market. An example of this was found in Mombasa, in a large firm which is a subsidiary of a multinational. The firm links with mother company to access technology and be superior to its competitor, which is a local firm. It also uses this link to secure markets for its products and has diversified into other packaging materials.

Application of Business Systems

Observations of many economies show difference in stages of growth. Some economies are growing, while others are either declining or stagnant. This is attributed to the recognition of the fact that the pace of development is a function of the institutional environment (Benson, 2001). Our research in Kenya has revealed a number of dynamics in line with this argument. In analysing firm linkages and business competition, our data shows that, firm linkages, competition and business rivalry to some extent is determined by the embedded institutional framework. In analysing linkages especially those related to sub-contracting, the study found out that sub-contracting within the metal sub-sector is justified by a number of factors, including: lack of skills, license, capacity, including equipment and tools, and high seasonal demand. However, lack of trust has contributed to large firms not being able to sub-contract production tasks to small firms. This has affected the link between large and small firms and their general output and contribution to the economy.

Metal products firms guard against competition especially from firms producing similar products. There is fear among firms of possible theft of technology. This makes firms protect leakage of technology to competitors. The situation is worsened by lack of awareness of patent rights. Technology transfer is an important aspect of business environment and ways and means have to be available for firms to access technology. Our findings show that it is almost impossible for small firms to access technology. Their options include relying on other firms who have technology, hiring individuals who have experience from larger firms or relying on some external support, which is limited.

Efficient exchange requires trust. As Ricketts (2001) argues, business can only take place if the transactors trust that each will respect some basic rules of honest dealing. In the absence of trust, there has to be recourse in the form of credibly threatened sanctions against breaches of contract. In most developing countries including Kenya, this task is undertaken by the government. However, regulations have not been efficient, especially their enforcement. This has contributed to poor regulatory business environment, making entrepreneurs very cautious when considering a potential trading partner. In the metal sub-sector, lack of trust is reflected in the reluctance of large firms to sub-contract to small firms. When contracts are not honoured, firms have nowhere to turn to since dispute resolution mechanisms are either non-existent or too cumbersome to follow.

Metal product firms, like many other firms in Kenya, rely on associations and network in responding to their business environment, that is, largely unpredictable. In particular, small firms rely on association for their welfare. Associations and social networks ensure their social security by assisting entrepreneurs to deal with medical and funeral expenses, access to finance, training, supplies, business sites, dealing with harassment by Local Authorities, solving disputes and sharing business information, lobbying and contributing to policy processes. Absence of this creates a hostile business environment that affects the performance of firms.

CONCLUSIONS

Some conclusions can be drawn from this chapter. Limited linkages characterize firms in the metal products sub sector. Due to the nature of competition, mistrust and rivalry in the sector, firms view linkages as only one of the ways of responding to changing market conditions. Most firms prefer the other alternatives to linkages, such as diversifying their products as a means of responding to competition or increasing staff to meet increased demand for the product. This shows that there is need for policy to address firm competition and competitiveness in the sector through improved infrastructure, security, logistics and official bureaucratic red tape, which reduces the competitiveness of firms in the sector.

The perceived lack of clear benefits or knowledge of such benefits from associations and mismanagement of existing associations have mainly acted to discourage firms, especially small firms from joining any associations. This has meant that firms in this sector do not therefore enjoy the potential benefits that association memberships bring to firms. This leads to high cost of production, declining market share for individual firms and low production, which is reflected in low capacity utilization characterized by firms in the sector. The limited linkages cut across firms of different sizes and are not restricted to any firm size.

REFERENCES

Aguilar, R. and Bigsten, A. 2002. "Regional Programme on Enterprise Development Survey 1993-95". In Bigsten, A. and Kimuyu, P. (eds.). *Structure and Performance of Manufacturing in Kenya*. Oxford: Centre for the Study of Kenyan Economies.

Beardshaw, J. and Palfreman, D. 1986. *The Organisation in its Environment*. Third Edition, London: Pitman Publishing Limited.

Benson, Bruce, L. 2001. "Knowledge, Trust and Recourse: Imperfect Substitutes as Sources of Assurance in Emerging Economies". *Economic Affairs*, March 2001.

Bigsten, A. 2002. "History and Policy of Manufacturing in Kenya". In Bigsten, A. and Kimuyu, P. (eds.). *Structure and Performance of Manufacturing in Kenya*. Oxford: Centre for the Study of Kenyan Economies.

Collier, P. and Gunning, W. 1999. "Explaining African Economic Performance". *Journal of Economic Literature, Vol. XXXVII (March 1999) 64-111*.

Coughlin, P. 1988. "Economies of scale, Capacity utilization and Import Substitution: A focus on Dies, Moulds and patterns". In Coughlin, P. and Ikiara, G.K. (eds.). *Industrialization in Kenya: In Search of a Strategy*. Nairobi: Heinemann; London: James Currey.

Coughlin, P. 1991. "The Steel Industry: Contradictory Policies, Government Inertia and Private Conflicts. In Coughlin, P. and Ikiara, G.K. (eds.). *Kenya's Industrialisation Dilemma*. Nairobi: Heinemann.

Departments of Economics, University of Gothenburg and University of Nairobi. 1994. *Limitations and Rewards in Kenya's Manufacturing Sector: A Study of Enterprise Development*. Mimeo: University of Gothenburg

Ellis, F. 2000. *Rural Livelihoods and Diversity in Developing Countries*. New York: Oxford University Press.

Graner, M. and Isaksson, A. 2002. "Export Performance in the Kenyan Manufacturing Sector". In Bigsten, A. and Kimuyu, P. (eds.). *Structure and Performance of Manufacturing in Kenya*. Oxford: Centre for the Study of Kenyan Economies.

Ikiara, G.K.; Kimuyu, P.; Manundu, M. and Masai, W. 2002. "Firm, Product Market and Technological Characteristics". In Bigsten, A. and Kimuyu, P. (eds.). *Structure and Performance of Manufacturing in Kenya*. Oxford: Centre for the Study of Kenyan Economies.

ILO/EAMAT. 1999. *Kenya: Meeting the Employment Challenges of the 21st Century*. Geneva

Isaksson, A. and Wihlborg, C. 2002. "Financial Constraints on Kenyan Manufacturing". In Bigsten, A. and Kimuyu, P. (eds.). *Structure and Performance of Manufacturing in Kenya*. Oxford: Centre for the Study of African Economies.

K'Obonyo, P.; Ikiara, G.K.; Mitullah, W.V.; Abuodha, C.; Ongile, G and McCormick, D. 1999. "Complying with Business Regulation in Kenya: a Benchmark Study of the Trade Licensing and Registration of Business Names Acts, 1997-1998". IDS Occasional Paper No. 64. Nairobi: University of Nairobi, Institute for Development Studies.

Kenya Association of Manufacturers (KAM). 2002.

Kenya, Republic of. 2000. *Economic Survey 2000*. Nairobi: Government Printer.

Kenya, Republic of. 1997. *National Development Plan 1997-2002*. Nairobi: Government Printer.

Kenya, Republic of. 1986. *Sessional Paper Number one of 1986 on Economic Management for Renewed Growth*. Nairobi: Government Printer.

Kinyanjui, M. and Mitullah, W.V. 1997. "Inter-Firm Dynamics in the Construction Sector". IDS Working Paper No. 296. Nairobi: University of Nairobi, Institute for Development Studies.

McCormick D. and Atieno R. 1997. Private Enterprise Development in Africa: Methodology for Research. Nairobi: University of Nairobi, Institute for Development Studies.

McCormick, D. and Atieno, R. 2002. "Linkages between Small and Large Firms in the Kenyan Food Processing Sector". In Van Dijk, M.P. and Sandee, H. (eds) *Innovation and Small Enterprises in the Third World*. Cheltenham,UK: Edward Edgar Publishing.

McCormick, D.; Mitullah, W.V. and Kinyanjui, M.N. 2001. "Enhancing Institutional Capacity for Policy Development, Dialogue and Advocacy: Role of Associations and Other Community Based Organisations". Nairobi: University of Nairobi, Institute for Development Studies.

McCormick, D. and Kimuyu, P. 2003. "Business Systems Theory: An African Perspective". Nairobi: University of Nairobi, Institute for Development Studies.

Meyanathan, D.S. and Munther, R. 1994. "Industrial Structures and the Development of Small and Medium Enterprise Linkages: An Overview". *EDI Seminar Series*. Washington D.C.: World Bank.

Mitullah, W.V. 1999. "Lake Victoria's Nile Perch Fish Cluster: Institutions, Politics and Joint Action". Working Paper No. 87. Sussex: Institute of Development Studies.

North, D. C. 1990. *Institutions, Institutional Change and Economic Performance.* Cambridge: Cambridge University Press.

Okech, B.; Mitullah, W.V. and Atieno, R. 2002. "Understanding Business Systems in Kenya: Firm Response to Changing Market Environment in the Metal Products Sector". Draft Report Presented at the Regional Workshop on Business Systems in Africa, 15-16 April, Nairobi, Kenya, April 2, 2002.

Parker, J and Torres, T. 1994. "Micro and Small Enterprises in Kenya: Results of the 1995 Baseline Survey". Gemini Project Contract Number DHR 5448-Q-45-9081-06. USAID.

Pedersen, P.O. 1996. "Flexibility and Networking: European and African contexts". In McCormick D. and Pedersen P. O. (eds.). *Small Enterprises: Flexibility and Networking in an African Context.* Nairobi. Longhorn Kenya.

Qualmann, R. 2002. "Why do(n't) they Innovate? Explaining the Diverse MSE Adjustment Strategies after an External Shock". In Dijk Van M.P. and Sandee H. (eds). *Innovation and Small Enterprises in the Third World.* Cheltenham, UK: Edward Edgar Publishing.

Ricketts, Martin. 2001. "Trust and Economic Organisation". *Economic Affairs,* March 2001.

Sodebom, M. 2000. "Constraints and Opportunities in Kenyan Manufacturing: A Report on the Kenyan Manufacturing Survey". Available at: *www.economics.ox.ac.uk/CSAEadmin/reports/main.html*

Henson, Spencer and Mitullah, W.V. 2004. "Kenya Exports of Nile Perch: The Impact of Food Safety Standards on an Export-Oriented Supply Chain". Policy Research Working Paper 3349, June 2004. Washington DC: World Bank.

UNIDO 2002. *Industrial Development Report 2002/2003.* Vienna: United Nations Industrial Development Organisation.

Chapter 9

Textiles and Clothing: Global Players and Local Struggles

Dorothy McCormick, Peter Kimuyu and Mary Njeri Kinyanjui

INTRODUCTION

The textile and clothing sectors offer excellent examples of the way in which local and global institutions interact to produce unique forms of industrialisation. Global institutions, including the Multi Fibre Arrangement (MFA),General Agreement on Tariffs and Trade (GATT), and World Trade Organisation (WTO), especially the Agreement on Textiles and Clothing (ATC), clearly affect Kenyan producers hoping to participate in world trade in textiles and/or clothing. Other lesser-known institutions, such as the barely studied international trade in second-hand clothing, have also had a major impact on these industries in Kenya. Regional organisations like COMESA and the East African Community (EAC) affect raw materials supplies and set the rules of regional trade in final products. Local institutions, such as knowledge, gender, ethnicity and entrepreneurship, affect the ways these industries are organised. Finally, firm level institutions determine firms' efficiency and their interactions with other industry players. The textile and clothing sectors are, therefore, extremely useful lenses through which to view Kenya's business system.

This chapter attempts to contribute to the understanding of Kenya's business system by analysing the full range of textile and clothing firms. The picture that emerges is of a multi-tiered industry that interacts in various ways with global, regional, and local institutions. Some parts of the industry are thriving, while others are gasping for survival or have all but succumbed to the forces of what many perceive to be unfair competition and ineffective institutional support.

The chapter draws on primary and secondary sources of information. Primary data, gathered in 2000-2001, came from two main sources: a series of in-depth interviews of 22 textile and clothing firms ranging in size from 5 to 2,000 workers, located in various parts of Kenya (see McCormick et al., 2001), and a survey of 125 micro and small-scale clothing manufacturers in Nairobi. This survey was designed to replicate an earlier study of 245 micro and small clothing producers, carried out in 1989 (see Kinyanjui and McCormick, 2003 for details of both surveys). Both sets of data were analysed using a combination of quantitative and qualitative techniques. Primary data were supplemented with various secondary sources of information.

A number of papers were produced that used results from such analysis. This chapter synthesises material from these and other papers in an attempt to shed light on Kenya's business system as seen from the perspective of the textile and garment sectors. The next two sections describe the textile sector, first in its global context and then in its specifically Kenyan form. The chapter then goes on to discuss each of the three tiers of firms: global exporters, firms exporting into regional markets, and those aiming at domestic markets. A final section draws conclusions from the analysis, focusing especially on the policy implications of the findings.

THE TEXTILE SECTOR IN GLOBAL CONTEXT

The textile and clothing industries were among the first manufacturing activities to take on a global dimension. Analysing these industries suggests that Kenya's business system is not confined within national borders, but is strongly influenced by global institutions. Before discussing these institutions, we first provide the reader with a brief overview of the textile sector as it exists in various countries of the world.

What is the Textile Sector?

The term 'textile sector' is used in two ways. In its comprehensive sense, it includes all aspects of textile and apparel production from the fibre stage to completed end-use products (see Figure 9.1). In a more limited sense, the term is used to designate only a portion of the textile industry, namely, the segment that manufactures fibres, yarns, fabrics, and selected finished products.[1]

The textile industry can be broken down into three main product groupings: fibres, intermediate components, and final products. Figure 9.1 shows these three segments and the linkages among them. The left-hand segment shows the main fibre groups of cotton, wool, and manufactured fibres. These undergo a spinning process, which results in yarn. The yarn is then used singly or in combinations to make the intermediate components shown in the centre segment: thread and cordage, woven fabric, and knit fabric. Some fibres also go directly, without spinning, into the manufacture of carpets and rugs. The right-hand segment of the diagram shows the most common end product groups: apparel, interior furnishings, industrial and other consumer products, and carpets and rugs. Of these, the apparel or clothing sector, is by far the most important. Approximately, 50% of all textile production goes into the manufacture of garments (Dicken, 1998: 285). The mix within each of the three segments varies from one country to another. Unfortunately, available data do not allow us to calculate the proportions for Africa.

---

1   Products like blankets, bed sheets, and certain knitted garments are included in the 'textile' classification.

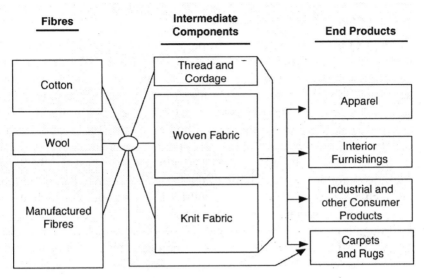

Figure 9.1: Typical Industry Structure

Adapted from Dickerson, 1999

Fibres are the raw materials for the textile industry. Natural fibres include cotton, wool, silk, linen, ramie, hemp, jute, and a few others. Manufactured fibres are further subdivided into two: cellulosic fibres, such as rayon and acetate, which come from trees and other natural cellulose sources, and synthetic fibres such as polyester, nylon, and acrylic, which are petrochemical derivatives. Both types of fibres are spun into various types of thread and yarn.

Fibre products are used to make intermediate components, including thread and cordage as well as woven and knitted fabric. Fabric usually requires additional dying and/or finishing to make it suitable for consumer use. Large textile mills often have integrated operations from yarn spinning through fabric finishing.

Finally, the intermediate components are made into end products. Of these, apparel is the largest user of fabric, followed by industrial and other consumer products, and interior furnishings, such as curtains, upholstery, and bed sheets. Carpets and rugs are made directly from fibre. In the past, wool was the main rug fibre, but now many rugs are made from manufactured fibres.

The apparel and, to a lesser extent, the interior furnishings segments are further subdivided according to the final user and the market. Apparel, for example, is categorised into women's wear, men's wear, children's wear, etc. Perhaps the most important distinction is between fashion items, which are seasonal and subject to rapidly changing styles, and standard items, such as socks and ordinary T-shirts, which change very little from one year to the next (Dicken, 1998). This latter distinction has direct repercussions on production and delivery times.

Global Institutions Shaping the Industry

Three groups of institutions can be considered under the broad umbrella of 'global' institutions, in the sense that they originate beyond Kenya's borders and have had an impact on the country's external as well as internal activities. The first group includes many of the changes brought about as a result of the World Bank/IMF Structural Adjustment Programmes (SAPs). The requirements and loan conditionalities laid down by these two bodies in the 1980s and 1990s led to significant changes in markets and the general business environment in Kenya. Two aspects of Kenya's SAPs are pertinent to the textile industry: liberalisation of foreign trade in goods and the freeing of the foreign exchange markets. Before trade reforms, Kenya had an inward-oriented industrialisation policy, which attempted to protect the array of import-substitution industries that had been formed from the 1950s through the 1980s (McCormick, 1999; Bigsten and Kimuyu, 2002). The textile and clothing sectors were major beneficiaries of the import substitution regime. In the early 1990s, when Kenya opened its markets by removing quantitative restrictions on imports and lowering tariffs, these industries immediately felt the pinch.

The second group of global institutions affecting Kenya's textile industry is the international trading regime for clothing and textiles, which includes the Multi-Fibre Arrangement and its related World Trade Organisation's (WTO) Textile Agreements. These set specific rules governing international trade in clothing and textiles by countries that are members of the WTO. The third is closely related to the second. It consists of new bilateral agreements, most notably, the African Growth and Opportunity Act (AGOA) of the US Government and the Cotonou Agreements.

International Trading Regime

Box 9.1: Textile Agreements

1961
Short Term Cotton Agreement

1962-1973
Long Term Cotton Agreement

1974-1994
Multi-Fibre Agreement (MFA)

1995-2005
Agreement on Textiles and Clothing of the Uruguay Round

The importance of textiles and clothing to national economies and, especially, their threatened status in industrialised countries in the second half of the 20th century gave rise to a set of special regimes to govern international trade.

By the mid 1950s, developing countries began to increase their exports, especially of cotton textile fabric and made-up products. In response, some developed countries negotiated agreements with individual governments to limit the quantities of exports of cotton textiles (Bagchi, 2001). Many bilateral agreements, however, are difficult to manage, so a multilateral solution was sought. The result was the Short Term Cotton Agreement, which was followed a year later by the Long Term Cotton Agreement (see Box 9.1). Both allowed countries to impose quotas on imports from particular countries when they caused disruption in the market.

By the 1970s, manufactured fibres had become an important component of the textile industry. Furthermore, in the United States, the wool textile industry wanted protection. There was, therefore, considerable pressure to expand the existing cotton agreements to cover other fibres. The Multi Fibre Agreement (MFA) came into existence in 1974 with the aim of including the trade in manufactured fibres and wool products within the restrictive framework of market disruption (Bagchi, 2001).

The MFA was a complex institution, with an equally complex interaction with the General Agreement on Tariffs and Trade (GATT). One of its main consequences was the development of a system of quotas on clothing and household textiles. The overall effect of these quotas was to increase prices in importing countries (mostly industrialised countries) and to suppress the growth of exports in many developing countries (Trela and Whalley 1990, Bagchi 2001). In particular, cases, however, countries benefited from quotas. For example, the development of the Mauritian garment industry happened, to some extent because several countries imposed quotas on Hong Kong, which prompted Hong Kong textile and clothing investors to look for alternative production sites (Cable, 1990).

Developing countries began to call for the end of the MFA as early as 1980. Their demand for liberalisation of the textile trade in real terms was the genesis of the mandate to end restrictive practices in the Uruguay Round of GATT negotiations (Bagchi, 2001). In the end, the Uruguay Round negotiated the Agreement on Textiles and Clothing (ATC), which provided for a ten-year phasing out of the MFA. The ATC requires all countries that are members of the World Trade Organisation (WTO) to integrate textiles and clothing into general WTO trading rules, which are essentially GATT rules. The process was allowed to take place in phases, but all textile items were to be integrated by the end of the ATC on 31 December 2004. The ending of import quotas has caused anxiety among countries that had benefited from their existence. Evidence from the first few months of 2005 suggests that this final liberalisation of the market of textile products has squeezed profits and forced firms to improve efficiency or close down (McCormick et al., 2006).

All of these developments took place within an overall international context in which tariffs levels were reducing while the use of non-tariff barriers was increasing. In 1940, the average tariff on manufactured products was around 40%; by the late 1990s, it stood at only around 4% (Dickens 1998: 92 ff.). Since the mid-1970s, there has been a marked increase in the use of non-tariff barriers. The import quotas discussed above are only one form of non-tariff barriers. Others include rules of origin, anti-dumping measures, special labelling and packaging regulations, and local content requirements.

Trade Preferences

By the late 1990s, it was clear to many that Africa's industrialisation was lagging seriously behind (Lall, 1995; 1999; Dicken, 1998; Bigsten and Kimuyu, 2002). After Structural Adjustment, many countries, including Kenya, hoped to industrialise through promotion of manufactured exports. Production of clothing for export seemed an obvious way to go. The industry is labour intensive, with fairly low capital requirements. Furthermore, its global organisation, as described in the previous section, makes it fairly easy to penetrate. Since, as we shall see, it is difficult for poor countries to produce competitively, trade preferences have become an important instrument for boosting export production.

Kenya's export trade in clothing is largely with the EU, the US, and the Africa Region, especially neighbouring countries. In nearly all cases, the trade is governed by bi-lateral or multi-lateral arrangements: the Cotonou Agreement for the EU, AGOA for the US, and COMESA or the EAC for African trade. Of these, AGOA seems to be having the greatest impact.

The Africa Growth and Opportunity Act (AGOA), was signed into law in October 2000. The bill gives duty-free access to the US market to a list of products originating in Africa. To qualify for benefits under AGOA, countries had to put into place a set of procedures designed, among other things, to prevent trans-shipment. In January 2001, Kenya became the first African country to meet all of the requirements for registration under the Act.

AGOA established its own rules of origin for goods traded under the Act. Specifically, it requires a double transformation. In the context of clothing, which is Kenya's main AGOA-traded textile product, this means that two transformations – from yarn into cloth and from cloth into clothing – must take place in a country in order for an item to qualify for duty-free import into the USA. Alternatively, an African clothing manufacturer may use US textiles or textiles produced in another AGOA-qualified country. Use of cloth manufactured in the US is not practical due to distance and costs, and firms have had difficulty in sourcing good quality African cloth at competitive prices. Application of this double-transformation requirement was first suspended for developing countries until 30 September 2004. This allowed African countries to produce clothing using fabric from China or other Eastern producers. The AGOA acceleration act of 2004 (AGOA II) extended the overall programme from 2008 until 2015. It also extended for three years, or until 30 September 2007, the sub-limit on third country fabric. In December 2006, this was further extended to 2012. The level of tariffs determines the value of the benefit. The US has an extremely complex tariff schedule running to thousands of pages (see http://dataweb.usitc.gov). Table 9.1 presents the rates of duty for a few articles, including those commonly produced by developing country garment firms.

The duty-free entry into the US offered by AGOA effectively means that African garments can be sourced more cheaply than comparable garments from non-AGOA countries. The benefit, however, varies from one product to another because of the varying tariff rates. In general, the higher the applicable rate of duty, the more valuable the benefit. Using the items listed in Table 9.1, we see that the benefit range from around 30% for items like T-shirts and blouses made of man-made fibres, to only 8% for babies' cotton knit sun suits and women's cotton skirts. The fact that articles made from man-made fabrics give the highest benefit has clear implications for the direction Kenya's textile industry needs take if it wishes to continue using the AGOA facility.

Table 9.1: *US Tariff Rates for Selected Items of Clothing, 2003*

Tariff Sub-Heading	Article	Rate of Duty (%)
Chapter 61 – Articles of Apparel and Clothing Accessories, Knitted or Crocheted		
6109.10.00	Cotton T-shirts	17.0
6109.90.10	T-shirts of man-made fibres	32.2
6111.20.60	Babies' cotton knit sun suits	8.2
6115.92.90	Cotton socks	13.6
Chapter 62 - Articles of Apparel and Clothing Accessories, Not Knitted or Crocheted		
6203.42.40	Men's cotton trousers or shorts	16.7
6204.52.20	Women's cotton skirts	8.2
6204.43.40	Women's synthetic fabric dresses	16.1
6205.20.20	Men's or boys' cotton shirts	19.8
6206.40.30	Women's or girls' blouses of man-made fibres	27.1
6207.21.00	Men's or boys' cotton pyjamas	9.0

Source: Harmonised Tariff Schedule of the United States (2003) (Supplement 1)

Evolution of Global Textile Industry

The textile sector has played a leading role in the development and evolution of worldwide economic and industrial history. Textile production led the Industrial Revolution from about 1750 onwards. It was the first sector to shift from skilled hand labour to production based on machines as well as the first to use technical inventions in large-scale factories, thereby transforming England from an agricultural to an industrial economy. Development of textile production into a factory system created the jobs that led to widespread employment of women. Poor working conditions in textile mills and later, in garment factories led to the first industrial reforms (Elson, 1994; Dickerson, 1999; Dicken, 1999). Similar processes occurred in other countries of Europe and North America until, by the beginning of the 20th century, the textile industry was well established in all industrialised countries. The process was then repeated in many developing countries from the mid-20th century. Substantial industries were developed, especially in East Asia.

Global patterns of textile and clothing production began to shift dramatically in the mid 1950s. Between 1953 and 1973, textile production in developing areas grew rapidly while industrialised countries' share of output began to diminish (Dickerson, 1999:168). Worldwide textile production slowed in 1973 in response to the sharp increase in oil prices. Dickerson (1999) argues that the year 1973 was a turning point for the textile industry, and that from that year on, the strongest textile production growth rates were in the developing and, later, the transition economies. In part, this shift is attributable to the relocation of manufactured fibre production from industrialised to less-developed countries. This happened mainly through licensing and subcontracting arrangements between firms in the North and the South (Elson, 1994).

By the 1980s, the developing countries – especially those in East Asia – were exhibiting strong growth in textile production. Low wages combined with good quality output gave the Asian textile industry a decided competitive advantage over the industrialised countries. As a result, the countries of the South, which in 1975 accounted for only 19% of world output in textiles, saw their share rise to 26% in 1990 and to over 40% by 1998 (Elson, 1994; ILO, 2000).

In the clothing industry, the shift from industrialised to developing countries was even more pronounced than in textiles. From only 12% of world output in 1970, developing countries' share of clothing production rose to 20% in 1990 and to over 50% in 1998 (Elson 1994, ILO, 2000). Clothing production is widely spread geographically. The largest concentration is in China, which had over 3.6 million workers producing clothing in 1998 (ILO, 2000:19). Distant followers of China are the United States, Mexico, the Russian Federation, Japan, Bangladesh, and Indonesia.

Many now conceptualise the clothing industry as a buyer-driven commodity or value chain (Gereffi, 1994; McCormick and Schmitz, 2002). In such chains, large retailers, brand-name merchandisers, and trading companies play a key role in setting up decentralised production networks in a variety of exporting countries (Gereffi, 1994: 216). Many fashion-oriented clothing companies do not own any production facilities. Instead, they make their name – and their profits – by designing fashion garments that carry their label. Factories, often in the developing world, that make to the buyer's exact specifications, carry out the actual production. The result is often a 'global garment' that was sewn in one country of fabric woven in a different country, using thread, buttons, and other materials from a third or even a fourth country.

Gereffi's (1994) buyer-driven commodity chain model posits a set of concentric circles representing the sourcing patterns of different levels of buyers. In this model, companies with expensive designer brands buy from an inner circle of premium-quality, high-value-added exporting countries, such as Italy, France, UK, and Japan. Department stores and specialty chains selling under their own label buy from the next ring of established exporters such as South Korea, Mauritius, and Taiwan. Mass merchandisers look farther out to find low cost standardised goods, and may approach producers in countries like Viet Nam, Egypt, Lesotho, or Kenya.

In all cases – from those buying only high quality to those emphasising low cost – buyers are looking for exact replication of sample garments, consistent quality, and reliable delivery times.

Trade in Second-Hand Clothing

Along with the rise in global trade in new clothing has come a related phenomenon – surging trade in second-hand clothes. Research in this area has been limited, but what exists suggests that the trade originates in affluent countries where individuals donate unwanted clothing to charity shops, church clothing drives, and recycling bins (Haggblade, 1990; Bigsten and Wicks, 1996). The sheer magnitude of the donations, combined with the new openness of developing country markets brought about by SAPs, has fuelled a new global industry consisting of exporters in developed countries feeding layers of wholesale and retail traders in developing countries, especially Africa and the former Eastern Bloc (Field, 2000; Baden and Barber, 2005).

Once the clothing reaches the African continent, it is distributed by local wholesale and retail traders according to complex mechanisms that take into account its style, condition and ultimate saleability. Second-hand garments attract considerable consumer interest. One reason is price: the prices of second-hand items are only 10 to 30 per cent of those of comparable new garments (McCormick et al., 1997; Field, 2000). Consumers are also attracted by the variety of second-hand clothing and by what many believe is its higher quality (McCormick et al., 1997). Second-hand clothing has, therefore, become a major competitor to new clothing in many countries of Sub-Saharan Africa, including Kenya, where low incomes often mean that new clothing is out of reach for majority of the consumers.

THE KENYAN TEXTILE SECTOR

Shaped by both the global institutions discussed above and its own national institutions, the Kenyan textile industry has evolved from a classic import substitution industry into a complex sector with firms of various types and sizes serving global, regional, and domestic markets. Key to its evolution has been the market liberalisation process that accompanied the country's structural adjustment programme.

National Institutions Shaping Kenya's Textile Industry

National institutions are critical to the functioning of business (Whitley, 1992; Pedersen and McCormick, 1999). Kenya's textile sector has been shaped by at least four sets of national institutions: the state, markets, the technology system, and the financial system (McCormick et al., 2001; 2002).

State and Government

The state and the organs of government have played a major role in Kenya's economy since independence. A number of institutions make up the state apparatus. At the highest level, we can speak of legislative, executive, and judicial branches of government. In Kenya, these translate into the Parliament, the Presidency and

Executive arms of the Ministries, and the Judiciary. More particularly, the organs with the greatest impact on the textile industry tend to be Parliament in its policy- and law-making functions, the Ministry of Trade and Industry, ministries responsible for tax collection, infrastructure, and internal security, and state-controlled organisations such as the Kenya Bureau of Standards.

One difficulty pervading government at all levels has been the combination of excessive bureaucracy and endemic corruption. A rigid and poorly paid bureaucracy has over the last two decades become more and more corrupt. This makes it difficult and expensive to do business in Kenya. The impact is felt on many fronts. For example, illegal and/or unaccustomed imports of garments find their way onto the market, where they compete unfairly with Kenyan goods. Some unscrupulous business people also try to benefit from Kenya's trade privileges by transhipping goods produced elsewhere. Corruption also raises transactions costs, as business people seeking licences or transacting other business with the government make extra payments and/or lose productive time in trying to obtain legitimate services.

A second difficulty is the negative effect on production costs of high taxation, poor infrastructure, and lack of security. These affect firms of all sizes in all industries. The government acknowledges that Kenya's tax in relation to GDP is higher than that for many low-income countries, and that, it is characterised by uneven and unfair taxes, a narrow tax base with very high rates, and low compliance (Kenya, 2003). Although Kenya once had a fairly well developed infrastructure, including one of the best road networks in Africa, railroad, electricity grid, port facilities, telecommunications, and piped water, much of this was allowed to deteriorate until, by the end of the 20th century, poor infrastructure was considered to be a major disincentive to potential investors and a threat to the realisation of the goal of industrialisation (Kenya, 1996). Like the infrastructure, the public security system also deteriorated to the point where the government could guarantee citizens neither personal security nor the security of their property. The new government blamed this on low morale in the police force, low professionalism, inadequate allocation of resources, and corruption within the police force (Kenya, 2003). Many have also recognised that Kenya's proximity to countries such as Somalia and Ethiopia that lack the ability to cooperate on border control, has exacerbated the security problem. Weak security is a deterrent to both local and foreign investment because it threatens the safety of capital and indirectly affects labour productivity. For example, workers may perform poorly or miss work because of security related incidents, and firms find it difficult to schedule night shifts because workers are reluctant to leave their homes exposed to robbers.

On a more positive note, Kenya has since the early 1990s had in place specific platforms designed to promote export production. Platforms serve the dual purpose of making it possible for enterprises to obtain inputs at world or border prices so that such firms can gain export price competitiveness, and removing negative trade protection from exports (Glenday and Ndii, 2003). There are three such platforms in Kenya, namely, Export Compensation, Manufacturing Under Bond, and Export Processing Zones. Several problems with the first of these caused it to be phased out in 1993. The first problem was that under the scheme, it was difficult to maintain the same level of compensation for different products. Some items were over-compensated while others were under-compensated. Lowering of duty rates in the 1990s was also incompatible with the compensation scheme. Furthermore, the scheme's simplicity made it fall into the category of prohibited subsidies susceptible to countervailing measures by importing countries under the WTO/GATT rules).[2]

The other two export platforms remain. Manufacturing-Under-Bond (MUB) was established in 1988 (Kenya, 1988). Under the programme, bonded factories can import plant equipment, spare parts and raw material duty-free to manufacture goods for export. The scheme also gives participating firms investment incentives in the form of favourable income tax treatment of capital expenditure, and zero-rating for VAT purposes of domestic input purchases. Initially, the special MUB incentives were restricted to new factories. Later, this was relaxed to give bonded manufacturers flexibility so that, they could relocate to rented premises and still qualify for the investment benefits. To control MUB, customs department has to verify inventories of imported raw materials, manufactured products, and waste or scrap material.

The Export Processing Zones (EPZ) legislation, passed in 1990, gives an even more generous incentive package designed to attract foreign investment. EPZ firms receive duty and VAT waivers on imports of plant equipment and raw materials, expedited licensing and reduced business licence fees, exemption from rent and tenancy controls, and a ten-year tax holiday followed by reduced tax rates for the next ten years (Kenya, 1990). There is, however, no exemption from Kenyan labour legislation. Export processing zones are gazetted as special purpose corporations that can only operate in a designated EPZ location, which may be a single factory or a unit in an EPZ industrial park (Glenday and Ndii, 2003). Kenyan firms can establish EPZ subsidiaries but are not allowed to do part of the business inside and another part outside the EPZ. Provisions were also made in the income tax act to control potential transfer pricing between EPZ enterprises and related domestic firms. EPZs are treated as outside the customs territory. Sales from Kenyan firms into the EPZ are treated as exports while those from EPZs to Kenyan firms are treated as imports that attract duties and taxes.

Technology System

As discussed in Chapter 1, the technology system includes the education, skills, and capabilities of workers, equipment used, work organisation, hours of work, interfirm linkages, and sources of technological innovation.

Technology varies considerably between textile and clothing production, and within clothing production, between those targeting the top of the range and those mass producing for low-end markets (ILO, 2000). Overall, the skill levels in the textile sector appear low: Most of the workers and managers have secondary level of

---

2   See WTO Agreement on Subsidies and Countervailing Measures, and GATT, Article XVI on Subsidies (World Trade Organisation, 1999).

education or less (Ikiara et al., 2002). Very few have university education and fewer still have technical education. The capability stock is therefore limited. Textile production is generally more capital and skill intensive than clothing production. This means that workers need higher levels of education and training. Within clothing production, firms desiring to improve quality need to introduce new machinery and to ensure that workers know how to use it properly. Surveys by the International Labour Office indicate that relatively unskilled machine operators, who are able to be trained to make standard garments, often cannot adapt to new technology and, as a result, have trouble meeting deadlines and quality standards (ILO, 2000: 106).

Technology also involves physical capital in the form of buildings, machinery, and small equipment. Generally speaking, the capital requirements for establishing a textile mill are more than those for setting up a garment factory. Furthermore, the requirements for a mill making woven fabric are generally more than those for a knitting mill. The differences have to do both with the cost of the machines and the nature of the scale economies. Nevertheless, such differences are not universal. A firm making embroidered T-shirts, for example, may use highly sophisticated computerised embroidery machines, while a small-scale weaver uses relatively inexpensive handloom technology.

Another aspect of in-firm production technology involves the hours of work, including length of the work shift, number of shifts per day, number of days worked per week, etc. In some cases, this is related to the nature of the production. Some processes, such as those used for making synthetic fibres, are continuous and are most efficiently done using continuous shifts. Others, such as garment production, are more easily adapted to an interrupted work schedule.

Production can also be organised between firms by means of subcontracting, licensing, and other cooperative arrangements. Subcontracting is very common in parts of the textile industry worldwide. In clothing, for example, work is often subcontracted to small workshops and even home workers (McCormick and Schmitz, 2002).

Studies have shown that the manufacturing sector in Kenya does not undertake any research and development, so that hardly any technological development takes place within the sector (Ikiara et al., 2002). Nor apparently is the industry making much use of existing formal training institutions. The government's Textile Training Institute, established in the 1970s, is hardly functioning. Although some universities have relevant degree programs, such as design and textile engineering, it is not clear where their graduates find jobs. One large clothing producer complained that polytechnic students on attachment wanted to become managers immediately, and were not interested in learning the various jobs on the factory floor. At still lower levels, the government has a system of trade tests, but these seem more oriented to self-employment than to industrial work. Most large firms train on the job. In some cases, the training is fairly comprehensive, with trainees learning a wide variety of skills. In others, they are trained only for a specific task.

At least one large EPZ factory offered free industrial training to local residents. The factory absorbed the best of the trainees into its workforce, and released the rest, presumably, to get jobs elsewhere. The factory owner had explored the possibility of having his programme accredited by the Ministry of Education in order to give participants a certificate that would be recognisable outside this factory. The Ministry, however, appeared uninterested and the factory owner eventually gave up trying. In short, the mechanisms for upgrading textile and clothing technology from within Kenya are in short supply, and those that exist are not being well used.

Opportunities for technological acquisition from abroad are restricted to licence agreements, technical assistance, and use of brand names. Use of foreign licenses is not common in Kenyan manufacturing. Although previous studies did not show any use of technical assistance in the textile and garments sector, it is expected that firms in the export processing zones are likely to use such assistance. Very few firms employ expatriates as general, production and technical managers. Research has shown that in the early part of 1990s, less than 10% of textile firms employed expatriate production managers (Bigsten and Kimuyu, 2002).

Labour and Gender

The labour and gender systems are intertwined in the textile industry, as in many productive activities in Kenya. The Kenya Government continues to make a sharp distinction between the "modern sector" and the "informal sector" in its documents. By the end of 2002, the "modern sector" employed about 1.7 million persons out of a total labour force estimated at over 15 million.[3] Employment in the "informal sector" is difficult to estimate precisely, but probably lies between three and five million.[4] Even in the so-called modern sector, terms and conditions of service vary considerably. Many factories have a relatively small proportion of workers on permanent terms, with full benefits, while the remainder are considered to be casual labourers. While the casualisation of the labour force may have a positive impact on the basic cost structure of textile products, it no doubt has the opposite effect in the long run because workers have little incentive to excel in situations where promotions are reserved for a small cadre of permanent staff.

Textile industries are often considered to be female, but the actual distribution of male and female workers differs from one country to another and within countries according to the specific activity. Women account for approximately 30% of world textile employment, and 74% of clothing employment (ILO, 2000). The proportions of male and female workers vary considerably from one region to another. Africa tends to have more male workers than other parts of the world in both textiles (76%) and clothing (36%). Africa also has considerable variability from one country to another in the gender distribution in both segments of the industry. For example, in Kenya, Ghana, and Zimbabwe, women make up less than 31% of the

---

[3] Own estimate

[4] The government estimate as of the end of 2002 was 5.086 million, but this was considerably higher than estimates based on what is considered to be an authoritative survey conducted in 1999, which yields a figure closer to 3 million.

workforce, while in Morocco and Mauritius, they comprise over three-quarters of the workers.

In Kenya, studies have shown that when all enterprise sizes are put together, nearly a third of all textile manufacturing firms are owned by women. However, there is an inverse correlation between firm size and female ownership, with women found more in micro and small-scale enterprises. About 17% of all industrial workers in the textile sector are female. Women are in the minority in activities such as spinning and weaving. In clothing production, long established factories favour male workers, whereas the new EPZ factories have followed the world trend of hiring mostly young women for their assembly operations.

The Evolution of the Kenyan Textile Industry

Kenya had a significant import-substituting textile and clothing industry (Pack, 1987; Coughlin, 1991) that collapsed in the early 1990s under the pressure of market liberalisation. The industry included textile plants producing yarn, woven fabric, and knitted fabric, as well as mixed factories making both knitted fabric and clothing. Pack (1987: 80) concluded that two large, relatively modern factories would have been able to export cloth 'if their purchased inputs were available at international prices and were not subject to tariffs, quotas, and the uncertain availability of specific qualities of fibres.'

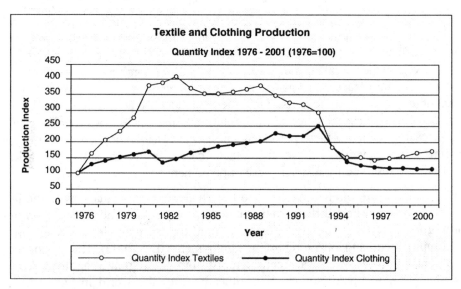

Figure 9.2: Textile and Clothing, 1976-2001

Source: Economic Survey, various years

Market liberalisation should have solved these problems, but instead, it gave rise to others. The rapid liberalisation of the market for cheap textiles brought about heavy adjustment costs, including a dramatic drop in aggregate output of almost 50% which, in turn, had implications for capacity utilisation and productivity (Lundvall et al., 2002). Firms coped with this by eliminating product lines and generally reducing the variety of offerings. This, in turn, sent some buyers to imported fabric where they could get the variety they wanted. In some cases, quality also suffered, as factories tried to stretch their limited financial resources. There was also a reluctance to invest in new plant and equipment because of political uncertainties. The resulting technological backwardness, combined with deteriorating infrastructure, reinforced the scale and quality problems. Overall production dropped sharply between 1993 and 1999 (see figure 9.2).[5] By the end of the 1990s, many of the textile mills that had been household words in Kenya – Rivatex, Raymonds, and Kicomi, among others – had closed or were on the verge of collapse.

The clothing industry suffered similar problems. Clothing production peaked in 1982, then dipped before rising slightly in the late 1980s. From 1989, the industry's production fell sharply until by 1997, the production index stood only 20% higher than it had been two decades earlier (McCormick et al., 1999).[6] Many of the factories have closed; others have shifted production into new lines that do not have to compete directly with imports. The clothing sector, however, differs from textiles in one important respect. Since the passage of the US African Growth and Opportunity Act in the year 2000, production for export has taken off. Export factories, spurred by AGOA, have enabled exports to the US to jump from US$ 39 million in 1999 to US$ 65 million in 2001 and an estimated US$ 128 million in 2002 (www.agoa.gov). Thirty new factories, most of which have been built with foreign investment, have opened since January 2001. Clearly this is a major accomplishment. But Kenya has to do more if it is to maintain its position when the special concessions extended to low income countries expire.

Our mapping of the industry revealed a structure with three tiers (see Table 9.2). The base of the structure is formed by approximately 60,000 thousand micro and small enterprises (MSEs) firms that produce for the domestic market. Most of these first tier firms make clothing from woven fabric. In Nairobi, about 4% of them make knitted garments, mostly cardigans and children's school sweaters. Some MSEs make other textile end products, including interior furnishings and industrial and other consumer products. A few speciality small enterprises produce hand-woven cloth that they use to make clothing, bags, table and bed covers.

The next tier consists of firms ranging in size from small to fairly large that produce mainly for the domestic market, with some forays into other countries of the region. Included here are many of the textile and garment firms established during the Import Substitution era that have survived liberalisation and continue to aim most of their production at the local market. Firms in this tier had between 10 and 400 workers at the time of our research, with most concentrated in the range of 50-150 workers. They include mills that spin natural and synthetic fibres into yarn,

---

5   The Quantity Index of Textile Production rose from 100 in 1976 to 252.0 in 1993, then dropped to 114.7 by 2001 (Kenya. *Statistical Abstract*, various years).

6   The Quantity Index of Clothing Production peaked at 406.8 in 1983 and again at 378.6 in 1989. It dropped to a low of 142.4 in 1997, then rose to 172.8 in 2001 (Kenya. *Statistical Abstract*, various years).

factories making cordage, rope and twine, mills making woven and knitted fabric, and manufacturers of end products, especially clothing. The clothing manufacturers produce knitted garments, such as socks and T-shirts, as well shirts, trousers, dresses, uniforms, etc. from woven fabric. Much of the woven fabric is imported, mostly from China and India.

Table 9.2: *Textile and Clothing Firms, by Tier*

Tier	Firms (N-approx.)	Firm size	Market(s)
1	60,000	MSE	Mainly domestic; less than 10% export some output to neighbouring countries
2	150	Small to large	Mainly domestic, with a minority of firms exporting to Africa or one or more European countries
3	45	Large to very large	Export to USA, Europe

Source: Own data, 2000; CBS et al., 1999; Kenya, 2001; EPZ Authority; Investment Promotion Council

Note: Tier 1 data is as of mid 1999; Tier 2 is for 2001; Tier 3 data is as of early 2003.

The third tier consists of large to very large export-oriented firms. In 2000, there were 15 such firms, all making clothing and mainly located in Nairobi or Mombasa. By 2003, their number had tripled, mainly in response to AGOA (see table 9.2). They range in size from 500 to 2,000 workers. These firms mainly operate as 'cut, make, and trim' contractors. They receive orders from abroad, but do neither design work nor supply procurement. Designs are supplied by the importer the local firm then makes and grades the patterns. The importer also sources fabric and most other inputs from Asia and has them shipped directly to the Kenyan producer. The main items bought in Kenya are packaging materials, though one firm was trying to work with a local supplier to upgrade the quality of thread to a level acceptable to the US buyers (McCormick et al., 2001).

TIER 1: MICRO AND SMALL GARMENT FIRMS

Micro and small enterprises are the backbone of garment production in Kenya. Although these firms are spread throughout the country, our study concentrated on those in Nairobi. We did this partly because of the size and variety of the garment producing sector in Nairobi, and partly because we wanted to take advantage of data from an earlier study that would allow us to compare the situation before and after Structural Adjustment. In order to put these Nairobi firms into context, we begin with a review of textile and garment MSEs in the country as a whole, drawing on secondary data.

National Profile

The 60,000 tier-one enterprises making clothing represent about 5 per cent of all micro and small enterprises, and over one-third of the manufacturing MSEs in

Kenya (CBS et al., 1999). The typical firm operates with the owner and one or two other workers. They are spread throughout the country, in cities, towns, and rural areas. Not surprisingly, given the overall concentration of the Kenyan population in the rural areas, nearly sixty percent of MSE textile employment is rural (CBS et al., 1999).

The typical owner of a garment MSE is an African woman. Most garment firms are African owned, though some Asians, especially those with a family tradition of garment making, are active (see Box 9.2). In garments, women own two-thirds of the firms. This gender distribution of firm ownership contrasts with that of small-scale manufacturing generally where two-thirds of the business owners are men. The proportion of female ownership is higher in the city and lower in rural areas, where the tradition of male tailors remains strong.

MSE garment firms can be categorised into three types: custom tailors, contract workshops, and mini-manufacturers (McCormick et al., 1997; McCormick, 1997). Custom tailors, the most common type, produce made-to-measure garments for individuals. They sometimes provide the fabric, but often use fabric supplied by the customer. Contract workshops produce in quantity to order, while mini-manufacturers produce in quantity for the market. The typical mini-manufacturer uses a variation of division of labour borrowed from larger mass producers. Most producers make sewn garments of woven fabric, but a minority (9.6 per cent) specialise in knitwear, especially cardigans and school sweaters. Many of the smallest firms, especially those in rural areas and the low-income areas of cities and towns, do mainly repairs and alterations.

Information on technology is scanty, but what is available suggests that most producers depend on foot-powered machines, even in situations where electricity is available (see Box 9.2). This may have to do with the wide availability and relatively low cost of such machines, as well as their use in many training programmes. Foot powered machines are mainly used for straight sewing. So, to some extent, their use limits the variety and quality of garment finishing, For certain jobs, like embroidery or the making of buttonholes, garment enterprises sub-contract or buy the services of more sophisticated machinery (Billetoft, 1996; McCormick et al., 1997).

Mainly because of their small size, most garment MSEs have a very simple internal organisation. Firms with employees sometimes have a basic division of labour that assigns the most sensitive work – buying materials and cutting cloth – to either the owner or a highly skilled senior tailor. Bigger MSEs can also divide out finishing work, such as hemming, sewing on buttons, and pressing the completed garment. In the typical one- or two-person firm, however, such duty assignments are not possible.

Box 9.2: Varieties of MSE Garment Making

One Asian family, with a longstanding tradition of garment-making, dominates the tailoring business in Voi, a town of some 16,000 people on the Nairobi-Mombasa highway. Three brothers are in charge of the business, which covers a wide range of activities: tailoring/dressmaking, retailing ready-made clothes and footwear, selling textiles, and somewhat unrelated, a combined hardware and garment store. Other local tailors depend on the Asian brothers for supplies, and these in turn get their textiles through relatives in Mombasa and Nairobi.

Source: Billetoft, 1996

Shinyalu, a small trading centre about 10 km from Kakamega in Western Province, is home to a cluster of about 15 textile businesses. The first textile business in the cluster was started in 1952. The enterprises mostly make women's clothes and school uniforms for the local community. Although there is electricity available, only three businesses use it for production. The rest rely on hand tools and foot-powered sewing machines. Many of the businesses have apprentices or trainees who engage in production while they learn. Most of these have completed primary school, and some have had basic training in the local polytechnic.

Source: McCormick and Kinyanjui, 2000

Kericho, a town of approximately 50,000 in Rift Valley Province, has three basic categories of garment production: small garment factories practicing a certain degree of serial production; custom tailors mainly sewing new garments; and repair tailors. One of the firms illustrates the possibility of graduation from custom tailoring into small-scale garment factories. The owner, a former *Jua Kali* tailor who began with just two workers, has developed his business into a factory employing about thirty people making aprons for tea pickers and bags for shops, and offering technical training, not only in tailoring, but also in other artisan trades. At the other end of the spectrum are the many small tailors who ply their trade in small shops and on verandas.

Source: Billetoft, 1996

Most small garment producers focus on the local market, drawing their customers from a fairly small radius. They make uniforms for local schools, choir robes for churches, dresses and trousers for people in the vicinity, and undertake repairs and alterations for those who come to them. In general, these small producers distribute their goods and services directly to the end user, whether a business, an institution, or an individual, rather than through any intermediary. Many complain of the inroads made into their markets by *mitumba*, though careful analysis suggests that *mitumba* are a problem mainly for those producing for the bottom end of the market, where the low price and relatively good quality of second-hand garments are a particularly attractive alternative (Billetoft, 1996; McCormick et al., 1997).

Some producers, especially those in Nairobi, are known to trade beyond the local area. For example, clothing producers have been trading across the borders with Tanzania and Uganda for many years. Many urban firms use their linkages to their rural homes or to friends and relatives in other places to find markets (McCormick, 1997).

Interfirm linkages are believed to be important for MSE growth and development (Schmitz, 1989; Rasmussen, 1992; Fafchamps, 1994; Barr, 1995; McCormick et al., 1997). Although national data on the linkages of garment firms are not available, we know that the main links for MSEs generally are with other MSEs and with individuals (CBS et al., 1999). Very few businesses have significant linkages with larger firms or with government. There are some linkages with other MSEs through associations, but garment enterprises seem less likely to join associations than other types of manufacturers. In part, this may be due to the fact that the main type of MSE association – the *Jua Kali* association – is strongly identified with male artisan trades such as metalwork, vehicle repair, and woodworking (King 1996; McCormick et al., 2001). Firms do, however, form informal networks, such as the ethnic networks that link the tailors in Voi to their suppliers (see Box 9.2).

Profile of Micro and Small Garment Firms in Nairobi

With this background, we turn to the data from our survey of Nairobi firms. The survey, concentrated on Nairobi, where in 2000 there were 6,323 enterprises employing nearly 10,000 people. Although enterprises in Nairobi may be somewhat different from their rural counterparts, the heavy concentration of garment producers made the city an ideal place to gather information on the business system in this industry.

The Nairobi garment entrepreneurs were similar in age, with a mean of 34.5 years, to other MSE owners. All had some education, and more than half (59.9 per cent) had secondary or above. Nearly half (46.4 per cent) belong to Kenya's largest ethnic group, the Kikuyu. The rest were Luo (24.8 per cent), Luhya (9.6 per cent), Kamba (8.8 per cent) and a wide variety of other groups. There was only one Asian in the sample and only two respondents (1.6 per cent) were citizens of a country other than Kenya.

Not surprisingly, most of the businesses (57.6 per cent) are located in Nairobi's populous Eastlands, an area known for its many MSEs (see McCormick, 1988) and containing two significant garment clusters (see McCormick et al., 1997). The rest are in the suburbs south and west of the city (19.2 and 14.4 per cent respectively), and in the Central Business District (CBD) (8.8 per cent).

The vast majority of businesses (90.4 per cent) are sole proprietorships, one is a private limited company, and the rest are partnerships. The enterprises range in age from one to 40 years, with a mean age of 8.9 years. The total number of regular workers per firm ranges from one to 16, with a mean of 2.7, making these businesses somewhat larger on average than the typical manufacturing MSE. Estimated annual turnover averages Kshs 169,087. Turnover figures, of course, must be treated with great caution. Our mean is based on only a little over half of the sample, and only about one-third (35.2 per cent) of the businesses keep what might be considered reliable income records. The rest keep receipts or lists that they never tally or no records at all.

Institutions Important to Nairobi's MSE Garment Producers

The research identified seven different sets of institutions that are important to the structure and functioning of MSE garment producers. Supply and product markets, firms, including firm-level institutions and inter-firm linkages, and the government are clearly the most important. Four others — the financial system, technology system, gender, and labour markets — also shape the operations of MSE garment producers.

Markets

The market is the institution with the greatest impact on micro and small garment producers. This is especially true of product markets. Even before the market liberalisation of the early 1990s, garment MSEs competed with each other, with larger enterprises, and to some extent, with second-hand clothes in the domestic market. Market liberalisation simply intensified the competition by expanding the range of goods available to potential MSE customers. In Nairobi, the mushrooming of 'exhibitions' featuring imported new clothing added to the competition of those custom tailors targeting middle class working women. The wide range of offerings in second-hand clothing affected garment producers at all levels, from mini-manufacturers mass producing relatively cheap items in the garment markets to higher level custom tailors in the city centre (McCormick et al., 1997; Kinyanjui and McCormick, 2003). Yet, the market for garments in Nairobi is far from perfectly competitive. As in most places, it is segmented according to age, income level, and garment type. More importantly, retailers are small and advertising is almost non-existent. This means that potential customers must get information about what is available where either by word of mouth or by observing shop windows. From the consumer's point of view, this form of search is both expensive and unsatisfactory. When it is combined with MSEs' well-known contract-enforcement and trust problems, the result is an imperfectly competitive market that gives rise to a variety of firm-level survival market strategies.

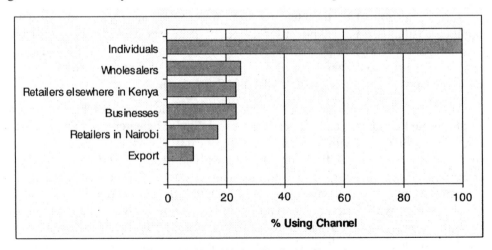

Figure 9.3: Use of Various Distribution Channels

All of the producers in our sample sell directly to individual consumers (see Figure 9.3). Many of them combine sales to individuals with other distribution channels, including wholesalers (24.8%), shops and markets elsewhere in Kenya (23.2%) and businesses buying for their own use (23.2%). A smaller proportion sells to Nairobi retailers (16.8%), including supermarkets and chain clothing stores. Exporters form the smallest group (8.8%), probably because of the greater challenges associated with selling into other countries (see McCormick et al., 2002).

The supply markets for MSE garment producers are closely linked to their distribution channels. Several examples will illustrate this. Custom tailors making for individuals either use material brought by the customer or source in small quantities from itinerant traders or retail shops. Such fabric is often African *kitenge*[7] cotton, which may be either local or imported, or imported synthetic. The makers of school or work uniforms use Kenyan fabric, which they source either from wholesalers or directly from the factory. Some tiny firms operating in low income suburbs use *mitumba*[8] as raw materials. One of these cut up T-shirts to make children's underwear. Most producers of cardigans and school sweaters use polyester yarn imported from China. Shops selling such yarn can be found in many markets, especially the large ones in Nairobi's Eastlands, where they cater for knitwear producers within the market. Although market liberalisation has led to the closure of many Kenyan textile mills, it has probably, on balance, expanded the range of choices available to fabric and yarn buyers.

Firms and Firm Linkages

In very small firms, it is often difficult to distinguish the firm from its entrepreneur. How small firms operate is, to some extent, dictated by the characteristics of their owners, including their level of education, their prior experience, their technical and/or managerial training, and their vision for the business. In all of these aspects, our data point to some shifts that have taken place in the past decade or so (see McCormick et al., 2002). In particular, among the owners of garment, MSEs are those without training in tailoring, some of whom are fairly well-educated entrepreneurs who are ready to shift product lines or even industries to take advantage of new opportunities.

Nairobi's micro and small garment producers operate largely without formal linkages to other firms, despite the fact that many are located in clusters where they are in close physical proximity. One-fifth of the firms subcontract the making of entire garments to other producers. A somewhat larger proportion subcontracts certain functions requiring specialised machinery. No firm reported receiving subcontracts from larger enterprises.

---

7   Kitenge is a Kiswahili word referring to brightly coloured cotton fabric of African design

8   Mitumba is a Kiswahili word referring to second hand clothes

When asked about membership in business associations, only six firms (4.8%) reported belonging to a *Jua Kali*[9] association, six (4.8%) to the Kenya Small Traders Association, one (0.8%) to the Kenya National Chamber of Commerce, and one (0.8%) to the Kenya Association of Manufacturers. Adjusting for firms with multiple memberships leaves only 11 firms (8.8%) that belong to any business association. Membership in other types of organisations is much higher. Many belong to credit groups: 40% of respondents belong to rotating savings and credit organisations and 19.2% to an NGO credit group. Others have joined welfare or social groups such as women's groups (33.6%), welfare groups (37.6%), clan associations (34.4%), and village associations (28.8%). This pattern of memberships is probably due to a combination of factors. One is the lack of services offered by the traditional business associations (McCormick et al., 2003). Another is the fact that *Jua Kali* associations – the type of association most accessible to MSEs – are not perceived as catering for female trades such as garment production. Third, busy entrepreneurs must allocate their time carefully. In many cases, attending a meeting means closing the business or leaving it in the hands of a trainee or employee who could take advantage of the situation. Attending a credit group meeting has obvious benefits, either for the business or for the entrepreneur's personal finances. The benefits of social groups such as welfare or clan associations are less immediately obvious, but earlier research suggests that they are an important form of social insurance (McCormick et al., 2001).

Even without formal associations, firms are involved in some forms of networking that enhance their business operations. For example, our in-depth interviews revealed that business owners collaborate on trips, both to distant markets in Kenya and to neighbouring countries. Several businesses will join together to fund the travel and accommodation expenses of one or two of their members who will take goods for the entire group. There are also informal arrangements for training one another's workers, using specialised equipment, and looking after the business of a colleague who is sick or away.

Government

The Kenya Government affects micro and small garment producers through both its broad policies and its licensing and regulatory measures. Before discussing these, it is useful to have a clear picture of how government relates to MSE garment producers. The Ministry that is currently responsible for all matters concerning MSEs is the Ministry of Labour and Human Resource Development, within which is housed the Department of Micro and Small Enterprises. The Ministry of Trade and Industry, nevertheless, maintains an 'informal' interest in these firms as part of the larger textile industry.

Two policy measures can be expected to have direct impact on MSE garment producers. The first, market liberalisation, has already been discussed. The second is its industrial policy which, officially at least, encourages and supports small-scale

---

9 *Jua Kali*, literally 'hot sun' in Kiswahili, is used in Kenya to describe micro and small businesses operating informally

production. As we saw in chapter 8, however, the impact of the MSE policies has been mixed at best.

When we consider matters of policy implementation, several problems emerge. One is the complicated matter of production space. Many garment firms in Nairobi operate from market stalls that were originally designed for the retailing of fruits and vegetables (McCormick et al., 1997). The markets are owned and managed by the Nairobi City Council. Most are at least 30 years old, overcrowded, and with few amenities. Although the stalls are too small and inappropriately configured for efficient production, business owners choose to be there because they offer a combination of affordability and security that compares favourably with most alternative locations. Government discussions of space for micro and small enterprises have tended to focus on either retail space for street traders or on *Jua Kali* sites. Very little attention has been paid to space for non-*Jua Kali* manufacturers.

A second knotty problem concerns imported clothing, both new and second-hand. New clothing is subject to tariffs, but these are not always charged, either because of corruption at the port of entry or because new items that are mixed into bales of second-hand clothes simply slide through the inspection process. Some of the new clothing is first quality, but some consists of seconds and factory rejects that are being sold at throw-away prices in order to clear them. As a result, these new clothes often sell at prices below what small producers can afford to charge for comparable items. The problem of second-hand clothes is compounded by the fact that for many Kenyans, new clothes are simply not an option and for others, a mix of *mitumba* and new clothes are the only way to stretch a very tight clothing budget. Government has recognised these problems and has taken measures to make the tariff structure on second-hand clothing more realistic. It now has to ensure that the tariffs on both new and second-hand clothes are actually applied as written.

Other Institutions

Our research revealed that other groups of institutions also have an impact on micro and small garment producers. These include gender, labour markets, the financial system, and the technology system. Nearly three-quarters (71.2%) of the garment MSEs in Nairobi are owned by women. Generally, since in MSEs, male owners tend to hire more male workers and female owners, more female workers (CBS et al., 1999), it would appear that MSE garment production should provide a significant source of jobs for women. Gender analysis of the survey data shows differences between male and female business owners in choice of product line, nature of start-up capital, and sources of raw materials (Kinyanjui, 2003). Interestingly, the analysis did not reveal any difference in the choice of distribution channels. Over three-quarters (78.7%) of the women in the study were married and presumably, had to combine domestic responsibilities with running their businesses. Despite this, there was no significant difference in the turnover figures for male and female business owners.

It is generally known that urban MSEs operate with a mixture of regular employees, casual workers, and trainees (McCormick and Abuodha, 2000). What the general statistics rarely reveal, however, are the variations in the labour system. Case studies suggest that most garment workers get their jobs through relatives and friends (McCormick and Muguku, 2003). Jobs are generally considered casual, but in some cases carry benefits such as annual leave and transport allowance. Remuneration varies from below minimum wage to more than three times the minimum, with the latter being earned by a skilled embroiderer. Some are paid on piecework basis and others on monthly salaries. Delays in payment of wages appear to be common. Hours of work range from eight to twelve hours daily, for six or seven days a week. Other than the long hours, working conditions are fair, with conditions in shops being better than those in the overcrowded garment markets.

Kenya's formal financial system is generally unfriendly towards small enterprise. It is not surprising, therefore, that the most common forms of finance for garment MSEs are self and informal sources. Own savings (54.4%), gift or loan from spouse (22.4%), and gift or loan from relatives (16.0%) were the most common sources of start-up capital. For business loans or credit, the most common sources were rotating savings and credit associations (40.0%), community based organisations (35.2%), supplier credit (24.8%), and NGO loans (23.2%). Only 4% of respondents had ever received a bank loan, and 5.6% had had a loan from a savings and credit organisation.

Technology in MSE garment producers varies considerably. Most use a 'make through' system of production, in which an operator makes an entire garment. There are some exceptions. In many firms, finishing is done by hand as a separate function. The embroidery that adorns some African dress is usually done by a skilled worker who specialises in that. Nevertheless, the assembly line operation that characterises larger enterprises is rare in MSEs, even in firms with several workers.

At the level of machines, the technology resembles that of garment MSEs generally, except that Nairobi firms make greater use of electric and specialised machines. Approximately half (54.4%) of the firms operate with foot powered machines only. The rest either use all electric machines or combine electric with foot powered machines. Some of this latter group have electric overlocks, buttonholers, and embroidery machines. The differences in machinery translate into differences in quality of output. For example, a firm that owns a dedicated buttonhole machine can make higher quality buttonholes than one that uses an ordinary household-type zigzag machine to make them. Some overcome their lack of machines by subcontracting specialised work such as overlock (33.6%), buttonhole making (25.6%), and embroidery (9.6%).

The discussion of Tier-one clothing producers suggests that their present situation is largely the result of the interaction of four groups of institutions: product markets, government, the financial system, and the technology system. Market liberalisation has shaped strategies, pushing many firms to seek niches, such as uniforms and African dress, where they can avoid competing head on with low priced substitutes. In addition to being the architect of liberalisation, Government has affected Tier-one clothing firms through its inconsistent and poorly implemented industrial policy and its failure to provide appropriate physical infrastructure. Weaknesses in the formal financial system have forced most businesses to self-finance. In many cases this results in lack of both working and investment capital. Finally, many Tier-one firms use only the most rudimentary technology. It is important to emphasise that these institutions do not operate in isolation, but are interlinked. Government shapes markets. An unfriendly financial system constrains investment and poor infrastructure contributes to low technology, which in turn affects product quality and competitiveness.

TIER 2: LARGER TEXTILE AND GARMENT PRODUCERS

The next tier of firms consists of those medium to large producers whose main market is domestic, but who may also sell some of their output into neighbouring countries or even the wider global market. Many of these are companies that were formed during the import-substitution era and are now struggling to find their way in the new liberalised markets. During our research, we interviewed 17 such companies (McCormick et al., 2001). They ranged in size from 10 to 1,500 workers. The two smallest, with 10 and 12 workers each, had shrunk as they struggled to survive following market liberalisation. The two largest made fabric as well as garments, and exported some of their output, in one case to the Region and in the other to Canada and Europe. The remaining firms ranged in size from 20 to 500 workers. Nine of them were producing solely for the domestic market, while three aimed at tourists and/or the Regional market. Their products included fibres, fabric, and both knitted and woven garments.

Responses to our questions concerning problems facing the industry fell into four broad groupings: high production and distribution costs, weak domestic demand, difficulty in accessing export markets, and low investment (see Table 9.3). Further discussions, especially respondents' identification of what they perceived to be the causes of their problems, offered insights into the institutions of Kenya's business system.

Table 9.3: *Larger Firms: Main Problems and Their Causes*

Problem	Main Causes	Contributing Factors
High production and distribution costs	Tax and tariff regime Transport cost High cost and uneven supply of electricity	Productivity and production technology Lack of viable textile industry Education and training
Weak domestic demand	Market liberalisation Globalisation	Small size of market
Difficulty in accessing export market	High production costs Unstable markets in neighbouring countries	Entrepreneurial networks Telecommunications system Trade information system Lack of viable textile industry
Low investment	General instability and insecurity Financial system	None named

Source: Own data, 2000-2001

Firms named three main causes of their high production and distribution costs: the tax and tariff regime, transport costs, and the high cost and uneven supply of electricity (see Table 9.3). In their view, Government was to blame for all three. Government's own tax and tariff regime contributed directly to high costs by making imported inputs too expensive. Transport costs were also a major issue. Several respondents gave a familiar example – the high cost of moving a container between Mombasa and Nairobi – to support their claim that importing fabric and sending their products to market were simply too expensive. Electricity was also named as a cause of high production costs. Kenya's electricity rates are significantly higher than those in many competing countries. At the time of our research, power rationing had forced many of the larger firms to generate their own electricity, further increasing their costs. Although rationing has disappeared, the price of electricity remains much higher than it is in, for example, South Africa.

Contributing to the high production and distribution costs are factors such as poor production technology, lack of a viable textile industry, and inappropriate education and training. Outmoded equipment in these firms is a real problem. Some are still using 1960s and 1970s machines because they are reluctant to invest in more modern equipment. The organisation of production is another aspect of the technology problem. Some firms use 'make through' processes. One owner explained that he had tried to change to 'chain' or 'line' processes that allow for greater efficiency, but his workers, many of whom had been with the firm for years, had refused. Poor technology contributes to what many business owners said was a serious problem underlying their high costs: labour productivity. They felt that Kenya is not able to benefit from the fact that it is a low wage country because the wage advantage is more than offset by low productivity. Two other issues believed to contribute to high costs were lack of a viable local textile industry and a weak education and training system. The former raises costs by pushing many firms to import their major raw material, while the latter is blamed for causing the increased use of expensive expatriate skills and for forcing firms to invest more than they should in in-house training for production workers.

The second major problem for the industry was weak domestic demand. Since these firms are rooted in the local market, they see domestic sales as the key to their survival. Their problems are similar to those of the Tier-one firms. They face low demand in the home market, which they blame on globalisation and Government's mishandling of market liberalisation, especially the unregulated imports of both new and used clothing.

The third major problem is difficulty in accessing export markets. Many owners realise that, with the opening of the home market to outsiders, Kenyan firms will have to seek new markets beyond the country's borders. Yet, when firms try to do this, they often experience difficulties. One of these is the high cost of production that has already been discussed. The second is neighbouring country markets. The same factors making Kenyan markets difficult for producers to penetrate also operate in Kenya's neighbours. Markets are small, people are poor, and imports of new and used clothing are taking a large share of the market. Some firms mentioned

COMESA and the East African Community as potentially useful in their efforts to export into the Region, but we saw little concrete evidence of benefits actually being experienced.

Finally, the industry suffers from low investment. As we have already discussed, local firms are reluctant to invest in new plant and equipment. Business owners blame Government for failing to create a secure and stable business environment that would encourage them to invest. The political violence that surrounded both the 1992 and 1997, high crime rates, especially in Nairobi, and continuing political uncertainty were considered to be serious problems at the time these interviews were carried out in 2000 and 2001. Several firms mentioned insecurity as a reason for not operating a night shift, citing both difficulties associated with workers' transport, and workers' reluctance to leave their houses empty at night

In such a climate, foreign investors are even more reluctant than locals to put money into the industry. Kenya's foreign direct investment in the 1980s and 1990s was significantly below what was expected. UNCTAD (2005) attributes this poor performance to poor or inconsistent economic policies, deteriorating infrastructure, rising corruption, and insecurity that together resulted in poor growth. By the year 2000, when our research was beginning, the cumulative effects of all of these ills were continuing to reduce Kenya's attraction as an investment destination. When the new government took over in 2003, it stated clearly that infrastructure, macroeconomic stability, and public security are necessary for development (Kenya, 2003). Progress towards these goals has, however been very slow.

At the time of our research, high interest rates and what firms perceived to be an unfriendly banking system were cited as a further deterrent to investment. The situation has improved somewhat in recent years with the bank overdraft rate dropping from 19.7% in 2001 to 11.1% in July 2004. The export segment of the industry, as we shall see, has been able to attract some investment because the advantages of access to the US market appear to outweigh the uncertainties of the investment climate and because foreigners, who are the main investors, are less dependent than Kenyans on the Kenyan banking system for finance.

In sum, this analysis suggests that three groups of institutions exert the strongest influence on the performance of Tier-two firms. The first consists of government institutions, especially the tax and tariff system, the physical infrastructure, and the internal security system. The second group includes the domestic and regional markets, while the third consists of the institutions making up the country's financial system. Contributing to their problems is the technology system, including the organisation of production within firms. Finally, some institutions that might be expected to exert a positive influence on the industry, such as regional trade agreements, appear to be making little difference.

TIER 3: KENYA'S GLOBAL GARMENT EXPORTERS

At the end of 2003, Kenya had 45 firms that could be termed Global Exporters (see Table 9.2). Fifteen firms, or one-third of the total, were "old exporters." Two-thirds were new entrants.

Background and Profile of the Global Exporters

Many of the "old exporters" were established in the late 1980s and early 1990s to exploit a window of opportunity by exporting to the US and Europe. Although Kenya was not a signatory to the MFA until May 1994, its status as a country without a US quota was its early export start. Between 1991 and 1994, the industry experienced a surge in investments, employment and export. In early 1994, however, the US government, claiming a disruption in the market for men's and boys' shirts and cotton pillowcases, imposed quotas on imports of these items from Kenya (Claxton, 2003; own data, 1997). The impact of the quotas was severe. Exports dropped significantly and a number of firms stopped operating. Some, however, found markets elsewhere, so that in the year 2000, there was an important, if small, export clothing sector. The new entrants did not exist when the fieldwork for this project was being carried out. Available information suggests that many are foreign investments, in contrast with earlier exporting firms which were largely based in Kenyan Asian capital.

The large exporters organise their production in ways that are similar to each other and comparable to large clothing factories elsewhere in the world. In several, pattern making is computerised, though we did not see any computer-aided cutting. Production uses an assembly line in which work in process moves from station to station, with each operator performing a specific task. The physical capital consists mainly of a set of stand-alone machines designed for specific purposes, such as testing fabric, assembling the body of a garment, making buttonholes, sewing on buttons, hemming, etc. Most firms operate one or two shifts.

The four older global exporters that were included in our study all operated under either the Export Processing Zones or Manufacturing-under-Bond schemes. They ranged in size from 500 to 2,000 workers. There were clear gender and ethnic dimensions to the factories' ownership and employment. All of the managers are male. Production workers were mixed. However, factories more recently opened seem to hire mainly young women, while the older ones more men, suggesting that in future, the typical factory will have more women workers. Many export-oriented factories, like most of Kenyan manufacturing, are owned and operated by Kenyan Asians. Expatriates from the Indian subcontinent hold key technical positions, such as production managers, accountants, and line supervisors. Workers, on the other hand, were Kenyans of African origin.

The firms produced mostly casual wear, such as sport shirts, shorts, and cotton trousers for both men and women. Their main markets were the US, Canada, and Europe. Customers are mainly importers who supply low-end retailers such as Target and K-Mart. Based on the nature of the buyers, Kenya appears to operate in the 'outer ring' of global markets, where buyers are interested in consistent quality at very low prices.[10] This position puts great pressure on firms to improve

---

10 Gereffi (1994) developed the notion of the structure of a country's apparel imports being depicted by a set of concentric circles, or rings. His most recent version, which covers the period 1990-2000, does not include

productivity and maintain their low cost profile. Although these firms were doing well, the export industry was growing very slowly at the time of our research.

Benefits, Concerns, and Related Institutions

Kenya's global exporters have benefited from the overall globalisation of the textile and clothing industries described above. The older exporters found markets largely because of Kenya's quota-free status under the MFA and its successor, the ATC. More recently, AGOA has provided an impetus to new investment.

As discussed above, Kenya was one of the first African countries to qualify for AGOA, and from its inception in early 2001, textiles have been Kenya's major AGOA export. Current AGOA rules have allowed Kenya and other low-income countries to import fabric for clothing production and still qualify for duty-free import into the US market. As suggested by the range of US tariff rates on items of clothing (see table 9.1), this duty exemption represents a significant advantage to Kenyan producers. Not only has it benefited existing firms, but it has attracted new investment that has resulted in the tripling of the number of large garment exporters. Nevertheless, a major problem remains. Kenya's textile industry is still not able to produce good quality woven fabric at competitive prices. Unless the textile segment of the industry can be rebuilt, Kenya may be unable to take advantage of AGOA's duty-free imports after 2007.

The expiration of the ATC, which took place on 1 January 2005, changed the rules of textile trade in significant ways. In 2004, an astute observer notes that the ending of the ATC was likely to enhance market access, expand trade, and intensify competition, but that, its precise effects on individual countries would depend on their own policies and conditions (Osakwe, 2004). Early post – MFA experience supports this. All of Africa's major AGOA exporters registered declines in export values between the first quarter of 2004 and the equivalent period of 2005. Overall, the decline was 17%, but there was considerable variation among countries, with Kenya's exports declining only 3% compared with 45% for South Africa, 17% for Lesotho, and 14% for Madagascar. (McCormick et al., 2006; Kaplinsky et al., 2006)

The integration of clothing and textiles into normal WTO rules should offer other benefits. The WTO provides much clearer rules than the MFA, and procedures for enforcing rights and obligations under its provisions have been strengthened. For example a country may take action against another country when it feels that its rights have been violated by the other's actions, or when it feels that another country has not met its obligations under the Agreements. The difficulty for countries like Kenya is that they lack the capacity to take the permitted action and even if they try, are likely to be out-manoeuvred by the large, well-staffed delegations of developed countries.

Kenya at all; probably because Kenyan trade was less than 1% of total US imports during that period (see Gereffi and Memedovic 2003).

At the micro level, Kenya's global exporters shared many of the concerns expressed by the Tier-two companies: high production and distribution costs, difficulty in accessing the export market, and low investment. Although they were not directly affected by the liberalisation of the domestic market for garments, they were concerned about input markets, especially the situation in the local textile industry. Like the Tier-two firms, they tended to place the responsibility for many of their difficulties on the government.

The most important state institutions are the Ministry of Trade and Industry and the ministries responsible for taxation, infrastructure, and internal security. Many of the points raised in interviews concerning the state were negative. Exporters blamed the state for their various troubles more often than any other national institution. Nevertheless, it is also important to highlight the positive side of some of these issues. Probably the most important of these is market liberalisation. The problems experienced in the liberalisation of product markets have, in many instances, overshadowed the benefits accruing to producers from the liberalisation of foreign exchange and supply markets. Prior to liberalisation of foreign exchange markets, exporters had to surrender their foreign currency to the Central Bank and then request allocations to be used in paying for equipment and supplies. This was an extremely cumbersome process that easily lent itself to corruption. No firm suggested a return to such controls.

The intense competition of global markets makes issues of technology and productivity especially pertinent to these firms. The technical skills in these factories come from a variety of sources. Although Kenya is beginning to produce its own textile engineers in university-based degree programmes, there is little in the way of high-level training in clothing production technology. Expatriate technical personnel are evident in textile factories. Managers, on the other hand, often have skills gained in post-secondary education, at either polytechnics or universities.

Workers' basic education varies. One factory that was starting up when we were conducting our interviews was hiring primary school leavers. Another said that it requires secondary education because the owners feel that this makes the workers better able to learn the skills they need. The workers and line supervisors are generally trained on the job. Labour productivity is a serious issue for exporters. Kenya is a low-wage country, with 1993 wage costs comparable to those in China and India (ILO, 1995). This should make Kenyan garments very competitive on the world market. This wage benefit is seriously undermined, however, by low productivity. Government does not collect productivity data, but a recent survey showed that the median value-added per worker in Kenyan manufacturing is US$ 2,733, down from US$ 3,337 in the 1990s. This compares with US$ 4,021 and US$3,369 in China and India respectively (Cotton et al., 2003). The average monthly cash earnings were US$ 250.22, and range from US$ 96.20 for unskilled production workers to US$ 712.52 for managerial staff.[11] The average monthly cash earnings for the textile and leather sub-sector were US$ 155.47, the lowest average for any sector.

Manufacturers interviewed for our study recognised the productivity problem. One of them claimed that garment industry productivity rates in the Far East were ten times those in Kenya, and that Indian productivity was five times Kenya's. The data above show that such claims are exaggerated. Chinese and Indian labour productivity rates were more like 47% and 22% better than Kenyan productivity. Nevertheless, poor productivity and lack of skills are real problems that require attention.

CONCLUSIONS AND POLICY IMPLICATIONS

In this chapter, we have synthesised information contained in papers produced under the business systems programme to describe the textile and garments sector and categorise firms in the sector. We then used such categorisation to shed light on the interplay between textile and garment firms and different levels of institutions. What does all of this tell us about the business system as experienced by firms in the textile industry?

First, we can conclude is that this industry is a clear example of what has been called the fragmented African business system (Pedersen and McCormick, 1999). The three tiers of firms are quite distinct, with few linkages and little interaction among them. The micro and small enterprises of Tier one have limited interactions among themselves, supply linkages with some of the Tier-two textile producers, and no contact with the global exporters. Tier-two firms are similarly isolated, though more of them belong to business associations. The exporters of Tier three are linked to global value chains, including external customers and suppliers, but have almost no linkages within Kenya.

Our second major conclusion is that firms in different tiers mostly deal with different institutions and organisations and, therefore, experience the business system differently. Markets are crucial for all three tiers, but for Tier 1, the market that matters is the domestic market, while Tier 3 firms are mainly concerned with global markets. Similarly, government policy and its implementation affect all three tiers, but the nature of the concerns and even the ministries that they deal with differ from tier to tier. The same is true of the financial system, the labour system, and the technology system.

With such differences, it is clear that very broad industrial policies and programmes are likely not only to be very expensive to implement, but may also fail to address the real problems of businesses in this industry. We propose instead a strategy aimed at achieving greater integration of the industry, while at the same time recognising that firms in all three tiers need to be supported. Among the initiatives that could be included in such a strategy are:

---

11 These findings were based on the first 100 firms from a survey that targeted 400 firms. This first set of 100 firms was dominated by large firms and may therefore not be fully representative.

i) Supporting linkages, especially subcontracting between small and larger firms

ii) Revitalising the fabric segment of the textile industry by offering incentives for investment.

iii) Targeting infrastructure support to the particular needs of large, medium, and small textile and garment firms

iv) Reviewing the EPZ and MUB legislation to eliminate provisions that work against the integration of the industry.

v) Improving government sponsored technical training programmes to better meet the needs of different parts of the industry

vi) Supporting research into labour productivity, innovation, new technologies, and other issues related to the competitiveness of various segments of the industry.

REFERENCES

Baden, Sally and Barber, Catherine. 2005. "The Impact of the Second-hand Clothing Trade on Developing Countries." Oxford: Oxfam.

Bagchi, Sanjoy. 2001. *International Trade Policy in Textiles: Fifty Years of Protectionism*. Geneva: International Textiles and Clothing Bureau.

Barr, Abigail. 1995. "The Missing Factor: Entrepreneurial Networks, Enterprises, and Economic Growth in Ghana." Centre for the Study of African Economies WPS/95-11. Oxford: University of Oxford CSAE Publishing.

Bigsten, Arne, and Kimuyu, Peter. 2002. *Structure and Performance of Manufacturing in Kenya*. New York: Palgrave.

Bigsten, Arne and Wicks, Rick. 1996. "Used Clothes Export to the Third World: Economic Considerations." *Development Policy Review* 14: 379-90.

Billetoft, Jorgen. 1996. *Between Industrialisation and Income Generation: The Dilemma of Support for Micro Activities: A Policy Study of Kenya and Bangladesh*. Copenhagen: Centre for Development Research.

Cable, Vincent. 1990. 'Adjusting to Textile and Clothing Quotas: A Summary of Some Commonwealth Countries' Experiences as a Pointer to the Future." In Hamilton, Carl B. (ed.). *Textiles Trade and the Developing Countries: Eliminating the Multi-Fibre Arrangement in the 1990s*. Washington: The World Bank.

Central Bureau of Statistics (CBS), International Centre for Economic Growth (ICEG), and K-Rep Holdings, Ltd. 1999. *National Micro and Small Enterprise Baseline Survey 1999*. Nairobi: K-Rep Development Agency.

Claxton, Jacklyn J. 2003. "The Implications of the African Growth and Opportunity Act for the Textile and Apparel Industry in Kenya". MA Thesis. University of Connecticut (Storrs, CT).

Cotton, L.; Elbadawi I.; Kimuyu, P.; Marchat, J. M.; Ngugi, R.; Ramachandran, V. and Shah, K.M. 2003. *Enhancing the Competitiveness of Kenya's Manufacturing Sector: The Role of the Investment Climate.* Nairobi: Kenya Institute of Public Policy Research and Analysis (KIPPRA) and RPED, Africa Private Sector Group; Washington: The World Bank.

Coughlin, Peter. 1991. "A Gradual Maturation of an Import-Substitution Industry: The Textile Industry". In Coughlin, Peter and Ikiara, Gerrison K. (eds.). *Kenya's Industrialization Dilemma..* Nairobi: Heinemann Kenya.

Dicken, Peter. 1998. *Global Shift.* Third Edition. London: Paul Chapman Publishing Ltd.

Dickerson, K. 1999. *Textiles and Apparel in the Global Economy.* Upper Saddle River, NJ: Prentice-Hall.

Elson, Diane. 1994. 'Uneven Development in the Textiles and Clothing Industry.' In Sklair, Leslie (ed). *Capitalism and Development.* London: Routledge.

Fafchamps, Marcel. 1994. "Industrial Structure and Microenterprises in Africa." *The Journal of Developing Areas* 29: 1-30.

Field, Simone. 2000. "The Internationalisation of the Second-hand Clothing Trade: The Case of Zimbabwe." African Studies Centre, Coventry University: Unpublished PhD Thesis.

Gereffi, G. 1994. 'Capitalism, Development and Global Commodity Chains.' In Sklair, Leslie (ed.). *Capitalism and Development.* London: Routledge.

Gereffi, Gary and Memedovic, Olga. 2003. "The Global Apparel Value Chain: What Prospects for Upgrading by Developing Countries." Sectoral Studies Series. Vienna: United Nations Development Organisation.

Glenday, G and Ndii, D. 2003. "Export Platforms in Kenya". In Kimenyi, M. S.; Mbaku, J. M. and Mwaniki, N. (eds.). *Restarting and Sustaining Growth and Development in Africa.* Aldershot, Ashgate.

Granér, M. and Isaksson, A. 2002. "Export Performance in Kenyan Manufacturing". In Bigsten, A and Kimuyu, P. (eds.) *The Structure and Performance of Manufacturing in Kenya.* Basingstoke and New York: Palgrave.

Haggblade. Steve. 1990. "The Flip Side of Fashion: Used Clothing Exports to the Third World." *Journal of Development Studies* 26: 505-521.

Ikiara, G.K.; Kimuyu, P.; Manundu, M. and Masai, W. 2002. " Firm, Product Markets and Technological Characteristics". In Bigsten, A. and Kimuyu, P. (eds.). *The Structure and Performance of Manufacturing in Kenya.* Basingstoke and New York: Palgrave.

International Labour Organisation (ILO). 1995. "Recent Developments in the Clothing Industry". Report I. Geneva :International Labour Office.

International Labour Organisation (ILO). 2000. *Labour Practices in the Footwear, Leather, Textiles and Clothing Industries.* Geneva: ILO.

Kaplinsky, Raphael; McCormick, Dorothy and Morris, Mike. 2006. "The Impact of China on Sub Sharan Africa". Agenda-Setting Paper Prepared for DFID China Office, Grant Reference Number AG4419. Institute of Development Studies, University of Sussex; Institute for Development Studies, University of Nairobi; School of Economics, University of Cape Town.

Kenya, Republic of. 1988. *Development Plan, 1989-1993.* Nairobi: Government Printer.

Kenya, Republic of. 1990. *Export Processing Zone Act (Cap 517, Rev 1993, Laws of Kenya).* Nairobi: Government Printer.

Kenya, Republic of. 1996. *Industrial Transformation to the Year 2020.* Nairobi: Government Printer.

Kenya, Republic of. 2003. *Economic Recovery Strategy for Wealth and Employment Creation, 2003-2007.* Nairobi: Ministry of Planning and National Development.

King, Kenneth. 1996. *Jua Kali Kenya: Change and Development in an Informal Economy, 1970-95.* Nairobi: East African Educational Publishers.

Kinyanjui, Mary Njeri. 2003. "A Gender Analysis of Small-Scale Garment Producers: Response to Market Liberalisation in Kenya." *African Geographical Review* 22: 49-59.

Kinyanjui, Mary N. and McCormick, Dorothy. 2003. "Value Chains in Small-Scale Garment Producers in Nairobi: Challenges in Shifting from the Old Global Regime of Import Substitution to a More Liberalised Global Regime." IDS Working Paper No. 536. Nairobi: University of Nairobi, Institute for Development Studies.

Kinyanjui, M. N. and McCormick, D. 2001. "E-Commerce in The Garment Industry in Kenya: A Review of Usage, Obstacles and Policies". Report prepared in connection with project entitled: 'E-Commerce for Developing Countries: Building an Evidence Base for Impact Assessment'.

Lall, Sanjaya. 1995. "Structural Adjustment and African Industry." *World Development* 23(12): 2019-2031.

Lande, Stephen; Gale, Michael R; Arora, Rajeev; and Sodhi, Navdeep. 2005. "Impact of the End of MFA Quotas on COMESA's Textile and Apparel Exports Under AGOA: Can the Sub-Saharan African Textile and Apparel Industry Survive and Grow in the Post-MFA World?" Report to USAID by Manchester Trade. Available at:
www.ecatradehub.com/reports/rp.downloads/2005.MFA.Final.report.pdf

Lundvall, Karl; Ochoro, Walter; and Hjalmarsson, Lennart. 2002. "Productivity and Technical Efficiency." In Bigsten, Arne and Kimuyu, Peter. 2002. *Structure and Performance of Manufacturing in Kenya*. New York: Palgrave.

McCormick, Dorothy. 1988. "Small Enterprise in Nairobi: Golden Opportunity or Dead End?" Unpublished Ph.D dissertation. Baltimore: The Johns Hopkins University.

McCormick, Dorothy. 1997. "Industrial District or Garment Ghetto? The Case of Nairobi's Mini-Manufacturers". In van Dijk, Meine Pieter and Rabellotti, Roberta (eds.). *Enterprise Clusters and Networks in Developing Countries*. London: Frank Cass.

McCormick, Dorothy. 1999. "Institutions and Industrial Development: A Case Study of Garments and Textiles in South Africa". Paper prepared for workshop on African Business Systems, Nairobi.

McCormick, Dorothy and Muguku, Charles W. 2003. "Labour and the Paradox of Flexibility: The Case of Small Garment and Metal Enterprises in Nairobi." Paper presented in Adger University College – Mzumbe University Conference, Dar es Salaam, 26-28 February 2003.

McCormick, Dorothy and Abuodha, Charles. 2000. "Differences Between Rural and Urban Enterprises." Unpublished.

McCormick, Dorothy; Kamau, Paul and Ligulu, Peter. 2006. "Post Multi Fibre Agreement Analysis of the Garment and Textile Sectors in Kenya". *IDS Bulletin 37(1): 80-88*.

McCormick, Dorothy and Kinyanjui, Mary Njeri. 2000. "Towards a Practical Understanding of Enterprise Clusters in Kenya." Final report submitted to International Centre for Economic Growth, Nairobi.

McCormick, Dorothy; Kinyanjui, Mary Njeri and Ongile, Grace. 1997. 'Growth and Barriers to Growth Among Nairobi's Small and Medium-Sized Garment Producers". *World Development* 25(7): 1095-1110.

McCormick, Dorothy; Kimuyu, Peter and Kinyanjui, Mary 1999 "Institutions and the Industrialisation Process: A Proposal for a Study of the Textile and Textile Products Industry in Kenya". IDS Working Paper No. 527. Nairobi: University of Nairobi, Institute for Development Studies.

McCormick, Dorothy; Kimuyu, Peter and Kinyanjui, Mary. 2001. "Kenya's Garment Industry: An Institutional View of Medium and Large Firms". IDS Working Paper No. 531. Nairobi: University of Nairobi, Institute for Development Studies.

McCormick, Dorothy; Kimuyu, Peter and Kinyanjui, Mary. 2002 "Weaving Through Reforms: Nairobi's Small Garment Producers in a Liberalised Economy". Paper presented at East African Workshop on Business Systems in Africa, Nairobi.

McCormick, D.; Mitullah, Winnie V. and Kinyanjui, Mary Njeri. 2003. "How to Collaborate: Associations and Other Community Based Organisations

Among Kenya Micro and Small-scale Entrepreneurs." IDS Occasional Paper No. 70. Nairobi: University of Nairobi, Institute for Development Studies.

McCormick, D.; Kimuyu, P. and Kinyanjui, M N. 2002, "Can Micro Enterprises Export? Preliminary Evidence from Nairobi's Garment Sector". Paper presented at the International Conference on Business Systems in Africa: Institutions in Industry and Agriculture at the Travellers Beach Hotel, Mombasa, Kenya. September 26 27, 2002.

McCormick, D. and Schmitz, H. 2002. *Manual for Value Chain Research on Homeworkers in the Garment Industry*. Sussex: Institute of Development Studies. Available at: www.ids.ac.uk

Osakwe, Chiedu. 2004. "Developments in the Multilateral Trading System in the Textiles and Clothing Sector." Paper presented at the Annual General Meeting of the International Wool and Textiles Organisation (IWTO), Evian France, 12 May 2004.

Pack, Howard. 1987. *Productivity, Technology, and Industrial Development: A Case Study in Textiles*. Washington: The World Bank.

Pedersen, Poul Ove and McCormick, Dorothy. 1999. "African Business Systems in a Globalizing World." *Journal of Modern African Studies* 37 (1): 109-136.

Rasmussen, Jesper. 1992. "The Local Entrepreneurial Milieu: Enterprise Networks in Small Zimbabwean Towns". Research Report no. 79. Department of Geography, Roskilde University in cooperation with Centre for Development Research, Copenhagen.

Schmitz, Hubert. 1989. "Flexible Specialisation: A New Paradigm of Small-scale Industrialisation?" Discussion Paper 261. Sussex: Institute of Development Studies.

Trela, Irene and Whalley, John. 1990. 'Unravelling the Threads of the MFA.' In Carl B. Hamilton (ed.). *Textiles Trade and the Developing Countries: Eliminating the Multi-Fibre Arrangement in the 1990s*. Washington: The World Bank.

UNCTAD. 2005. *Investment Policy Review: Kenya*. United Nations Conference on Trade and Development. Available at: www.unctad.org. Accessed 11 September 2006.

Whitley, R. 1992. *Business System in East Asia*. London: Sage.

Chapter 10

The Smallholder Tea Industry in Kenya: Networks, Markets and Livelihoods

Mary Omosa

INTRODUCTION

It is argued that the interplay between market forces, government policy and social structure continues to shape and re-shape the tea market. In the midst of what seems like expanded choices arising from the liberalisation of the tea industry, producers are constantly making decisions. Some of these decisions present dilemmas that come to impact on everyday practices, tea marketing included. The decisions that producers finally take draw from several experiences, some local and others that are based on activities taking place in far-away places. To this end, we seek to answer the following set of questions. Who are the actors in the tea market and how are they organised? What are the ongoing interactive processes within and beyond the tea catchments areas? How do actors in the tea industry construct, reproduce and transform formal linkages? What is the resultant business system in the context of the tea market? Hence, this chapter focuses on the nature of linkages between the tea market and rural livelihoods and how this actually comes to influence business practices.

Underlying the notion of the business system theory is recognition that businesses operate in a specific environment and with a wide variety of institutions (Pedersen and McCormick, 1999:2). However, the specificity of this environment has remained unclear to the extent that some key variables are often left out while attempting to explain the type of business systems that exist. Yet, if institutions constitute 'the rules of the game' as argued by North (1990), a study on business systems must by a necessity looked at both the formal and the informal rules governing the institutions within which these businesses operate. This would entail looking at both internal and external forces in an attempt to explain the way individual businesses operate vis-à-vis what is recommended to take place. For instance, tea growers operate in a fairly structured industry with rules and regulations that touch on almost every step that a farmer must take in the growing and marketing of green leaf. This structure is a product of externally driven requirements and standards, many of which are assumed to be non-negotiable.

However, studies now suggest that in spite of an apparent uniformity in business rules and regulations, actual practices and experiences vary from place to place (cf. Pedersen and McCormick, 1999:3). This means that business operations and smallholder tea production and marketing in particular will vary with people's economic base and more importantly, the social structure within which these activities take place. Some of these factors are rooted in a people's history. But, whereas it could be assumed that a common history produces similar experiences, actual outcomes are dependent on how the individuals concerned interweave these experiences with their every-day lives, in an attempt to operate in a market economy.

The actual outcome of people's engagement in business is a product of several interactions. At the heart of these considerations is the interplay between networks, markets and livelihoods. *Livelihoods* is here used to refer to efforts aimed at making a living and this includes attempting to meet various consumption and economic necessities, coping with uncertainties, responding to new opportunities and making a choice between different value positions (Long, 1997:11). In other words, in making decisions about tea marketing, households will interweave their own perceptions and experiences with how a given strategy operates. This is bound to affect outcomes. As such, common strategies, tea marketing included, will be variously executed and, results will differ and levels of success will be interpreted and experienced differently.

Among smallholder tea producers, the choice of where and when to sell one's green leaf is subject to who knows what, what it is that they know, what image they would want to project of themselves, and the value system informing this perceived identity (cf. Wallman, 1984:28). But, while this tends to suggest that the strategies that households engage in with regard to tea marketing are pre-determined, this is not always the case. As a social and economic activity, tea marketing takes place in a dynamic environment and one in which 'new' ideas and opportunities are always emerging. As such, the marketing strategies that people identify with will change or be seen to have changed for various reasons. In this regard, Wallman has identified time, information and identity as the other equally important elements that come into play in shaping livelihoods, businesses included, in addition to the more conventional factors of production, namely, land, labour and capital (Wallman, 1984).

Any attempt to understand how people organise and interact with markets must be seen in a wider context. This includes looking at the type of opportunities that markets portend and how these are perceived at the household level. Some of the forces that may contribute to how people run their businesses include externally stimulated processes such as policy guidelines and other planned interventions. However, despite a possible uniformity in these interventions, the interface between the tea commodity market and rural livelihoods must be analysed in the light of the choices that households make in an attempt to meet their consumption and economic necessities, and the context in which these operations take place. This context could be social, cultural, political or economic in nature. To this end, the environment of the people being studied is fundamental to understanding African businesses and the tea industry in particular. This refers to the totality of people's surrounding and it includes the broad political and economic structures and the immediate physical, social and cultural environments where people live and work (cf. Hebinck, 2002).

Resources and businesses are inter-linked and this relationship is central to the direction of outcomes resulting from various engagements, interactions with markets included. The level of caution with which producers handle markets is dependent on the type of vulnerabilities within which those concerned must operate. These include the need to pay attention to the processes that shape endeavours, and the activities of institutions and individuals that appear external to the communities under consideration but who, nevertheless, influence what goes on. Hence, the totality of the context in which tea producers conduct their businesses is crucial to our understanding and ability to delineate the interplay between rural livelihoods and people's response to business opportunities and how these come to shape their business environment and attendant practices.

In seeking to understand the nature of the linkages between tea producers and markets, our focus in this chapter is on network building and knowledge construction within the smallholder tea industry. Discussions are based on field interviews and a random survey of 60 smallholder tea producers from 12 of the 45 buying centres serving under Kebirigo Tea Factory and 50 *Soko Huru* dealers operating within the Nyamira-Kericho tea corridor. The selection of Kebirigo Tea factory, one of the 45 KTDA factories in the country, was guided by the existence of a variety of markets open to tea producers who are otherwise expected to sell their green leaf through designated KTDA factories. Some of these potential markets include multi-national tea factories, *Soko Huru* traders and fellow growers. And in an attempt to fully understand the intricacies surrounding tea marketing, key personnel from both the KTDA and multi-national companies were also interviewed. Some of the staff included: Buying Clerks, Leaf Base Managers, Factory Managers, and KTDA Directors.

THE TEA INDUSTRY IN KENYA: A HISTORICAL OVERVIEW

Tea was first planted in Limuru, Kiambu District, Kenya in 1903 and later spread to other districts on a commercial basis in the 1920s (KTDA, 1990; Omosa, 2002b; Omosa, 2003; Swynnerton, 1953). However, it was not until early 1950s when tea was first introduced to African areas on experimental basis under the auspices of the Special Crops Development Authority (SCDA). In 1952, tea growing was introduced among smallholders on a pilot basis in Kirinyaga, and in 1957, a tea factory was constructed for purposes of processing green leaf from small-scale growers. From these nucleuses, the crop spread to other districts that were considered suitable for tea growing. In 1964, the Special Crops Development Authority was replaced with the Kenya Tea Development Authority (KTDA). This was followed by the introduction of field extension services for smallholder tea growers and the establishment of two marketing boards, namely: Central Province African Tea Growing and Marketing Board (CPATGMB), and the Nyanza and Rift Valley Provinces African Tea Growing and Marketing Board (NRVPATGMB).

Several changes have, however, continued to take place in the tea industry. The most radical shift involved the privatisation and liberalisation of the tea sector that culminated in a change over from the Kenya Tea Development Authority to the Kenya Tea Development Agency Limited, for the express purpose of handing over power to tea growers. These changes culminated in the incorporation of the Kenya Tea Development Agency Limited in the year 2002.

The Kenya Tea Development Agency

The Kenya Tea Development Authority (KTDA) was established as a State Corporation in 1964 to take over from the Special Crops Development Authority (SCDA) with the primary mandate of managing the smallholder tea sector, demarcated as growers with less than 10 hectares of land under tea. At inception in 1964, KTDA inherited about 19,000 tea growers, cultivating 4,700 hectares of tea and producing 2.8 million kilograms of leaf annually. Four decades later, KTDA has grown to a membership of over 360,000 tea producers accounting for a total of 82,230 hectares of land under tea and an annual leaf production in excess of 500 million kilograms (KTDA, 2003).

Table 10.1: *Growth in the Tea Industry*

Year	No. of Growers	Area Planted (HA)	Production (Kgs)
1964	19,000	4700	2,800,000
2003	36,000	82,230	500,000,000

The KTDA runs 45 of the 83 tea processing factories in the country. In general, the smallholder sub-sector under the KTDA contributes 57 percent of the national tea output. Some of the services that the KTDA continues to render to smallholder tea producers include the management of tea factories, green leaf transportation, procurement of production goods, and marketing and payment of tea proceeds to growers (Kenya, 1999a:8).

Following the privatisation of the KTDA, all the 28 smallholder tea growing districts participated in elections. A total of 11,368 farmers were elected representatives to leaf collection centres, 255 directors to tea factory boards, 12 to the Kenya Tea Development Agency, and 11 to the Tea Board of Kenya (KTDA, 2003).

Other players in the industry include the Kenya Union of Smallholder Tea Growers, The Tea Research Foundation, The Nyayo Tea Zones Development Corporation, The Kenya Tea Growers Association, the East African Tea Trade Association, and the Kenya Government. Several changes have, however, continued to take place in the tea industry, the latest being the liberalisation of the tea sub-sector. One of the emerging consequences of liberalisation of the tea sector is the mushrooming of private traders, commonly known as *Soko Huru.*

Other companies closely associated with KTDA include Majani Insurance Brokers, the KTDA Farmers' Company, and the Kenya Tea Packers Limited. In spite of the said liberalisation, KTDA remains a monopoly with respect to the marketing and processing of tea from smallholder growers.

KTDA has since been described as the boldest and most ambitious agricultural programme in the country. Within the first decade of its establishment, smallholder tea production became the most profitable economic activity. Two decades later, Kenya was the leading black tea exporter in the world and the largest tea producer, after India and Sri Lanka (Finance, 2000:24; AFTTA, 1994).

The Tea Management Structure

Prior to the liberalisation of the tea industry in Kenya, the sector was divided into three: large-scale growers, medium-scale growers, and small-scale growers. These three groups are differentiated at the level of acreage under tea, manufacturing, marketing and transportation. (Kenya, 1999a; Kenya, 1999b; Kenya, 2000).

Large-Scale Growers are mainly multi-national companies with their own factories and marketing channels. Some of these large-scale companies depend on out-growers for the supply of green leaf. Out-growers are largely made up of medium-scale tea growers. The small-scale sub-sector consists of smallholder tea farmers with less than 10 hectares of land under tea. All small-scale tea growers process and market their green leaf through KTDA-run factories. However, all the three sub-sectors sell most of their processed tea through the Mombasa tea auction.

The *Smallholder Tea Growers* constitute the first entry point into the tea commodity market (see Figure 10.1). The growers provide their factory with green leaf and this is sold through *Leaf Buying Centres*. Each centre is charged with the responsibility of collecting leaf from farmers and delivering this to the designated processing factory. An elected committee known as a Tea Buying Centre Area Committee, drawn from registered farmers, manages leaf-buying centres. This committee consists of five tea growers elected by and from among tea growers registered with the specific tea factory for delivery of green leaf.

A Tea Buying Centre Area Committee aims to foster tea development in their respective areas in liaison with tea extension officers. The committee achieves this by promoting good tea husbandry practices; supervising green leaf grading, weighing and collection; receiving, distributing and monitoring the use of farm inputs; and undertaking anything else that is deemed beneficial to tea growers. Each factory has several tea buying centres.

Leaf Buying Centres are coordinated by a Leaf Base and this is managed through a *Leaf Base Committee*. The committee advises and co-ordinates buying-centre committees and the movement of leaf carriers. The committee also estimates and advises the factory on farm inputs, leaf collection, weighing scales and other managerial concerns. The Leaf Base Committee consists of six members elected from among tea growers. The leaf base manager and tea extension manager attend as ex-officio.

The fourth level in this hierarchy is the Tea Factory. Upon receiving the green leaf, the factory processes it into black (made) tea, which is then transported, to Mombasa for auction. Each factory is expected to keep a record of its made tea and organise for transportation to the auction. Once sales are made and completed, the factory organises for payments to farmers through the leaf base buying centres. Some of the tea is sold at the factory door to farmers for domestic consumption. The Tea Factory Board engages in policy formulation, implementation of resolutions of the general meetings, procurement, and appointment of a management agent, personnel, brokers and auditors.

Tea Board Of Kenya
(Registering, Licensing and Regulation)

KTDA HQs
(Policy and Management)

KTDA Tea Factory
(Board of Directors)

Leaf Base Committee
(Tea Leaf Base Committee)

Leaf Buying Centre
(Tea Buying Centre Area Committee)

Smallholder Tea Grower
(Household)

Figure 10.1: Tea Management Structure

The *KTDA Board of Directors* is composed of, among others, representatives of smallholder tea farmers. These are selected on the basis of zones and a zone elects one director to the KTDA board. Each zone comprises three factories. The Board of Directors comprises a minimum of 13 and a maximum of 19 directors, 12 of who are elected by the shareholders. These directors are in-charge of policy and management.

All tea growers and manufacturers must register with the *Tea Board of Kenya*. Large-scale growers register directly while smallholders register using the factories through which they sell their green leaf. Licensed factories are required to maintain a register of growers falling under them on behalf of the Tea Board. For the continued validity of registration, growers are forbidden to sell green leaf to any person other than to the manufacturing factory specified in the application and with whom they are registered.

Manufacture of tea is undertaken under licence from the Tea Board of Kenya. The primary consideration is availability of adequate leaf. The aim is to ensure that processing factories do not operate below capacity and that there is no conflict with regard to the source of leaf. This licence is renewed annually at a fee. The Tea Board of Kenya consists of representatives from both the growers and processors of tea. The Tea Board is charged with the registration, licensing, regulation, control and improvement of the cultivation, processing and marketing of Kenyan tea. The government, however, remains an interested party and continues to render support by providing guarantees on external loans borrowed by KTDA on behalf of the smallholder tea farmers.

Tea Production and Export Volume

By 1930, total area under tea covered only 4,047 hectares with an annual production of 1,814,836 kilograms of made tea. However, acreage under tea grew rather rapidly and by independence in 1963, over 21,400 hectares of land were under tea (Kenya, 1999b; The East African, 1999). This has remained the case for the last nine years. In 1997, over 117,000 hectares of land were under tea. This rose to more than 118,400 hectares in 1998; 124,200 hectares in 1999; and 126,200 hectares in 2000. A more significant rise was experienced in 2001 when acreage under tea rose to 131,581 hectares. By the year 2004, the area under tea was in excess of 136,700 hectares, and this rose to 141,315 hectares in 2005 (Tea Board of Kenya, 2003; 2006), making Kenya the third largest producer of tea in the world. Comparatively, smallholder producers account for over two thirds of the acreage under tea (Figure10.2).

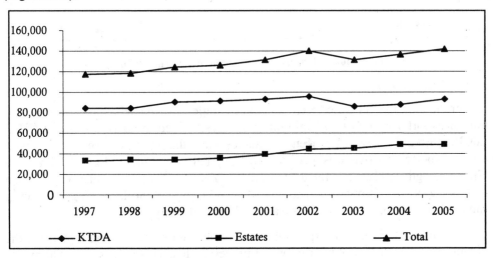

Figure 10.2: Area under Tea (Hectares)

Source: Tea Board of Kenya

Production figures suggest that although tea output is generally on the increase, there are periods when this fluctuates considerably. For instance, while tea output rose from 221,000 metric tons in 1997 to 294,000 metric tons in 1998, this dropped to 249,000 metric tons in 1999. In 2000, national production stood at a mere 236,000 metric tons. There was, however, a significant increase in 2001 when production rose to 295,000 metric tons. Although this gain was followed by a sizeable drop, to about 287,100 metric tons in 2002, production again rose to 293,670 metric tons in 2003, and 324,608 metric tons in 2004 (Tea Board of Kenya, 2004; 2006). These fluctuations are largely attributed to poor weather conditions.

Cumulatively, the smallholder tea sub-sector accounts for more than one half of the tea produced in the country although unit output seems higher within the estates sub-sector (Figure 10.3).

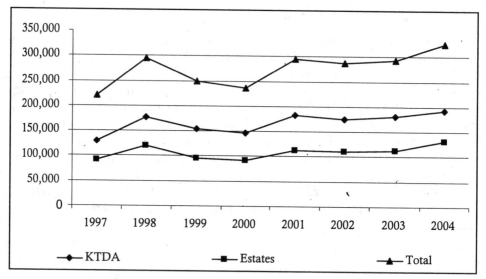

Figure 10.3: Tea Production by Company of Origin (Metric Tons)

Source: Tea Board of Kenya

Tea production has remained Kenya's largest single foreign exchange earner with an annual export volume of 272 million kilogram's, valued at Kshs. 34 billion (KBC 2003). Current Tea Board of Kenya statistics show that over 90 percent of Kenya's tea is exported to overseas markets, mainly, Pakistan (24%), Egypt (17%), the United Kingdom (16%), Afghanistan (13%), Yemen (7%), and Sudan (5%). Most of this tea is sold through the Mombasa Auction, the second largest tea auction in the world after Colombo in Sri Lanka (Tea Board of Kenya, 2004).

The volume of Kenya's tea exports has experienced a general increase. In 1997, the country exported 198,000 metric tons of processed tea. This rose to 263,000 metric tons in 1998. Although the country recorded a drop in exports in subsequent years (242,000 in 1999 and 217,000 in 2000), it was able to rise to a high of 270,000 metric tons in 2001 and 275,255 metric tons in 2002 (Figure 10.4). Much as there was a drop in the volume of exports in 2003 (to about 269,900 metric tons), this rose to over 333,500 metric tons in 2004 and 349,900 metric tons in 2005 (Tea Board of Kenya, 2006).

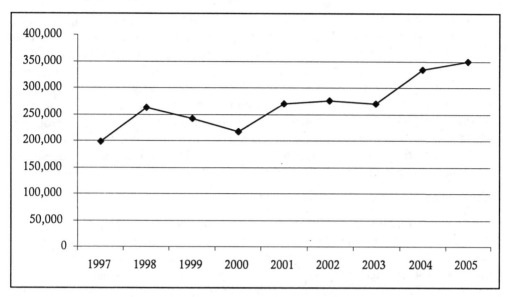

Figure 10.4: Tea Exports (Metric Tons)

Source: Tea Board of Kenya

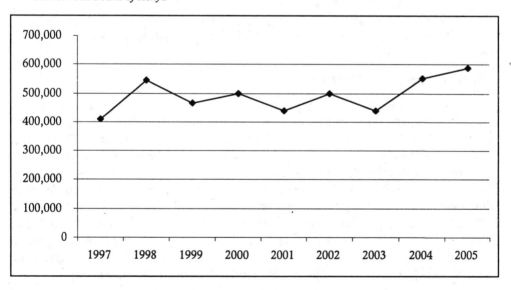

Figure 10.5: Tea Exports (Value US$)

Source: Tea Board of Kenya

The value of Kenya's tea exports fluctuates beyond variations in volume output. Indeed, fluctuations in pricing have sometimes occasioned higher returns for lower volume and vice versa. In effect, this means that tea producers and smallholder growers in particular have to contend with fairly unpredictable returns. This situation is complicated further by currency fluctuations (Figure 10.5).

Despite these problems, tea production remains a major source of livelihood for a majority of rural dwellers living in growing areas. Indeed, East Africa is the only region in the world where the tea crop is available year round. Furthermore, there are opportunities to expand the area under tea both through planting and per hectare exploitation (The East African, 1999). These comparatively favourable growing conditions have continued to make tea farming fairly attractive. Among smallholder producers, tea farming has remained a steady source of cash income. The crop also commands a fair amount of social capital among local communities. This is evidenced by the fact that tea growers are often well to do, progressive people and likely to be the ones taking up positions of leadership within the community.

THE SMALLHOLDER TEA INDUSTRY

We focus the remaining sections of this chapter on how the smallholder tea market is organised. In particular, discussions are centred on the type of linkages that producers maintain with KTDA, their main market outlet, and what shapes and governs these linkages and how. Special attention is paid to what underlies the behaviour of smallholder producers and whether this lies within the realm of the 'formal' or the 'informal' and why. The general aim is to bring out the interactions between smallholder tea producers and buying institutions and how these come to influence the operations of these institutions, sometimes to the point of departing from assumed or formalised procedures. One of the emerging questions therefore is, who are these smallholders and, how have they organised their participation in the tea commodity market?

Characteristics of Smallholder Producers

In the Kebirigo KTDA Factory catchment area, a considerable proportion of the growers were women most of who were *de facto* heads of household. Many of the growers were in the forties and the oldest person was 80 years old. There were, however, young tea growers, many of who were aged between 31 and 40 years (Figure 10.6). In other words, involvement in the tea industry seems to come about with the attainment of certain requirements, one of which is adulthood. Women dominate among the relatively young tea growers while male producers tend to be concentrated among older growers. Comparatively, women enter the tea industry very early in their lives mainly because a majority of them are generally engaged in agricultural production while their male counter-parts tend to move into agriculture only when they retire from wage employment and/or other off-farm engagements.

Most tea producers had moderate levels of education. Only four of the sixty smallholder tea producers interviewed had attained college or university level of education. Instead, the majority of the producers had only between primary and secondary school level of education; two were illiterate. Moreover, these literacy levels among smallholder tea growers were found to vary with gender. Male producers were the most educated while their female counterparts dominated among the least educated tea growers (Figure 10.7).

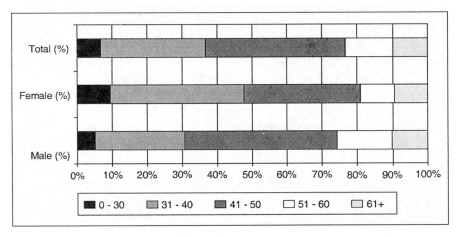

Figure 10.6: Producers' Age Distribution by Gender

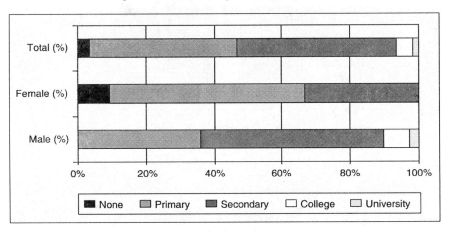

Figure 10.7: Producers' Level of Education by Gender

The characteristics of the smallholder producers are not unique to the tea sector. What is different, however, is how these characteristics influence the activities of smallholder tea producers, especially with regard to the marketing of green leaf. For instance, differentiation in assets is likely to influence whether farmers sell their tea crop through the formal market or not. Similarly, the levels of exposure will regulate the nature of risks that tea producers choose to take and the usefulness of market information to the way that they conduct their businesses. Therefore, the interplay between commodity markets and rural livelihoods is mediated through a people's socio-economic characteristics. One area where these variations are manifest is in how people choose to utilise available land.

Land under Tea

On average, among smallholders, tea occupies only about one half of the size of land available to most households. Many of the tea growers interviewed had put less than 1.2 acres of land under tea, out of an average land holding of about 3 acres. The remaining portions were under coffee and/or staple food crops such as maize, sorghum and finger millet. This suggests that diversification is one of the primary tools tea growers employ to be able to control and survive the various institutional challenges that accompany being engaged in markets. However, levels of diversification vary. Growers with less than one acre of land under tea diversified less as compared to those with between one and two acres of land, who tended to aim at striking a balance between various land uses. Area under tea reduced rather drastically among tea growers with four acres of land or more (cf. Figures 10.8 and 10.9).

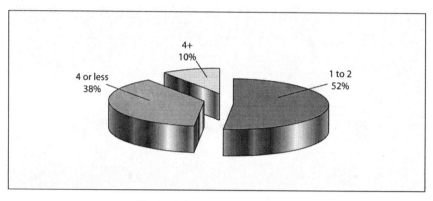

Figure 10.8: Area under Tea (Acres)

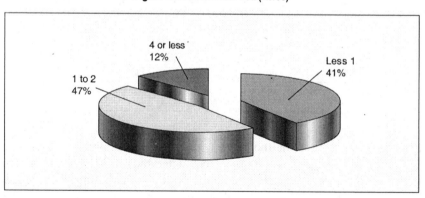

Figure 10.9: Total Land Holdings (Acres)

These cropping patterns suggest that specialisation within farming as an enterprise is subject to availability of resources. Tea growers with limited land sizes diversify less and the scope seems to increase with availability of land as a major input. Nevertheless, tea is a primary commodity among growers with limited land sizes, much unlike the common assumption that such households would limit themselves primarily to food crop production.

Entry into Tea Production

Although the principal reason underlying entry into tea farming seems to be monetary gain, there is diversity in the forces propelling this movement. For some of the growers, this economic decision was made in a social context, centred on advice received or the desire to be seen to be doing what everybody else in the community is engaged in primarily. On the other hand, some of the growers entered tea farming due to the influence of external forces. This suggests that the relationships that smallholder tea growers maintain with market outlets and the decision to carry on with tea production is governed by the reasons that influence their entry into tea farming, and some of these originate from outside of their immediate environment.

In general, those interviewed became tea producers almost as soon as they had access to their own piece of land and some cash money with which to purchase seedlings, one of the key inputs. Nevertheless, most tea growers advanced different reasons as to why they entered tea farming. For some, this followed advice they received from extension workers, most of which centred on the benefits of being a tea grower. For others, this sort of advice came from parents. The rest of the respondents, however, indicated that they entered tea farming following a market glut for pyrethrum or because they had witnessed the economic benefits that tea farming had brought to their fellow producers. Others simply took over from where their parents had left.

No matter the reasons behind making entry into the tea market, the actual decision seems to be based on some deliberate planning. Indeed, for about two thirds of the tea growers (61%), the initial capital required to cultivate tea was derived from savings. Only less than one tenth (7%) of the growers took a loan to be able to enter the tea commodity market. Even then, a fair proportion of these growers (32%) depended on other sources, and for most of them, this referred to inheriting already grown tea bushes from parents or spouses (Figure 10.10).

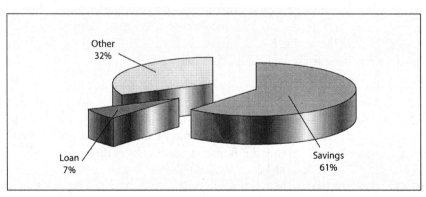

Figure 10.10: Source of Initial Capital for the Tea Crop

Again, entry into the tea market is as a result of both social and economic networks. For some people, this could only become possible through savings or linking up with economic institutions while for others, all they needed was social ties with endowed relatives. The category of tea growers that gained access to already existing tea bushes had the added advantage of exposure to tea farming, besides the fact that theirs was a mature crop and therefore a source of instant cash. Hence, such growers are likely to link up with markets rather differently as compared to those with no prior knowledge of the industry. In other words, the decision to enter into tea farming as an enterprise goes beyond access to the primary factors of production, such as land and start-up capital, to include one's knowledge base. This social input may, however, remain latent especially where enterprises are dependent on pooling resources such as in the processing of tea from smallholder farmers. In the next two sections, we look at how the smallholder tea market is organised and what this portends for the tea industry.

Buying Centres: Tradition, Compliance and Competition

The Leaf Buying Centre is the smallest unit in the KTDA marketing hierarchy (Figure 10.11). The Centre constitutes the point at which the smallholder tea grower meets with the KTDA representatives for purposes of selling their green leaf. These centres are open Monday through Friday between 9 a.m. and 4 p.m. although actual observations revealed that many times this went on into the night. A Leaf Buying Clerk, an employee of the KTDA, manages a Leaf Buying Centre. On the other hand, an elected Leaf Base Committee represents the tea growers who sell their produce through a specified Leaf Buying Centre. Representatives of tea growers are elected from among KTDA registered tea growers able to deliver up to 2,000 kilograms of tea per year. Emphasis seems to be put on the volume of tea delivered on the assumption that this connotes both area covered and productivity levels.

In areas where tea is widely cultivated such as Kebirigo, most growers were within a distance of one kilometre from the nearest tea-buying Centre. Nevertheless, some producers delivered tea to centres other than the closest one because they owned dispersed pieces of land but preferred to continue using one central registration or market outlet. But, for the same reason, other tea growers maintained more than one registration due to their having several pieces of land under tea or because they wanted to share out incomes at source between husband and wife or amongst several wives. Whichever the outlet, the activities at the Buying Centre demonstrate further the kind of business environment in which the smallholder tea industry operates.

On arrival at the green Leaf Collection Centre, growers queue to have their leaf inspected for quality before proceeding to have it weighed and the quantities entered into their records by the Leaf Collection Clerk. The Leaf Collection Clerk retains the original receipt while the farmer takes a copy with him/her. The weighed leaf is then put out in spread beds awaiting the arrival of gunny bags aboard the green leaf carrier truck. Up to this point in time, the green leaf is still the responsibility of the growers. Growers therefore organise themselves such that a few of them take care of leaf already weighed to avoid withering or theft. Once the transport is availed, this leaf is then packaged into gunny bags each weighing no more than 15 kilograms for transportation to the factory for processing. At this point in time, the KTDA factory assumes responsibility and farmers only await payments from the factory. The buying factory fixes the price of green leaf delivered based on the quality of made tea that the factory is able to produce and its level of demand on the market.

Figure 10.11: The Smallholder Tea Commodity Chain

In spite of being a seemingly easy market structure, the tea leaf collection centres constitute a life-world, largely because of the interactions that take place between formalised and non-formalised rules and regulations. Firstly, most queues comprise of women and children but in the vicinity are several men. The latter category of persons are the actual or declared owners who come along to ensure that the leaf delivered from their farms gets actually sold to the KTDA in their names. Secondly, this category of persons is the one to engage the Leaf Collection Clerk in negotiations necessary to ensure that the sale is smooth and to their advantage. This involves ensuring that the Collection Clerk is not unnecessarily strict while checking on the quality of tea delivered and more importantly, that the declared weight of leaf delivered is the actual amount. If disputes arise during this process, there is always a member of the Leaf Collection Centre Committee to arbitrate between the KTDA green-leaf buying clerk and the farmer concerned. The same committee member ensures general order during the selling of green leaf and he/she is charged with the responsibility of answering any questions that producers may have regarding their green leaf and general on-farm husbandry practices. In the event that the KTDA buying clerk rejects one's green leaf for any reason arising from quality control, the seller seeks alternative markets.

In 2001, smallholder tea growers sold their green leaf to the KTDA at Kshs. 25 per kilogram less various charges including fertilisers, transportation and related expenses, and a number of local government levies. Some of this money was paid monthly to the farmer at a flat rate of Kshs. 7.50 per kilogram of green leaf sold and the balance thereto was paid annually. This back pay, popularly known as *bonus* money, constituted the balance from the Kshs. 25 less the above listed deductions and payments already received on a monthly basis. Only the price changes but the procedure remains same year after year.

Most tea growers continue to sell green leaf through the KTDA because they are by Law, registered with the KTDA as their market outlet. The KTDA has also continued to be a favourite outlet for smallholder tea growers because buying centres are designated and reachable. Indeed, the tradition around the KTDA seems to favour the organisation further in terms of being fairly established and with no long-term competitor. Some of the growers derive satisfaction from the fact that payments are regular and monthly and this enables them to plan for their money better. Other incentives include the fact that the KTDA has a back payment commonly known as *bonus*, prices per kilogram are seen as generally better, and farmers receive inputs on credit alongside extension services. However, almost all growers complained about poor tea prices and the fact that deductions are rather many. In spite of this, only a few of the tea growers had knowledge of what determines the price of processed tea and whether, as growers, they are represented at the tea auction. Moreover, barely one fifth of the growers knew what comprises the Tea Act.

Nevertheless, most tea growers (78%) indicated that they planned to expand acreage under tea. The centrality of tea production as a source of livelihood among smallholder farmers is reinforced further by the fact that over one half of the growers did not have any other source of income. In other words, their economic future, among other things, lay with tea production. The question however is, whether smallholder tea growers are in a position to take their rightful place in a liberalised economy.

Generally, smallholder tea farmers actively participate in the affairs of the industry at least to the point where they are able to deliver and sell their green leaf through the KTDA. However, whether these growers concern themselves or even have knowledge of the tea market beyond the buying centres where they deliver their green leaf varies. In spite of discussions in the media and elsewhere about the need to liberalise the tea industry, most tea growers were taken by surprise when tea marketing was liberalised. Only about 38 percent of the smallholder tea growers reported that they were adequately prepared for the liberalisation of the industry. This group explained that the apparent competition arising from emerging markets had resulted in an increase in the price of green leaf. They also argued that liberalisation had given smallholder producers the power to manage the factories under their jurisdiction efficiently and it is this that has contributed to better tea prices.

Growers that felt that they were not adequately prepared for the liberalisation of the tea sector argued that the process was highly politicised and they did not play any role in determining the outcome. Instead, they were only informed that the government had withdrawn from the sector by granting the farmer more powers in decision making. As a consequence, most of these growers felt that liberalisation had brought about responsibilities that they were not adequately prepared for, among them, the fact that they are now entirely responsible for the operations of their factories, some of which are too small to break even. It was also reported that liberalisation had brought about a parallel market and this is detrimental to the smallholder tea industry.

THE SOKO HURU TRADE: INFORMAL CONTRACTS, NETWORKS AND COMPETITION

Prior to the liberalisation of the tea industry, growers did not have much of a choice regarding where to sell their green leaf. Smallholder tea growers sold their green leaf through the KTDA only. Currently, who to sell to and when varies with the season, a specific household's financial needs, and availability of alternative markets. In all instances, the farmer's decision is guided by how each of the market outlets is organised and the extent to which growers are able to manipulate set rules and regulations to suit circumstances as they unfold. In other words, tea growers continue to sell their green leaf through both formal and informal outlets and this decision is determined on the basis of events of the day and without necessarily disengaging from any one of these market outlets permanently. The emergent alternative market to the KTDA is commonly referred to as *Soko Huru*, a free flowing but fairly structured segment of the tea market that runs parallel to the KTDA.

Interface between Soko Huru and KTDA

Soko Huru is made up of several players, among them, out-growers, brokers, agents and the small-scale producers (Omosa, 2002a). Out-growers are large-scale tea producers who are registered with the Kenya Tea Growers Association to deliver green leaf to multi-national tea factories. Some of the out-growers obtain part of the green leaf that they sell to these factories from small-scale tea growers who cannot sell directly to multi-national companies. It is this out-sourcing that brings about the need for brokers and agents. Brokers form the linkage between small-scale tea growers and out-growers and they play a key role in the *Soko Huru* trade. It is them who source green leaf from small-scale tea growers and then deliver it to multi-national factories on behalf of the out-growers who contract them. In almost all cases, brokers depend on agents to reach the small-scale tea growers.

As is evident from Figure 10.12, green leaf from small-scale growers finds its way to multi-national tea factories through three main outlets. The first and most intense is where agents solicit green leaf from small-scale growers on behalf of brokers. Upon making cash payments, the brokers deliver the green leaf to out-growers who then deliver this to the multi-national tea companies with whom they are registered. On the other hand, some brokers solicit green leaf from small-scale growers without using an agent and then deliver this directly to the processing factory but under the name of a registered out-grower, with whom this broker has an agreement. The third line of purchase involves out-growers who buy green leaf directly from small-scale growers and deliver it to the multi-national factory without the assistance of agents or brokers.

On the other hand, some small-scale tea growers operate in *Soko Huru* by leasing out their tea farm to registered out-growers or other traders for a specified period of time. Once they agree on a price, the out-grower may get his own labour to pick the leaf or the small-scale farmer may pick his/her own leaf and deliver it all to the out-grower. On the part of the out-grower (or any other person leasing in land under tea), the incentive is ready access to green leaf at a time when it is in short supply. At this point, the tea trade operates with the bare minimum of linkages. There is also a time when a broker is given money by an out-grower to go and source leaf and deliver it to the factory on behalf of an out-grower. The broker may or may not use an agent.

In all instances, agents and small-scale growers do not deliver green leaf directly to the multi-national factories, largely because of logistical constraints. These include lack of a working capital to invest in the purchase and transportation of green leaf.

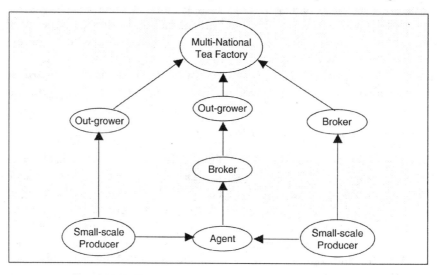

Figure 10.12: The Linkages between Various *Soko Huru* Operators

Many of the agents and brokers claimed that they were introduced to the *Soko Huru* trade by KTDA green leaf buying clerks in response to requests from brokers and out-growers to find them reliable persons to work with. Others, however, joined through being introduced by brokers who knew them and considered them to have good public relations. In addition, people who get considered for the position of agent also need to come from the locality where the green leaf is to be obtained. In 2001, agents were paid at a daily rate of between Ksh.100 and Kshs.150, exclusive of lunch, and all of them reported that they went into *Soko Huru* because it pays well and they were jobless. On the other hand, brokers were paid on commission or they drew their profits by re-selling the green leaf to out-growers at a negotiated margin.

Apparently, there is some interdependence between the *Soko Huru* trade and the KTDA green leaf market to the extent that employees deal with one another more as collaborators than competitors. This relationship is, however, full of contradictions. The KTDA Leaf Buying Clerks complained continuously about the damage that *Soko Huru* was causing their market. They felt that *Soko Huru* is an unfair competitor because it reaps where it did not sow with regard to the provision of support services to small-scale tea producers such as extension, farm inputs and infrastructure development.

On the other hand, a general ranking of the problems facing *Soko Huru* suggests that the KTDA is one of the biggest impediments to the advancement of this trade, largely because of the restrictions that the KTDA puts on small-scale tea growers. Paradoxically, agents came second on the list of impediments and ahead of even the local administration. The question however is, who is engaged in *Soko Huru* and what governs entry into this trade?

The Soko Huru Market

In spite of a seeming spontaneity, the *Soko Huru* market is fairly organised and structured. Nevertheless, this structure is neither fixed nor smooth. What happens and when it does happen is determined by the supply and demand configuration and the eventual direction is a function of existing networks and how well they are reinforced and sustained. Hence, much as the *Soko Huru* operators do not have a written contract with the producers from whom they purchase green leaf on a constant basis, there are many unwritten rules that tend to guide and stabilise these operations. These rules vary with the green leaf supply-demand configuration.

The *Soko Huru* operators have fairly definite routes that they follow every day, and most of these are designated KTDA buying centres and major markets. The choice of these buying points is deliberate and guided by the consideration that this gives them easy access to producers and their green leaf, especially what may be rejected by the KTDA. At these buying centres, the agents inspect the leaf while awaiting brokers or out-growers. Generally, the brokers do not negotiate the price with the producers because the entire group of dealers has an agreed upon price (of seven shillings per kilogram of green leaf by then) and nobody is allowed to undercut the other. Dealers who dare undercut others face assault or their vehicles are blocked from reaching the factories, the final point of sale.

The *Soko Huru* operations are fairly networked and peaceful with each dealer having a demarcated territory, and a majority of them visit between one and two centres at any one time. However, some go to as many as 12 buying centres. In spite of being quite regular, only one out of the fifty dealers interviewed reported having a written contract with the producer from whom he buys the green leaf. The rest depend on monopolising and frequenting buying centres from which they obtain their green leaf. In August 2001, the dealers interviewed handled an average of 35,000 kilograms of green leaf, ranging between 200 and 240,000 kilograms.

When there is scarcity of leaf, agents apply all sorts of methods to ensure that producers sell green leaf to their preferred outlets. For instance, the agents make sure that producers can trust them and their networks by buying from them regularly, by paying instantly or on time, and by appearing fair in determining the amount of green leaf received. They also entice these producers using persuasive language and by ensuring that they are not mistreated in the course of weighing. Some of the agents reported that they select green leaf growers on the basis of economic means with the hope that the needy ones will be easy to influence and contain. They also go for growers who are known to them and who therefore have a relationship to keep. When all else fails, the agents employ propaganda against their competitors.

However, the amount of green leaf purchased is also determined by cash at hand, the willingness of the farmer to sell to *Soko Huru*, the carrying capacity of the vehicles in use and the amount of leaf that the out-grower in question is expected to deliver to the processing factory. In the case of the latter, out-growers are allowed to exceed their daily capacity whenever their fellow suppliers are unable to meet designated quotas. This means that each of the out-growers and their agents and brokers will keep watch over the performance of their competitors with the intention of filling in their daily quota. In some instances, this may entail taking a chance at the factory gate and in the event that there is no such room, the green leaf is discarded.

Like the tea growers from who they buy, most of the *Soko Huru* operators that sell directly to the factories have no written contract with the buyers of their green leaf. Many of the *Soko Huru* operators are commissioned on a daily basis with or without the capital with which to purchase green leaf. Others just go ahead and purchase green leaf from the tea growers in anticipation of selling to brokers or out-growers. In spite of these arrangements, only about one half of the *Soko Huru* operators were able to sell all the green leaf that they purchased, largely due to limited processing capacity at the factory level. The left-over leaf is taken back home and discarded in the farm or it is dumped on the roadside. Much as no studies have been conducted to establish the actual coverage of the *Soko Huru* market vis-à-vis the KTDA one, it is clear that *Soko Huru* is now a major player in the tea industry.

Although *Soko Huru* involves several people, some actually serve the interests of the same 'master'. All the green leaf purchased through *Soko Huru* ends up with multi-national companies operating in the surrounding areas. These *Soko Huru* participating processing factories are found within a radius of 12 to 40 kilometres. However, only out-growers registered with these multi-national companies and who have the approval of the Tea Board of Kenya can sell green leaf to these companies. Therefore, the brokers sell the green leaf that they purchase to out-growers on a day-to-day basis or on a monthly account whereby some of them actually deliver green leaf directly to the factories but under the name of an out-grower. On the other hand, some agents work for brokers or out-growers or both depending on the demand for green leaf. Purchased green leaf is stuffed into sisal sacks and transported in pickup trucks, which must be roadworthy and registered with the receiving factories. In response to the question on where they sell their green leaf, slightly over one third (35%) of the operators stated that they sold directly to multi-national companies and a similar number sold through brokers (33%) and out-growers (31%). Only a few operators sold through several of these outlets (2%) simultaneously.

The relationship between small-scale tea growers and the various *Soko Huru* operators that they come into contact with is sometimes full of mistrust. Growers gave accounts of operators who exploited longstanding relationships to con them out of their green leaf. Such operators seek green leaf on credit from growers and refuse to honour their pledge. Others literary take off with the money as soon as they weigh and receive leaf. In both instances, such operators thereafter change routes or personnel and growers are left with no alternative for redress.

Soko Huru agents too had their story to tell. They reported that there are times when brokers take leaf on credit and the agents stand surety. Thereafter some of these brokers avoid routes where they have debts and this ruins the agent's relationship with his clientele. On other occasions, when leaf is in plenty, brokers and out-growers become so choosy that most growers are not able to sell. Yet, growers operate on the belief that leaf that is sold to *Soko Huru* has no quality requirements and they therefore expect the brokers to just buy. When leaf is rejected, it is the agents who face the wrath of the growers. This becomes quite challenging as their survival hinges on the co-operation of tea growers. This is also heightened in instances where brokers fail to collect leaf because of strict quarters, poor transport, or any other factor that may bar them from going to collect leaf from regular clients.

Evidently, the marketing decisions within the smallholder tea industry are arrived at in the context of who is making the decision and when. As such, some tea growers sell only to the KTDA while others combine this with *Soko Huru*. In both instances, the grower aims to maximise efforts and this is guided by what that particular market is able to offer and when. Therefore, even when tea growers know about some of the overriding advantages of selling through the KTDA, they still find it necessary to sell to *Soko Huru* for practical reasons. Whereas these two market outlets seem to co-exist and some of the off-shots of competition are already benefiting the tea farmer, it is not clear what the future holds for the smallholder tea industry.

CONCLUSION

We set out to understand the operations of the smallholder tea industry and how, from the point of view of the tea farmer, various activities are linked. The main aim was to demonstrate how these interactions and perceptions come to shape general operations, and especially subsequent performance of the tea market, and what this tells us about doing business with smallholder tea growers. Discussions have shown that even what looks like very informal operations have formalised origins, which have been re-worked over time, sometimes unconsciously. Access to correct information, however, emerges as a key contributory factor to the re-constructions that smallholder tea growers subject formal market operations to. There is, therefore, need for smallholder tea growers to have access to the right information, especially that which could enable them become competitive players in the industry. Currently, much of the evidence points towards limited access to crucial information, particularly in the area of marketing. Emerging patterns suggest the need to improve the quality of information that tea growers get and much of this depends on ensuring that their representatives throughout the various structures are themselves well informed.

REFERENCES

AFTTA, 1994. *East African Tea Trade Association. Constitution, Rules and Regulations*. Mombasa: Tea Trade Centre.

East African, The. 1999 "East African Tea Trade Association". *The East African*, December 6 -12.

Finance, Magazine. 2000. "From KTDA to Tea Factory Companies". *The Finance Magazine* International. May 18th, 2000:24-31.

Hebinck, P. 2002. "The Sustainable Livelihoods Framework". Draft report to IFPRI, Washington, D.C. May.

KBC, Kenya 2003. "Tea Tops Kenya's Foreign Earner". Kenya Broadcasting Corporation. Web Posted. Available at: http://www.kbc.co.ke. August 6.

Kenya, Republic of. 1999a. *Sessional Paper No.2 of 1999 on the Liberalisation and Restructuring of the Tea Industry*. Nairobi: Government Printer.

Kenya, Republic of 1999b. *Sessional Paper No. 2 of 1999 on the Liberalisation and Restructuring of the Tea Industry. Reforms in the Tea Board of Kenya and Privatisation of the Kenya Tea Development Authority*. Ministry of Agriculture. Nairobi: Government Printers.

KTDA, The. 2003. *The Kenya Tea Development Agency Limited*. Available at:

http://www.kenyaweb.com/agriculture/boards/ktda.html.

KTDA, The. 1990. *Kenya Tea Development Authority. Annual Report and Statement of Accounts 1989-1990*. Nairobi: KTDA.

Long, N. 1997. "Agrarian change, Neo-liberalism and Commoditisation. A Perspective on Social Value". In Haan, H. de and Long, N. (eds.) *Images and Realities of Rural Life*. Wageningen Perspectives on Rural Transformations. Assen: Van Gorcum pp. 226-244

North, D. 1990. *Institutions, Institutional Change and Economic Performance*. Cambridge: Cambridge University Press.

Omosa, M. 2003. "The Interplay between Commodity Markets and Rural Livelihoods: A Focus on the Tea Industry in Rural Kenya". IDS Working Paper No. 538. Nairobi: University of Nairobi, Institute for Development Studies.

Omosa, M. 2002a. "Soko Huru Trade: A Socio-Economic Analysis of the Tea Commodity Chain". A Paper presented at the IDS/CDR Business Systems Workshop. April 15-16, 2002. Holiday Inn, Nairobi.

Omosa, M. 2002b. "Negotiating Formal Institutions: A Focus on Smallholder Tea Farming". Proceedings of the IDS/CDR International Conference on Business Systems in Africa. September 26-27, 2002. Mombasa, Kenya.

Omosa, M. 1993. "Rural-rural Development Disparities". In *Wajibu* Vol. 8 No. 3.

Pedersen, P. O. and McCormick, D. 1999. "African Business Systems in a Globalising World". *The Journal of Modern African Studies*. 37 (1):109-135. Cambridge University Press.

Stern, N.H. 1972. "An Appraisal of Tea Production on Smallholdings in Kenya". Mimeo, Paris, France.

Swynnerton, R.J.M. 1953. *A Plan to Intensify the Development of African Agriculture in Kenya*. Nairobi: Government Press.

Tea Board of Kenya, The. 2003; 2004; and 2006. *The Tea Board of Kenya*. Available at: http://www.teaboard.or.ke

Wallman, S. 1984. *Eight London Households*. London: Routledge.

Chapter 11

Steaming Cups!
Policy Reforms and Problems in the Coffee Trade in Kenya

Karuti Kanyinga

INTRODUCTION

Businesses do not operate in a vacuum. A variety of social-cultural, political and economic factors influence the way businesses operate. This implies that interaction of factors within the broader environment affects how business operates. Analyses of these factors, however, tend to focus on the state and markets; other environmental factors are either assumed away or presumed to be same for all firms (Pedersen and McCormick, 1999). But a wide range of institutions (as well as organisations) affect how businesses operate. Political institutions and values as well as organisations, for instance, may cause formulation of policies that would affect how businesses operate. Furthermore, social-cultural institutions may constrain operation of business systems sometimes resulting in growth or collapse of businesses. That is, businesses operate within a system shaped by a range of factors, institutions and values as well as organisations.

The above notwithstanding, there is little understanding of how policies affect operation of agricultural business systems especially at the local level. There is little understanding of how policies impact on production processes and marketing of agricultural commodities at the local level. Analysis tends to place emphasis on macro and global levels, yet the local has significant implications for operation of business at these other levels. Secondly, the focus of analysis has been on the outcome of interaction between the state and the market and what this implies for the agricultural sector. Relatively little attention is given to how these factors shape commodity production and marketing at the local level, yet these are very important elements of local economies. Analysis of economic liberalisation reforms and its implications for organisation of agricultural business system in Sub-Saharan Africa has continued to suffer this bias. There is neglect of how market reforms have affected commodity production and trading at the local level.

Globalisation and attendant liberalisation policies have impacted on how local businesses operate. They have impacted on organisation of agricultural labour, production relations, and trading patterns. In some cases, liberalisation has fundamentally altered the structure around which businesses operate as well as altered the structure of production relations. Some studies now show that farmers have abandoned exchange labour and labour parties for hired labour and that social-negotiation has given way to contract as a labour recruitment strategy (Ponte, 2000). In spite of this, there is limited knowledge on how liberalisation has impacted on trading of agricultural commodities and organisation of local agricultural markets at the local level. Importantly, reforms focusing on reduced roles of state institutions from the agricultural sector have implications for how the sector is organised.

A point worth emphasising is that in Kenya, the state has been central in the development of the agricultural sector from the colonial period. Until very recently, the state has been central in the production, processing and marketing of the principal cash crops. For instance, in the coffee industry, through state-owned and/or controlled agencies, the government influenced how coffee was grown, processed and marketed. Marketing was monopolised by the state-owned Coffee Board of Kenya (CBK) while Kenya Planters Cooperative Union (KPCU), a body in which the state had overwhelming influence, facilitated processing and milling of coffee before taking it to CBK for auction. But state control of the agricultural sector, like elsewhere in Africa, had its own difficulties which contributed to reduced growth of the agricultural sector. This resulted in the increased pressures for liberalisation in line with other policies inspired by the World Bank and the International Monetary Fund (IMF) through Structural Adjustment Programmes (SAPs).

Studies now show that liberalisation policies have had several consequences on the agricultural sector and the commodity markets in particular (Ponte, 1998; 2002; Ikiara et al., 1993; Nyangito, 1998). In the coffee industry, the reforms targeted the government's control of coffee production, processing, marketing and exports. The government, through new policy initiatives, opened up the space for participation of different actors in the various stages of coffee production, milling and marketing. Importantly, and in line with foreign exchange policy changes, planters were allowed to open foreign exchange retention accounts. Growers with fewer than two hectares of land under coffee were licensed as planters. This resulted in the proliferation of new actors involved in coffee trading. Nonetheless, there is limited knowledge on how the coffee market changed under liberalisation and the impact of liberalisation policies on agricultural markets at the local level. There is need to understand the evolving forms of economic and social relations in the sector. Focus towards this direction is important because of the centrality of agriculture in the country's economic development and the fact that Kenya is an agrarian society.

In this chapter, we discuss the changes that have taken place in coffee trading in Kenya after implementation of liberalisation measures. The discussion seeks to answer the following questions: who are the new actors in the coffee business system and how have they evolved? Who gains from the 'new coffee business system' and what does this imply for development of the coffee industry at the local level? The chapter generally examines the implications of these changes for the development of the coffee industry and business in general. Data are drawn from field research conducted in two coffee growing districts – Meru and Nyeri – of Kenya in 2001 and 2002. Field research comprised interviews with small and large-scale farmers; primary cooperative societies; and coffee traders in the districts. The two districts are some of the most important coffee producing regions in the country. In both districts, coffee has been a major cash crop alongside tea. Meru also has a long history of coffee growing having been among the first districts where the colonial government allowed controlled growing of coffee outside the areas scheduled for white settlement, which included Nyeri. Meru thus pioneered in small scale African coffee holdings while Nyeri was the core of White settlers' large-scale holdings.

COFFEE SECTOR IN KENYA

Coffee is a significant agricultural commodity in Kenya. It is renown for fine quality throughout the world. Kenya coffee's fine quality fame has contributed to its fetching relatively better prices compared to other growers of Arabica coffee (Mwangi and Ndii, 2003). In some cases, buyers obtain Kenya coffee to mix with other brands so as to produce a fine blend. As a result of this fame, coffee husbandry has been emphatic on quality. Quality is emphasised from the level of selecting seedlings and preparation for planting all the way to delivery of cherry to a pulping plant and subsequent fermentation. Quality is also enhanced through an elaborate system of grading in which bean size and taste are the chief elements. But the quality of coffee is not the same everywhere in the country. Adherence to quality procedures and effectiveness of enforcement mechanisms varies from cooperative society or even coffee estate to another. Hence, coffee quality differs from one place to another. Quality is dependent on the effectiveness of the coffee management control system put in place by the cooperatives, estates, and the pulping factories. One factor behind the relatively high quality of smallholders' coffee compared to estates' coffee is the fact that smallholders are organised into cooperatives in which there are clear procedures for quality and mechanisms for enforcing these procedures. Of note in this regard is that coffee from smallholder farms is of relatively superior quality than coffee from the estates. To compensate for this and to improve on quality, the estates buy coffee from the smallholders for the purpose of mixing with that from their farms.

At the domestic level, coffee is important for several reasons. It is a major foreign exchange earner and is an important source of income and employment for many households – both those farming coffee and those not. Coffee farming is a source of livelihood for between 500,000 and 700,000 small-holders in the coffee agro-ecological zones and another over 4000 medium and large estate coffee producers (Kenya, 2001b). In terms of hectares, it is estimated that about 162,000 hectares are under coffee. Of this amount, estates and small-scale holdings account for 39,000 and 122,000 hectares respectively.

In the period between 1975 and 1986, coffee constituted over 40% of the total exports value. By 1992, this dropped to 9% of the total exports due to low prices in the international market and other factors such as poor management of the agricultural sector, and poor leadership of the cooperatives around which coffee trading was organised. Following liberalisation in the early 1990s, production began to increase and contribution to exports value showed improvement – 15% in 1995 and 20% in 2000. Coffee also comprises about 22% of agricultural export earnings. These trends imply continued importance of coffee in the overall economy.

Historical Profile

Production of coffee in Kenya has a long history. Brought from Tanzania and Malawi by the Roman Catholic Church and the Church of Scotland missionaries respectively, coffee was first experimented in Bura, Kibwezi and later on in Nairobi. Commercial farming started in the colonial Kiambu in 1900 but farming was restricted to settler farmers only. The colonial administration locked out Africans from coffee farming on argument that they could not observe strict crop husbandry that was required for growth of quality coffee. However, in 1930, the administration allowed controlled coffee farming by select Africans in some parts of Meru and Kisii. Other areas were locked out of coffee farming. Overall, coffee farming remained an economic activity for the settlers. By 1936, many White settlers had established themselves as commercial coffee farmers in various parts of Kenya (McMahon, 1984:19; CBK 1996). Very few Africans were allowed to produce Coffee.

The Swynnerton Plan of 1954 opened the farming of coffee to more Africans by removing administrative and legislative restrictions (Maitha, 1974:23; McMahon, 1984: 19; CBK, 1996). This notwithstanding, the Plan did not remove restrictions on strict crop husbandry standards that provided the excuse for the colonial government to lock out Africans from coffee farming. This restriction meant two things: that only a few Africans would participate in coffee farming, and that large-scale settler farmers would continue to dominate coffee farming and trading. This domination continued to the post-colonial period. Smallholder production picked up after the post-colonial government began to emphasise production through cooperative societies and expansion into areas suited for coffee production.

During the colonial period, the government and settler farmers established institutions to support coffee production, processing and marketing. In 1909, settlers established the Coffee Growers Association (CGA) for the articulation of their interests. In 1917 the Coffee Planters Union (CPU) replaced the CGA and began to demand for formation of a marketing board. In 1933, the Legislative Council enacted formation of a Coffee Board to oversee production, quality and marketing in the country. Following this, in 1935, the government again formed the Kenyan Coffee Auctions Limited (KCA). The first auction of Kenyan coffee took place in September 1935. In 1944, the government started a research centre in Ruiru to inform coffee production practices. This initiative became the origins of Coffee Research Foundation. A marketing board was also established in 1946 to address marketing concerns.

From the outset, the government played a very central role in the production and marketing of coffee. It regulated production, processing, and marketing. This was due to several reasons including the need by the colonial administration to promote the colonial settler economy by ensuring little or no competition between settlers and black Africans. It was also in line with the evolving centrality of the state in governing economic development both in the colonies and at the centre.

The post-colonial government assumed this legacy. It continued to control and regulate economic development as it became the most important agent for development. Several legislations paving room for state control of the different sectors were introduced where they did not exist. The agricultural sector, which had grown to become the backbone of the economy, received significant attention in this regard. One emphasis that the government placed in the development of the agricultural sector at the time was development of small-scale holdings in coffee farming. Through credit schemes and extension services, the importance and number of smallholder agricultural farmers rapidly increased. In the coffee industry, the government encouraged these farmers to form cooperative societies in order to increase efficiency in production as well as to get maximum benefits. We now discuss the main institutions involved in the production and marketing of coffee prior to liberalisation. Problems associated with the state's involvement in the sector are also outlined.

PRE-LIBERALISATION PRODUCTION AND TRADING

Production and marketing of coffee prior to liberalisation involved several institutional actors. These included the producers, the cooperative societies, the milling actors and the marketing board. The relation among these players was maintained by the functions that each played. However, both the small and large-scale estate producers were the most important players in the production. Trade of coffee also was under the control of cooperative societies and marketing boards. The cooperatives were only important in terms of collecting coffee and delivering through the Unions for milling by the Kenya Planters Cooperative Union (KPCU). They were also important in receiving payments on behalf of the farmers (for details see Nyoro, 1994; Coffee Board of Kenya, 1996; Coffee Research Foundation, 1994; Institute of Economic Affairs, 2000). The estates delivered directly to the KPCU. Coffee Board of Kenya (CBK) would then sell the coffee, through Kenya Coffee Auctions, to exporters. Proceeds to farmers would follow the same chain, (Figure 11.1).

Production

For the purpose of preparing for coffee farming, a farmer was required to get a farm license from CBK. The farmer would then register with the local cooperative society and the society would assign a registration number. This registration number would later be required for getting credit facilities in the form of inputs and general support services. After registration, the cooperative society would provide certified seedlings. Usually, the societies germinated seedlings under careful supervision and subsequent certification by CBK/CRF. Staff from Coffee Research

Foundation (CRF) trained staff from the cooperative societies on the correct germination procedures while agricultural extension workers supervised and/or monitored use of correct procedures in germinating and planting the seedlings suited for different types of soils in areas suited for coffee farming. Thus, control Quality was inbuilt at the very early stages of coffee production.

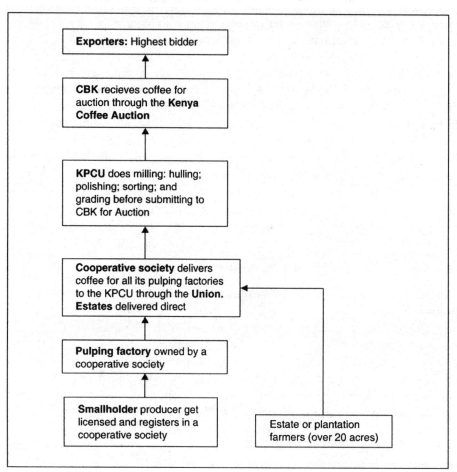

Figure 11.1: Pre-liberalisation Linkages in Coffee Farming and Marketing

The law was also used to ensure quality control in coffee farming. The law provided what was required of the farmer in coffee production and marketing. Importantly, the law restricted growth of coffee only in areas suited for coffee production. Agricultural extension officers assisted farmers in determining the type of seedlings required in different areas. They also ensured that farmers adhered to correct spacing between the seedlings. The law prohibited inter-cropping and uprooting of coffee trees. Through the law, farmers maintained quality and farm discipline.

The smallholder farmers registered with cooperative societies for purposes of processing coffee collectively. Each cooperative society had pulping factories where farmers would deliver their coffee cherry. However, one could deliver only to a factory owned by the members' cooperative society. Those who had several holdings scattered in different locations could pick cherry and deliver to the nearest factory owned by the cooperatives society in which they were members.

At the pulping factory, the cherry would be sorted into various grades or classes ranging from class one to class three with class one being the highest quality grade. Specially trained employees would examine the beans keenly and direct the farmer on how to sort the beans into good quality beans, fair quality, and dry or poor quality beans. Thus, farmer would sort a day's delivery into the various 'quality categories'. Each class of beans was pulped and fermented separately. After pulping, washing and sun drying would follow. A pulping plant had its source of clean water for this purpose. All these processes were labour intensive; farmers provided the bulk of the required labour while the cooperatives employed support staff to assist in the day-to-day operations such as sun drying, packaging and storage.

These processes were supervised through an elaborate governance structure comprising elected and administrative officials. Each pulping plant would have an elected representative(s) to oversee, on behalf of members, the different aspects of processing such as the grading system and quality control. They were also charged with the responsibility of ensuring that collective labour regulations were strictly adhered to. Favours, biases and corrupt behaviour on the part of administrative staff or farmers would be reported to the representatives who would then forward the complaints to the management committee. In other words, self-regulation was central in the organisation of coffee production and trading especially at this level.

The estates had their own pulping plants. Estate owners were also required by law to have a licence to operate a farm. They used to pulp their own coffee. Because of strict control by the government, there was no relationship between the estates and the smallholder factories. Nonetheless, production of coffee in the estates was also labour intensive; smallholders supplied labour if they were proximate to their location.

Processing: Cooperative Societies and Unions

Unions and cooperatives were important for the smallholders. Unions were an amalgamation of several societies. They were established under the Cooperative Act for the purposes of supervising operations of the member factories and to ensure reduction in processing and handling costs (Nyoro, 1994: 19). Cooperatives assisted in collective processing of farmers' coffee. They received coffee from the different pulping points and transported it for milling on behalf of the farmers. They also received payment on behalf of the farmers. The cooperatives, in this case, were meant to facilitate coffee production and marketing and ensure efficiency in all stages.

The management of the cooperatives and the Unions was in the control of the farmers themselves through their representatives. Farmers elected their representatives into the Committee that was responsible for the management of the society. The Committee would make decisions on issues such as how much would be deducted from farmers for the purpose of administration of the societies and Unions, the number of workers required for certain period, coffee development programmes, and other administrative issues. The members were also responsible for articulating farmers' grievances to the Unions as well as to the administrative officials. The Committee members receive financial allowances and other privileges such as exemption from collective labour in the pulping factories. Some of those interviewed for this study pointed out that the Committee members had certain important privileges that cut them above the ordinary peasants. The responsibility to make important decisions made the Committee positions very competitive. They pointed out that it was only the wealthy peasants who vied for positions to become officials. Some respondents observed that elections for Committee membership were like any other election. Local elites viciously fought for these positions. They would use their wealth to out-compete each other.

Elections of such officials were made difficult by entry of local political factors. In some of these cases, local politicians aligned with certain candidates for key committee positions in order to ensure that they had a firm grip on the management of the cooperatives. This was necessitated often by the need to have the numeric strength of the cooperatives as a base of support. Struggle over such numbers, therefore, occasioned vicious conflicts and deep politicisation of the cooperative societies. As a result of this, local political factionalism would spill into the elections and subsequently into the management of the cooperatives. Again, where this was the situation, there would always be an opposition team waiting to wrest power from the incumbent management teams. Such conflicts had negative consequences on the management of the cooperatives as organisations. Embezzlement of funds and general mismanagement of resources became a characteristic of many coffee cooperative societies.

Annual general meetings for each cooperative society provided farmers with the opportunity to raise questions concerning management of the society and their factories. Farmers would use the annual general meetings to question how the cooperatives or even the Union and the pulping plants were managed. In most cases, those who lost in the competition over Committee positions would organise themselves into an opposition faction through which members articulated their positions. The coffee political factions therefore had important functions. They were an important means for providing 'checks and balances' on the governance of the local cooperatives as well as ensuring accountability of elected officials.

In some places, the elected officials lacked basic education. They would be elected on account of their relative success in businesses or on account of having relatively large coffee holdings. Such qualities often attracted attention from other ordinary farmers. In the words of local respondents, these qualities simply made them look like they could lead others. This situation obtained in the 1970s. Respondents in both Meru and Nyeri generally noted that teachers, the clergy and retired civil servants, among others, became interested in the local politics of coffee from the early 1980s. This was the period following the coffee boom. From then on, the struggle over cooperatives became much more intense and continued to intensify with the entry of local political factors. It may be argued therefore that the local elites and other notables became much more interested in the coffee industry because committee membership was a gainful occupation.

In the meantime, the Unions assisted the cooperative societies by providing technical advisory services. This included recruiting and training management staff and providing bookkeeping services. Unions also negotiated credit facilities with the banks for the societies. The societies would later use this to provide farm inputs to the farmers. The technical role played by the Unions has been on decline since the liberalisation. However, in some cases, the Unions have disappeared altogether. Others have diversified into other economic activities.

Milling and Marketing

Kenya Planters Cooperative Union (KPCU) provided milling services to both the smallholders and estate farmers. It was established as a service organisation to mill farmers' coffee, provide advisory services to farmers and to provide them with credit facilities. KPCU had a milling monopoly that was founded in law: the law required that coffee parchment be delivered to a commercial miller where it would also be graded before being taken to Coffee Board of Kenya for sale. The law also allowed private planters who wished to mill their own coffee to do so provided they got a licence from CBK. However, very few licenses were given.

Farmers, both smallholders and large-scale estate farmers, had a role in the management of KPCU. They elected their representatives to the KPCU's governing board. These representatives were the avenues through which farmers' cooperative societies articulated their problems to the milling body. In spite of the KPCU being a farmers' body, the government had an overwhelming influence on its management especially because of its relationship with the state controlled Coffee Board of Kenya (CBK). On several occasions in the 1980s, for instance, the government influenced both hiring and firing of chief officers of the farmers' body. In line with the trend of appointment to public positions, those appointed to head KPCU were individuals loyal to senior politicians allied to powerful individuals in government. Political patronage as a method of appointing senior managers in both KPCU and CBK gradually led to mismanagement and embezzlement of funds. To ensure that the management of KPCU was in the hands of loyal individuals, senior politicians in government infiltrated the local electoral processes to ensure that only loyal individuals would be elected to represent farmers in the board of KPCU. The same approach was used in the composition of CBK and the Cooperative Bank, the bank which both KPCU and CBK used to process payments to farmers.

After milling, the KPCU delivered coffee to CBK for marketing. CBK in turn offered the coffee for sale through a contracted broker – Kenya Coffee Auctioneers Ltd (KCA) – in a centralised coffee auction. Buying of coffee at the auction was through competitive bidding. After the bidding process was through, the winning dealer would get authority from the CBK to export the coffee. The payment procedure to the farmers was usually that the grower was paid an initial payment within 14 days after milling. Payment for coffee bought in the auction was done within seven days from the date of the winning bid. Payments were made after levies, taxes, deductions for marketing costs, milling charges and co-operative societies processing costs in case of small-scale farmers. This meant that the farmer would get at least two instalments; the first after coffee milling and the second or final payment after the auctioning. This mode of payment provided the smaller holder farmers with opportunities to plan for investments and attend to other basic household needs. Some respondents argued that they considered this form of payment as a way of saving money; they were always guaranteed of these payments and therefore they would plan their investments with certainty about the security of the source of funding. To them, delays in payment were often attributed to the inability of their elected officials to follow up the payments with KPCU and the Coffee Board of Kenya. On the other hand, elected officials, aware that delays in payment to farmers would cost them their seats, often organised to get bank loans or credit facilities awaiting payments from KPCU. Respondents among some cooperative societies in Meru, pointed out that this resulted in high indebtedness and subsequent high turnover of committee members because of their inability to find ways and means of paying the debts.

The above discussion clearly shows that quality control is an important aspect of coffee production and processing in the period before liberalisation. The cooperatives had inbuilt mechanisms for enhancing quality production using especially the coffee cherry collection points in the various pulping plants. Overseeing quality thus was an inbuilt feature of the local cooperative societies around which all smallholder coffee production was organised. The second important observation is that the peasants had a role in the management of the industry. This was the function played by their elected officials. The elected officials, however, lacked basic management skills. Some were elected in these positions because of their successes in coffee farming or local businesses. Mostly, those elected were the local notables. Over time and with increasing importance of coffee after the coffee boom of the 1970s, local elites became active participants in local coffee politics. They turned to competing for local committee positions, which many saw as any other gainful occupation.

POST-LIBERALISATION: WHAT IS NEW?

What has liberalisation of the economy done for the coffee sector? Has the structure of production and trading changed in any significant manner? In 1992 the government announced a major policy change in the coffee industry. The change underlined a three-phased liberalisation of the sector with the focus on production, marketing, financing and farmer payment system. The first phase aimed at introducing auctioning of coffee in US dollars at the Nairobi coffee auction. There was also introduction of foreign currency retention accounts.

The second phase included introduction of optional direct sales at the coffee auction. Societies and Estate owners were given the option to choose between the old pool system of payment and a new one that involved direct payment (out of the pool payment) immediately after the sale of coffee. The third phase concerned liberalisation of the coffee milling. This required licensing of more commercial millers to compete against KPCU, and give farmers more choices in the milling and marketing of their coffee. This phase also involved making of rules and regulations for commission agents. The section that follows examines the change that has taken place over the years. These are discussed from the production chain upwards. Figure 11.2 shows the new linkages.

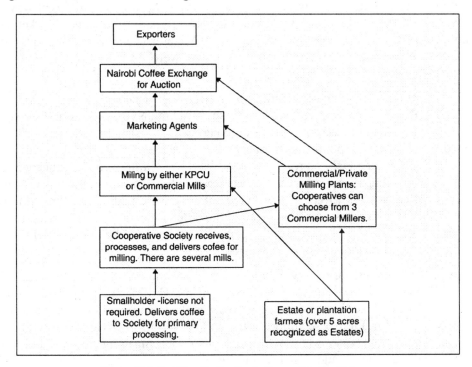

Figure 11.2: Post-liberalisation Production and Trading Linkages

The regulatory structure of the coffee sector has remained the same even after liberalisation. Figure 11.2 show that the structure and linkages have not undergone significant changes. Farmers continue to deliver coffee to the cooperative societies receives for primary processing. The cooperatives in turn deliver coffee for milling. Unlike in the past when KPCU was the only milling plant, liberalisation opened the space for new private commercial mills – Thika Coffee Mills and SOCFINAF (liberalisation also allowed establishment of private mills. These do not mill coffee from the cooperative societies. Estates own some of the private mills).

A second feature of the post-liberalisation period is the licensing of 'new marketing agents'. Whereas in the past Coffee Board of Kenya was the only body marketing coffee, the law now provides for new marketing agents. However, from around 2001 the commercial millers were allowed to operate as the marketing agents on interim basis. The millers thus continued to operate as 'new marketing agents'. From the marketing agents, coffee is taken to the Nairobi Coffee Exchange for auction, after which it is exported. Liberalisation, therefore, did not mean radical restructuring of the trading linkages. It nonetheless eroded the monopoly of both the

KPCU and the CBK as the main actors in the coffee processing and marketing space.

Moreover, liberalisation was a slow and contested process both at the local and at the national level. It involved extensive consultations at all levels from the primary cooperative society level to the national level. The process was surrounded by a variety of forces. Different actors evolved to inform the process in different ways. At the same time, the regulatory structure tended to remain the same. Marketing continued to be done through the cooperatives. A major change, however, was at the level of processing. Several coffee millers were licensed and additional marketing agencies given licences.

A shown in figure 11.2, under liberalisation, licensing of new farms is no longer required under the law. Respondents for this study in both Nyeri and Meru observed that even prior to liberalisation, this requirement was not strictly followed. In the view of some of the respondents, 'farmers simply pretended that they were adding to their original holdings'. They 'knew well that they did not require a licence to expand their holdings'. Apparently, this was a gap in the legislation; the law did not demand coffee farmers to get a new licence if they were adding seedlings to an existing holding. Farmers used this legal gap to extend their holdings. Agricultural extension officers would provide the required technical advice to ensure the seedlings were of quality and appropriate to the locality.

An even more interesting observation is that farmers and cooperative societies did not any longer insist on quality seedlings from the Coffee Research Foundation (CRF) in Ruiru. While the cooperative societies argued that transport costs incurred in travelling to Ruiru to get seedlings or the costs of technical advice were too high to be met by members, some farmers simply said that 'engaging in the search for quality seedlings was an additional cost to the already high costs incurred in coffee production'. CRF was also said to be lacking certain varieties when farmers require them probably because the demand for seedlings from the Foundation has been on decline. Those who wanted seedlings resorted to preparing their own nurseries using the beans from their own farms. Others bought from private estates if they happened to have them. This led to situations in which a single holding would have different varieties of coffee trees including varieties meant for different types of soil. On the whole, there was no strict adherence to quality guidelines in selecting seedlings, as was the case in the past. High cost of production and general neglect of coffee farming rules are to blame for this. Poor returns to investment in coffee, on the other hand, are the main culprit. Farmers, as well as their respective cooperative societies, voiced concern about the poor returns, which they blamed for everything going wrong in the sector.

Farmers were not getting inputs from the cooperative societies because the societies have collapsed and/or have broken up into different societies. Others were re-constituting anew. Credits for inputs, which the cooperatives used to provide in the past, were no longer available. And even if it was available, some respondents stated that they went for credit because of the generally high costs of coffee production. Local shopkeepers are the main source of inputs for farmers still interested in using inputs. Other farmers were improvising with locally available materials for example, manure instead of industrial fertiliser. A few got inputs from the societies that were capable of providing inputs. Most of these societies, however, did not have regular supplies because demand was uneven. Where societies supply inputs, they required the farmers to pay using a cash check-off system in which the cost of inputs supplied to a farmer was deducted from the farmer's payment. The problem, however, was that some farmers do not pay the cooperatives when they were required to do so. They absconded on payment using different registration numbers. In some instances, a household would have more than one registration account or account name in the same cooperative society. A spouse would use one account name to acquire inputs, while the other would be used to deliver coffee to the society. Payment would usually be made through the account name used for delivery of coffee. The amount of cherry delivered to the account used for inputs would certainly be less than the amount delivered to the account where the family expects payments from. To most respondents, farmers began absconding on payment in tandem with declining income from coffee. In view of many, the farmers' investment in coffee was not paying off yet the law prevented them from uprooting or intercropping. It was generally difficult to sustain heavy familial investments in coffee holdings in terms of labour and materials. To avoid wholesome deductions of the costs incurred in buying inputs, farmers had to circumvent the regulation using different account names in the cooperative society. Still, there were farmers who could not sustain their membership in the cooperative societies owing to familial demands for basic needs which declining proceeds from coffee could not meet. Some of these farmers were highly indebted to the cooperative societies. Unable to pay debts to the societies, they absconded from participation in cooperative societies. They became the most important source of coffee for private dealers and estates. They turned to selling their coffee to the local coffee traders at the farm gate. They defaulted on payment to the cooperative society and withdrew from the cooperatives altogether.

Overall, circumvention of society regulations by farmers had the effect of indebtedness on the part of the cooperative societies. Several cooperative societies got into indebtedness with banks, which had lent money for inputs and credit facilities. Neither the state nor the cooperative societies developed mechanisms to follow up on the farmers that owed money to the cooperatives. Poor self-regulations within the cooperative societies and poor law enforcement mechanisms generally contributed to the collapse of some of the cooperative societies.

What ought to be noted at this stage is that the strict control and regulations that centred on quality of production in the coffee sector are thawing away. Over the years, use of quality seedlings and emphasis on quality process of production, including use of inputs, has been responsible for the fame of Kenya coffee in the world market. The loosening of quality control that is evolving in tandem with withdrawal of the state in the main stages of coffee production is undermining the quality of coffee produced by smallholders. It is also evident, at least for the moment, that the cooperative societies do not have the capacity to enforce self-regulations in the production process. Problems around internal governance have undermined efficiency of some of the cooperative societies leading to collapse of some of them. Moreover, the committee system is meant to take up this responsibility. The committees, however, tend to lack the capacity to do so. They depend increasingly on social sanction, which may not work in a purely economic setting.

Coffee Production

Coffee production in Kenya has been fluctuating. From about 51,000 metric tons in 1990, production rose to about 62,000 metric tons in 1994 and declined to 29,000 metric tons in 2001. The quality of coffee has also been on decline. Coffee in class one to three constituted only about 9 percent of total production in the 2000/2001 period. This marked a decline from about 20 per cent in the previous period (Kenya, 2001a). Field findings from the two regions, Meru and Nyeri, show that production did not increased significantly. Figures for Meru region clearly show that coffee production in each district in Meru (the region has three administrative districts: Meru Central, Meru South and Meru North) was on decline. Although records for all the years in the region were difficult to obtain, available records show that production in the entire region was uneven.

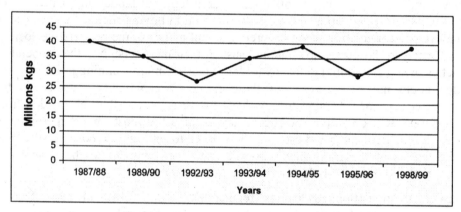

Figure 11.3: Meru Central Coffee Production Figures

Source: Records from the Cooperative Societies in Meru Central

In Meru Central, production stood at 40 million Kgs in 1987/88 periods and decreased to 35 million Kgs in 1988/89 period. Then this dropped to about 26 million Kg in 1992/93 period before rising to 39 million Kgs in the 1994/95 period. Thereafter, production declined but gradually rose again in 1998/1999 period (see figure 11.3).

These figures clearly show that coffee production did not improve in any significant way in the district. Coffee production in the district was stagnant for almost one decade. Farmers in the area underlined that 'there are very few people interested in expanding their holdings and also few farmers uprooting their coffee trees because the law prevented them from doing so'. Some of those interviewed observed that they had turned to dairy keeping and to small-scale horticultural farming because they could not rely on coffee income. Some planted fodder crops in the coffee holdings for dairy animals while others planted horticultural crops on the sides of the holdings. One may argue that although legal restrictions prevented people from removing their coffee trees from their holding, the farmers in the district evolved different approaches to circumvent the law. Furthermore, the legal restrictions did not lead to increased coffee production. The law simply caused stagnation in levels of production.

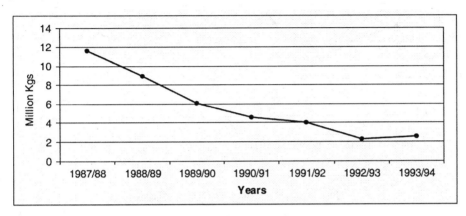

Figure 11.4: Meru North Coffee Production Figures

Source: Records from the Cooperatives Societies in Meru North

Production in Meru North district shows the sharpest decline from the late 1980s (see Figure 11.4). Production in the district was on the decline from the late 1980s to around 1993/1994 period. The district had three cooperative societies and in all of them, farmers complained about how coffee farming had become insignificant in terms of household incomes. Many complained that they could not depend on coffee to pay fees or attend to basic familial needs. There was thus widespread neglect of coffee holdings in many parts of the district. Indeed, in most cases around Nyambene hills, many farmers had intercropped their holdings with food crops and with little care about the legal provisions about inter-cropping. Some of them pointed out that in the past, it was the responsibility of agricultural extension officers to monitor how farmers were taking care of coffee holdings but such services were no longer available. They pointed out that Provincial Administration officials had not bothered to ask anyone and therefore everybody had taken to turning coffee holdings into food crop holdings. In the upper parts of Nyambene hills, many farmers had turned into Miraa (khat- or a stimulant plant) farming. In these areas, the stimulant plant was grown widely in all areas that used to produce coffee. With a daily income many times that of coffee, planting miraa became a major occupation for many peasants in the area and the main alternative. It out-competed both tea and coffee in the area.

Meru South witnessed a fluctuation similar to other regions (see figure 11.5). Like in Meru Central, production in Meru South was fluctuating throughout the 1990s. There was neither significant increase nor decrease especially after 1992/1993 period. For about five years from 1993, production appears not to have improved in any significant manner. Again in this district, many farmers had turned to dairy keeping and horticulture away from coffee. In the view of many respondents, it was not possible to pay attention to coffee farming because of poor coffee prices. People had, therefore, turned to agricultural activities in which they were guaranteed regular incomes.

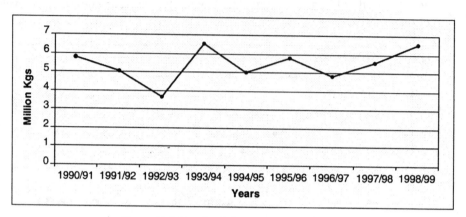

Figure 11.5: Meru South Coffee Production Figures

Source: Records from Cooperative Societies in Meru South

Coffee production in Nyeri also appear to have assumed a similar trend; no significant growth in production. Figure 11.6 shows this trend in the district.

Production in Nyeri was also not impressive. There was decline from 1995 to 1997 period. From then on, production picked to the level similar to the one in around 1991/92 period. This generally suggests poor growth in production.

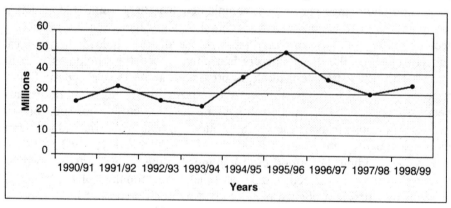

Figure 11.6: Nyeri Coffee Production Figures

Source: Records from Cooperatives Societies in Nyeri

These figures for both Meru and Nyeri are evidence of sluggish growth in coffee production as well as rapid decline in some areas. One observation arising from these figures then is that coffee production/farming is no longer highly valued in areas that used to have it as the most important cash crop. There have been no incentives for farmers to increase their size of holdings and/or increase on yields.

Respondents were pointing to a trend in which many were intercropping coffee or uprooting it altogether. Others have been subdividing holdings among family members without adding the acreage under coffee. Many have not bothered to rehabilitate their holdings: they see no cause to do it.

With regard to liberalisation of the coffee industry, there is need to reiterate that it did not occasion any significant recovery in production of coffee. In some places, there was slight improvement in production figures. Others showed rapid decline. A conclusion that can be made here is that recovery of coffee production is going to be slow even though liberalisation has been introduced. Farmers lack capital to rehabilitate their farms (for those who retained them after the fall of prices in the 1980s) while others have shifted focus to other activities such as horticultural and dairy farming. Still, one may want to add that there is no correlation between liberalisation and production figures shown above given that the trend towards a decline in production had started way before liberalisation measures were introduced. That is, one may not see the consequences of liberalisation in the sector until all the policy reforms have been implemented.

A related observation is that policy reforms in the coffee industry should not be seen in isolation from the broader economic policies and in particular, agricultural policies. Notably, broader social-economic policies are required to spur growth in the sector. Introducing reforms pertaining to a single sector in the context in which sectors are interlinked will not produce the desired results. Moreover, there are important legal restrictions that appear to be constraining utilization of holdings, and yet, these restrictions are not contributing to coffee production. Liberalisation policies, therefore, have clearly failed to interlink sectoral policies; hence, continued neglect and sluggish growth of coffee.

Liberalisation, Cooperative Societies and Mills

One component of the coffee industry highly affected by the growing withdrawal of the government from the sector is the cooperative societies. In both Nyeri and Meru, many of the old cooperatives broke up into smaller cooperative societies. Reasons for the split included general disillusionment with the management of the societies and the resultant consolidation of different factions each seeking to stamp its character on the management of the society. Others were the result of disagreements over where to mill the coffee. While some would prefer continued milling with KPCU, others argued for milling through the newly licensed players. Again, some farmers were in favour of smaller and better-managed units than big cooperatives with excessive overheads. This resulted in many cooperatives splitting into very small units.

In Nyeri and Meru, the trend was towards transforming each pulping factory (and the members delivering cherry to that factory) into a cooperative society. In January 2001, for instance, Mukurweini cooperative society with a membership of 19,000 members and 28 pulping factories, split into 13 cooperative societies. The split was brought about by disagreements over leadership; there had developed several factions within the cooperative. Each of these factions pursued different positions regarding the management of the society. Those supporting the split argued that 'farmers were paying heavily for the maintenance of a large cooperative society'. A split into smaller units would enable 'members to pay less for overheads and, at the same time, give individual farmers an opportunity to participate directly in making management decisions'. According to them, decisions could be made without consulting members in the large cooperative. A smaller group would take less time in making decisions concerning especially where to mill farmers' coffee. These arguments finally led to the split of the giant cooperative society. Mutation process is not yet over. Some of the new societies prefer splitting further — again, depending on the nature of factions involved in the conflict over split.

This trend was also witnessed in Meru district. In Meru central, 14 cooperative societies split into 52 societies. In Meru North, three societies split into 30 cooperative societies each with its own management team. Here, like in Nyeri, the basic unit for the new societies is the local pulping factory. The split of the cooperatives also meant distribution of assets among the new cooperative societies. In all cases, however, distribution of assets was accompanied by conflicts between the different societies. Sometimes, local electoral politics spilled over into these conflicts thereby deepening the tensions. The split has thus been simply acrimonious; each group seeking to get maximum benefit. Split of the cooperatives into smaller units was said to have resulted into individual cooperative societies being vulnerable; they cannot manage price risks as they did in the giant cooperative.

Overhead costs for the smaller units, contrary to arguments by factions supporting the split, increased because each of them has to hire new officers to manage the society. Each had to elect a management committee and put operating framework in place. The costs for supporting a management staff for these new cooperative societies were undoubtedly high. In each of the new societies, farmers elected committee members from among themselves. The Committee also recruited the administrative staff who were charged with day to day operations of the society. The management committee (elected from among the Committee members) is responsible for making policies at the society level and monitors the administrative staff. Thus, the Committee members have certain important management duties that are almost similar to those of the employees. A conflict of attribution between the Committee and administrative staff is a common feature in the new societies.

Membership in some of the new societies was also too low to have adequate coffee production to support and run a society in a profitable manner. This also had certain implications for the pulping capacity of the new societies; for example, the capacity for some of them was under-utilised (under 500,000 kg) because the society did not have members with sufficient amount of coffee to support a pulping plant on their own.

The Unions had become the victims of this development. Some wound up while others were afloat because of the diversified investments they had made before the liberalisation process. In Meru district, only the Meru Central Farmers Union was in operation and active in supporting the societies that remained in its membership. The Union had diverse investments including flour milling and dairy production in addition to coffee support services. Those that relied on coffee support services wound up. The Unions depended on exploitation of farmers' primary societies; they levied high fees for the support services provided to the societies. The splits in these societies and the reconstitution of the societies meant limited role for the Unions. Because of this, the societies were outsourcing the services previously provided by the Unions on their own. The Unions were unlikely to re-emerge given that the societies were now selling their coffee directly without going through the Unions.

As already mentioned, one important outcome of liberalisation was licensing of new commercial millers in addition to KPCU. There are now five milling outlets in the country. Three of which are commercial: KPCU; Thika Coffee Mills and SOCFINAF. The private include Gatatha and Kibubutu and they mill their own coffee. The entry of new millers resulted in increased milling capacity from 140,000 metric tonnes in 1993 to 230,000 metric tonnes by end of 1996 (Kenya, 2001a). But milling capacity increased in the midst of declining production. This meant heightened competition among the millers over whatever coffee was available. KPCU was certainly more advantaged in this competition given its infrastructure.

The new entrants devised different strategies, some unethical, to access farmers' coffee. Some of them were buying coffee directly from farmers while others supported different 'leadership factions' in the cooperative societies so that they could use their influence to take farmers' coffee to their mills. It is in connection with this that some of those interviewed blamed the new millers for the split of some of the cooperative societies. They argued that the officers in these milling plants, unable to compete with KPCU, turned to bribing the management committees in the cooperative societies so that they can be contracted to mill the coffee for them. Scouting for coffee led therefore to playing one faction against the other and sometimes financing the split itself. When there were such splits, the new millers got at least one faction to work with.

In addition to bribing the committee members, the millers allegedly hired people to disrupt annual general meetings in the cooperative societies where they felt their faction would lose in the event of a vote on where to deliver coffee. Since such choice was sometimes made in the annual general meetings and/or by the management committee, the crafty millers through local agents had to scout for support from among some of the members. This had the effect of intensifying the conflicts among the farmers as well as deepening the divisions between farmers and the management committees.

New Local Traders

At the local level, there were coffee traders who bought coffee from smallholders in order to sell to other traders including estate farmers. Speculators emerged; they bought coffee from smallholders at farm gates and at very low price. They delivered the same cherry to the societies where they were registered as members or sold to estate farmers altogether. The price the traders paid farmers was usually lower than what the farmers had received in the last payment in their cooperative societies. In addition to buying directly from farmers, some traders requested the farmers to deliver to their registered accounts in the cooperative societies. After delivery, the farmer would present a receipt of delivery to the trader for payment. This method was quite common in areas where the provincial administration and the local co-operative societies were against the buying and selling of coffee outside of registered pulping plants or societies.

There were cases of estates buying coffee from farmers. They bought from smallholders sometimes because of the quality of their coffee and for the purpose of mixing it with that from their own farms in order to improve on the latter's quality. In Meru, this was common among estate farms in Meru North. Estate farmers employed agents and lined them up on the roads leading to the pulping factories and/or cooperative societies. They carried weighing machines, empty bags and money for the day (enough determined by how they plan to transport the coffee to the estate). Sometimes the agents walked early in the morning around farm holdings to negotiate with farmers the price they would pay for the coffee once picked. In most cases, they visited holdings where they were certain the farmer would be picking coffee. Prices were negotiated even before the start of picking. Once they had agreed on payments, the agents would move to another holding for similar negotiations. They only came back to pick the coffee and to make payments to the farmer at the farm gate. Coffee-for-cash-payment had become so common that many smallholders were involved in it in all the areas.

Poor peasants were eager to sell to them. Some divided their coffee into two separate portions every day they were picking coffee. One was meant for sale to the private trader to get cash money on the spot. The second portion was meant for the cooperative society. The latter was used as a saving: if prices improved, then the farmer would benefit. If the prices were poor, then the farmer would have compensated this with the sale to the private traders no matter the price.

Some farmers preferred selling their coffee to the cooperatives in spite of the problems around their management. They observed that selling to cooperatives provided opportunities to do planning for the coffee earnings. Secondly, the cooperatives provided one with credit facilitates or inputs that they would use to improve their farms. Private traders did not give such facilities. In their view, the only problem with the societies was delays in payments and mismanagement. They expected these to be resolved with time.

In general one may argue that the local traders were speculators. The majority bought coffee from smallholders on the assumption that prices would increase. Others bought in order to sell to estate farmers who are not keen to be seen buying from smallholders. This notwithstanding, traders were an important source of income for the smallholders. Many of them made distress sales in order to attend to pressing needs at home. Some of the farmers complained that it took long to get money if they delivered to the local societies and therefore they found it better to sell to those ready to give cash. Moreover, they were generally uncertain about how much they would finally get from their societies. There were those who argued that the societies were highly indebted owing to mismanagement and, therefore, they (farmers) were not ready to assist in paying the debts they did not contribute to.

Traders generally did not give attention to quality; they preferred quantity. The more they bought the better for their proceeds. Since most of them had no time and space to check on the quality of what they receive from farmers, they insist on paying as little as possible. This of course had implications for the quality of coffee that was delivered to estate farmers; it was of relatively less quality than that from cooperative societies. The evolvement of traders at this level thus had compromised coffee quality.

It is worth noting that liberalisation evolved a situation where enforcing some of the regulations is difficult. Significant, new traders emerged at the local level to buy coffee from farmers at the farm gates without constraints. Although regulations so not allow such trading to take place, CBK has very little or no capacity to enforce regulations in the sector. After losing the leverage it had in coffee marketing, the board did not have sanctions. One may argue then that liberalisation weakened the mechanisms for regulating activities in the coffee sector and this would impact on quality.

CONCLUSION

The discussion has pointed out that coffee production in Kenya has been emphatic on quality. Quality control has been an important feature in coffee production from the early stages of planting seedlings to the stage of processing of coffee berries. Prior to liberalisation, the government coffee agencies had a role in enforcing quality controls. Agricultural extension officers visited the fields to provide both technical advice on crop husbandry and to monitor quality procedures. This was an important role played by government agencies. Cooperative societies complemented this service by recruiting staff to supervise quality procedures at the pulping factories. Every Cooperative Society had a Management Committee that made decisions regarding management of the Cooperative Society. The Committee also had a role to play in enhancing quality; the Committee supervised the administrative staff to ensure quality procedures were adhered to. This was all important given that the coffee earnings depended on the quality of coffee delivered. It was the responsibility of the Committee, therefore, to ensure they complemented government efforts in ensuring they got the best out of their society.

Liberalisation reforms, however, appear to have evolved new conditions through which farmers were neglecting quality. There were new traders in the market whose main concern was the amount of coffee they bought from farmers rather than the class or grade of coffee. Moreover, the conditions under which new traders bought coffee from the farm gates were not sufficient to foster quality controls. Firstly, they collected coffee already packed in bags at the farm gate. Given that they had to collect coffee from several holdings, they generally did not have sufficient time for quality checks. Liberalisation reforms, arguably, contributed to the shift of attention from quality.

An important observation is that, in spite of liberalisation, production of coffee has not increased. Fluctuation in output continued to characterise production since the early 1990s. Although this might not be attributed to liberalisation because such a fluctuation in production had begun to show even in the 1980s, it is important to note that liberalisation has not accelerated growth in production. Many farmers are yet to go back to coffee. They moved into new cash crops. Some crops earn them many more times than coffee. Incentives to go back to coffee farming are, therefore, not anchored in policy reforms alone as this may not spur growth in production. It is evident that factors outside the broad policy environment may have a role to play in this regard. Cash-on-delivery, for instance, has become an important incentive for farmers selling coffee to new traders. Cash upon delivery of coffee indeed may be argued to be gradually eroding the basis of existence of new cooperative societies.

Liberalisation has had an effect on the structure of cooperative societies. Licensing of new milling plants has occasioned intense conflicts within the societies sometimes leading to splits into smaller cooperative societies formed around the pulping plants. There are several leadership factions, which the new actors and institutions are scouting to gain support from. The rivalry between the milling plants, for instance, has spilled over into the governance of local cooperative societies occasioning deep divisions among members. Factions in the leadership of the coffee industry are now a common feature.

Institutions that emerged in the coffee industry through the new policy reforms appeared to be plunging the industry into governance problems. Smallholder coffee farmers as well as the estate farmers appeared ill equipped to resolve some of these problems. Similarly government coffee institutions lost their influence in the sector; they are not able to regulate the sector. They have weak mechanisms for enforcing regulations. Furthermore, the new actors have no direct relations with the state institutions in the coffee sector to suffer the consequences of any sanctions imposed by the government to ensure compliance with the law and coffee regulations.

The state appears to be withdrawing from some of its responsibilities without preparing farmers to take charge of the sector. Whether this is a transition period or note, it is clear that policy reforms in the sector should be seen within a broader social-political and economic context. The coffee sector reforms should not be implemented without reference to broader macro-economic and political reforms. They should be linked to the broader social-political and economic context because the sector does not operate in isolation. Activities in the coffee sector are anchored in a broader context comprising various dimensions. The 'coffee cup will continue to steam' as long as policies in the sector are not linked to the broader social-political and economic context on which coffee production and marketing is anchored.

REFERENCES

Coffee Board of Kenya (CBK). 1996. *Report of the Task Force on Liberalisation of the Coffee Industry*. Nairobi: Coffee Board of Kenya.

Coffee Research Foundation (CRF) 1994. "Coffee Production and Marketing under a Liberalized System in Kenya". A Report Prepared by a Technical Committee appointed by CRF.

Ikiara, G; Jama, M. A. and Amadi, J. O. 1993. "Agriculture Decline, Politics and Structural Adjustment in Kenya". In Gibbon, P. (ed.). *Social Change and Economic Reform in Africa*. Uppsala: Nordic Africa Institute.

Institute of Economic Affairs. 2000. *Our Problems, Our Solutions: An Economic Policy Agenda for Kenya*. Nairobi: Institute of Economic Affairs.

Kenya, Republic of. 2001a. "Sessional Paper No. 2 of 2001 on Liberalisation and Restructuring of Coffee Industry: Reforms in the Coffee Board of Kenya, Coffee Research Foundation and Privatization of Coffee Marketing Services of the Board". Nairobi: Government Printer.

Kenya, Republic of. 2001b. "Coffee Act, 2001 No. 9 of 2001". Nairobi: Government Printer.

Maitha, J. 1974. *Coffee in the Kenyan Economy: An Econometric Analysis*. Nairobi: East African Literature Bureau.

McMahon, G.1984. "International Commodity Agreement and a Small Developing Country: The Case of Kenya and the International Coffee Agreement". PhD Thesis, University of Ontario.

Mwangi, G. and Ndii, D. 2003. "Who is on the Act? Coffeecrats, Buccaneers and Kenya's Black Gold". In Briefing paper No1/2003. Nairobi: Kenya Leadership Institute.

Nyangito, H. 1998. "Agricultural Sector Performance in a Changing Policy Environment". A Paper Presented for the Annual IPAR National, 15-16 April 1998.

Nyoro, J. K. 1994. "Processing and Marketing Coffee in a Liberalised Market". In proceedings of a conference on Market Reforms, Agricultural Production and Food Security, Egerton University, June 1994.

Nyoro, J. 1999. "Challenges Facing the Coffee Industry and Way Forward". A Paper Presented to Coffee Stakeholders Meeting organized by KIPPRA, 17th Feb 1999, Nairobi.

Pedersen, P. O. and McCormick, D. 1999. "African Business Systems in a Globalising World". *Journal of Modern African Studies* 37(1): 109-135.

Ponte, S. 2002. "Quality and Trade Governance in Global Value Chains: The Case of Coffee Originating in East Africa". Paper prepared for a conference on Business Systems in Africa. Nairobi: Institute for Development Studies, Mimeo.

Ponte, S. 2000. "From Social Negotiation to Contact Strategies of Farm Labour Recruitment in Tanzania under Market Liberalization". *World Development* 28 (6):1017-1030.

Ponte, S. 1998. "Policy Reforms, Market Failures and Inputs Use in African Smallholder Agriculture", A Paper Presented at the Annual Meeting of the African Studies Association, Chicago, October 29-November 1, 1998.

Chapter 12

Trade and Transport: Business Linkages and Networks

Patrick O. Alila, Meleckidzedeck Khayesi, Walter Odhiambo and Poul Ove Pedersen

INTRODUCTION

Trade and transport are important leading producer services in Kenya. At both the domestic and international levels, trade contributes significantly in terms of generating output and employment. In Kenya, trade and transport is responsible for the creation of many jobs especially in the informal sector and forms an important component of the service sector. Furthermore, trade is often a country's biggest single source of finance. Exports from Kenya, for example, accounted for about 55% of the country's GDP in the period 1997-2000.

For trade to flourish, there is a need for an effective and reliable transportation system. Transport provides a crucial link in the chain of productive activities and facilitates access to and movement of goods and services for effective trade to take place domestically and internationally. Without a strong and functional transportation and communication system, countries are unlikely to have vibrant domestic markets and to reach international markets, thus curtailing their abilities to exploit potentials. Kenya's experience in the recent past has clearly shown that a run down and ineffective transportation and communication system severely affects performance in trade and reduces competitiveness. The poor state of infrastructure in Kenya has severally been blamed for the high cost of doing business in the country which has made the country's exports uncompetitive (Alila et al., 2003).

Although global trade and the spread of economic activities within and across borders have grown fairly fast in recent years, new developments in the enabling and space-shrinking technologies of transportation and communication are fundamentally transforming space-time relationships (Fitzisimmons, 2002). The outcome has been the emergence of global production networks in which manufacturing is highly spatially dispersed. In this kind of system for which transport and communication is crucial, raw materials and components used in producing a particular product may come from two different countries with the assembly and marketing in a third country.

Moreover, technological and other socio-economic changes have altered significantly the trade and transportation systems within national boundaries notably, in terms of changes in the trade and transportation networks and also in the functions of the actors. Indeed, new actors are emerging and new functions being crafted. For instance, containerisation – a modern technological device in warehousing and distribution – has sent ripples in the organisation of trade and transport. Containerisation has surmounted the physical and time constraints and in the Kenyan context weakened the links between heavy industries and rail. The pattern and style of trade in Kenya and many countries has also changed mainly due to trade liberalisation, with far reaching consequences for the overall economic framework for trade and transport.

The purpose of this chapter is to analyze the scope, pattern and trends of the interrelated services of trade and transportation in Kenya. We briefly review the historical and institutional origins of trade and transport, present an economic profile of the actors, and assess the nature and impact of technological and socio-economic changes on trade and transport networks. The study adopts a network or business system perspective and examines the key actors in trade, particularly wholesale and retail enterprises. In transport, rather than pay attention to infrastructure per se, we focus on transport operators and organizers as well as logistics.

The chapter is based on secondary and primary information collected in the period 1999-2002 as part of the CDR/IDS African business systems project. The primary information was obtained through a series of interviews carried out in a number of locations in Kenya and focusing on trade and transport agents (including individual traders, enterprises, institutions and the state). The secondary information was obtained from published official sources and research reports.

TRADE AND DISTRIBUTION IN KENYA: THREE FORMATIVE PERIODS

The Colonial Period: Era of Exclusivity

The present state of trade and transport in Kenya is a product of numerous processes and activities dating back to the colonial period. The historical origin of trade and transport in Kenya is, therefore, an important foundation to subsequent developments worth bearing in mind. First, we examine the development of commerce and trade through three formative phases: colonial, post-independence and reform periods. Secondly, the development of the transport system in Kenya is examined, focusing on the main modes: road, railway, water and pipeline.

Literature on the development of commerce and industry during the colonial era in Kenya contains evidence that the economy was largely divided into three hierarchically distinct racially-based compartments. There was first the Europeans who occupied the immensely productive agricultural land or the "White"

Highlands, with a monopoly of cash crop farming and political administrative power. The second group comprised of the Asians who dominated trade. There were then the majority native Africans, who, on the basis of apartheid-like segregation colonization policy, were bundled into the native reserves. The reserves were overcrowded and Africans forced into uneconomic subsistence farming and supply of labour to the modern sector of the economy. The general impression in the literature is that the three groups acted virtually like exclusive economic enclaves to the extent that there were for example, no Africans and Asians farming in the "White" Highlands, which was the preserve for Europeans, or Africans in retail trade in towns where Asians were given an upper hand. There was, however, some exchange between them in that, for instance, the Africans were expected to earn their living by working on the European farms and in Asian shops and residence, while the Asians peddled products from the European sector and abroad, and marketed African agricultural produce.

The predominance of the Asian community in trade has a history that dates back to the nineteenth century. Himbara (1993) has provided an excellent account of the emergence of the Indian merchants in Kenya. It all started with Indian merchants based on the East Coast of Africa who traded in goods originating from Europe and the Far East. These merchants would supply goods to the East African hinterland and also get from them goods which they sold abroad. This connection established what turned out to be major trade and distribution networks in Kenya subsequently resulting in the emergence of an Asian dominated merchant class in Kenya.

A major impetus to the development of trade in the country came with the building of the railway from the late 1890s. To build the railway, the British government brought in a large number of Indian workers. After the completion of the railway, most of the Indians went back but a number were left behind, some deep in the hinterland where they had started businesses, preceding in most cases, the establishment of the local government structures. It is thus not surprising even today to find Indian businesses in small trading centres deep in the hinterland of Kenya. A close network of merchants and Indian firms was thus established, which later moved into other areas such as money lending, manufacturing and banking. By 1920s, some East African Indian merchants had been able to move beyond retail into more of actual production. Companies such as the Kenya Aluminium Ltd (Kalu Works) and the Chandaria family of companies (now Comcraft) were established around this time (Lawrence, 1960 quoted by Himbara, 1993). This network of Indian merchants and industrialists are largely given credit for the emergence of the current countrywide arrangements of trade and distribution in Kenya. According to Mangat (1969):

> "These petty Indian merchants were the real founders of Indian commercial enterprises in the interior of East Africa- and helped to create trade, first in a small way and then in a large way, in areas where none had existed previously. With considerable fortitude and perseverance, they pioneered the establishment of dukas, of local trading centres and Indian bazaars in different districts; and by introducing the local populations to a variety of imported goods and later the rupee currency, they provided an incentive to greater local

production as well as the transition from a barter-to money based economy".
(Mangat, 1969 quoted in Himbara, 1993:101)

The Indian networks, did not, therefore, only introduce the local population to imports but were also instrumental in their local distribution. According to Hollingsworth (1960), no commodity could be distributed to the native customers in the interior without an Indian agency. The dominance of the Indians went on undeterred in most of the colonial period despite the Europeans' silent disapproval.

Post-independence: Empowering the Africans

At independence in 1963, the incoming African government felt strongly that there was a lot to be changed in commerce and industry (Himbara, 1993). The need for promotion of the indigenous African cause in commerce and industry was spelt out in virtually all policy documents and pronouncements at that time. It was indicated that although the government appreciated the role of foreign capital and large non-African investments, including the Asian component, there was a need to correct imbalances as a result of the inequities suffered by the African in particular under the colonial regime. To do this, the government embarked on what was subsequently known as the Kenyan Africanisation programme. It was a multi-faceted programme notably, including a land settlement programme for Africans as the initial step, due to the fact that land was and remains a highly emotive political issue on which a violent struggle was waged and independence won from the British.

To address the gaps in the area of commerce, the government saw the need to adopt a two-pronged approach in which with one hand, it enacted legislations, and with the other, created institutions to offer Africans chances for participation. By 1967, the government in quick succession had passed four important pieces of legislation. These were the Landlord and Tenant Act of 1966, the Immigration Act of 1967, the Trade Licensing Act of 1967, the Import, Export and Essential Supplies Act of 1967. The objective of the first two was to ensure that Africans had access to business premises and to control the inflow of foreigners who could take up opportunities meant for Africans. This was then seen as an effective way of ensuring that the native population had access to trade opportunities. The objective of the Trade Licensing Act was to exclude non-Africans from trading in the non-central areas. This was directed towards Asian traders who had already penetrated the hinterland. The Act specifically stipulated that non-citizens do not conduct business in specified goods in any place that is not a general business area.

The Act prohibited non-Africans from conducting trade in the main streets in urban centres in Kenya. In a fast move, quit notices were given to non-citizen owned shops and non-citizen employees. These shops were then turned over to Kenyans of African origin.

Parallel to this, the government created a number of institutions to empower the African to go into business. These included the Industrial and Commercial Development Corporation (ICDC), the Industrial Development Bank (IDB), and the Kenyan Industrial Estates (KIE). Others were the Development Finance

Corporation of Kenya (DFCK) and the Joint Loan Boards (JLBs). The ICDC, DFCK, IDB and JLBs were charged with the responsibility of availing loans to Kenyans, essentially Africans, to start and expand both large and small enterprises in varied sub-sectors of the economy. KIE, which was initially a subsidiary of ICDC, was given the responsibility of providing sheds and machinery to African entrepreneurs.

In the area of commerce, the government created the Kenya National Trading Corporation (KNTC) on which the Import and Export and Essential Supplies Act of 1976 bestowed monopoly power in wholesale and retail trade. The corporation dealt in basic commodities such as sugar and salt, later expanding its activities to other goods including bicycles. The KNTC, with its monopoly powers, appointed agents who, as it turned out, were mainly of African origin. This was seen as the most effective way of nurturing African businesses by directly ensuring that they handled the most essential commodities.

The impact of the Africanisation programme has been a subject of critical analysis. There are those who believe that there were some achievements despite constraints (see for example Swainson, 1990). Among the achievements that have been cited is the increased number of local African investors in commerce and industry. The access by Africans to credit has been cited as an indication of success of the programme. Through the credit institutions that the government created, local investors, including traders were able to secure loans for their businesses. This saw the Africans at least gaining a foothold into business. This success was, however, achieved at the expense of Asian businesses (though one can argue that this was the objective of the Africanisation programme). Many Asian businesses, particularly in retail, were closed down and the few who could survive moved on to industries. As Nowrejee (2001:51) indicates:

> "Asian African Businesses during the period were ignored by government and left to fend for themselves; there were certainly more urgent issues to tend to, or so thought the government. However, those fewer businesses grew steadily, and due to the effect of all the above legislation on retail businesses, an increasing amount of Asian African business was now in industrial enterprises."

There are those analysts who, however, believe that the Africanisation programme was a failure. Himbara (1994), for example, argues that the policy failed because of the shortcomings of the parastatal organisations that 'possessed neither the technical skills nor the financial resources to accomplish their goals'. The fragmented nature of the Kenyan government elite and their entrenched interests was also another reason for the poor success of the strategy. The other effects of the Africanisation programme in trade were largely due to the legislation that had been enacted and the working of the empowering institutions. According to Swainson (1978), access to capital in Kenya was not even and that certain segments of the African entrepreneurs benefited more than the others. Thus, according to the author, the KNTC became "an instrument by the emergent bourgeoisie to penetrate the wholesale and retail sectors, which had formerly been the exclusive preserve of non-citizens."

This assertion brings into the picture an important feature of distributorship in the post independence period: that wholesale and retail was uneven both by tribe and by implication, region, given the regional settlement of tribes in Kenya. Only those with political leverage were able to get distributorships from KNTC. Trade and distribution in the country thus turned into a patronage resource. The literature on Kenyan capitalism has shown that during the 1970s, the leading distributorships in the country were held by the Kikuyu community. This continued in most of the Kenyatta regime but with the political re-alignments that characterized the Moi regime, changing the situation to the benefit of other ethnic groups, especially the Kalenjin, was high on the political agenda.

The Structural Adjustment Phase

By around 1984, there were clear signs in the aftermath of the oil crises of the 1970s and the droughts of the 1980s that a major crisis was looming in the economy of Kenya. Among the leading signs was the collapse or underperformance of most of the financial institutions that were put in place to help African entrepreneurs. Indigenous banks such as Continental Finance, Jimba Credit and the Rural and Urban Finance were put under receivership and eventually wound up. The economic fundamentals, particularly the rate of unemployment and inflation, were also indicative of major economic problems. The establishment of parastatals by the government had resulted in an over-extended public sector with a low elasticity of output. Entrenched rigidities were also evident in the budgetary process. The fiscal deficit was running at about 9 percent of the GDP. As a prescription to turn around the economy, the government started in 1986 to implement the IMF/World Bank instigated structural adjustment programmes. The reforms put in place a number of policy changes some of which had direct and others indirect implications for trade and distribution. We discuss below some of the relevant policy changes.

Tariff reforms

For most of the post-independence period, the government pursued the *import-substitution strategy* to industrial development under a high tariff wall that ensured that there was very little competition from imports. On realising in the early 1980s that there was no more scope for further import-substitution, the government changed gear to an export promotion strategy that saw the reduction and abolition of tariffs. What this meant, from the perspective of trade and distribution enterprises, was that goods from other countries would now freely be imported into the country. The possibility of competition and even complementarity between different goods and between distribution channels, both local and imported, became options.

Elimination of price controls

Up until 1994, the government controlled the prices of most agricultural and manufactured goods in the country. This meant that the actors in trade and distribution systems knew with certainty what prices and margins they were to receive. In 1994, the government abolished the price control system replacing the Price Control Act with the Restrictive Trade Practices, Monopolies and Price

Control Act. The new Act was to focus more on monopolies and collusive tendencies. The rationale for price decontrol was the belief by the government that price controls reduced incentives to invest both in industry and commerce.

Parastatal enterprise reforms

An important component of the structural adjustment programme was to reform the parastatal sector. In 1996, the IMF approved a loan for Kenya under the Enhanced Structural Adjustment Facility (ESAF) to support the government economic reform programme. This was to be used among other things, to complete the privatisation of a number of key enterprises including Kenya Airways, National Cereals and Produce Board (NCPB) and contracting out the container terminal of the Kenya Ports Authority and the Kenya Post and Telecommunications Corporation. The government was also to divest in a large number of other non-strategic parastatals. Among the enterprises registered for privatisation was the Kenya National Trading Corporation (KNTC), as often it remained in place and its mandate largely unclear. There has been at the same time considerable reluctance by the government to privatize parastatals like the Kenya Telecommunication Corporation.

Development of the informal sector

Although the government had policies to encourage the Africanisation of commerce and industry, policy on small enterprises did not initially envision informal sector enterprises. The official stance towards the micro and small enterprises (MSE) sector only started taking shape with the publication of the International Labour Office (ILO) report in 1972. Soon after, official policy documents began to reflect the change in attitude. However, there was hardly any concrete programmatic support for the sector until the publication of Sessional Paper No 1 of 1986. In this document, the government underscored the importance of the sector in terms of its potential to bring about balanced rural-urban development and create non-farm employment based on its unique characteristics.

The 1986 Sessional Paper was followed by Sessional Paper Number 2 of 1992 on Small Enterprises and *Jua Kali* Development in Kenya. The latter paper outlined several policy recommendations, which covered the three areas in the previous strategy paper namely: an enabling environment, credit for the MSEs and non-financial promotional programmes. In addition, gender related policies were outlined. It should be noted, however, that government support of the informal sector has almost entirely focused on small-scale producers, although about two-thirds of the small enterprises in the country are traders (Pedersen, 2006).

ESTABLISHMENT OF THE TRANSPORT SYSTEM IN KENYA

Transport has a long and eventful history in Kenya dating back to pre-colonial establishment of caravan trade, which was superseded by the construction of the railway to Kisumu that resulted in the establishment of a colony. This went hand in hand with setting up of "White" Highlands and African reserves which became the concentration of human settlement and the destination of human traffic flow. The transport system is made of five modes: road, railway, airway, water and pipeline.

These modes of transport have a history spanning both the colonial and independence periods. A brief historical development of each mode of transport is presented below.[1]

Overland Transport

The origin and development of the road system in Kenya in relation to economic, social and political forces has greatly influenced its present pattern. Three stages or phases in the development of the road system, 1890-1920, 1920-1940, and 1940-present, have been identified (Ogonda, 1986; 1992; 1998).

The first stage of road development, 1890-1920, started with the construction of Mackinnon-Sclater roads extending from Kibwezi to Mumias through Busia to Uganda. A number of important interior centres emerged served by both the road and railway systems: Nairobi, Nakuru, Eldoret, Nyeri and Kisumu. This stage of road growth and development was concomitant with the setting up of the British administration and the first and second phases of the establishment of European settlement in Kenya. In the second stage, 1920-1940, routes that were constructed were essentially lateral interconnections, notably, Thika-Kitui road and Gilgil-Thompson Falls road. This stage coincided with the phase of ex-soldiers settlement scheme. Some considerable progress was made in road construction in the 1930s to serve mining and tea growing areas. By 1940, closer networks of roads were concentrated in western Kenya, the Kenya highlands and at the coast (Ogonda, 1986; 1992a). The third stage, 1940 to present, saw the development of routes between the most important centres. Some sections of the main roads with heavier traffic were butumised, for example, Nairobi-Thika and Nairobi-Nakuru. The Rural Access Roads Programme (RARP) and Special Roads Programme (SRP) of the 1970s and 1980s contributed to the expansion and improvement of rural road network.

At the time of independence in 1963, Kenya had an estimated road network of 150,600 kms, consisting of 41,800 km of classified roads and 108,800 of unclassified roads (Kenya, 1997). The network is, however, still not well distributed throughout the country. There is a dense road network in the coastal, central and western parts of Kenya. There is a sparse road network in the northern, north-eastern and southern parts of the country. The rural areas generally have poor road networks.

Kenya had a higher standard of road transport infrastructure and lower transport costs than most countries in Sub-Saharan Africa up to the mid-1980s. The situation has changed, as there has been deterioration in the quality of the road network in the past 10-15 years. The poor state of roads is largely due to inadequate maintenance, and gradual erosion of public sector capacity to effectively plan, finance and manage basic road infrastructure (Kenya, 1997). Other factors contributing to road

---

1 A more detailed discussion of the development of the Kenyan transport and logistics system is found in Alila et al., (2005).

deterioration are increased traffic volume, high axle loads, overloading and inadequate capacity in railway transport (Kenya, 1997). The financial constraints facing Kenya have contributed to lack of funds to maintain the roads as revenues have not been allocated for maintenance on a dedicated basis because of government's budgetary constraints (Kenya, 1997).

The development of the railway system started with the construction of the Uganda Railway in 1896 from the port of Mombasa through Nairobi to its terminus, Kisumu, which was reached in 1901. The Uganda Railway and the road into the interior thus established the initial framework on which the Kenya road network and the rail branch lines evolved during the years of the establishment of the British administration and white settlement in Kenya (Ongaro, 1995). Rail branch lines were built to Central Kenya (Nanyuki), Western Kenya (Butere), North Rift (Eldoret) and to the Tanzanian Border (Taveta).

Air and Water Transport

Air and water transport played relatively minor roles in the overall transport pattern of Kenya during the colonial period compared to rail and road transport (Ogonda, 1992). The need for landing grounds for aeroplanes arose much later than the need for road network. The first land aeroplane had its inaugural flight from Wilson Airport to England in 1930. Wilson Airport was the original base of the East African Airways, then operated as a private company. In 1946, the company was established as a public corporation with its capital subscribed to jointly by Kenya, Uganda and Tanzania.

Presently, there are three main airports: Moi International Airport (Mombasa), Jomo Kenyatta International Airport (Nairobi) and Eldoret Airport. Kenya Airways was created in 1977 as the local successor to East African Airways (EAA), after the break up of the East African Community. There is a domestic air route network serving a number of airstrips throughout the country.

Water transport was an important medium of linkage for the coastal trading population for many years before and during the colonial period. Many of the streams and estuaries along the coast are navigable for short distances inland by crafts and dhows. But major rivers such as the Tana and Galana tumble in falls and cataracts and are of less use as waterways for much of their courses. However, the Tana River, when in flood, can be navigable for 500 kilometres upstream from the coast.

In the mainland, many of the streams are of no great size, have intermittent courses or have deeply incised gorges, and are of less importance as navigable waterways. Of the inland waterways, only Lake Victoria has been used as an important commercial link with the neighbouring countries. The first steamship on Lake Victoria was launched in Kisumu in 1901 to carry goods and passengers from the railhead to ports in Uganda and Tanzania. Within Kenya, little wharfs for smaller vessels were built at Port Victoria, Asembo Bay, Kendu Bay, Homa Bay etc.

Pipeline Transport

For a long period of time, there was a discussion that a pipeline be constructed between Mombasa and Nairobi to ease the movement of oil (Kenya, 1970). This has been realized and there is a 449-km Mombasa-Nairobi oil pipeline. This pipeline is operated by Kenya Pipeline Company which came into being in 1978. The oil pipeline has now been extended to western Kenya, with three outlays at Nakuru, Kisumu and Eldoret. There is a proposal to extend the pipeline to Kampala, under the aegis of the East African Co-operation agreement. It is thought that this extension will minimize damage to Kenyan roads by heavy tankers transporting petroleum products to neighbouring countries (Kenya, 1997).

THE KENYAN TRADE AND DISTRIBUTIONS SYSTEM: KEY ACTORS AND LOGISTICS[2]

The aim of the analysis of the trade and distribution system is to outline the emergent patterns and provide insights into the size and nature of trade and distribution in Kenya. The key actors in the system include the producers/importers, wholesalers and agents, retailers, and the consumers. In addition, the government, through policies and regulations, which determine the business environment, is a leading actor. It is important that these actors are well understood and their role in the system spelt out since outcomes of trade and distribution emanate from their transactions.

Wholesalers and Retailers

A distribution channel is a set of institutions, agencies and establishments through which a product moves from the producer to the consumer. Wholesalers play an important role in the product distribution channels. First, they serve as a crucial information channel linking the producers and the consumers. Through their contacts, wholesalers collect valuable information from the consumers through retailers and pass the same to producers and vice versa. Second, wholesalers play a major role in financing the chain since they, unlike agents, have to take physical possession of the goods. They, therefore, have to arrange for working capital. Third, the wholesalers are also very important in arranging the logistics in the chain, particularly transportation and storage. Lastly, wholesalers/distributors may provide specific services to their clients, such as the financing of purchases, customer service and technical support, marketing services such as advertisement and promotion, technical or logistical advice, and installation and repair services. Wholesale firms often employ workers to visit customers, install or repair equipment, train users and offer advice. After customers buy equipment, such as industrial machinery, assistance often is needed to integrate the products into the customers' workplace.

---

2   The information used in this section was obtained from both primary and secondary sources. The primary data collection involved a series of surveys in 6 major Kenyan towns in 2000/2001. The interviews covered agents in trade and distribution enterprises comprising of directors, wholesalers and retailers, together with key officials in the relevant government departments.

There are two types of wholesalers/agents. First, there are the bulk-creating wholesalers/agents who buy in small quantities from different producers and sell to retailers or sub-wholesalers. These types of traders operate mainly in the agricultural sector. The trader may be a private person, a cooperative society or even a state agency like the National Cereals and Produce Board (NCPB). In contrast, there are the bulk-breaking wholesalers who buy in bulk, typically from a few producers and sell in small quantities to the retailers and sometimes, directly to consumers. Most wholesalers dealing in household goods fall under this category.

The interviews conducted were not only to understand how wholesale trade is organized but also to have a feel of the dynamics in the sector. The following important characteristics of wholesale firms emerged from the survey[3]:

- Wholesale activities in Kenya are spread over a wide range of activities. These include the buying and selling of household merchandise, shoes, textile and garments, pharmaceutical, office equipment, pharmaceuticals and building materials. Other important activities are buying and selling agricultural inputs, motor vehicle spare parts, petroleum and petroleum products, metal and wood products among others.

- Most of the wholesale enterprises in Kenya are micro and small. From the survey, only 11% of the sampled enterprises were medium or large. However, unlike retailers, most wholesale firms fall in the formal sector of the economy.

- The legal status of the surveyed firms is shown in Table 12.1. It is evident that most wholesale firms are registered as limited liability companies (over 50%). The other forms of legal status are sole proprietorship (21%) and partnership (17%). The legal status of enterprises in trade is important as far as contracts and their enforcement are concerned.

Table 12.1: *Survey Results of the Legal Status of Wholesale Enterprises in Kenya*

Legal status	Type of wholesaler			Total
	Merchant/ Distributor	*Sales Branch*	*Agent/ distributor*	*Total*
Sole proprietor	16(20)		1(1)	17(21)
Partnership	12(16)	1(1)		13(17)
Limited liability company	30(38)	15(19)	2(2)	47(59)
Subsidiary of foreign firm	1(1)	1(1)		2(2)

Source: Survey data – Figures in parentheses are percentages

- Kenyans of Asian origin own most of wholesale enterprises in the country. The enterprises were mainly set up and managed as family enterprises. This is a very common phenomenon of Asian-owned businesses in Kenya.

---

3 For detailed discussion of the results of the Study, see Alila et al (2002).

- A number of firms combined wholesale and retail business, thereby making a pure wholesale business a rare phenomenon

Retail outlets can be differentiated by the size of the establishments involved (large, small, micro etc.) and whether they fall in the formal or informal sectors. The establishments range from the large supermarkets to itinerant traders who move around hawking their wares. While most of the larger enterprises fall within the formal sector, the majority of the smaller enterprises fall within the informal sector.

Supermarkets[4]

Supermarkets have increasingly become an important retailing outlet in urban centres. As well as selling the usual range of processed food and household consumables, supermarkets in Kenya have moved into clothing, hardware, furniture, pharmaceuticals and a wide range of consumable durables. The large supermarkets in the country are also stocking fresh produce. Although most of these supermarkets are located in urban centres, they are proliferating beyond the urban centres into suburban areas, smaller towns, and poorer rural areas.

To cater for the diverse customers in different locations, there has been different sizes of supermarkets in various localities. The most elaborate are two supermarket chains, Uchumi and Nakumatt, which have several outlets in the major towns. Uchumi, for example, has currently 80 stores in different locations. Among these are at least four hypermarkets[5]. There are also some specialized departmental stores which operate with the supermarket principle e.g. Deacons, which specializes mainly in imported clothes which are sold through a chain of outlets in urban centres.

Our analysis of the supermarkets in Kenya revealed that:

(i) Although the number of supermarkets has increased phenomenally in the last few years, the sub-sector is still controlled by a few large players.

(ii) Supermarkets have introduced an element of competition in trade and distribution in Kenya. Not only do the supermarkets compete amongst themselves but also with other retail outlets. Competition is both in terms of prices (price offers) and non-price factors such as quality of service.

(iii) Supermarkets and the larger retail outlets prefer to purchase directly from the manufacturers both locally and internationally. Supermarkets also prefer to import directly, leaving out agents in order to keep cost low. One characteristic that supermarkets consequently have in common is that they enjoy enormous bargaining power, which means an advantage over other retailers.

---

4   A supermarket is a self-service grocery store that sells food, beverages and other goods. They are located in urban centres and in shopping malls. They cover areas between 4,000 and 25000 square ft.

5   This is a supermarket with over 50,000 square ft. These are always located out of Central Business District (CBL) with extensive car parks. Examples are the Ngong Road Hyper and Langata and Nakumatt Hyper in Westland's and on Mombasa road.

(iv) The rapid rise of supermarkets has implications for the development of the retail sector, and particularly, the food retail sector. This and related issues are discussed in detail in the last section of this chapter.

Manufacturers/distributors with own outlets

Like elsewhere in the world, there are manufacturing firms and also importers in Kenya who maintain own retail outlets. In this case, the firm maintains its own fully owned distributors in strategic parts of the country. Typically, such a company will have a head office (mainly in Nairobi) with strategic outlets in major towns. The company will then operate through its distributors but often sets up strategic relationships with independent dealers. This type of arrangement is common with producers and importers of household items, electronics and auto spares parts. Most goods in this kind of arrangement are sold strictly on cash basis. There are possibilities for credit but this is often "out-sourced" i.e. the company offers the goods through established credit system such as SACCOs or through hire purchase companies.

A common retail arrangement akin to the one above is the sale of petrol and petroleum products through the numerous petrol stations spread all over the country. There are currently five petroleum companies across the country: Shell/BP, Caltex, Total/Elf, Kenol/Kobil and Mobil. These companies are either entirely owned by multinationals or part-owned by local consortia. The petroleum companies typically purchase petroleum from the refinery in Mombasa (or import directly) and transport to depots via pipeline or lorries. From the depots, the products are distributed to dealers throughout the country. The stations are either owned by the company or franchised to local dealers. There are, however, strict rules and regulations that dealers must abide by to operate such stations. Exit and entry is at the discretion of the company. There is, however, an increasing number of local petroleum products outlets owned wholly by indigenous entrepreneurs but relatively smaller in size.

Trade and distribution through credit

There are in Kenya a number of outlets that use the instalments or higher purchase system that enables the customers to pay for the product on an instalment, regular part-payment basis. After giving a certain amount as the down or initial payment, the customers are allowed to pay the rest of the money part by part over a specified period. There are also shops which provide a specialized service where no extra charge is kept over the normal cash price if all the dues are paid within a few months, usually two months. Higher purchase facilities enable low-income groups to purchase items which they would otherwise not be able to afford.

Kenya has experienced a fast growth in hire purchases outlets in the last few years. In 1990, seven urban centres in the country had higher purchase outlets. Today, hire purchase outlets can be found in some 33 towns offering relatively easy access to a wide range of products to both rural and urban populations. Items stocked by the higher purchase shops include television sets, video players, furniture, sewing machines and other consumer durables. Most of the outlets operate their own consumer finance schemes, mainly for salaried customers (e.g. teachers, civil servants, employees of rural companies) or those able to put up the collateral. Some companies, not bona fide hire purchase companies, are also selling their products through hire purchases or instalment payments. For example, three petroleum products in the country sell liquefied petroleum gas (LPG) cooker cylinders through targeted SACCOS or company debit systems. A battery distributor has also entered into credit arrangements with a major Kenyan bank to provide finance for its products and also deals with a hire purchase company on an exclusive basis.

Provision and retail shops

Provision stores were and are still dominant retail outlets in Kenya. These are located in the various urban and rural centres in Kenya. Provision shops, which are mainly owned by entrepreneurs of African origin, stock mainly household food items and drinks, soap and related items. These shops form important outlets for a wide range of consumer products. However, these outlets are currently facing a lot of competition from mainly supermarkets which are not only selling at relatively lower prices but also stocking a wide range of items. It is becoming a common occurrence that these outlets, when there are discount offers in the supermarkets, buy certain items to replenish their stock. There are also other specialized retail outlets in the country selling clothes and shoes, pharmaceutical products (pharmacies), agricultural inputs (stockists) etc. These are also dotted all over the country although they are more concentrated in the major towns and in the rural centres. Most of these outlets are licensed and are run by local entrepreneurs, both of African and Asian origin.

Kiosks and Itinerant traders

An important feature of trade in Kenya is the existence of numerous kiosks, canteen and other informal trade outlets countrywide, in rural as well as in urban centres. These outlets stock predominantly household goods, food and other items such as drinks, cigarettes, and sweets. Kiosks are typically sole proprietor establishments, which are run by the owners. Kiosk operators are required by law to obtain licences from the local authorities although quite a number of them in different parts of the country do not secure licences.

A fast growing phenomenon with implications for urban development is the mushrooming of itinerant traders or hawkers. In Nairobi and other urban centres, there are thousands of people who take their wares to open spaces thereby creating temporary open-air markets. These traders provide an enormous management challenge to councils because they have no fixed abode and are not licensed. It is therefore, difficult to control their numbers let alone the quality and authenticity of what they peddle. The physical confrontation between the council officers and the hawkers in Nairobi and other towns reflects the enormity of the challenge. This raises an important issue of business space in Kenya.

Although the survey for this study did not target such traders, they stock all kinds of goods ranging from clothes (new and second hand) to fresh agricultural produce. These commodities are both locally produced and imported. That the hawkers played an increasingly significant role in trade in Kenya is evident from the fact that such traders are selling mainly imported goods in offices, at traffic lights, restaurants and pubs.

Logistics: The Transport Sub-sector

There are a number of segments and actors each having a share in the freight transport logistic chain in Kenya. There are of course overlapping and competitive roles among the segments. The segments outlined are road freight, railway transport, shipping and non-motorized transport. We also include container freight highlighting the overlap shipping, railway and road transport. These segments are examined to demonstrate the dynamics of operation.

Road freight transport

Road transport is the dominant mode of transport in Kenya with respect to value of output and earnings. It is by far the most spatially widespread and commonly used mode of transport, especially when the non-motorized transport in the rural areas is taken into consideration. In the period 1996-2000, transport from road formed over 30% of the transport value, far exceeding earnings by the other competing modes such as the railway (Table 12.2).

Table 12.2: *Value of Output of the Transport Sector in Kenya, 1996-2000 (in Kshs Millions)*

Mode	1996	1997	1998	1999	2000
Road	18,528	18,994	17,414	18,552	21,503
Railway	3,672	3,000	4,096	5,206	5,954
Water	7,346	7,868	7,784	7,432	7,608
Air	10,812	11,858	14,026	20,002	23,025
Pipeline	4,614	4,802	5,282	5,728	6,194
Services incidental to transport	3,622	4,964	4,036	3,274	3,750
Total	*48,594*	*51,486*	*52,638*	*60, 194*	*68,034*
Road as a % of total	*38*	*37*	*33*	*31*	*32*

Source: Kenya (2001)

The road freight segment is complex with respect to ownership of trucks, organisation, zone of operation, management and demand and supply of the service. With respect to ownership, it is notable that the road freight business is fully in the hands of the private sector. There was, however, a government parastatal known as the Kenya National Transport Company (KENATCO), which operated freight trucks and taxis until it was sold in 1996 due to financial difficulties and government policy of privatisation. The company currently operates only taxi services. The collapse of the state parastatal opened the way for many small-and-medium-sized Kenyan operators to enter the transport market (Anyango, 1997).

There are basically two modes of delivery of transport services in Kenya. The first is the case where enterprises own their own trucks. This is a very common mode of delivery in Kenya, particularly among the medium-large manufacturing and trading enterprises. The prevalent practice among the large firms is to have a transport department to take care of logistics and maintenance of the fleets. In the smaller firms maintenance is commonly out-sourced. The practice in Kenya is that trucks that are meant for own use are registered separately and issued with a separate license (License C). Discussions during the survey, however, revealed that trucks licensed for owner-use only can still be hired out. This applies particularly to wholesalers who own trucks for their businesses but which they hire out for transporting bulky goods. The second mode of delivery of road transport services is through hiring from specialised transport trucking companies, which can be large or small, private business or public service. We examine in turn each of these elements of road transport in Kenya.

Large truckers

These are firms that typically have large fleets of vehicles and employ a large number of persons as managers, drivers and conductors. The interviews for this study established that the fleet size ranged between 20 and 100 mostly large vehicles with an average of 40. In terms of the size of the workforce, the range was between 50 and 150 workers, mainly drivers and loaders.

A large share of the large trucking firms is located in the urban areas. The large truckers serve both the national and international routes mainly to Uganda, Rwanda, Burundi and the Democratic Republic of Congo. Spatially, the large truckers are concentrated on the main transit corridors and cross-border markets. The goods from the region to the outside world are mainly agricultural products, e.g. coffee, tea, flowers and fruits and vegetables. This reflects the regions' agricultural orientation. The imports include malt, chemicals, machinery and equipments, fertilizers, and vehicles. The large transporters generally operate on long-term contractual arrangements with a number of firms and organisations for the transport of raw materials, finished products and recently, emerging relief supplies for the poor and displaced persons.

A challenge which the large transporters face is the difficulty to secure return freight. This has meant that for the return trip, the trucks are empty, thus making the total cost for the journey high. Some of the large firms have local agents to look for return freight and inform the head office to re-route or deploy the trucks to pick it up. The majority of the large firms however do not have this kind of arrangement. Truck drivers, however, with or without the authority of the trucks owners occasionally carry goods on the way back.

Small truckers

Transport for hire in Kenya is dominated by small transport businesses. As of 1997, they were estimated to own 60-70 percent of the vehicle fleet and carried about 75% of the available cargo (Anyango, 1997). These truckers operate mainly in local or regional markets, e.g. a district, province or town. The number of vehicles varies from a single truck to seldom more than ten. Some trucks (though few) are operated by the owners while most employ drivers and turn boys. The vehicles vary in capacity from one to 15 tonnes.

While some small transporters have longer term contracts, the majority operate on the spot market. The spot market is essentially an assemblage of individually owned trucks parked at a designated business site for collective bargain and action. In such a market, truck operators are found at waiting points where they are hired depending on the availability of goods to transport. Some operators have regular clients who look specifically for them but generally a prospective client negotiates the terms with the driver or operator or agent/broker. There may be a loose organisational structure for negotiations in some sites but in others, there is open competition and scrambling for prospective clients by the truck operators and agents.

The spot market trucks tend to carry a variety of goods ranging from industrial to household goods. The needs in their markets are varied and so, they are rarely specialized. There are, however, a few cases of specialization. For example, there are small spot market trucks in Nairobi that concentrate on transport of building materials such as sand. Others concentrate on agricultural produce, mainly horticultural products. The price negotiated in most cases is based on the distance to be covered rather than on tonnage. Where a broker is involved in the negotiation of the terms, a commission of about 10 per cent of the agreed price is paid.

Public Transport

Public bus and matatu transport also play an important role in the movement of goods and persons especially in the relatively short-distance inter-urban and rural transport. The matatu mode of transport, since its official recognition in 1973, has grown in importance. This is largely because the bus and truck transport system has been inadequate in both rural and urban areas in Kenya. The emergence of the matatus has, thus, partly filled the transport vacuum and play an important role for both passenger and freight movement (Khayesi, 1993; 2001; Ogonda, 1992; Mbuthia, 2002). It is not unusual to see a Matatu overloaded not just with passengers but also with goods. This is a common feature in the rural distribution system as well as for itinerary trading systems. Indeed, most urban and rural retailers of agricultural and households goods use this mode of transport to transport their wares. The rates paid on matatus are based on the distance and the bulkiness of the commodity being transported.

Public buses are also used to transport goods between towns and between rural and urban centres. The quantities carried by this mode are limited for buses designed for passenger transport. Nevertheless, urban to rural traders dealing mainly in second-hand clothes and certain household goods find them quite useful. Buses have also been used to transport agricultural products from rural areas to the urban market.

Railway transport

The railway in many countries plays an important role especially in the transport of bulky goods. But for Kenya, there has been a generally downward trend in the volume of freight. The decline in the freight of the Kenya Railways is largely a result of the loss of monopoly over transport goods for parastatals. For a long period, the Kenya government had directed that all parastatal organisations that handled bulky commodities such as coffee and tea be transported by railway (Irandu, 2000). The monopolistic protection by the government ensured freight but railway transport had also historically been protected from road transport. It was by a deliberate policy of the colonial government that roads were essentially to feed the railway network and not to compete with it. This has since changed, especially with liberalisation which has opened the railway to stiff competition from road transport. As a result, rail transport has lost both in freight and revenue.

Currently, about 70% of the total freight traffic from Mombasa to Nairobi and beyond goes by road. Of the 30% going by rail, 24% goes to Embakasi and only 6% to other destinations. Kenya Railways has a rate structure, which is used flexibly, and has higher prices for up going (Mombasa to Nairobi) traffic than for down going (Nairobi to Mombasa). Turn–around time between Mombasa and Nairobi is normally 5-7 days, although it is reported that 3 days is achievable occasionally.

Shipping

Shipping lines and the boat operators are crucial in providing sea and lake transport. Then there are the shipping agents and the ports which essentially facilitate water transport. The shipping industry consists of general freight and bulk freight. General freight has traditionally been transported by shipping lines serving specific routes, e.g. between Europe and East Africa, while the bulk traffic is carried in full loads in chartered tramp boats. However, shipping in Kenya is dominated by foreign lines having local agents representing them in the country. The role of the shipping agent is to serve the ships when they are in port and to secure freight for it. There are about 10-15 shipping agencies based in Mombasa, Kenya's main port. The agencies are typically Kenyan firms. These firms may serve a number of different shipping lines. However, there has been a trend for the shipping lines to establish their own agencies or buy a local agent which then only serves them. For example, P&O Nedloyd acquired Mackenzie Maritime while MSC acquired Oceanfreight. The Kenya Shipping Agency is a third variant of the same. It started as a parastatal (though it had nothing to do with the Kenya National Shipping Line) but is now privatized to a Kenyan owned company.

There are two main shipping ports in Kenya, in Mombasa and Kisumu. The port of Mombasa is the only international port in Kenya and is also the largest port in East Africa. Apart from a small but growing air freight, practically all of Kenya's overseas foreign trade passes through the Mombasa port. In addition, the port also serves as a transit point for part of the transit traffic to Uganda, Rwanda, eastern Democratic Republic of Congo, northern and north-western Tanzania and Sudan. The bulk, about 50% of the imports consist of liquids. Exports of liquid bulk are much smaller than imports and have dropped from 12-13% of the imports to only 5% of the imports.

Transit traffic to the neighbouring countries increased from 10-15% of the total throughput during the late 1980s to 20-30% during the late 1990s, but with a high peak in 1996 when it reached 51% of the total traffic. The import component of the transit traffic has over this period recorded the highest increase. This has been largely due to food aid and war imports bound for the lake region. This has since slackened somewhat as imports have reduced to 20-30% of the total imports. The transit traffic in Mombasa depends on the efficiency and rate structures of the port but also on the degree of competition especially from the Dar es Salaam port. Although labour productivity in Mombasa has been increasing, and the average number of port days per ship has decreased during the late 1990s, the waiting time in the port is still long due to inefficient custom clearance and unavailability of railway wagons in the port (Anyango, 1997). The port has also been associated with corruption and related malpractices that may have diverted traffic to competing ports.

The second port in Kenya, Kisumu, incepted in 1899, is closely associated with trade and economic activities in the lake towns of Kisumu, Mwanza, Musoma, Jinja and Entebbe (Ogonda and Onyango, 1994). The port, which is managed by the Kenya Railways Corporation, handles both through and lake-bound traffic. Through traffic consists of imports and exports to and from the neighbouring countries of Tanzania and Uganda. Goods are brought by railway and road to be put into vessels plying the lake. About three quarters of the goods trans-shipped through the port are mainly for local consumption within the lake and a quarter for transit to Uganda and other countries. The main goods transhipped through the port are: petroleum products, maize, groundnuts and simsim, beans, second hand clothes, cement, wheat, machinery, sugar, telephone posts, iron sheets, plastic ware, hides and skins, coffee, cotton bales, cotton seed and beer.

Freight

The use of containers has been one of the most significant developments in trade and transport in recent times. During the 1980s and the 1990s, the import of general freight to Kenya was mostly containerized. Also, an increasing share of the bulky exports including tea and coffee, which have traditionally been transported in bags, have been containerized 'at the shipping line convenience' in order to fill empty containers. Figure 12.1 shows the development of the container throughput at Mombasa since 1987. It is evident from the figure that use of containers for imports has gradually risen from about 55,000 in 1987 to 112,000 in 2000. Similarly, the use of containers for exports rose from about 55,000 in 1987 to 106,000 in 2000. The rapid increase in full containers over the period resulted in a corresponding increase in the export of empty containers.

The container traffic to and from Mombasa port is carried either by road or railway. A large share of the containers are also stripped or stuffed at the port and the freight moved by truck without the container. There are several reasons for this. Firstly, custom regulations often require containers to be emptied for inspection and then it may not pay to fill them again. This has proved to be a cumbersome process both for the port authorities and the users. There are plans in Kenya to introduce container-scanning equipment that will make opening of containers unnecessary. Secondly, many containers are consolidated, that is, contain freight belonging to different owners and therefore have to be split. Thirdly, and perhaps more important, transport costs are cheaper without containers because there can be more freight on the truck without the container, partly because one does not need to carry the container and partly because it is easier to carry overweight without the container.

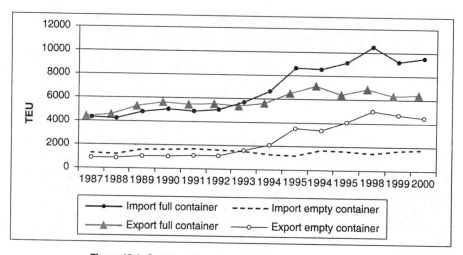

Figure 12.1: Container Throughput in Mombasa Port (1987-2000)

Source: Kenya Ports Authority, Annual Bulletin of Ports Statistics (Various Issues)

Non-motorised Rural Transport

The concern with non-motorised emanated from concern in the analysis to capture the complete spatial coverage of the transport system serving trade in the rural sector. The rural area is where the majority of the Kenyan population lives and earn their living from agriculture, which is the dominant sector of the economy. Agricultural commodities are of course necessary inputs for both industry and trade. Moreover, it is in the rural sector that most micro and small enterprises are located, and increasing in numbers, as recent surveys have shown. There was indeed compelling emerging evidence of heavy reliance on non-motorised transport by the large number of consumers, agricultural commodity producers, micro and small enterprise owners especially in the remote rural areas. The study therefore found it necessary to establish the composition and spatial operations of non-motorised transport and the role it plays in rural trade.

The non-motorised modes of transport, unlike motorised, engine propelled vehicles, comprise bicycles (boda boda), "mkokoteni", hand-carts, human porters, walking and animal carts. The use of both motorised and non-motorised vehicles is for movement of goods and people. However, in terms of quantity/weight of goods transported, they can carry much less than motorised vehicles carrying bulky goods.

Flexibility is also a major advantage of non-motorised mode in terms of travel routes and reach into the remote areas, following footpaths and tracks which may occasionally be constructed, but are often made by users through routine passage. There is ownership of bicycles, handcarts etc by individual operators but these can also be hired by the operators at a fee from a fleet owner who may not necessarily be involved in actual operation. The physical requirements of operation, particularly of *boda boda* and handcarts, make these exclusively young male businesses. But it should be remembered that women are predominant when it comes to human porters, partly due to the culturally influenced greater role in the provision of labour for agricultural production and produce marketing.

The *boda boda* operators in particular have introduced a number of rules and procedures as well as organisation into their operations. There are registration requirements, dress code (uniform), identification, operation from a specific location (stage) and membership of a credit and welfare association. In any case, the order being gradually established is good for the business and is already resulting in trust between *boda boda* operators and MSE operators. There is already a growing trend observed in Siaya district of MSE owners entrusting *boda boda* operators to collect and deliver goods already paid for in wholesale shops or even giving them money for purchase and delivery of the goods to their shops/kiosks. Thus, wholesalers and retailers are linked up and there is a possible reduction of costs to small rural entrepreneurs who often order stock in relatively small quantities.

In view of the fact that some of the remote areas may be inaccessible to motorised transport, by also ferrying passengers, non-motorised transport serves an increasingly indispensable linkage role between rural localities and outside world. Those travelling to and from urban centres are picked and taken right up to their gates/doorsteps and/or furnished with vital information regarding their travel route and transport available.

In the rural towns, particularly on designated market days, one can observe a clearly marked division of labour between motorised and non-motorised transport operators and also a distinction between large and small traders. The merchandise, including maize, cabbages, beans, tomatoes, second-hand clothes, etc arrive at the market in a pick-up or a lorry hired or owned by a large trader. The small traders then ferry small quantities to their kiosks/stalls using non-motorised transport. The options include handcarts, wheel barrows, human porters, *boda boda* and boarding a matatu with the merchandise as personal luggage.

There are indications that the use of non-motorised transport is on the increase countrywide and a useful purpose served. The *boda boda* routes in the rural areas are increasing while bicycle traffic in rural towns and even large urban centres continue to grow. The emerging issue of concern in terms of provision and availability of producer services is failure to plan for this increase. In the urban areas, failure to plan for bicycle routes, and poor terrain on rural paths and tracks mean a high frequency of crushes resulting in damage to goods and injuries to human beings.

EMERGING DYNAMICS IN TRADE AND TRANSPORT IN KENYA

The trade and transport sub-sector in Kenya, like other sectors of the economy, is quite dynamic and responds to changes both in the national and global environment. The enterprises in the sub-sector are largely profit motivated and their typical reaction will be to cut costs and to improve profit margins. The reactions will definitely vary depending on the size of the enterprises and the line of activities. There are, in any case, noticeable trends emerging due to changes in the Kenyan trade and transport sub-sector. We describe some below.

Competitive Distributive Trade

In line with the liberalisation of the economy, the trade sub-sector in Kenya has undergone major structural changes. This has resulted in the emergence of new players. The number of supermarkets and department stores as well as large retail outlets called hypermarkets has increased dramatically in the last few years. With the establishment of these outlets, the small retail outlets are now facing very stiff competition in terms of lower prices and a variety of products allowing for under the same roof shopping for household needs. However, in spite of the more competitive environment, the survey for this study has shown that the small outlets (kiosks and provision stores) remain the most popular shopping outlets especially for groceries. Although the spread of supermarkets has been fast, this is so far an urban phenomenon and they have not been able to push out the small retail outlets.

With regard to marketing of agricultural products, the large supermarkets in the country have already moved into direct sales of fresh agricultural products. This again puts them in direct competition with other traditional outlets like agricultural retail markets and other informal outlets. The direct marketing of agricultural produce by the large marketing outlets is expected to increase in the long run. This expansion has immediate implications for agro-food systems in the urban area and rural livelihoods (Weatherspoon and Reardon, 2003). The effect is that, the supermarkets are taking over the most dynamic segments of the food retail market, the urban areas. In the long run however, besides the promotion of strong linkages between agricultural production and consumer demands, this trend is expected to increase value-added through improved packaging and grading activities at the farm level.

Development of New Distribution Modes

Partly as a result of the liberalisation of the economy and the need to generate self-employment in Kenya, new and distinct modes of distributorship have emerged in Kenya. The two notable ones are direct sales and 'exhibitions'. Direct selling involving one-to-one contact with customers is growing in popularity as a marketing tool in Kenya. First are the hawkers who operate as individuals and purchase goods from importers and sell to customers. These types of hawkers will also be found in the central business districts of major towns selling wares on street pavements and alleys. The second type of hawkers are disguised as "promotion agents" and sell wares on behalf of larger importers, in most cases, registered firms.

This is usually done on commission basis. This distribution mode in Kenya is a typical case of formal establishments using informal outlets. Yet a third type is the hawkers specializing in second hand clothes and shoes. Rather than locate in particular markets, these traders prefer to move around with their wares and search of buyers

The latest forms of retail outlets are the so called "exhibitions". These are typically "shopping malls" with 10-20 small shops (cubicles) selling mainly imported clothes and garments, shoes, mobile telephones, toys, perfumes and electronic equipments. To understand the development and dynamics in this innovative marketing channel, a survey of 40 exhibition shops was carried out in the major urban centres in Kenya. Specifically, the survey covered Nairobi, Nakuru, Mombasa, Kisumu, Eldoret and Kericho. The survey yielded a number of important findings.

(i) Most of the enterprises are fairly recent having been established only in the last 2-6 years, the oldest enterprise having been established in 1996 while a large number were established in the survey year (2002). That most of the organisations are recent and dealing with imported products points to the fact that the enterprises are partly a response to the liberalized environment in the country. Trade liberalisation made importation easier and enterprising Kenyans are now moving to other countries to import 'cheap' goods to sell locally.

(ii) The enterprises are mainly sole proprietorships which are predominantly run by the owners. A few of the enterprises are partnerships of 2-3 people. The majority of the enterprises were established from the personal savings of the owners. Most of the enterprises have no employees as owners run the businesses themselves. Some, however, have engaged shop attendants.

(iii) The business premises are rented from landlords who have in the last few years changed the use of their premises. The landlords are mainly Kenyans of Asian origin. Rents for the stalls are in the range from Kshs. 1200-2000 per square metre per month.

There are clear indications that exhibition centres are doing booming business and that these enterprises and the African owners are becoming an important component of the business system in Kenya. Hence, they deserve recognition. Customers are attracted to the centres because they stock the latest fashion at affordable prices. Consumers in Kenya tend to prefer imported goods, believed to be of better quality, and being able to find under one roof required merchandise for adults and children, men and women etc, as in a departmental store. This is unlike most big shops exclusively for children, men and women only, and therefore an advantage for the centres serving a variety of customer needs. The growing demand for goods in these exhibition centres shows that generally the African enterprises are thriving. It can be argued that this trend is an increasing realisation, through private sector initiative, of what the government tried through legislation by setting up Kenya National Trading Corporation (KNTC) to promote Africanisation of commerce but did not quite succeed.

Outsourcing of Transport and Logistic Services

A trend emerging, especially among large-scale enterprises, is outsourcing of transport services. The traditional model for most Kenyan enterprises has been the reliance on in-house transport and logistic services. To do this most companies have full fledged transport and logistics departments operating with self-owned equipment to cater for their needs. As maintenance costs for aging trucks in their own account transport rise, outsourcing becomes a more attractive alternative. Logistical support involves many activities which may be the subject of outsourcing. These include warehousing services, product processing and packing and transportation or distribution services. Thus in Kenya, and indeed in other countries, a growing number of companies are outsourcing transport and logistic services instead of producing the services themselves. This development has been apparently motivated by the search for greater efficiency traceable to the poor economic performance which has depressed demand in the country and hastened the need for changes.

Both public and private enterprises in Kenya have attempted outsourcing of transport and logistic services. An example of a large public enterprise that is changing transport arrangement is the Pyrethrum Board of Kenya. Initially, the board had its own in-house transport service consisting of a fleet of vehicles to collect pyrethrum from farmers. Presently, the Board is moving towards hiring transport because of the high administrative and operational costs involved. The Board has made the decision to concentrate on its core business activity of pyrethrum marketing. Likewise, other public enterprises like the Kenya Tea Development Authority are considering different options of providing transport services, including outsourcing.

It is in the private sector, however, that outsourcing of transport and logistic services has been more pronounced. A number of large firms in Kenya have signed contracts with logistics providers such as Tibbet and Britten Kenya Limited. The company, which is part of the United Kingdom based Tibbet and Britten Group Plc., has contracts with firms such as Unilever Kenya (formerly East African Industries), East African Packaging Industries (EAPI), East African Breweries (EABL) and the British American Tobacco (BAT). These companies, and many others, have realized great savings in outsourcing warehousing and distribution services enabling them, for instance, to concentrate more intensively on their core competencies like manufacturing and marketing. It is important to note here that there are at any rate, very few logistic service firms in Kenya today.

Integration of Trade and Transport

An emerging trend in the trade and transport sub-sector in Kenya is the attempt of the traders and producers to provide transport as an added service to their customers. This is more important amongst the small-scale traders and producers. The results of the survey showed that 62% of wholesalers relied on transport provided by the manufactures while only 21% used their own transport. The remaining 17% used hired transport services, including courier, air and sea transport. For the retailers, 60% indicated that wholesalers or the producers delivered their supplies to them. Only 27% of the respondents had their own means of transport while 13% hire their own transport or use public means. It is evident from these results that the provision of transport to customers has become an important component of producer services.

An Integrated Transport System with `End of the Road' Pathways only Option

The dominant mode of transport countrywide in Kenya is road transport, broadly grouped into two types, namely, motorized vehicles (although a considerable share of the freight carried on motorable rural roads is often carried on the head or on non-motorized vehicles) and non-motorized. This classification, in conformity to type of infrastructure is meant for use by each mode of transport. Thus, constructed or motorable roads are generally for motorized vehicles while the non-motorized types depend on pathways. The latter, some constructed but mostly non-constructed, is the predominant infrastructure found in the rural hinterland. It is indeed the case that the majority of the rural communities in Kenya do not have direct access to recognizable roads. They rely on pathways as the viable, if not the only option, depending on precise location.

The general outlook, nevertheless, is one of an integrated transport system. There are inter and intra-linkages between and amongst motorized and non-motorized transport depending on distance, load type and weight, road and/or pathway to destination and the consumer preference based on affordability. The common trend is to use motorized transport within a road network area, and ultimately, resort to non-motorized type at the end of the road where there are only pathways. This is a familiar common practice for most rural dwellers. Nevertheless, it has also become the order of the day in congested informal urban settlements, and estates where roads have fallen into disrepair or blocked by illegal constructions. The participation and involvement of different agents and means of transport at different segments or parts of the transport chain reveals complementary, and sometimes, competitive arrangements that are seeking to satisfy the varying demand for transport.

Use of Information and Communication Technology (ICT)

In an increasingly global market driven by rapid technological changes, business will need to leverage ICT technologies to develop new competitive advantages. E-commerce is already revolutionizing the way trade is conducted. Globally, E-commerce is mainly used by businesses to coordinate between the purchasing operations of a company and its suppliers; by logistical planners and transportation companies that warehouse and move products; by sales organisations including retailers and wholesalers which sell products directly to consumers (Gold and Rao, 2000).

Although the actual use of ICT remains low compared to other developing countries like India and Thailand, its adoption in businesses in Kenya is fairly fast. The main users of the internet in Kenya are larger, well established firms who are using it to place orders, obtain acknowledgements and confirmation of prices, specifications, getting pre-shipment inspection and shipping documents and even sending and receiving invoices. About 80% of the large enterprises sampled in this study indicated that they had access to the internet and were actually using it. However, only a few, about 12%, had set up their own home pages although the majority indicated that they were actually in the process of doing so or were thinking about it. The enterprises with internet connections included large supermarkets, large retail shops and petrol stations.

The use of ICT by the small and micro enterprises, although low, is also picking up quite fast. From our survey, only a handful of these enterprises had access to and used the internet. Most retail and wholesale outlets have no internet connection. While some of them have telephone connections, they are not used to access it because of lack of computers. However, telephone connectivity for most business, especially in the rural areas, remains quite illusive. An important development, presumably, as a response to the low telephone connectivity is the increasing use of mobile telephones. The small and micro enterprises have found the use of the mobile phones relatively convenient and affordable. Transport companies are also finding mobiles quite useful as they have a wider coverage than radio calls. The adoption of ICTs in trade and transport has a number of potential effects. One is that, the use of ICT is likely to transform the supply chains which may in some cases, imply a diminishing role of some traditional actors. ICT is also likely to lead to better services at reduced costs and increased competition and wider markets. All these are likely to impact positively on trade and transport in the country.

CONCLUSIONS

The objective of this chapter was to analyse the scope and status of the interrelated services of trade and transportation in Kenya. Specifically, the analysis sought to show that the present pattern of trade and transport in Kenya is an outgrowth of many factors. The chapter also sought to point out the major trends in trade and transport within the context of globalisation and liberalisation. The following conclusions emerged from the analysis:

(i)   Historical factors, dating as far back as the pre-colonial period, have played an important role in shaping the current pattern of trade and transport in the country. In many ways, the current systems of trade and transport are relics of modes set up many years ago.

(ii) Over the years, the government has used legislation to achieve certain social as well as economic objectives in the trade environment in Kenya. By enacting legislation such as the Landlord and Tenant Act of 1966, the Immigration Act of 1967, the Trade Licensing Act of 1967 and the Import, Export and Essential Supplies Act of 1967, the government sought, among other things, to ensure the active participation of Africans in commerce and industry. To achieve almost similar objectives, the government also established a large number of institutions such as the Industrial and Commercial Development Corporation (ICDC), the Industrial Development Bank (IDB), and the Kenyan Industrial Estates (KIE). Others were the

Development Finance Corporation of Kenya (DFCK) and the Joint Loan Boards (JLBs). These played an important role in Africanising commerce and industry in the country.

(iii) Policies, and particularly the structural adjustment programmes pursued by the government, have played an important role in shaping the current patterns of distribution and trade. Policies such as import liberalisation, decontrol of prices and the restructuring of public enterprises have altered the economics of trade in the country.

(iv) As a result of the policies, legislation and the changing socio-economic environment, trade and in particularly wholesale and retail, has transformed itself in the following respects:

(a) Ownership: A sizeable share of merchandise retail trade, which was hitherto in the hands of Indians, is now predominantly African. A good number of Indians have moved to industrial and other ventures.

(b) New actors and new channels have entered the scene with the result that there is now increased competition.

(c) New networks and relationships have developed in the sector. The general trend is a move away from individual based networks to organisational networks

(v) Trade in the country is set to transform even further with the advent of the Internet. The Internet is likely to lead to the transformation of the supply chains leading to better services, reduced costs, increased competition and access to wider market. This is already happening in other countries.

REFERENCES

Alila, P.O.; Pedersen, P.O.; Odhiambo, W. and Khayesi, M. 2003. "Trade-Related Business Services in Eastern Africa: Kenya Country Study". Report to OECD, Paris.

Alila, P.O.; Khayesi, M.; Odhiambo, W and Pedersen, P.O. 2005. Development of African Freight Transport – the Case of Kenya. DIIS Working Paper no. 2005/6. Copenhagen: Danish Institute of International Studies.

Anyango, G. 1997. "Comparative Transportation Cost Analysis in East Africa". Technical Paper No. 22 SD Publication Series Office of Sustainable Development, Bureau for Africa. Washington DC: USAID.

Gold, R.N and Rao, B.J.R. 2000. *Electronic Commerce: Its Growing Importance in Trade and the Developmental Implications*. Commonwealth Secretariat.

Himbara, D.1993: "Myths and Realities of Kenyan Capitalism". *Journal of Modern African Studies* 31(1):93-107.

Himbara, D. 1994. "Failed Africanisation of Commerce and Industry in Kenya" *World Development* 22(3): 469-482.

Fitzsimmons , J. 2002. *The Role of Services in the Economy.* Austin, USA: University of Texas.

Hollingsworth L.W. 1960. *The Asians of East Africa.* London: Macmillan.

Irandu, Evaristus, M. 2000. "A Study on Improving Railway Transport in Kenya: Policy Options and Achievements to Date". Final Report prepared for Technoserve Inc. Nairobi.

Kenya, Republic of. 2001. *Economic Survey 2001.* Nairobi: Government Printer.

Kenya, Republic of. 1997. *National Development Plan, 1997-2001.* Nairobi: Government Printer.

Kenya, Republic of. 1970. *National Development Plan 1970-74.* Nairobi: Government Printer.

Kenya, Republic of. (Various Issues) *Statistical Abstracts.* Nairobi: Government Printer.

Khayesi, M. 1993. "Rural Household Travel Characteristics: the Case of Kakamega District". *Journal of Eastern Africa Research and Development* 23:88-105.

Khayesi, M. 2001. "Matatu Workers in Nairobi, Thika and Ruiru: Career Patterns and Conditions of Work". In Alila P.O. and Pedersen, Poul Ove (eds.). *Negotiating Social Space: East Africa Micro Enterprises.* Trenton, NJ: Africa World Press, Inc pp. 69-96.

Mangat, J.S. 1969. *The History of Asians in East Africa-1886-1945.* London: Oxford University Press.

Mbuthia, S. 2002. "An Analysis of Farm Level Transport Needs and Provisions in Mwea Tebere Irrigation Scheme, Kirinyaga District, Kenya". MA Thesis, Department of Geography, Kenyatta University, Nairobi.

Nowrojee, P. 2001. "Asian African Business-the National Perspective". *INFRA-Les Cashiers*, No 20 pp 49-57, Nairobi.

Ogonda, R.T. 1986. "The Development of the Roads System in Kenya". PhD thesis, University of Nairobi

Ogonda, R.T. 1992. "Transport and Communication in the Colonial Economy". In Ochieng, W.R. (ed.). *An Economic History of Kenya.* Nairobi: E.A Educational Publishers, pp. 129-145.

Ogonda, R.T. and Onyango G.M. 1994. "The Port and Town of Kisumu, Kenya: Past Present and Future Development". *African Urban Quarterly* 9 (1& 2): 85-108.

Ongaro, S.A.L. 1995. "Transport as a Medium for Spatial Interaction: A Case of Kenya's Railway Network". MA thesis, Department of Geography, University of Nairobi.

Pedersen, P. O. 2006. "Trade and traders: a dynamic factor in the small- and micro-enterprise sector in Kenya and other countries in eastern and southern Africa". African Journal of Business and Economic Research 1,1: 66-94.

Swainson, N. 1978. "Company Formation in Kenya Before 1945 with Particular Reference to the Role of Foreign Capital". In Kaplinsky, R. (ed.). *Readings on the Multinational Corporation in Kenya.* Nairobi: Oxford University Press.

Swainson, N. 1980. *The Development of Corporate Capitalism in Kenya.* London: Heinemann.

Swainson, N.1990. "The Rise of National Bourgeoisie in Kenya". *Review of African Political Economy* 4 (8): 39-54.

Weatherspoon, D.D and Reardon, T. 2003. "The Rise of Supermarkets in Africa: Implications for Agrifood Systems and the Rural Poor". *Development Policy Review* 21 (3):333-355.

Part III
Conclusions

Chapter 13

Business in Kenya: Institutions, Interactions, and Strategies

Patrick Alila, Dorothy McCormick and Mary Omosa

INTRODUCTION

This chapter looks at what it takes to enhance business operations in Kenya. The success of businesses is seen to lie with having a supportive policy environment, facilitating bureaucracy, productive inter-firm linkages, local context and improved physical infrastructure. The chapter focuses on the analysis of interactions as revealed by the sectoral studies: interactions between business and government, business and society, and businesses with each other. This leads to an examination of the incentive structure and investment patterns within the business system, which, in turn, suggest the elements of a strategy for building a more competitive business system.

GOVERNMENT POLICY IMPACTING ON KENYAN BUSINESS

In a business system, there is a wide range of actors comprising business entities or firms, government, non-governmental organisations, associations and groupings, as well as individuals. The proper working of a business system depends on the interaction of these different actors to effectively play their roles which may be formal and/or informal. The actors are generally "in business" and the type and scope of business transactions determine the nature and level of interactions between the various actors.

The interaction between government and business is generally an ongoing process, taking place on a regular daily basis. This is mainly because both have to deal with the public and therefore are in effect having the same "client" in common. In broad terms, the public is the consumer of government-provided public goods. At the same time, business enterprises market their merchandise and services to the very same public who constitute the consumers or their customers. Thus, the purpose for government and business relationship to the public, whether separately or both together, forms the basis of their interaction. It is furthermore, a useful indicator of the nature and scope of the three-way link between government, business and the public in which global actors play a major role particularly in matters of development assistance and foreign investment. The key parameters shaping the interactions between government and business include market liberalisation, privatisation, good governance, public goods and services, development capital and policy implementation.

Market: Liberalisation and Privatisation

The market is arguably the major interface for business and government interactions. It is the channel through which enterprises secure returns from the sale of merchandise. For government, market transactions are the primary source of revenue. Market and government have therefore, a mutual interest and regularly interact concerning the proper working of the market in terms of order in business dealings and the growth of the market. To this end, there are rules set up governing the operations of the market. For instance, the rules determine participation in the market by individuals and groups stipulating market boundaries, permitting or barring entry, imposing taxes/rent or granting exemptions, restricting or allowing expansion of a business firm, sanctioning engagement of labour and remuneration, levying penalties for default in transactions, stipulating global regional requirements of engagement, etc.

In Kenya, the major turning point for market operations, with far reaching consequences for government interaction with business and still taking root, were the liberalisation policy reforms of the 1990s. In contrast to preceding years of control and virtual government omnipresence in the market, there was a dramatic switch to a new era of a free market or *"soko huru"* of the tea and coffee farmers. The fundamental idea was that government should concentrate on its core business of providing public services and not undertake production or commerce in competition with or to the exclusion of private sector business firms.

The relevant policy prescription was and still remains privatisation, divesture and free movement of prices, which meant an enhanced role for private sector enterprises in commercial ventures and a significant reduction of government involvement in such ventures mainly through parastatal reforms. The resulting general policy context of interaction between government and business is mutual agreement on the necessary policies supportive of private enterprise and implemented by government. In this connection, the basic issue is government going out of private business and the critical role of government becomes regulatory such that the operation of firms in the market is on the basis of the rule of law. A case in point is agricultural sector regulatory boards for production and marketing of cash crops already taking up a leading role. This is in contrast to past historical practice of the government's direct involvement in both production and marketing, especially in the marketing of these commodities in the overseas markets.

Governance: The Persistent Problem of Government Control

The liberalisation policy reforms of the 1990s were, beyond the economic dimension, also a turning point in the political sphere. The reforms marked a new phase of democratisation and decentralisation politics that brought about major changes in forms of government and business interaction. Liberal democracy ideology, increasingly embraced in Kenya and other African countries, was instrumental in the rejection of authoritarian regimes which had been in power for decades and which insisted on highly restricted business voice, and people's will generally, in policy and decision-making.

Good governance fast became a rallying call and government was persistently urged by the proponents of liberalisation to provide an enabling environment, mainly for micro and small enterprises. The basic idea is putting in place a political process in which the relationship between government and people is participatory and interactive, involving state actors, together with the private sector and civil society as stakeholders. Specifically for business, the merits of good governance should be seen to lie in the fact that it promotes efficient services delivery and investment opportunities.

The Kenyan experience, however, shows that the continued government involvement in commercial business has been a major stumbling block to good governance practices. For instance, Government, save for limited concessions remains adamant and not conforming to privatisation and divesture for key parastatals dealing in energy and communications products and upholding joint ventures in the financial sector. The government allowing civil servants to still engage and compete with private businessmen is a major shortcoming, especially with regard to investment and supply ventures. The consequence has been inefficiency and corruption making business undertakings in Kenya expensive and adversely affecting investment growth.

Public Service Undertakings by Government and Business

The core business of government is public service, which makes interaction with business mandatory. The services can be provided of the government's own accord, and/or business owners and others in need can place demands for their provision, pointing to a two-way interaction premise. The leading service, which is also a determining factor for business undertakings and even the very existence of government, is upholding the rule of law. As discussed in Chapter 2, this takes various forms including maintaining law and order, contract enforcement, provision of security, setting up regulatory frameworks, setting quality standards, labour laws enactment and ensuring obedience, etc.

The government has a major role in human capital development, essentially as a public service to the private sector. The population gaining skills and knowledge from technological advances is a key government concern not only to serve business but also for overall development and growth. It is in the same vein that government provides crucial welfare services in education, health, water, human rights, gender balance, etc. Also, the government has a major responsibility for building physical infrastructure.

It needs to be emphasized that the provision of these services has not been left completely to the government. The private sector, including business firms, has assumed a significant role working in partnership with government or independently. The basic rationale for such involvement is corporate social responsibility on the part of business, essentially to give back part of the earnings towards community social development. In recent past, however, the private sector has taken up the provision of certain public services, notably, roads maintenance, security, education, and health care due to lack of resources on the part of government and therefore, failure to provide them.

It is owing to the need for services that various fora have been set up in which there is regular interaction between government and business. There are in Kenya, a number of business associations such as Kenya Association of Manufacturers (KAM), NCBDA, *Jua Kali* Associations and clubs like Rotary and Lions. These relate to the relevant government departments or committees to lobby for policy, make material or financial contributions or just be supportive, in writing or verbally, to government efforts. The interaction can take place at the individual enterprise level, groups of enterprises/business people, local authority and national level. In the best of cases, government reciprocates by offering similar support to private-sector initiatives.

Development Capital: The Challenges of Government – NGOs Partnership and Rivalry

The interaction between government and business has markedly intensified in recent years leading to concerted action. This often results in partnership, but some rivalry persists especially over increasingly scarce resources. Specifically, a major contributing factor has been the changing purposes, access, coupled with global politics of capital to finance development, currently viewed as people-centred. The key concern, according to this view, is the improvement of quality of life of the majority poor and the process to remain sustainable. It is this concern which has given currency to the present notion of development capital, channelled through a partnership between mainly global actors such as European Union (EU), United Nations (UN), World Bank/IMF and individual Western and Asian countries providing assistance/aid, with the recipients essentially, the governments and people of the developing countries'.

The form government and business interaction takes will largely depend on the agenda of provider(s) of development capital. The overriding preference for assistance to the private sector for investment to promote free market ideals can only mean competition and even conflict with government when it is pushing for social welfare priorities in areas of food security and epidemics. It is, however, often the case that the requirement of material supplies including technology being sourced from the country of origin of the assistance inevitably means joint effort and collaboration/partnership between government and business. Likewise,

316

resources/capital directly channelled to NGOs and CBOs on the ground give rise to a similar pattern of government and business interaction.

Thus, through development capital, multilateral agencies, bilateral agencies, NGOs and CBOs constitute a major interface of government and business interaction. The concerns for the people in the political and economic liberalisation development agenda are noble. However, questions remain unresolved regarding the future of the people in their economy without clear plans and policies, for ownership and control of business by the indigenous population. A related issue is tension over government sovereignty brought about by actions of powerful global actors including multinational corporations that tend to perpetuate external dependency, instead of allocation of development capital such that government and business interaction leads to home-grown policies and sustainable development. Policies however well formulated must ultimately be implemented for the intended gains to be realised. A major issue of serious concern in relation to development capital for Kenya is a very low policy implementation rate, especially in the case of development projects. Any improvement in the implementation record is likely to enhance business activity.

BUSINESS AND SOCIETY: NORMS, VALUES AND SOCIETAL EXPECTATIONS

The theoretical background and empirical chapters in the volume have argued and emphasised that institutions are a dominant factor having direct influence in the way businesses operate. Formal and informal rules are embodied in institutions and these are applied to different levels of mix, varied sequencing and degree of enforcement in the course of business operation, and ultimately, shape the structure and organisation of the various types of business. It is, however, also the case that African values and norms that are culturally rooted and locally embedded continue to direct the way individuals conduct business. At yet another level, while business practices derive from the cultural beliefs and practices of the business owner(s), these are also continuously influenced and shaped by the socio-political and economic contexts within which businesses operate.

Therefore, whereas it is the case that norms, values and societal expectations propel businesses this process must be understood in its local context. For instance, it is important to look beyond legislation in an attempt to understand what differentiates various businesses and especially what accounts for their performance.

It is also true that in business, people feel more tied to family or social institutions than to formal ones. This explains why livelihoods, and in particular, identity and aspirations are important to the performance of businesses. Similarly, these factors also explain why businesses with seemingly identical opportunities end up performing variedly. Indeed, the very perception of what is an opportunity is dependent on a people's norms and values and what society expects of them. Hence, depending on who is involved, what would appear to be an opportunity to be exploited may be perceived by some as taking advantage of an unfortunate situation.

317

In Kenya, it is actually the case that cultural norms and values, key components of institutions, and societal expectations have continued to guide and determine the performance of businesses. The resulting effect is all encompassing, embracing virtually all business transactions. Cultural norms and values determine the choice of a particular enterprise, who does business with whom as well as factors governing business links including personal relationships, and how working arrangements are instituted within and between businesses as going concerns. Therefore, the interaction between business and society, an integral part of the business system, is best understood from the point of view of how norms, values and societal expectations shape businesses in Kenya.

Taking Initiatives in Business

Entry into business is an outcome of social, economic and political processes both at the national level and as experienced by the individual. This is true for the type of business enterprise chosen and how it is organized. It is, however, also the case that one's knowledge is important in making the decision to enter business, in the selection of the business itself, and the extent of operations. The values and norms that direct the way individuals conduct business in Kenya are culturally rooted and locally embedded. However, while business practices derive from the cultural beliefs and practices of the proprietor, these are continuously influenced and shaped by the socio-political and economic contexts within which they operate. Indeed, this explains why some businesses tend to blossom at the same time as others face reductions in operations and profits, and without any visible fundamental changes in clientele or the formal business environment.

There is a widespread tendency among most people to choose businesses that are already tried out. This is based on the thinking that what is already in existence is well understood from the experience of others especially relatives and friends. The risks are, therefore, lower coupled with the belief that the market is assured. There is, however, a fallacy underlying such a view evidenced by the fact that particular sectors tend to be saturated, especially for MSEs, whereby in some instances, there are more traders than buyers. In the rural areas, this remains a big challenge especially in the case of seasonal, perishable commodities such as fish, tea, horticultural crops, bananas and mangoes. The implication is finding innovative ways when going into and doing business, especially the need to diversify the range of products and at the same time, closely monitoring changing market demands.

Engaging in business demands certain minimum resources. In the agricultural sector for example, these include land and start up capital. The latter is particularly important because it determines the scale at which businesses operate, whether they grow at all, and combined with working capital, they constitute a major reason for most businesses remaining small. It is, however, also the case that even when individual businesses make profit and could grow, there is a tendency to spread risk through diversification. This then means that when businesses remain small, it is not in itself necessarily an indicator of non-viability. Rather, this could be a value preference by the entrepreneur in terms of successfully remaining in business or a livelihood strategy to cope with seasonality, risk or both (see McCormick, 1993).

It is evident also that businesses are gendered. For instance, most on-farm coffee and tea business operators are women whereas the metal sub-sector is male dominated. These patterns are historical and largely resulting from formal training and socialisation. In addition, they are a function of the gender power relations subsequently governing resource allocation and distribution, notably land ownership, wage employment and credit access. Businesses that require a substantial amount of capital attract fewer women as do those that require too much mobility. But as would be expected, a few persons manage to overcome some of the socio-cultural barriers, and bolstered by ongoing socio-economic changes undertake activities that are out of the ordinary. Globally, this accounts for the presence of some women in male dominated sectors such as metal and transportation. In Kenya, we note that many of the exhibitions described in Chapter 10 are owned by women who travel to destinations like Dubai and Turkey to source merchandise.

In contrast, gender remains a negative factor specifically for women thereby constraining their participation in business. There is conclusive evidence of little or no access to credit from formal financial institutions by women and overall limited business opportunities to be exploited by women. Women, compared to men, tend to engage in fewer and only certain types of enterprises.

Business Interactions

Nearly all business investment in Kenya is financed from family or internal sources. This is especially true of the micro and small enterprises that form the backbone of the Kenyan business systems. Among these, 90% got their start-up capital from their own funds or from their families, and 80% got all additional capital from the same sources (CBS et al., 1999). Even among large firms, however, there is a reluctance to borrow from formal sources (Söderbom, 2002). This means that both initial and further investment in Kenyan businesses is largely constrained by the availability of resources from family sources, and more importantly, this comes to shape the nature of business-society relationships that we observe.

The choices of whom to do business with are thus largely based on individual(s) preference but have to take into account business operations requirements defined and determined by legislation. Smallholder tea producers are, for instance, expected by law to sell green leaf through the Kenya Tea Development Authority (KTDA) but end up engaging in *Soko Huru* while maintaining legal links with KTDA. The actual decision is apparently influenced by circumstances that pertain to the local individual businesses, specifically their financial needs and availability of alternative markets in a rural context. A similar pattern is observed in the coffee sub-sector. Therefore, whereas it is the case that norms, values and societal expectations propel businesses, this process must be understood in its local context. It is important to look beyond legislation in trying to understand what differentiates various businesses locally.

Business linkages are generally an expression of social relationships based largely on personal relations, trust and reciprocity, rather than pure market relations. The latter relations are sometimes depicted to be impersonal competition ruled by prices of goods and services and determined in turn by their ever changing supply and demand in the market place. However, the reality is that even in situations where businesses out-source transport services, for example, the tendency is to arrange procurement from known persons' businesses, notably, acquaintances, friends and even relatives. The practice does not, however, preclude compliance with statutory requirements such as tender procedures, registration, inspection and licensing.

A common thread of argument running through the empirical chapters in this volume is that social institutions facilitate businesses. A case in point is family networks and friendships providing start up capital, serving as a source of crucial ideas, and information generally, and even determining the line of business one takes as well as ways to go about it. Thus, the social institutions largely based on family and kinship systems, end up blending with, and could inject synergy into formal institutions, with positive consequences for business operations. These African social institutions are well recognised even in economic development initiatives and have also become an integral part of business on the continent, Kenya included.

However, social values and norms can also obstruct business. This happens when they negate bureaucracy and, therefore, frustrate attempts to enforce rules and regulations due largely to varying and sometimes divergent expectations. For instance, there are those relating to the expectation to provide financial assistance to kin and friend, and the need to maintain working capital and good business practices. At the same time, it is recognised that norms and values, and indeed institutions generally, are not static. In the dynamics of change, therefore, negative change may be superseded by a positive shift in one institution or more, culminating in positive consequences on all the various aspects of business operations logically leading to favourable profitable outcomes for the business.

Performance of Businesses

There have been explanations offered in an attempt to account for varied performance of businesses that in essence, argue that performance is dependent on management and style of leadership. The operations of a business and its probability of success or failure are a function of business goal and structure on the one hand, and management capacity subsuming leadership style on the other. African businesses specifically have shown relatively greater reliance on who leads them and the person's own preferred leadership style, such that the success of a business may not exactly be dependent on the rational functioning of the bureaucracy. Rather, two identical businesses in terms of a rational bureaucratic structure could end up with divergent performance outputs on account of management and leadership styles. As discussed in Chapter 2, it is often the case that different styles of management exist because they are embedded in the persons' socio-cultural orientation. This could be at the level of cultural identity or a perspective on business which could have emanated from days of schooling and training. Style of management is furthermore informed by the specific interests of the individuals at the helm of the different organisations. This could be a logical explanation for situations in which businesses appear to be diverging from their central policy position(s) which are precipitated by what the chief executive finds acceptable but which may or may not be sound business practice. Increasingly, however, businesses are beginning to identify with social philanthropy, both as a genuine desire to give to society but also as a marketing strategy.

A significant issue in relation to leadership and management is whether growth in a business is in the direction of diversification or specialisation. Larger businesses sub-contract to both smaller and like-minded larger firms in an attempt to diversify for purposes of spreading risks. It could also be due to the need to expand networks, and even to go around legislation. Therefore, some of the companies that seem to out-source are actually purchasing from themselves. This gives them required confidence with regard to quality and availability, and at the same time ensures that where procurement procedures apply, they are seen to be in compliance with the legal requirements. Generally, and as evidenced from the metal sector study Chapter 8, specialisation varies with level of skills. Therefore, businesses that draw on highly skilled personnel tend to specialise more. But specialisation is subject to availability of resources and most businesses specialise following years of experience and possibly, an accumulation of sufficient working capital. For instance, tea farmers with limited land diversify on their land use less, as compared to farmers with larger parcels of land. It is, however, also the case that even in the face of limitations, diversification is a key feature for certain resource constrained enterprises. Yet, the level of diversification is also socially couched.

However, some of the risk spreading mechanisms such as sub-contracting, expanding or opening new product lines, venturing into new markets and increasing or reducing staff, are not always the first options for a number of businesses. The implication is that some of the decisions businesses make remain unpredictable and are only made on account of the circumstances prevailing at a particular moment in time. This points to leadership as a key factor in the survival of business in terms of timely and decisive actions to remain in business. It is in this light that the fate of different enterprises due to the marked impact of liberalisation policies on business should be understood. For some, the changes act as an incentive for management to make the required turn-around while in other circumstances, the changes mark the beginning of poor performance leading to a downward spiral.

The quality of leadership, and the selection process in particular, affect the way businesses are run. In cases where such businesses are run as partnerships, disagreements lead to break-ups culminating in the emergence of even smaller enterprises. This is particularly evident in the coffee sub-sector where marketing societies have experienced extremely acrimonious and even violent break-ups. The resulting effect has been huge losses of assets and no longer being able to enjoy advantages that go with a large membership of cooperative society and/or union.

BUSINESSES INTERACTING WITH EACH OTHER

Businesses interact with each other in a variety of ways. They compete, they link, they network; relations between them are sometimes friendly, sometimes hostile, often wary. This research cannot claim to have captured all forms of interaction, but it has highlighted several of these that in our view, are important for understanding Kenya's business system.

Local, Regional, and Global Markets

Kenyan producers participate in markets that have changed drastically since the early 1990s. The major turning point was the market liberalisation that accompanied Kenya's broader processes of structural adjustment. Although this affected different sectors in somewhat different ways, the impact of liberalisation was felt throughout Kenya and the East African region. As the globalisation of markets and production systems everywhere intensified, goods from all over the world, but especially from South Africa and various parts of Asia, found their way onto the markets of Kenya and her neighbours.

By the time research for this book was being carried out, between year 2000 and 2003, competition had intensified, local markets were much more diverse, some old actors had disappeared or changed drastically, and new participants had emerged. Our examination of the textile and metal sectors as well as the study of domestic trade revealed greatly heightened competition, due both to the increase in imports of new and second-hand goods and to the proliferation of MSEs. At the low end of the market, second-hand clothing competes directly with Kenyan made goods. In the middle and upper income urban markets, vendors of imported new clothing compete with custom tailors for customers. In the case of the metal industry, competition comes both from imported metal products and plastic substitutes. In both production and trade, the roots of intense competition among MSEs go deeper than particular items entering or leaving the market. The combination of small markets and the proliferation of tiny businesses, often producing almost identical goods and services, locks firms into competition for whatever demand there is.

Liberalisation has made markets more diverse, not only in terms of the goods and services being exchanged, but also in their structure and organisation. As noted in Chapter 10 on trade, as the limited choices that characterised the import substitution era gave way to a wider variety of local and imported goods, new forms of business, such as the "exhibitions", "hyper" supermarkets, and second-hand vehicle dealers began to appear. A few businesses began interacting electronically. Ventures like *E-sokoni* linked traders and service providers to potential customers. Such efforts are, however, still modest compared to the vast majority of trade, which is carried on by businesses that deal with each other face-to-face. Liberalisation also transformed the markets for coffee and tea, and the previously dominant actors now coexist with parallel structures involving private traders.

Markets in neighbouring countries also liberalised, creating heightened competition and depriving Kenyan manufacturers of some assured outlets. Traders going to Uganda, for example, faced competition from imported new and second-hand items similar to that at home. At the same time, the reopening of borders with Tanzania restored some markets that had been closed since the late 1970s.

As globalisation has put pressure on large firms to become internationally competitive, it has at the same time created new business opportunities in, for example, logistics and transport. External initiatives, such as the Africa Growth and Opportunity Act (AGOA) of the US government, opened up new markets and linked manufacturers producing in Kenya to importers abroad. These created new types of interactions between businesses, with foreign importers bringing detailed specifications for products, especially garments, to be made in Kenyan factories. These changes have made Kenyan markets freer, more diverse, and competitive than before. Producers, traders, and consumers are generally happy with the trend, but many express concern that liberalisation has had its down side.

Four main issues emerged from the sectoral studies on these concerns: Quality, contracts and opportunism, poor information flow, and unfair competition. Issues of quality were most apparent in the coffee sector, but they were also mentioned in the textile study. In coffee, Government's withdrawal from agricultural extension, the fragmentation of cooperative societies, and the entry of private traders and millers into the chain have weakened the previously strong quality control system. There was general concern that low or irregular quality could have a serious impact on Kenya's good name for top grade Arabica coffee. Garment producers also raised issues of quality, but in the context of competition. They were concerned that competing imports were not being held to the same standards for quality, informational labelling, and so forth as Kenyan made items.

Almost every facet of the study raised issues of contracts and opportunism. The coffee study showed that the fact that farmers can abscond without paying the cooperative society for inputs provided has led to the collapse of some cooperatives. Tea farmers recounted stories of *soko huru* operators who conned them out of green leaf, while tea agents told of brokers who cheated them by failing to pay for leaf taken on credit. Traders, transporters, and other producers provided their own examples. It appears that the rapid transformation of the institution of the market has not been accompanied by the development of supporting economic institutions to ensure the fairness of transactions and give injured parties reliable mechanisms for redress.

The flow of market information varies considerably from one sector to another and from one level of market to another. Once coffee, for example, reaches the auction, price and quality information is readily available. Farther down the chain, however, information delays are very common. Information and Communication Technology (ICT), which could help bridge the information gap, is not yet widely used for this purpose by small farmers. Yet farmers who lack up-to-date price information are an easy prey for unscrupulous traders. Medium-sized garment and textile firms cited lack of information as one of the reasons why they had difficulty accessing export markets. We also observed that potential buyers of the products of garment and metal MSEs have no clear way of locating those selling particular items or of ascertaining the quality of products on offer. Unless they are ready to invest considerable time and effort in searching, they must rely on known sources or referrals by persons they feel they can trust.

Some complaints of unfair competition are linked to quality issues and the perception that imported goods escape the quality controls imposed on items produced in Kenya. Garment manufacturers also charged that many imports enter the country without paying duty. In the metal sector, some firms were accused of failing to pay VAT or using fake papers for exports. Although such allegations came mainly from the garment and metal sectors in this study, they are frequently heard with regard to products as diverse as sugar and auto spares.

Business Associations, Networks, and Linkages

Large and small firms tend to belong to different business associations. National associations such as the Kenya Association of Manufacturers (KAM), the Kenya National Chamber of Commerce and Industry draw their membership mainly from medium and large firms. Others, such as Nairobi's Central Business District Association, have a diverse membership linked by common concern for issues in their immediate business environment. Still others, such as Rotary and Lions Clubs as well as the welfare and credit groups favoured by the owners of micro and small firms, are not business associations, though they include many business people among their members.

The major associations have some sectoral committees, but sectoral associations hardly exist, probably because of the small size of the industrial sector. An exception to this is the association started by the exporting garment producers. At their height, coffee cooperative societies carried out many of the functions of a sectoral association: training, provision of technical and market information, promoting product quality, and offering a forum for advocacy regarding issues affecting the sector. Since liberalisation, however, the cooperatives appear to lack the capacity for most of these functions.

Associations of all types and sizes offer business people a forum for discussing issues of common concern. Kenyan associations focus more on advocacy than on providing services to members. Not surprisingly, the associations dominated by larger firms have a stronger voice. They have had some success in, for example, influencing the tariff structure on second hand clothing, but have been less successful in securing changes in what may be the most fundamental aspects of the business environment: infrastructure and internal security.

Not all firms see associations as useful. Although the larger garment firms are members of KAM and other national associations, few garment MSEs belong to any association. Small metal enterprises are more likely to belong to a *Jua Kali* association. Some, however, choose to remain on the sidelines, expressing the view that most associations are mismanaged.

Kenyan business is characterised by a multitude of informal networks. Many, but not all, are ethnically based. Networking sometimes leads to more formal business linkages, such as subcontracting, outsourcing, cooperating in production, or joining together in marketing trips. The research suggests that the fact that the formal institutions of contracts and contract enforcement are weak and subject to manipulation leads business persons at all levels to prefer to deal with people they know personally or who have been recommended by someone they know. It also favours linkages that do not involve the pooling of money. For example, several small metal work businesses may put together a production line to enable them to fill a large order, but they are hesitant to form a single business or cooperative that would require them to operate from a common account.

The research suggests that the nature of business linkages varies from one sector to another. The *soko huru* networks of the tea industry are not identical to the new coffee trading networks. A significant minority of metal firms subcontract some part of their work to others. Garment firms rarely subcontract, but small firms trying to access distant markets sometimes collaborate on marketing trips. Traders link with individuals and small firms that serve as "promotion agents" to sell goods on commission. Transporters are benefiting from the trend towards the outsourcing of transport and logistic services.

Linkages also vary by size of firms and the ethnicity of the owner. In general, subcontracting is more common among small than among large firms. Among metal firms, the reasons for subcontracting and its direction also vary with size. Certain trading and transport linkages tend to be "large to small" while others are between firms of similar size. Kenyan Asian businesses, which are on average larger than African ones, may be linked to the businesses of other family members by overlapping directorships. This form of linkage appears to be less common among firms whose owners are of African origin.

Although other research has suggested that large firms are wary of buying from or subcontracting to small ones because of delivery and quality problems, these did not emerge as constraints in our study. Rather, medium and large firms most often said that they did not subcontract simply because they had adequate resources to produce in house. To some extent, this is a legacy of the import-substitution era, which encouraged vertical integration and investment in excess capacity. Reluctance to subcontract may also be a matter of preference. Firms may prefer to operate independently or they may not find the available contractors acceptable as partners.

Businesses and Financial Organisations

Although interactions between businesses and financial organisations were not the focus of this investigation, a few points emerging from the textile study are worth noting. Micro and small enterprises finance their businesses from their own or family resources, and rarely deal with the formal financial system. Although medium and large scale firms are able to obtain bank loans, many business owners believed the cost of credit to be excessive and so preferred to finance their businesses internally. Businesses argued that liberalisation of the financial sector had been badly executed, and that instead of creating competitive markets, it had allowed a few large banks to exercise oligopoly power. Micro and small firms were more likely to interact with rotating savings and credit associations, community based organisations, suppliers, and micro-finance organisations than with any part of the formal financial system.

Overall, the trend for all but the largest firms is towards self-financing. This gives firms a sense of independence and the security of not being burdened by debt.

Nevertheless, self-financing means that a firm's ability to expand or take advantage of new markets is limited by funds already in the firm or available from family resources. For the vast majority of very small firms whose owners have little in the way of financial resources, this is a severe limitation. It is compounded by the fact that, not only can entrepreneurs not borrow for the business, they are also usually unable to borrow for any other purpose. This means that the business capital is at risk whenever there is a family emergency.

CONCLUSIONS: THE KENYAN BUSINESS SYSTEM

This investigation has revealed that the Kenyan business system contains various incentives that lead to certain types of investment arrangements and disincentives, that is, negative incentives that discourage certain types of activities. Both incentives and disincentives come from various sources not only within Kenya, but also from the global business context. Government is generally the main source of both financial and coercive incentives, while local communities tend to give social incentives. External markets also provide financial incentives for investment. In some cases, the signals are clear: invest, do not invest. More often, however, the incentives shape investment behaviour more subtly by encouraging certain types of investments over others.

Incentive Structure

Overall, the Kenyan incentive structure seems to favour investment that has three main characteristics: Financed from family or internal sources; Urban based; Short-term and high yielding. The picture in most sectors conformed to this overall pattern, though there were a few sectoral variations as well as differences between medium-to-large firms and their small and micro counterparts.

Nearly all business investment in Kenya is financed from family or internal sources. This is especially true of the micro and small enterprises that form the backbone of the Kenyan business systems. Among these, 90% got their start-up capital from their own funds or from their families, and 80% got all additional capital from the same sources (CBS et al., 1999). Even among large firms, however, there is a reluctance to borrow from formal sources (Söderbom, 2002). This means that both initial and further investment in Kenyan businesses is largely constrained by the availability of resources from family sources.

Incentives exist for business investment on a sub-national regional basis and mostly tend to take place in urban manufacturing firms rather than rural businesses. The first and probably the strongest of these incentives is infrastructure, including roads, electricity, and water supply. It is evident from the discussion of electricity and water in chapter 5 and the comments of business owners in the textile and metal sectors, that both the uneven distribution and the poor condition of Kenya's infrastructure are serious problems. Such problems are most acute in rural areas. Urban MSEs are, for example, twice as likely to have access to electricity, as are rural MSEs (CBS et al., 1999). Large businesses, which usually cannot operate without electricity, must either provide their own power or locate elsewhere. Textile manufacturers who reported self-provisioning in water made it clear that this was costly and affected both their competitiveness and their ability to undertake other investments.

In the case of rural investment, this is mostly in the agricultural sector, particularly, the growing of various types of cash crops. Our study focused on coffee and tea. However, investment in floriculture and horticulture has in recent years become important. Tea was the one area in which social incentives were mentioned. Some respondents acknowledged that they grow tea at least in part because they want to be seen to be doing what everyone else in the community is doing (chapter 10).

Finally, there exists a collection of incentives and disincentives that favour short-term high yielding investments. These include coercive measures, such as the harassment experienced by many micro producers, as well as incentives flowing from macro-economic variables such as inflation and foreign exchange rates, the uncertainties created by the prevalence of disease, lack of affordable insurance, and lack of reliable government services. By implication, this incentive structure works against the building of a strong manufacturing sector, discourages investment in higher level technologies, and deters the continuation of Kenya's reputation for high quality coffee or tea. On the positive side, these same incentives have encouraged the development of new forms of trade and the use of locally available raw materials.

Investment Pattern

Investment requirements are usually higher and start-up procedures more onerous for manufacturing than for trade and service enterprises. For this reason, the uncertainties that have been observed in the Kenyan economy are likely to discourage investment in large manufacturing. The research suggests that within the manufacturing sector, there is a clear tendency towards light manufacturing requiring relatively low investment. There is, for example, new investment in clothing firms, but little in the more capital and technology intensive textile sub sector.

Agribusiness market liberalisation, general economic uncertainties, and the precariousness of rural life seem also to be working against the investments required for maintaining Kenya's reputation for high quality coffee and tea. In both the coffee and tea sectors, old systems with in-built quality control procedures have either been replaced or reduced in importance. New structures have arisen that promise small-holders immediate payment, but much less attention is paid to the quality of the product delivered. As a result, farmers have little incentive to invest in the best seedlings, fertilizers, or other inputs.

Government offers few positive incentives to business investment. The main programmes, EPZ (and MUB, aim at encouraging production for export. As argued in the discussion of the textile sector, these can be reinforced by external incentives such as AGOA, which promises a ready market for Kenyan exports. The tax and other incentives built into these programmes also influence the nature and location of investment. Moreover, by affecting participating firms' linkages with suppliers and other firms in their sector, these programmes also influence industrial investment more generally. At present, for example, it is not possible for a firm that is not exporting all or nearly all of its output to locate within an Export Processing Zone). This reinforces the fragmentation of the business by denying many small and medium scale firms access to the superior infrastructure of the EPZs. Small and medium scale firms are further constrained because the EPZ and MUB regulations makes it very difficult for them to link with exporting firms through subcontracting relationships.

In the case of trade and services market, liberalisation has offered many more positive incentives to investment. Whole new lines of trade, such as booming wholesale and retail trade in second-hand clothing and vehicles, have emerged since markets were liberalised in the early 1990s. Supermarkets, exhibitions, 'car bazaars', and other new types of trading enterprises, have appeared. Interestingly, liberalisation has brought about an anomaly in the transport sector as we saw in chapter 12. On the one hand, large firms have responded to competition by outsourcing transport and logistic services. On the other, some small and medium producers, also responding to intensified competition, are now offering transport services as a way of winning customers. The growth of non-motorised transport is a direct result of escalating cost of transport for different businesses.

Strategies for a More Competitive Business System

Small units far outnumber large ones in the Kenyan economy, and most of these would be classified as micro, or very small. Small enterprises have a mean of less than two workers, and small holdings in the tea sector averaged only three acres. Medium and large-scale firms, while less numerous, nevertheless play an important role in some sectors and markets. In this study, we have seen the importance of large metal firms in making certain products, such as iron roofing sheets. We have also noted that large garment manufacturers in the Export Processing Zones are able to meet the quantity requirements of buyers for the US market. It appears clear, therefore, that a good strategy promoting business will provide a conducive environment for units of various sizes.

Our review suggests that an appropriate strategy for strengthening Kenya's business system will have five main components. Their broad directions are similar for all firms, but their specific applications or action plans may differ from one sector or firm size to another. The five key components are:

(i)   Improve security so as to promote investment;
(ii)   Improve infrastructure and public services;
(iii)   Encourage linkages between various segments of the business system;
(iv)   Improve the economic and regulatory institutions that support business transactions;
(v)   Ease firms' tax burdens.

Improve Security

Both small and large firms are concerned about security. Both recognise that insecurity resulting from high levels of crime and violence discourages investment and raises the cost of doing business. Some of the increased expenses are direct, such as the cost of hiring a guard or private security firm or the loss of money through theft. In other cases, security concerns influence choices in ways that lower incomes or increase costs. We have already seen examples of how in the garment industry, security considerations influence small firms' choice of premises and large firms' decisions about multiple shifts. The ethnic clashes that have erupted in various parts of the country at different times have, among other things, disrupted existing businesses and slowed investment in new ones. Government has the primary obligation to deter crime, punish criminals, and provide security in the face of warring factions. In carrying out these responsibilities, government needs to be pro-active and to include in its planning all segments of the business community.

Improve Infrastructure and Public Services

Complaints about the extent and condition of Kenya's infrastructure are commonplace (World Economic Forum, 2004; Bigsten and Kimuyu, 2002). In the sectors studied, poor infrastructure was a matter of concern, though firms of different sizes and sectors differed in their emphases. Electricity was a major problem, especially for manufacturing firms. Many small producers in both the metal and garment sectors lack electricity altogether or operate with pirated lines. For them, the problem is access. All of the larger firms are connected to the electricity grid, but complained of the high power tariffs, unreliable service, and the costs associated with providing backup generators. Although electricity was not mentioned by smallholder tea and coffee farmers, it is a matter of concern for those in other agricultural activities such as dairy and horticulture. The obvious conclusion is that both the quality and the extent of electricity service need improvement if business is to perform well.

The second aspect of infrastructure that emerged as a major issue is the condition of the roads. The problem is most severe for transporters and manufacturers located inland that use the port of Mombasa for importing raw materials or exporting finished products. Transporters must pay for frequent vehicle repairs, high fuel costs on bad roads, and earn reduced income on account of delays. Such costs are passed on to transport users, including smallholders and small traders. Manufacturers suffered from production delays, high transport costs, and difficulties in meeting export schedules. Improvements to the road network are clearly an urgent need if Kenya is to attract and hold investment. Certain groups of firms find other aspects of infrastructure and public services problematic. As we have seen, textile firms in Mombasa need a better water supply, many small garment and metal producers suffer from poor premises, and waste management services are lacking in many urban areas.

Encourage Linkages

One of the assumptions underlying the presentation of networks, linkages, associations, and social capital in chapter 2 of this book is that the business system will be healthier if firms are connected to each other, to government, and to the society in a variety of ways. A business system is conceptualised as essentially a social system of production. Yet, as we have seen in the sectoral chapters, some of the expected linkages are missing or do not function in the expected ways. The result is a fragmented business system in which information does not flow as it should and many opportunities for strengthening market linkages and/or accessing new markets go unexploited. It is, however, difficult to encourage linkages in a setting where businesses mistrust both each other and the institutions that are meant to support transactions.

Improve Economic and Regulatory Institutions

The institutional environment is critical for firms of all sizes and types. Two institutional issues emerged strongly from the research. The first is the complex issue of trust, contracts, and recourse in case of abuse. The research suggests that mistrust between businesses, between business and government, and between businesses and their customers is very common. Furthermore, mechanisms for seeking redress in the event of abuse of trust are either missing or difficult to use. As a result, businesses of all sizes and in all sectors take a variety of measures to reduce their exposure to opportunistic behaviour. Most small firms prefer to operate as sole proprietorships rather than put trust in partners. Small manufacturers ask for significant deposits before beginning an order. Owners of large firms are very reluctant to give credit and often get their suppliers from a network of carefully chosen individuals. Even when written contracts are used, the parties know that should the other default, collection will be difficult or impossible. Addressing this problem will require reducing the costs and red tape associated with the current legal system and, perhaps, developing new simpler mechanisms for dealing with small commercial claims.

The second institution has to do with the regulatory environment. Small firms in particular have experienced arbitrary harassment, evictions, and rent seeking on the part of government. Gaps, inconsistencies, and erratic enforcement not only cause immediate harm to individual businesses, but they also encourage harmful opportunistic behaviours that perpetuate mistrust and weaken the entire business system. Government must set the pace for an improved institutional framework first, by reviewing laws relevant to business and the mechanisms for enforcing them, and second, by setting an example of consistent, fair, and timely enforcement of all business regulations. It may also be necessary to change regulations that permit politicians and civil servants to engage in business activities related to their government responsibilities, so that all appearance of conflict of interest and/or corruption is removed. Individual businesses, business associations, and civil society can help by publicly supporting government's efforts to create and uphold strong and trustworthy economic institutions.

Ease Tax Burden

The tax burden is quite heavy for some firms, while others manage to escape nearly all taxation. The smallest firms, while not officially exempt from tax, usually pay no more than the VAT on items they purchase or import duties embedded in some imported raw materials. At the other end of the size spectrum, exporters operating under EPZ regulations are granted a ten-year holiday from income taxes, exemptions from duties on imported raw materials, and other concessions. This means that the heaviest burden of business taxation falls on firms in the medium to large range, many of whom are producing for the local and regional markets. These are the same firms that have struggled to stay afloat in the uncertain period of market liberalisation. We encourage a careful examination of alternatives to the present income tax system, with a view towards creating incentives for investment in businesses that can be expected to generate employment for unskilled workers and for encouraging the location of business enterprises in small towns and rural trading centres.

Final Word

The theoretical and empirical chapters in this book demonstrate that there is diversity in the type and nature of businesses operating in Kenya. This diversity is reflected at the level of operation, macro versus micro, and in the range of business activities covered. Three interaction arenas are evident, in terms of whom businesses engage: government-business; business-business; and, business-society. In this concluding chapter therefore, we looked at some of the key features of businesses in Kenya. The aim is to be able to respond to the question: is there a Kenyan business system and what underlies the observations made and why?

Discussions began with an overview of the policy framework and a historical account of some of the policies that have shaped business operations in the country. It is observed that the regulatory framework serves not only as an incentive but also as a determinant of who can engage in what business and when. Historical factors have a particular bearing on who could do business, where and with whom and around what activity. Nevertheless, some of the businesses are trans-national and have no internal geopolitical boundaries. A key feature then is the nature of the incentive structure and investment patterns emerging from the Kenyan business environment.

Another salient feature is the extent to which businesses are formal entities, regulated by impersonal rules and regulations and governed by profits. Generally, norms, values and societal expectations emerge as key components of business operations. These are reflected in the choices made with regard to type of enterprise, partners and size, and they come to determine the extent of success or failure of businesses. Yet, there is no uniformity.

This effort to describe Kenya's business system has been revealing. The system's underlying social norms and values as well as the ways that businesses interact with government and one another give the Kenyan business system a form and structure that both facilitates and impedes business activity. This should not be surprising, because the same has been shown to be true in East Asia, Europe, and Latin America. The true test of this research, therefore, lies in the use that will be made of the findings, not only by government in shaping policy, but also by business associations, firms, civil society and individual entrepreneurs. Each has a clear role to play in enabling business to contribute to the development of the economy and the wellbeing of all Kenyans.

REFERENCES

Bigsten, Arne and Kimuyu, Peter. 2002. *Structure and Performance of Manufacturing in Kenya.* New York: Palgrave.

Central Bureau of Statistics (CBS), International Centre for Economic Growth (ICEG), and K-Rep Holdings Ltd. 1999. *National Micro and Small Enterprise Baseline Survey, 1999.* Nairobi: K-Rep Development Agency.

McCormick, Dorothy. 1993. "Risk and Firm Growth: The Dilemma of Nairobi's Small-scale Manufacturers." IDS Discussion Paper No.291. University of Nairobi, Institute for Development Studies.

Södebom, M. 2002. "Investment Behaviour". In Bigsten, A. and Kimuyu, P. (eds). *Structure and Performance of Manufacturing in Kenya.* New York: Palgrave.

Index